DIARY IN AMERICA, SERIES

by

Frederick Marryat

Introduction.

After many years of travel, during which I had seen men under almost every variety of government, religion, and climate, I looked round to discover if there were not still new combinations under which human nature was to be investigated. I had traversed the old country until satisfied, if not satiated; and I had sailed many a weary thousand miles from west to east, and from north to south, until people, manners, and customs were looked upon by me with indifference.

The press was constantly pouring out works upon the new world, so contradictory to each other, and pronounced so unjust by the Americans, that my curiosity was excited. It appeared strange to me that travellers whose works showed evident marks of talent should view the same people through such very different mediums; and that their gleanings should, generally speaking, be of such meagre materials. Was there so little to be remarked about America, its government, its institutions, and the effect which these had upon the people, that the pages of so many writers upon that country should be filled up with how the Americans dined or drank wine, and what description of spoons and forks were used at table? Either the Americans remained purely and unchangedly English, as when they left their father-land; or the question required more investigation and deeper research than travellers in their hasty movements have been able to bestow upon it. Whether I should be capable of throwing any new light upon the subject, I knew not, but at all events I made up my mind that I would visit the country and judge for myself.

On my first arrival I perceived little difference between the city of New York and one of our principal provincial towns; and, for its people, not half so much as between the people of Devonshire or Cornwall and those of Middlesex. I had been two or three weeks in that city, and I said: There is certainly not much to write about, nor much more than what has already been continually repeated. No wonder that those who preceded me have indulged in puerilities to swell out their books. But in a short time I altered my opinion: even at New York, the English appearance of the people gradually wore away; my perception of character became more keen, my observance consequently more nice and close, and I found that there was a great deal to reflect upon and investigate, and that America and the American people were indeed an enigma; and I was no longer surprised at the incongruities which were to be detected in those works which had attempted to describe the country. I do not assert that I shall myself succeed, when so many have failed, but at any rate, this I am certain of, my remarks will be based upon a more sure foundation—an analysis of human nature.

There are many causes why those who have written upon America have fallen into error: they have represented the Americans as a nation: now they are not yet, nor will they for many years be, in the true sense of the word, a nation—they are a mass of many people cemented together to a certain degree, by a general form of government; but they are in a state of transition, and (what may at first appear strange) no amalgamation as has yet taken place: the puritan of the east, the Dutch descent of the middle states, the cavalier of the south, are nearly as marked and distinct now, as at the first occupation of the country, softened down indeed, but still distinct. Not only are the populations of the various states distinct, but even those of the cities: and it is hardly possible to make a remark which may be considered as general to a country, where the varieties of soil and of climate are so extensive. Even on that point upon which you might most safely venture to generalise, namely, the effect of a democratical form of government upon the mass, your observations must be taken with some exceptions, arising from the climate, manners, and customs, and the means of livelihood so differing in this extended country.

Indeed the habit in which travellers indulge of repeating facts which have taken place, of having taken place in America, has, perhaps unintentionally on their part, very much misled the English reader. It would hardly be considered fair, if the wilder parts of Ireland, and the disgraceful acts which are committed there, were represented as characteristic of England, or the British empire; yet between London and Connaught there is less difference than between the most civilised and intellectual portion of America, such as Boston and Philadelphia, and the wild regions, and wilder inhabitants of the west of the Mississippi, and Arkansas, where reckless beings compose a scattered population, residing too far for the law to reach; or where if it could reach, the power of the government would prove much too weak to enforce obedience to it. To do justice to all parties, America should be examined and portrayed piecemeal, every state separately, for every state is different, running down the scale from refinement to a state of barbarism almost unprecedented; but each presenting matter for investigation and research, and curious examples of cause and effect.

Many of those who have preceded me have not been able to devote sufficient time to their object, and therefore have failed. If you have passed through a strange country, totally differing in manners, and customs, and language from your own, you may give your readers some idea of the contrast, and the impressions made upon you by what you saw, even if you have travelled in haste or sojourned there but a few days; but when the similarity in manners, customs, and language is so great, that you may imagine yourself to be in your own country, it requires more research, a greater degree of acumen, and a fuller investigation of cause and effect than can be given in a few months of rapid motion. Moreover, English travellers have apparently been more active in examining the interior of houses, than the public path from which they should have drawn their conclusions; they have searched with the curiosity of a woman, instead of examining and surveying with the eye of a philosopher. Following up this wrong track has been the occasion of much indiscretion and injustice on their parts, and of justifiably indignant feeling on the part of the Americans. By many of the writers on America, the little discrepancies, the mere trifles of custom have been dwelt upon, with a sarcastic, ill-natured severity to give their works that semblance of pith, in which, in reality, they were miserably deficient; and they violated the rights of hospitality that they might increase their interest as authors.

The Americans are often themselves the cause of their being misrepresented; there is no country perhaps, in which the habit of deceiving for amusement, or what is termed hoaxing, is so common. Indeed this and the hyperbole constitute the major part of American humour. If they have the slightest suspicion that a foreigner is about to write a book, nothing appears to give them so much pleasure as to try to mislead him; this has constantly been practised upon me, and for all I know, they may in some instances have been successful; if they have, all I can say of the story is that "*se non e vero, e si ben trovato*," that it might have happened. (Note 1.)

When I was at Boston, a gentleman of my acquaintance brought me Miss Martineau's work, and was excessively delighted when he pointed out to me two pages of fallacies, which he had told her with a grave face, and which she had duly recorded and printed. This practice, added to another, that of attempting to conceal (for the Americans are aware of many of their defects), has been with me productive of good results: it has led me to much close investigation, and has made me very cautious in asserting what has not been proved to my own satisfaction to be worthy of credibility.

Another difficulty and cause of misrepresentation is, that travellers are not aware of the jealousy existing between the inhabitants of the different states and cities. The eastern states pronounce the southerners to be choleric, reckless, regardless of law, and indifferent as to religion; while the southerners designate the eastern states as a nursery of overreaching pedlars, selling clocks and wooden nutmegs. This running into extremes is produced from the clashing of their interests as producers and manufacturers. Again, Boston turns up her erudite nose at New York; Philadelphia, in her pride, looks down upon both New York and Boston; while New York, clinking her dollars, swears the Bostonians are a parcel of puritanical prigs, and the Philadelphians a would-be aristocracy. A western man from Kentucky, when at the Tremont House in Boston, begged me particularly not to pay attention to what they said of his state in that quarter. Both a Virginian and Tennessean, when I was at New York did the same.

At Boston, I was drinking champaign at a supper. "Are you drinking champaign?" said a young Bostonian. "That's New York—take claret; or, if you will drink champaign, pour it into a *green* glass, and they will think it *hock*; champaign is not right." How are we to distinguish between right and wrong in this queer world? At New York, they do drink a great deal of champaign; it is the small beer of the dinner-table. Champaign become associated with New York, and therefore is not *right*. I will do the New Yorkers the justice to say, that, as far as *drinks* are concerned, they are above prejudice: all's right with them, provided there's enough of it.

The above remarks will testify, that travellers in America have great difficulties to contend with, and that their channels of information have been chiefly those of the drawing-room or dinner-table. Had I worked through the same, I should have found then very difficult of access; for the Americans had determined that they would no longer extend their hospitality to those who returned it with ingratitude—nor can they be blamed. Let us reverse the case. Were not the doors of many houses in England shut against an American author, when from his want of knowledge of conventional *usage*, he published what never should have appeared in print! And should another return to England, after his tetchy, absurd remarks upon the English, is there much chance of his receiving a kind welcome? Most assuredly not; both these authors will be received with caution. The Americans, therefore, are not only not to blame, but would prove themselves very deficient in a proper respect for themselves, if they again admitted into their domestic circles those who eventually requited them with abuse.

Admitting this, of course I have no feelings of ill-will toward them for any want of hospitality toward me; on the contrary, I was pleased with the neglect, as it left me free, and unshackled from any real or fancied claims which the Americans might have made upon me on that score. Indeed, I had not been three weeks in the country before I decided upon accepting no more invitations, even charily as they were made. I found that, although invited, my presence was a restraint upon the company; every one appeared afraid to speak; and when anything ludicrous occurred, the cry would be—"Oh, now. Captain Marryat, don't put that into your book." More than once, when I happened to be in large parties, a question such as follows would be put to me by some "free and enlightened individual":—

"Now, Captain Marryat, I ask you before this company, and I trust you will give me a categorical answer, Are you, or are you not about to write a book upon this country?" I hardly need observe to the English reader, that, under such circumstances, the restraint, became mutual; I declined all farther invitations, and adhered to this determination as far as I could without cause of offence, during my whole tour through the United States.

But if I admit, that after the usage which they had received, the Americans are justified in not again tendering their hospitably to the English, I cannot, at the same time, but express my opinion as to their conduct toward me personally. They had no right to insult and annoy me in the manner they did, from nearly one end of the Union to the other, either because my predecessors had expressed an unfavourable opinion of them before my arrival, or because they expected that I would do the same upon my return to my own country, I remark upon this conduct, not from any feeling of ill-will or desire of retaliation, but to compel the Americans to admit that I am under no obligations to them: that I received from them much more of insult and outrage than of kindness; and, consequently, that the charge of ingratitude cannot be laid to my door, however offensive to them some of the remarks in this work may happen to be.

And here I must observe, that the Americans can no longer anticipate lenity from the English traveller, as latterly they have so deeply committed themselves. Once, indeed, they could say, "We admit and are hospitable to the English, who, as soon as they leave our country, turn round and abuse and revile us. We have our faults, it is true: but such conduct on their part is not kind or generous." But they can say this no longer; they have retaliated, and in their attacks they have been regardless of justice. The three last works upon the Americans, written by English authors, were, on the whole, favourable to them; Mr Power's and Mr Grund's most decidedly so; and Miss Martineau's, filled as it is with absurdities and fallacies, was *intended*, at all events to be favourable.

In opposition to them, we have Mr Cooper's remarks upon England, in which my countrymen are certainly not spared; and, since that publication, we have another of much greater importance, written by Mr Carey, of Philadelphia, not, indeed, in a strain of vituperation or ill-feeling, but asserting, and no doubt to his own satisfaction and that of his countrymen, proving, that in every important point, that is to say, under the heads of "Security of Person and Property, of Morals, Education, Religion, Industry, Invention, Credit," (and consequently Honesty,) America is in advance of England and every other nation in Europe!! The tables, then, are turned; it is no longer the English, but the Americans who are the assailants; and such being the case, I beg that it may be remembered, that many of the remarks which will subsequently appear in this work have been forced from me by the attacks made upon my nation by the American authors; and that, if I am compelled to draw comparisons, it is not with the slightest wish to annoy or humiliate the Americans, but in legitimate and justifiable defence of my own native land.

America is a wonderful country, endowed by the Omnipotent with natural advantages which no other can boast of; and the mind can hardly calculate upon the degree of perfection and power to which, whether the states are eventually separated or not, it may in the course of two centuries arrive. At present all is energy and enterprise; everything is in a state of transition, but of rapid improvement—so rapid, indeed, that those who would describe America now, would have to correct all in the short space of ten years; for ten years in America is almost equal to a century in the old continent. Now, you may pass through a wild forest, where the elk browses and the panther howls; in ten years, that very forest, with its denizens, will, most likely, have disappeared, and in their place you will find towns with thousands of inhabitants; with arts, manufactures, and machinery, all in full activity.

In reviewing America, we must look upon it as showing the development of the English character under a new aspect, arising from a new state of things. If I were to draw a comparison between the English and the Americans, I should say that there is almost as much difference between the two nations at this present time, as there has long been between the English and the Dutch. The latter are considered by us as phlegmatic and slow; and we may be considered the same, compared with our energetic descendants. Time to an American is everything, (Note 2) and space he attempts to reduce to a mere nothing. By the steamboats, rail-roads, and the wonderful facilities of water-carriage, a journey of five hundred miles is as little considered in America, as would be here a journey from London to Brighton. "*Go ahead*" is the real motto of the country; and every man does push on, to gain in advance of his neighbour. The American lives twice as long as others; for he does twice the work during the time that he lives. He begins life sooner: at fifteen he is considered a man, plunges into the stream of enterprise, floats and struggles with his fellows. In every trifle an American shows the value he puts upon time. He rises early, eats his meals with the rapidity of a wolf, and is the whole day at his business. If he be a merchant, his money, whatever it may amount to, is seldom invested; it is all floating—his accumulations remain active; and when he dies, his wealth has to be collected from the four quarters of the globe.

Now, all this energy and activity is of English origin; and were England expanded into America, the same results would be produced. To a certain degree, the English, were in former times, what the Americans are now; and this it is which has raised our country so high in the scale of nations; but since we have become so closely packed—so crowded, that there is hardly room for the population, our activity has been proportionably cramped and subdued. But, in this vast and favoured country, the very associations and impressions of childhood foster and enlighten the intellect and precociously rouse the energies. The wide expanse of territory already occupied—the vast and magnificent rivers—the boundless regions yet remaining to be peopled—the rapidity of communication—the dispatch with which everything is effected, are evident almost to the child. To those who have rivers many thousand miles in length, the passage across the Atlantic (of 3,500 miles) appears but a trifle; and the American ladies talk of spending the winter at Paris with as much indifference as one of our landed proprietors would, of going up to London for the season.

We must always bear in mind the peculiar and wonderful advantages of *country*, when we examine America and its form of government; for the country has had more to do with upholding this democracy than people might at first imagine. Among the advantages of democracy, the greatest is, perhaps, that *all start fair*; and the boy who holds the traveller's horse, as Van Buren is said to have done, may become the president of the United States. But it is the *country*, and not the government; which has been productive of such rapid strides as have been made by America. Indeed it is a query whether the form of government would have existed down to this day, had it not been for the advantages derived from the vast extent and boundless resources of the territory in which it was established. Let the American direct his career to any goal he pleases, his energies are unshackled; and, in the race, the best man must win. There is room for all, and millions more. Let him choose his profession—his career is not checked or foiled by the excess of those who have already embarked in it. In every department there is an opening for talent; and for those inclined to work, work is always to be procured. You have no complaint in this country, that every profession is so full that it is impossible to know what to do with your children. There is a vast field, and all may receive the reward due for their labour.

In a country where the ambition and energies of man have been roused to such an extent, the great point is to find out worthy incitements for ambition to feed upon. A virtue undirected into a wrong channel may, by circumstances, prove little better than (even if it does not sink down into) actual vice. Hence it is that a democratic form of government is productive of such demoralising effects. Its rewards are few. Honours of every description, which stir up the soul of man to noble deeds—worthy incitements, they have none. The only compensation they can offer for services is money; and the only distinction— the only means of raising himself above his fellows left to the American—is wealth; consequently, the acquisition of wealth has become the great spring of action. But it is not sought after with the avarice to hoard, but with the ostentation to expend. It is the effect of ambition directed into a wrong channel. Each man would surpass his neighbour; and the only great avenue open to all, and into which thousands may press without much jostling of each other, is that which leads to the shrine of Mammon. It is our nature to attempt to raise ourselves above our fellow-men; it is the main-spring of existence— the incitement to all that is great and virtuous, or great and vicious. In America, but a small portion can raise themselves, or find rewards for superior talent, but wealth is attainable by all; and having no aristocracy, no honours, no distinctions to look forward to, wealth has become the substitute, and, with very few exceptions, every man is great in proportion to his riches. The consequence is, that to leave a sum of money when they die is of little importance to the majority of the Americans. Their object is to amass it while young, and obtain the consideration which it gives them during their lifetime.

The society in the United States is that which must naturally be expected in a new country where there are few men of leisure, and the majority are working hard to obtain that wealth which almost alone gives importance under a democratic form of government. You will find intellectual and gentlemanlike people in America, but they are scattered here and there. The circle of society is not complete: wherever you go, you will find an admixture, sudden wealth having admitted those who but a few years back were in humble circumstances; and in the constant state of transition which takes place in this country, it will be half a century, perhaps, before a select circle of society can be collected together in any one city or place. The improvement is rapid, but the vast extent of country which has to be peopled prevents that improvement from being manifest. The stream flows inland, and those who are here today are gone to-morrow, and their places in society filled up by others who ten years back had no prospect of ever being admitted. All is transition, the waves follow one another to the far west, the froth and scum, boiling in the advance.

America is, indeed, well worth the study of the philosopher. A vast nation forming, society ever changing, all in motion and activity, nothing complete, the old continent pouring in her surplus to supply the loss of the eastern states, all busy as a hive, full of energy and activity. Every year multitudes swarm off from the east, like bees: not the young only, but the old, quitting the close-built cities, society, and refinement, to settle down in some lone spot in the vast prairies, where the rich soil offers to them the certain prospect of their families and children being one day possessed of competency and wealth.

To write upon America *as a nation* would be absurd, for nation, properly speaking, it is not; but to consider it in its present chaotic state, is well worth the labour. It would not only exhibit to the living a somewhat new picture of the human mind, but, as a curious page in the Philosophy of History, it would hereafter serve as a subject of review for the Americans themselves.

It is not my intention to follow the individualising plans of the majority of those who have preceded me in this country. I did not sail across the Atlantic to ascertain whether the Americans eat their dinners with two-prong iron, or three-prong silver forks, with chopsticks, or their fingers; it is quite sufficient for me to know that they do eat and drink; if they did not, it would be a curious anomaly which I should not pass over. My object was, to examine and ascertain *what were the effects of a democratic form of government and climate upon a people which, with all its foreign admixture, may still be considered as English.*

It is a fact that our virtues and our vices depend more upon circumstances than upon ourselves, and there are no circumstances which operate so powerfully upon us as government and climate. Let it not be supposed that, in the above assertion, I mean to extenuate vice, or imply that we are not free agents. Naturally prone to vices in general, circumstances will render us more prone to one description of vice than to another; but that is no reason why we should not be answerable for it, since it is our duty to guard against the besetting sin. But as an agent in this point the form of government under which we live is, perhaps, the most powerful in its effects, and thus we constantly hear of vices peculiar to a country, when it ought rather to be said, of vices peculiar to a government.

Never, perhaps, was the foundation of a nation laid under such peculiarly favourable auspices as that of America. The capital they commenced with was industry, activity, and courage. They had, moreover, the advantage of the working of genius and wisdom, and the records of history, as a beacon and a guide; the trial of ages, as to the respective merits of the various governments to which men have submitted; the power to select the merits from the demerits in each; a boundless extent of country, rich in everything that could be of advantage to man; and they were led by those who where really giants in those days, a body of men collected and acting together, forming an aggregate of wisdom and energy, such as probably will not for centuries be seen again. Never was there such an opportunity of testing the merits of a republic, of ascertaining if such a form of government could be maintained—in fact, of proving whether an enlightened people could govern themselves. And it must be acknowledged that the work was well begun; Washington, when his career had closed, left the country a pure republic. He did all that man could do. Miss Martineau asserts that "America has solved the great problem, that a republic can exist for fifty years;" but such is not the case. America has proved that, under peculiar advantages, a people can govern themselves for fifty years; but if you put the question to an enlightened American, and ask him, "Were Washington to rise from his grave, would he recognise the present government of America as the one bequeathed to them?" and the American will himself answer in the negative. These fifty years have afforded another proof, were it necessary, how short-sighted and fallible are men—how impossible it is to keep anything in a state of perfection here below. Washington left America as an infant nation, a pure and, I may add, a virtuous republic; but the government of the country has undergone as much change as everything else, and it has now settled down into anything but a pure democracy. Nor could it be otherwise; a republic may be formed and may continue in healthy existence when regulated by a small body of men, but as men increase and multiply so do they deteriorate; the closer they are packed the more vicious they become, and, consequently, the more vicious become their institutions. Washington and his coadjutors had no power to control the nature of man.

It may be inquired by some, what difference there is between a republic and a democracy, as the terms have been, and are often, used indifferently. I know not whether my distinction is right, but I consider that when those possessed of most talent and wisdom are selected to act for the benefit of a people, with full reliance upon their acting for the best, and without any shackle or pledge being enforced, we may consider that form of government as a republic ruled by the most enlightened and capable; but that if, on the contrary, those selected by the people to represent them are not only bound by the pledges previous to their election, but ordered by the mass how to vote after their election, then the country, is not ruled by the collected wisdom of the people, but by the majority, who are as often wrong as right, and then the governing principle sinks into a democracy, as it now is in America. (Note 3.)

It is singular to remark, notwithstanding her monarchical form of government, how much more republican England is in her institutions than America. Ask an American what he considers the necessary qualifications of a president, and, after intellectual qualification, he will tell you firmness, decision, and undaunted courage; and it is really an enigma to him, although he will not acknowledge it, how the sceptre of a country like England, subject to the monarchical sway which he detests, can be held in the hand of a young female of eighteen years of age.

But upon one point I have made up my mind, which is that, with all its imperfections, democracy is the form of government *best suited to the present condition of America*, in so far as it is the one under which the country has made, and will continue to make, the most rapid advances. That it must eventually be changed is true, but the times of its change must be determined by so many events, hidden in futurity, which may accelerate or retard the convulsion, that it would be presumptuous for any one to attempt to name a period when the present form of government shall be broken up, and the multitude shall separate and re-embody themselves under new institutions.

In the arrangement of this work, I have considered it advisable to present, first, to the reader those *portions* of my diary which may be interesting, and in which are recorded traits and incidents which will bear strongly upon the commentaries I shall subsequently make upon the institutions of the United States, and the results of those institutions as developed in the American character. Having been preceded by so many writers on America, I must occasionally tread in well-beaten tracts; but, although I shall avoid repetition as much as possible, this will not prevent me from describing what I saw or felt. Different ideas, and different associations of ideas, will strike different travellers, as the same landscape may wear a new appearance, according as it is viewed in the morning, by noon, or at night; the outlines remain the same, but the lights, and shadows, and tints, are reflected from the varying idiosyncrasy of various minds.

My readers will also find many quotations, either embodied in the work or supplied by notes. This I have considered necessary, that my opinions may be corroborated; but these quotations will not be extracted so much from the works of English as from *American* writers. The opinions relative to the United States have been so conflicting in the many works which have been written, that I consider it most important that I should be able to quote American authorities against themselves, and strengthen my opinions and arguments by their own admissions.

Note 1. *Paragraph from a New York paper*. That old, deaf English maiden lady, Miss Martineau, who travelled through some of the states, a few years since, gives a full account of Mr Poindexter's death; unfortunately for her veracity, the gentleman still lives; but this is about as near the truth as the majority of her statements. The *loafing* English men and women who visit America, as penny-a-liners, are perfectly understood here, and Jonathan amuses himself whenever he meets them, by imposing upon their credulity the most absurd stories which he can invent, which they swallow whole, go home with their eyes sticking out of their heads with wonder, and print all they have heard for the benefit of John Bull's calves.

Note 2. The clocks in America—there rendered so famous by Sam Slick— instead of the moral lessons inculcated by the dials in this country, such as "Time flies," etcetera, teach one more suited to American feeling:—"Time is money!"

Note 3. And in this opinion I find that I am borne out by an American writer, who says—"It is true, indeed, that the American government, which, as first set up, was properly republican—that is, representation in a course of salutary degrees, and with salutary checks upon the popular will, on the powers of legislation, of the executive, and the judiciary,—was assailed at an early period of its history, and has been assailed continuously down to the present time, by a power called democracy, and that this power has been constantly acquiring influence and gaining ascendency in the republic during the term of its history."—(*A Voice from America to England*, by an American Gentleman, page 10.)

Volume One—Chapter One.

I like to begin at the beginning; it's a good old fashion, not sufficiently adhered to in these modern times. I recollect a young gentleman who said he was thinking of going to America; on my asking him, "how he intended to go?" he replied, "I don't exactly know; but I think I shall take the fast coach." I wished him a safe passage, and said, "I was afraid he would find it very dusty." As I could not find the office to book myself by this young gentleman's conveyance, I walked down to St. Katherine's Docks; went on board a packet; was shewn into a superb cabin, fitted up with bird's-eye maple, mahogany, and looking-glasses, and communicating with certain small cabins, where there was a sleeping berth for each passenger, about as big as that allowed to a pointer in a dog-kennel. I thought that there was more finery than comfort; but it ended in my promising the captain to meet him at Portsmouth. He was to sail from London on the 1st of April, and I did not choose to sail on that day—it was ominous; so I embarked at Portsmouth on the 3rd. It is not my intention to give a description of crossing the Atlantic; but as the reader may be disappointed if I do not tell him how I got over, I shall first inform him that we were thirty-eight in the cabin, and 160 men, women, and children, literally stowed in bulk in the steerage. I shall describe what took place from the time I first went up the side at Spithead, until the ship was under weigh, and then make a very short passage of it.

At 9:30 a.m.—Embarked on board the good ship Quebec; and a good ship she proved to be, repeatedly going nine and a-half knots on a bowling, sails lifting. Captain H— quite delighted to see me—all captains of packets are to see passengers: I believed him when he said so.

At 9:50.—Sheriff's officer, as usual, came on board. Observed several of the cabin passengers hasten down below, and one who requested the captain to stow him away. But it was not a pen-and-ink affair; it was a case of burglary. The officer has found his man in the steerage—the handcuffs are on his wrists, and they are rowing him ashore. His wife and two children are on board; her lips quiver as she collects her baggage to follow her husband. One half-hour more, and he would have escaped from justice, and probably have led a better life in a far country, where his crimes were unknown. By the bye, Greenacre, the man who cut the woman up, was taken out of the ship as she went down the river: he had very nearly escaped. What cargoes of crime, folly, and recklessness do we yearly ship off to America! America ought to be very much obliged to us.

The women of the steerage are persuading the wife of the burglar not to go on shore; their arguments are strong, but not strong enough against the devoted love of a woman.—"Your husband is certain to be hung; what's the use of following him? Your passage is paid, and you will have no difficulty in supporting your children in America." But she rejects the advice—goes down the side, and presses her children to her breast, as, overcome with the agony of her feelings, she drops into the boat; and, now that she is away from the ship, you hear the sobs, which can no longer be controlled.

10 a.m.—"All hands up anchor."

I was repeating to myself some of the stanzas of Mrs Norton's "Here's a Health to the Outward-bound," when I cast my eyes forward.

I could not imagine what the seamen were about; they appeared to be *pumping*, instead of heaving, at the windlass. I forced my way through the heterogeneous mixture of human beings, animals, and baggage which crowded the decks, and discovered that they were working a patent windlass, by Dobbinson—a very ingenious and superior invention. The seamen, as usual, lightened their labour with the song and chorus, forbidden by the etiquette of a man-of-war. The one they sung was peculiarly musical, although not refined; and the chorus of "Oh! Sally Brown," was given with great emphasis by the whole crew between every line of the song, sung by an athletic young third mate. I took my seat on the knight-heads—turned my face aft—looked and listened.

"Heave away there, forward."

"Aye, aye, sir."

"'Sally Brown—oh! my dear Sally.'" (Single voice).

"'Oh! Sally Brown.'" (Chorus).

"'Sally Brown, of Buble Al-ly.'" (Single voice).

"'Oh! Sal-ly Brown,'" (Chorus).

"Avast heaving there; send all aft to clear the boat."

"Aye, aye, sir. Where are we to stow these casks, Mr Fisher?"

"Stow them! Heaven knows; get them in, at all events."

"Captain H—! Captain H—! there's my piano still on deck; it will be quite spoiled—indeed it will."

"Don't be alarmed, ma'am; as soon as we're under weigh we'll hoist the cow up, and get the piano down."

"What! under the cow?"

"No, ma'am; but the cow's over the hatchway."

"Now, then, my lads, forward to the windlass."

"'I went to town to get some toddy.'"

"'Oh! Sally Brown.'"

"'T'wasn't fit for any body.'"

"'Oh! Sally Brown.'"

"Out there, and clear away the jib."

"Aye, aye, sir."

"Mr Fisher, how much cable is there out?"

"Plenty yet, sir.—Heave away, my lads."

"'Sally is a bright mulattar.'"

"'Oh! Sally Brown.'"

"'Pretty girl, but can't get at her.'"

"Avast heaving; send the men aft to whip the ladies in.—Now, miss, only sit down and don't be afraid, and you'll be in, in no time.—Whip away, my lads, handsomely; steady her with the guy; lower away.—There, miss, now you're safely *landed*."

"Landed am I? I thought I was *shipped*."

"Very good, indeed—very good, miss; you'll make an excellent sailor, I see."

"I should make a better sailor's *wife*, I expect, Captain H—."

"Excellent! Allow me to hand you aft; you'll excuse me.—Forward now, my men; heave away!"

"'Seven years I courted Sally.'"

"'Oh! Sally Brown.'"

"'Seven more of shilley-shally.'"

"'Oh! Sally Brown.'"

"'She won't wed—'"

"Avast heaving. Up there, and loose the topsails; stretch along the topsail-sheets.—Upon my soul, half these children will be killed.—Whose child are you?"

"I—don't—know."

"Go and find out, that's a dear.—Let fall; sheet home; belay starboard sheet; clap on the larboard; belay all that.—Now, then, Mr Fisher."

"Aye, aye, sir.—Heave away, my lads."

"'She won't wed a Yankee sailor.'"

"'Oh! Sally Brown.'"

"'For she's in love with the nigger tailor.'"

"'Oh! Sally Brown.'"

"Heave away, my men; heave, and in sight. Hurrah! my lads."

"'Sally Brown—oh! my dear Sally!'"

"'Oh! Sally Brown!'"

"'Sally Brown, of Buble Alley.'"

"'Oh! Sally Brown.'"

"'Sally has a cross old granny.'"

"'Oh—!'"

"Heave and fall—jib-halyards—hoist away."

"Oh! dear—oh! dear."

"The clumsy brute has half-killed the girl!—Don't cry, my dear."

"Pick up the child, Tom, and shove it out of the way."

"Where shall I put her?"

"Oh, any where just now; put her on the turkey-coop."

"Starboard!"

"I say, clap on, some of you *he* chaps, or else get out of the way."

"Sailor, mind my band-box."

"Starboard!"

"Starboard it is; steady so."

Thus, with the trifling matter of maiming half-a-dozen children, upsetting two or three women, smashing the lids of a few trunks, and crushing some band-boxes as flat as a muffin, the good ship Quebec was at last fairly under weigh, and standing out for St. Helen's.

3 p.m.—Off St. Helen's; ship steady; little wind; water smooth; passengers sure they won't be sick.

3:20.—Apologies from the captain for a cold dinner on this day.

4 o'clock.—Dinner over; every body pulls out a number of "Pickwick;" every body talks and reads Pickwick; weather getting up squally; passengers not quite so sure they won't be seasick.

Who can tell what the morrow may bring forth? It brought forth a heavy sea, and the passengers were quite sure that they were seasick. Only six out of thirty-eight made their appearance at the breakfast-table; and, for many days afterwards, there were Pickwicks in plenty strewed all over the cabin, but passengers were very scarce.

But we had more than sea-sickness to contend with—the influenza broke out and raged. Does not this prove that it is contagious, and not dependant on the atmosphere? It was hard, after having sniffled with it for six weeks on shore, that I should have another month of it on board. But who can control destiny? The ship was like a hospital; an elderly woman was the first victim—then a boy of twelve years of age. Fortunately, there were no more deaths.

But I have said enough of the passage. On the 4th of May, in the year of our Lord 1837, I found myself walking up Broadway, among the free and enlightened citizens of New York.

Volume One—Chapter Two.

A visit, to make it agreeable to both parties, should be well timed. My appearance at New York was very much like bursting into a friend's house with a merry face when there is a death in it—with the sudden change from levity to condolence. "Any other time most happy to see you. You find us in a very unfortunate situation."

"Indeed I'm very—very sorry."

Two hundred and sixty houses have already failed, and no one knows where it is to end. Suspicion, fear, and misfortune have taken possession of the city. Had I not been aware of the cause, I should have imagined that the plague was raging, and I had the description of Defoe before me.

Not a smile on one countenance among the crowd who pass and repass; hurried steps, careworn faces, rapid exchanges of salutation, or hasty communication of anticipated ruin before the sun goes down. Here two or three are gathered on one side, whispering and watching that they are not overheard; there a solitary, with his arms folded and his hat slouched, brooding over departed affluence. Mechanics, thrown out of employment, are pacing up and down with the air of famished wolves. The violent shock has been communicated, like that of electricity, through the country to a distance of hundreds of miles. Canals, railroads, and all public works, have been discontinued, and the Irish emigrant leans against his shanty, with his spade idle in his hand, and starves, as his thoughts wander back to his own Emerald Isle.

The Americans delight in the hyperbole; in fact they hardly have a metaphor without it. During this crash, when every day fifteen or twenty merchants' names appeared in the newspapers as bankrupts, one party, not in a very good humour, was hastening down Broadway, when he was run against by another whose temper was equally unamiable. This collision roused the choler of both.

"What the devil do you mean, sir?" cried one; "I've a great mind to knock you into *the middle of next week.*"

This occurring on a Saturday, the wrath of the other was checked by the recollection of how very favourable such a blow would be to his present circumstances.

"Will you! by heavens, then pray do; it's just the thing I want, for how else I am to get over next Monday and the acceptances I must take up, is more than I can tell."

All the banks have stopped payment in specie, and there is not a dollar to be had. I walked down Wall Street, and had a convincing proof of the great demand for money, for somebody picked my pocket.

The militia are under arms, as riots are expected. The banks in the country and other towns have followed the example of New York, and thus has General Jackson's currency bill been repealed without the aid of Congress. Affairs are now at their worst, and now that such is the case, the New Yorkers appear to recover their spirits. One of the newspapers humorously observes—"All Broadway is like unto a new-made widow, and don't know whether to laugh or cry." There certainly is a very remarkable energy in the American disposition; if they fall, they bound up again. Somebody has observed that the New York merchants are of that *elastic* nature, that, when fit for nothing else, they might be converted into *coach springs*, and such really appears to be their character.

Nobody refuses to take the paper of the New York banks, although they virtually have stopped payment;—they never refuse anything in New York;—but nobody will give specie in change, and great distress is occasioned by this want of a circulating medium. Some of the shopkeepers told me that they had been obliged to turn away a hundred dollars a-day, and many a Southerner, who has come up with a large supply of southern notes, has found himself a pauper, and has been indebted to a friend for a few dollars in specie to get home again.

The radicals here, for there are radicals, it appears, in a democracy—

"In the lowest depth, a lower deep—"

are very loud in their complaints. I was watching the swarming multitude in Wall Street this morning, when one of these fellows was declaiming against the banks for stopping specie payments, and "robbing a poor man in such a *w*illanous manner," when one of the merchants, who appeared to know his customer, said to him—"Well, as you say, it is hard for a poor fellow like you not to be able to get dollars for his notes; hand them out, and I'll give you specie for them myself!" The blackguard had not a cent in his pocket, and walked away looking very foolish. He reminded me of a little chimney-sweeper at the Tower Hamlets election, asking—"Vot vos my hopinions about primaginitur?"—a very important point to him certainly, he having no parents, and having been brought up by the parish.

I was in a store when a thorough-bred democrat walked in: he talked loud, and voluntarily gave it as his opinion that all this distress was the very best thing that could have happened to the country, as America would now keep all the specie and pay her English creditors with bankruptcies. There always appears to me to be a great want of moral principle in all radicals; indeed, the levelling principles of radicalism are adverse to the sacred rights of *meum et tuum*. At Philadelphia the ultra-democrats have held a large public meeting, at which one of the first resolutions brought forward and agreed to was—"That they did not owe one farthing to the English people."

"They may say the times are bad," said a young American to me, "but I think that they are excellent. A twenty dollar note used to last me but a week, but now it is as good as Fortunatus's purse, which was never empty. I eat my dinner at the hotel, and show them my twenty dollar note. The landlord turns away from it, as if it were the head of Medusa, and begs that I will pay another time. I buy every thing that I want, and I have only to offer my twenty dollar note in payment, and my credit is unbounded—that is, for any sum under twenty dollars. If they ever do give change again in New York it will make a very unfortunate change in my affairs."

A government circular, enforcing the act of Congress, which obliges all those who have to pay custom-house duties or postage to do so in specie, has created great dissatisfaction, and added much to the distress and difficulty. At the same time that they (the government) refuse to take from their debtors the notes of the banks, upon the ground that they are no longer legal tenders, they compel their creditors to take those very notes—having had a large quantity in their possession at the time that the banks suspended specie payments—an act of despotism which the English Government would not venture upon.

Miss Martineau's work is before me. How dangerous it is to prophecy. Speaking of the merchants of New York, and their recovering after the heavy losses they sustained by the calamitous fire of 1835, she says, that although eighteen millions of property were destroyed, not one merchant failed; and she continues, "It seems now as if the commercial credit of New York could stand any shock short of an earthquake like that of Lisbon." That was the prophecy of 1836. Where is the commercial credit of New York now in 1837?!!!

The distress for change has produced a curious remedy. Every man is now his own banker. Go to the theatres and places of public amusement, and, instead of change, you receive an IOU from the treasury. At the hotels and oyster-cellars it is the same thing. Call for a glass of brandy and water and the change is fifteen tickets, each "good for one glass of brandy and water." At an oyster-shop, eat a plate of oysters, and you have in return seven tickets, good for one plate of oysters each. It is the same every where.—The barbers give you tickets, good for so many shaves; and were there beggars in the streets, I presume they would give you tickets in change, good for so much philanthropy. Dealers, in general, give out their own bank-notes, or as they are called here, *shin plasters*, which are good for one dollar, and from that down to two and a-half cents, all of which are redeemable, and redeemable only upon a general return to cash payments.

Hence arises another variety of exchange in Wall Street.

"Tom, do you want any oysters for lunch to-day?"

"Yes!"

"Then here's a ticket, and give me two *shaves* in return."

The most prominent causes of this convulsion have already been laid before the English public; but there is one—that of speculating in land—which has not been sufficiently dwelt upon, nor has the importance been given to it which it deserves; as, perhaps, next to the losses occasioned by the great fire, it led, more than any other species of over-speculation and over-trading, to the distress which has ensued. Not but that the event must have taken place in the natural course of things. Cash payments produce sure but small returns; but no commerce can be carried on by this means on any extended scale. Credit, as long as it is good, is so much extra capital, in itself nominal and non-existent, but producing real returns. If any one will look back upon the commercial history of these last fifty years, he will perceive that the system of credit is always attended with a periodical *blow up*; in England, perhaps, once in twenty years; in America, once in from seven to ten. This arises from their being no safety valve—no check which can be put to it by mutual consent of all parties. One house extends its credit, and for a time, its profits; another follows the example. The facility of credit induces those who obtain it to embark in other speculations, foreign to their business; for credit thus becomes extra capital which they do not know how to employ. Such has been the case in the present instance: but this is no reason for the credit system not being continued. These occasional explosions act as warnings, and, for the time, people are more cautious: they stop for a while to repair damages, and recover from their consternation; and when they go a-head again, it is not quite so fast. The loss is severely felt, because people are not prepared to meet it; but if all the profits of the years of healthy credit were added up, and the balance sheet struck between that and the loss at the explosion, the advantage gained by the credit system would still be found to be great. The advancement of America depends wholly upon it. It is by credit alone that she has made such rapid strides, and it is by credit alone that she can continue to flourish, at the same time that she enriches those who trade with her. In this latter crisis there was more blame to be attached to the English houses, who *forced* their credit upon the Americans, than to the Americans, who, having such unlimited credit, thought that they might advantageously speculate with the capital of others.

One of the most singular affections of the human mind is a proneness to excessive speculation; and it may here be noticed that the disease for (such it may be termed) is peculiarly English and American. Men, in their race for gain, appear, like horses that have run away, to have been blinded by the rapidity of their own motion. It almost amounts to an epidemic, and is infectious—the wise and the foolish being equally liable to the disease. We had ample evidence of this in the bubble manias which took place in England in the years 1825 and 1826. A mania of this kind had infected the people of America for two or three years previous to the crash: it was that of speculating in land; and to show the extent to which it had been carried on, we may take the following examples:—

The city of New York, which is built upon a narrow island about ten miles in length, at present covers about three miles of that distance, and has a population of three hundred thousand inhabitants. Building lots were marked out for the other seven miles; and, by calculation, these lots when built upon, would contain an additional population of one million and three-quarters. They were first purchased at from one hundred to one hundred and fifty dollars each, but, as the epidemic raged, they rose to upwards of two thousand dollars. At Brooklyn, on Long Island, opposite to New York, and about half a mile distant from it, lots were marked out to the extent of fourteen miles, which would contain an extra population of one million, and these were as eagerly speculated in.

At Staten Island, at the entrance into the Sound, an estate was purchased by some speculators for ten thousand dollars, was divided into lots, and planned as a town to be called New Brighton; and had the whole of the lots been sold at the price for which many were, previous to the crash, the original speculators would have realised three million of dollars. But the infatuation was not confined to the precincts of New York: every where it existed. Government lands, which could only be paid for in specie, were eagerly sought after; plans of new towns were puffed up; drawings made, in which every street was laid down and named; churches, theatres, hospitals, rail-road communications, canals, steam-boats in the offing, all appeared on paper as if actually in existence, when, in fact, the very site was as yet a forest, with not a log—but within a mile of the pretended city. Lots in these visionary cities were eagerly purchased, increased daily in value, and afforded a fine harvest to those who took advantage of the credulity of others. One man would buy a lot with extensive *water privileges*, and, upon going to examine it, would find those privileges rather too extensive, the whole lot being *under water*. Even after the crisis, there was a man still going about who made a good livelihood by setting up his plan of a city, the lots of which he sold by public auction, on condition of one dollar being paid down to secure the purchase, if approved of. The mania had not yet subsided, and many paid down their dollar upon their purchase of a lot. This was all he required. He went to the next town, and sold the same lots over and over again.

To check this madness of speculation, was one reason why an act of Congress was passed, obliging all purchasers of government lands to pay in specie. Nevertheless, government received nine or ten millions in specie after the bill passed. Now, when it is considered what a large portion of the capital drawn from England was applied to these wild speculations—sums which, when they were required, could not be realised, as, when the crisis occurred, property thus purchased immediately fell to about one-tenth of what was paid for it—it will be clearly seen that, from this unfortunate mania, a great portion of the present distress must have arisen.

The attempt of General Jackson and his successors, to introduce a specie currency into a country which exists upon credit, was an act of folly, and has ended in complete failure. (See note 1.) A few weeks after he had issued from the Mint a large coinage of gold, there was hardly an eagle to be seen, and the metal might almost as well have remained in the mine from whence it had been extracted. It was still in the country, but had all been absorbed by the agriculturists; and such will ever be the case in a widely extended agricultural country. The farmers, principally Dutch, live upon a portion of their produce and sell the rest. Formerly they were content with bank bills or Mexican dollars, which they laid by for a rainy day, and they remained locked up for years before they were required. When the gold was issued, it was eagerly collected by these people, as more convenient, and laid by, by the farmers' wives, in the foot of an old worsted stocking, where the major part of it will remain. And thus has the famous gold-currency bill been upset by the hoarding propensities of a parcel of old women. (See note 2.)

Note 1. One single proof may be given of the ruinous policy of the Jackson administration in temporising with the credit of the country. To check the export of bullion from our country, the Bank of England had but one remedy, that of rendering money scarce: they contracted their issues, and it became so. The consequence was, that the price of cotton fell forty dollars per bale. The crop of cotton amounted to 1,600,000 bales, which, at forty dollars per bale, was a loss to the southern planters of 64,000,000 of dollars.

Note 2. A curious proof of this system of hoarding, which immediately took place upon the bank stopping payment, was told me by a gentleman from Baltimore. He went into a store to purchase, as he often had done, a canvas shot-bag, and to his surprise was asked three times the former price for it. Upon his expostulating, the vendors told him, that the demand for them by the farmers and other people who brought their produce to market, and who used them to put their specie in, was so great, that they could hardly supply them.

Volume One—Chapter Three.

Fifty years ago, New York was little more than a village; now, it is a fine city with three hundred thousand inhabitants. I have never seen any city so admirably adapted for commerce. It is built upon a narrow island, between Long Island Sound and the Hudson River, Broadway running up it like the vertebrae of some huge animal, and the other streets diverging from it at right angles, like the ribs; each street running to the river, and presenting to the view a forest of masts.

There are some fine buildings in this city, but not many. Astor House, although of simple architecture, is, perhaps, the grandest mass; and next to that, is the City Hall, though in architecture very indifferent. In the large room of the latter are some interesting pictures and busts of the presidents, mayors of the city, and naval and military officers, who have received the thanks of Congress and the freedom of the city. Some are very fair specimens of art: the most spirited is that of Commodore Perry, leaving his sinking vessel, in the combat on the Lakes, to hoist his flag on board of another ship. Decatur's portrait is also very fine. Pity that such a man should have been sacrificed in a foolish duel!

At the corner of many of the squares, or *blocks* of buildings, as they are termed here, is erected a very high mast, with a cap of liberty upon the top. The only idea we have of the cap of liberty is, the *bonnet rouge* of the French; but the Americans will not copy the French, although they will the English; so they have a cap of their own, which (begging their pardon), with its gaudy colours and gilding, looks more like a *fool's cap* than any thing else.

New York is not equal to London, nor Broadway to Regent Street, although the Americans would compare them. Still, New York is very superior to most of our provincial towns, and, to a man who can exist out of London, Broadway will do very well for a lounge—being wide, three miles long, and the upper part composed of very handsome houses; besides which, it may almost challenge Regent Street for pretty faces, except on Sundays. (On Sundays the coloured population take possession of Broadway.) Many of the shops, or *stores*, as they are here called, (for in this land of equality nobody keeps a shop), have already been fitted up with large plate-glass fronts, similar to those in London, and but for the depression which has taken place, many more would have followed the example.

Among the few discrepancies observable between this city and London, are the undertakers' *shops*. In England they are all wooden windows below and scutcheons above; planks and shavings within—in fact, mere workshops. Here they are different: they have large glass fronts, like a millinery or cut-glass shop with us, and the shop runs back thirty or forty feet, its sides being filled with coffins standing on end, mahogany and French polished. Therein you may select as you please, from the seven feet to receive the well-grown adult, to the tiny receptacle of what Burns calls, "Wee unchristened babe." I have, however, never heard of any one choosing their own coffin; they generally leave it to their relatives to perform that office.

I may here remark, that the Americans are sensible enough not to throw away so much money in funerals as we do; still it appears strange to an Englishman to see the open hearse containing the body, drawn by only one horse, while the carriages which follow are drawn by two: to be sure, the carriages generally contain six individuals, while the hearse is a sulky, and carries but one.

The New York tradesmen do all they can, as the English do, to attract the notice of the public by hand-bills, placards, advertisements, etcetera; but in one point they have gone a-head of us. Placards, etcetera, may be read by those who look upwards or straight-forward, or to the right or to the left; but there are some people who walk with their eyes to the ground, and consequently see nothing. The New Yorkers have provided for this contingency, by having large marble tablets, like horizontal tomb-stones, let into the flag pavements of the *trottoir* in front of their shops, on which is engraven in duplicate, turning both ways, their names and business; so, whether you walk up or down Broadway, if you cast your eyes downwards so as not to see the placards above, you cannot help reading the inscriptions below.

Every traveller who has visited this city has spoken of the numerous fires which take place in it, and the constant running, scampering, hallooing, and trumpeting of the firemen with their engines; but I do not observe that any one has attempted to investigate the causes which produce, generally speaking, three or four fires in the twenty-four hours. New York has certainly great capabilities, and every chance of improvement as a city; for, about one house in twenty is burnt down every year, and is always rebuilt in a superior manner. But, as to the causes, I have, after minute inquiry, discovered as follows. These fires are occasioned—

1st. By the notorious carelessness of black servants, and the custom of smoking cigars all the day long.

2nd. By the knavery of men without capitol, who insure to double and treble the value of their stock, and realise an honest penny by setting fire to their stores. (This is one reason why you can seldom recover from a fire-office without litigation.)

3rd. From the hasty and unsubstantial way in which houses are built up, the rafters and beams often communicating with the flues of the chimneys.

4th. Conflagrations of houses not insured, effected by agents employed by the *fire-insurance companies*, as a punishment to some, and a warning to others, who have neglected to take out policies.

These were gravely stated to me as the causes of so many fires in New York. I cannot vouch for the truth of the last, although I feel bound to mention it. I happen to be lodged opposite to two fire-engine houses, so that I always know when there is a fire. Indeed, so does every body; for the church nearest to it tolls its bell, and this tolling is repeated by all the others; and as there are more than three hundred churches in New York, if a fire takes place no one can say that he is not aware of it.

The duty of firemen is admirably performed by the young men of the city, who have privileges for a servitude of seven years; but they pay too dearly for their privileges, which are an exemption from militia and jury summons. Many of them are taken off by consumptions, fevers, and severe catarrhs, engendered by the severe trials to which they are exposed: the sudden transitions from extreme heat to extreme cold in winter, being summoned up from a warm bed, when the thermometer is below zero—then exposed to the scorching flames—and afterwards (as I have frequently seen them myself), with the water hanging in icicles upon their saturated clothes. To recruit themselves after their fatigue and exhaustion they are compelled to drink, and thus it is no wonder that their constitutions are undermined. It is nevertheless a favourite service, as the young men have an opportunity of shewing courage and determination, which raises them high in the opinion of their brother citizens.

I made a purchase at a store; an intelligent looking little boy brought it home for me. As he walked by my side, he amused me very much by putting the following questions:—

"Pray, captain, has Mr Easy left the King of England's service?"

"I think he has," replied I; "if you recollect, he married and went on shore."

"Have you seen Mr Japhet lately?" was the next query.

"Not very lately," replied I; "the last time I saw him was at the publisher's."

The little fellow went away, perfectly satisfied that they were both alive and well.

Volume One—Chapter Four.

The dogs are all tied up, and the mosquitos have broke loose—it is high time to leave New York.

The American steam-boats have been often described. When I first saw one of the largest sweep round the battery, with her two decks, the upper one screened with snow-white awnings—the gay dresses of the ladies—the variety of colours—it reminded me of a floating garden, and I fancied that Isola Bella, on the Lake of Como, had got under weigh, and made the first steam voyage to America.

The Hudson is a noble stream, flowing rapidly through its bold and deep bed. Already it has many associations connected with it—a great many for the time which has elapsed since Henrick Hudson first explored it. Where is the race of red men who hunted on its banks, or fished and paddled their canoes in its stream? They have disappeared from the earth, and scarce a vestige remains of them, except in history. No portion of this world was ever intended to remain for ages untenanted. Beasts of prey and noxious reptiles are permitted to exist in the wild and uninhabited regions until they are swept away by the broad stream of civilisation, which, as it pours along, drives them from hold to hold, until they finally disappear. So it is with the more savage nations: they are but *tenants at will*, and never were intended to remain longer than till the time when Civilisation, with the Gospel, Arts, and Sciences, in her train, should appear, and claim as her own that portion of the universe which they occupy.

About thirty miles above New York is Tarry Town, the abode of Washington Irving, who has here embosomed himself in his own region of romance; for Sleepy Hollow lies behind his domicile. Nearly opposite to it, is the site of a mournful reality—the spot where poor Major André was hung up as a spy.

You pass the State prison, built on a spot which still retains its Indian name—Sing Sing—rather an odd name for a prison, where people are condemned to perpetual silence. It is a fine building of white marble, like a palace—very appropriate for that portion of the *sovereign* people, who may qualify themselves for a residence in it.

I had a genuine Yankee story from one of the party on deck. I was enquiring if the Hudson was frozen up or not during the winter? This led to a conversation as to the severity of the winter, when one man, by way of proving how cold it was, said—"Why; I had a cow on my lot up the river, and last winter she got in among the ice, and was carried down three miles before we could get her out again. The consequence has been that she has milked nothing but *ice-creams* ever since."

When you have ascended about fifty miles, the bed of the river becomes contracted and deeper, and it pours its waters rapidly through the high lands on each side, having at some distant time forced its passage through a chain of rocky mountains. It was quite dark long before we arrived at West Point, which I had embarked to visit. A storm hung over us, and as we passed through the broad masses piled up on each side of the river, at one moment illuminated by the lightning as it burst from the opaque clouds, and the next towering in sullen gloom, the effect was sublime.

Here I am at West Point.

West Point is famous in the short history of this country. It is the key of the Hudson river. The traitor Arnold had agreed to deliver it up to the English, and it was on his return from arranging the terms with Arnold, that André was captured and hung.

At present, a Military College is established here, which turns out about forty officers every year. Although they receive commissions in any regiment of the American army when there may be vacancies, they are all educated as engineers. The democrats have made several attempts to break up this establishment, as savouring too much of *monarchy*, but hitherto have been unsuccessful. It would be a pity if they did succeed, for such has been the demand lately for engineers to superintend railroads and canals, that a large portion of them have resigned their commissions, and found employment in the different States. This consideration alone is quite sufficient to warrant the keeping up of the college, for civil engineers are a *sine quâ non* in a country like America, and they are always ready to serve should their military services be required. There was an inspection at the time that I was there, and it certainly was highly creditable to the students; as well as to those who superintend the various departments.

When I awoke the next morning, I threw open the blinds of my windows, which looked out upon the river, and really was surprised and delighted. A more beautiful view I never gazed upon. The Rhine was fresh in my memory; but, although the general features of the two rivers are not dissimilar, there is no one portion of the Rhine which can be compared to the Hudson at West Point. It was what you may imagine the Rhine to have been in the days of Caesar, when the lofty mountains through which it sweeps were not bared and naked as they now are, but clothed with forests, and rich in all the variety and beauty of undisturbed nature.

There is a sweet little spot not far from the college, where a tomb has been erected in honour of Kosciuscko—it is called Kosciuscko's Garden. I often sat there and talked over the events of the War of Independence. Many anecdotes were narrated to me, some of them very original. I will mention one or two which have not escaped my memory.

One of the officers who most distinguished himself in the struggle was a General Starke; and the following is the speech he is reported to have made to his men previous to an engagement:—

"Now, my men,—you see them ere Belgians; every man of them bought by the king of England at 17s. 6d. a-head, and I've a notion he'd paid too dear for them. Now, my men, we either beats them this day, or Molly Starke's a widow, by G—d." He did beat them, and in his despatch to head-quarters he wrote—"We've had a dreadful hot day of it, General; and I've lost my horse, saddle and bridle and all."

In those times, losing a *saddle* and *bridle* was as bad as losing a horse.

At the same affair, the captain commanding the outposts was very lame, and he thought proper thus to address his men:—

"Now, my lads, you see we're only an outpost, and we are not expected to beat the whole army in face of us. The duty of an outpost, when the enemy comes on, is to go in, *tree*ing it, and keeping ourselves not exposed. Now, you have my orders; and as I am a *little lame*, I'll go in first, and mind you do your duty and come in after me."

I passed several days at this beautiful spot, which is much visited by the Americans. Some future day, when America shall have become wealthy, and New York the abode of affluence and ease, what taste may not be lavished on the banks of this noble river! and what a lovely retreat will be West Point, if permitted to remain in all its present wildness and grandeur!

I re-embarked at midnight in the steam-boat descending from Albany, and which is fitted out as a night boat. When I descended into the cabin, it presented a whimsical sight: two rows of bed-places on each side of the immense cabin, running right fore and aft; three other rows in the centre, each of these five rows having three bed-places, one over the other. There were upwards of five hundred people, lying in every variety of posture, and exhibiting every state and degree of repose—from the loud uneasy snorer lying on his back, to the deep sleeper tranquil as death. I walked up and down, through these long ranges of unconsciousness, thinking how much care was for the time forgotten. But as the air below was oppressive, and the moon was beautiful in the heavens, I went on deck, and watched the swift career of the vessel, which, with a favouring tide, was flying past the shores at the rate of twenty miles an hour—one or two people only, out of so many hundreds on board of her, silently watching over the great principle of locomotion. The moon sank down, and the sun rose and gilded the verdure of the banks and the spires of the city of New York, as I revelled in my own thoughts and enjoyed the luxury of being alone—a double luxury in America, where the people are gregarious, and would think themselves very ill-bred if they allowed you one moment for meditation or self-examination.

Volume One—Chapter Five.

Stepped on board of the Narangansett steam-vessel for Providence. Here is a fair specimen of American travelling:— From New York to Providence, by the Long Island Sound, is two hundred miles; and this is accomplished, under usual circumstances, in thirteen hours: from Providence to Boston, forty miles by railroad, in two hours—which makes, from New York to Boston, an average speed of sixteen miles an hour, stoppages included.

I was, I must confess, rather surprised, when in the railroad cars, to find that we were passing through a *church-yard*, with tomb-stones on both sides of us. In Rhode Island and Massachusetts, where the pilgrim-fathers first landed—the two States that take pride to themselves (and with justice) for superior morality and a strict exercise of religious observances—they look down upon the other States of the Union, especially New York, and cry out, "I thank thee, Lord, that I am not as that publican." Yet here, in Rhode Island, are the sleepers of the railway laid over the sleepers in death; here do they grind down the bones of their ancestors for the sake of gain, and consecrated earth is desecrated by the iron wheels, loaded with Mammon-seeking mortals. And this in the puritanical state of Rhode Island! Would any engineer have ventured to propose such a line in England? I think not. After all, it is but human nature. I have run over the world a long while, and have always observed that people are very religious so long as religion does not interfere with their pockets; but, with gold in one hand and godliness in the other, the tangible is always preferred to the immaterial. In America everything is sacrificed to time—for time is money. The New Yorkers would have dashed right through the church itself; but then, *they* are publicans, and don't *pretend* to be good.

Boston is a fine city, and, as a commercial one, almost as well situated as New York. It has, however, lost a large portion of its commerce, which the latter has gradually wrested from it, and it must eventually lose much more. The population of Boston is about eighty thousand, and it has probably more people of leisure in it (that is, out of business and living on their own means) than even Philadelphia; taking into the estimate the difference between the populations. They are more learned and scientific here than at New York, though not more so than at Philadelphia; but they are more English than in any other city in America. The Massachusetts people are very fond of comparing their country with that of England. The scenery is not unlike; but it is not like England in its high state of cultivation. Stone walls are bad substitutes for green hedges. Still, there are some lovely spots in the environs of Boston. Mount Auburn, laid out as a Père la Chaise, is, in natural beauties, far superior to any other place of the kind. One would almost wish to be buried there; and the proprietors, anxious to have it peopled, offer, by their arrangements as to the price of places of interment, a handsome premium to those who will soonest die and be buried—which is certainly a consideration.

Fresh Pond is also a very romantic spot. It is a lake of about two hundred acres, whose water is so pure that the ice is transparent as glass. Its proprietor clears many thousand dollars a year by the sale of it. It is cut out in blocks of three feet square, and supplies most parts of America down to New Orleans; and every winter latterly two or three ships have been loaded and sent to Calcutta, by which a very handsome profit has been realised.

Since I have been here, I have made every enquiry relative to the sea-serpent which frequents this coast alone. There are many hundreds of most respectable people, who, on other points, would be considered as incapable of falsehood, who declare they have seen the animals, and vouch for their existence. It is rather singular that in America there is but one copy of Bishop Pontoppidon's work on Norway, and in it the sea-serpent is described, and a rough wood-cut of its appearance given. In all the American newspapers a drawing was given of the animal as described by those who saw it, and it proved to be almost a *fac-simile* of the one described by the Bishop in his work.

Now that we are on marine matters, I must notice the prodigious size of the lobsters off Boston Coast: they could stow a dozen common English lobsters under their coats of mail. My very much respected friend Sir Isaac Coffin, when he was here, once laid a wager that he would produce a lobster weighing thirty pounds. The bet was accepted, and the admiral despatched people to the proper quarter to procure one: but they were not then in season, and could not be had. The admiral, not liking to lose his money, brought up, instead of the lobster, the affidavits of certain people that they had often seen lobsters of that size and weight. The affidavits of the deponents he submitted to the other party, and pretended that he had won the wager. The case was referred to arbitration, and the admiral was cast with the following pithy reply, *"Depositions are not lobsters."*

Massachusetts is certainly very English in its scenery, and Boston essentially English as a city. The Bostonians assert that they are more English than we are, that is, that they have strictly adhered to the old English customs and manners, as handed down to them previous to the Revolution. That of sitting a very long while at their wine after dinner, is one which they certainly adhere to, and which, *I* think, would be more honoured in the breach than the observance; but their hospitality is unbounded, and you do, as an Englishman, feel at home with them. I agree with the Bostonians so far, that they certainly appear to have made no change in their manners and customs for these last hundred years. You meet here with frequent specimens of the Old English Gentleman, descendants of the best old English families who settled here long before the Revolution, and are now living on their incomes, with a town house and a country seat to retire to during the summer season. The society of Boston is very delightful; it wins upon you every day, and that is the greatest compliment that can be paid to it.

Perhaps of all the Americans the Bostonians are the most sensitive to any illiberal remarks made upon the country, for they consider themselves, and pride themselves, as being peculiarly English; while, on the contrary, the majority of the Americans deny that they are English. There certainly is less intermixture of foreign blood in this city than in any other in America. It will appear strange, but so wedded are they to old customs, even to John Bullism, that it is not more than seven or eight years that French wines have been put on the Boston tables, and become in general use in this city.

It is a pity that this feeling towards England is not likely to continue; indeed, even at this moment it is gradually wearing away. Self-interest governs the world. At the declaration of the last war with England, it was the Northern States which were so opposed to it, and the Southern who were in favour of it: but now circumstances have changed; the Northern States, since the advance in prosperity and increase of produce in the Southern and Western States, feel aware that it is only as manufacturing states that they can hold their rank with the others. Their commerce has decreased since the completion of the Erie and Ohio canals, and during the war they discovered the advantage that would accrue to them, as manufacturers, to supply the Southern and Western markets. The imports of English goods have nearly ruined them. They now manufacture nothing but coarse articles, and as you travel through the Eastern countries, you are surprised to witness splendid fabrics commenced, but, for want of encouragement, not finished. This has changed the interests of the opponent States. The Southern are very anxious to remain at peace with England, that their produce may find a market; while the Northern, on the contrary, would readily consent to a war, that they might shut out the English manufactures, and have the supply entirely in their own hands. The Eastern States (I particularly refer to Massachusetts, Connecticut, and Rhode Island) offer a proof of what can be effected by economy, prudence, and industry. Except on the borders of the rivers, the lands are generally sterile, and the climate is severe, yet, perhaps, the population is more at its ease than in any other part of the Union; but the produce of the States is not sufficient for the increasing population, or rather what the population would have been had it not migrated every year to the West and South. They set a higher value upon good connections in these poor States than they do in others; and if a daughter is to be married, they will ask what family the suitor is of, and if it bears a good name, they are quite indifferent as to whether he has a cent or not. It is remarkable, that if a man has three or four sons in these States, one will be a lawyer, another a medical man, another a clergyman, and one will remain at home to take the property; and thus, out of the proceeds of a farm, perhaps not containing more than fifty acres, all these young men shall be properly educated, and in turn sent forth to the West and South, where they gain an honourable independence, and very often are sent to Congress as senators and representatives. Industry and frugality are the only entailed estate bequeathed from father to son. Yet this State alone manufactures to the value of 86,282,616 of dollars in the year. As a general axiom it may fairly be asserted, that the more sterile the soil, the more virtuous, industrious, and frugal are the inhabitants; and it may be added, that such a country sends out more clever and intelligent men than one that is nominally more blessed by Providence. The fact is, without frugality and industry the Eastern States could not exist; they become virtues of necessity, and are the basis of others; whilst, where there is abundance, vice springs up and idleness takes deep root.

The population of Massachusetts is by the last returns 701,331 souls. I rather think the proportion of women to men is very great.

An energetic and enterprising people are naturally anxious for an investigation into cause and effect, a search into which is, after all, nothing but curiosity well directed, and the most curious of all men is the philosopher. Curiosity, therefore, becomes a virtue or a small vice, according to the use made of it. The Americans are excessively curious, especially the mob: they cannot bear anything like a secret,—that's *unconstitutional*. It may be remembered, that the Catholic Convent near Boston, which had existed many years, was attacked by the mob and pulled down. I was enquiring into the cause of this outrage in a country where all forms of religion are tolerated; and an American gentleman told me, that although other reasons had been adduced for it, he fully believed, in his own mind, that the majority of the mob were influenced more by *curiosity* than any other feeling. The Convent was *sealed* to them, and they were determined to know what was in it. "Why, sir," continued he, "I will lay a wager that if the authorities were to nail together a dozen planks, and fix them up on the Common, with a caution to the public that they were not to go near or touch them, in twenty-four hours a mob would be raised to pull them down and ascertain what the planks contained." I mention this conversation, to shew in what a dexterous manner this American gentleman attempted to palliate one of the grossest outrages ever committed by his countrymen.

Volume One—Chapter Six.

Crossed over to New Jersey, and took the railroad, to view the falls of the Passaic River, about fifteen miles from New York. This water-power has given birth to Patterson, a town with ten thousand inhabitants, where a variety of manufactures is carried on. A more beautiful wild spot can hardly be conceived; and to an European who has been accustomed to travel far in search of the picturesque, it appears singular that at so short a distance from a large city, he should at once find himself in the midst of such a strange combination of nature and art. Independent of their beauty, they are, perhaps, the most singular falls that are known to exist. The whole country is of trappe formation, and the black rocks rise up strictly vertical. The river, which at the Falls is about one hundred and twenty yards wide, pours over a bed of rock between hills covered with chestnut, walnut, pine, and sycamore, all mingled together, and descending to the edge of the bank; their bright and various foliage forming a lovely contrast to the clear rushing water. The bed of black rock over which the river runs, is, at the Fall, suddenly split in two, vertically, and across the whole width of the river. The fissure is about seventy feet deep, and not more than twelve feet wide at any part. Down into this chasm pour the whole waters of the river, escaping from it, at a right angle, into a deep basin, surrounded with perpendicular rocks from eighty to ninety feet high. You may therefore stand on the opposite side of the chasm, looking up the river, within a few feet of the Fall, and watch the roaring waters as they precipitate themselves below. In this position, with the swift, clear, but not deep waters before you, forcing their passage through the rocky bed, with the waving trees on each side, their branches feathering to the water's edge, or dipping and rising in the stream, you might imagine yourself far removed from your fellow-men, and you feel that in such a beauteous spot you could well turn anchorite, and commune with Nature alone. But turn round with your back to the Fall—look below, and all is changed: art in full activity—millions of reels whirling in their sockets—the bright polished cylinders incessantly turning, and never tiring. What formerly was the occupation of thousands of industrious females, who sat with their distaff at the cottage door, is now effected in a hundredth part of the time, and in every variety, by those compressed machines which require but the attendance of one child to several hundreds. But machinery cannot perform everything, and notwithstanding this reduction of labour, the romantic Falls of the Passaic find employment for the industry of thousands.

We walked up the banks of the river above the Fall, and met with about twenty or thirty urchins who were bathing at the mouth of the cut, made for the supply of the water-power to the manufactories below. The river is the property of an individual, and is very valuable: he receives six hundred dollars per annum for one square foot of water-power; ten years hence it will be rented at a much higher price.

We amused ourselves by throwing small pieces of money into the water, where it was about a fathom deep, for the boys to dive after; they gained them too easily; we went to another part in the *cut*, where it was much deeper, and threw in a dollar. The boys stood naked on the rocks, like so many cormorants, waiting to dart upon their prey; when the dollar had had time to sink to the bottom the word was given—they all dashed down like lightning and disappeared. About a minute elapsed ere there was any sign of their re-appearance, when they came up, one by one, breathless and flushed (like racers who had pulled up), and at last the victor appeared with the dollar between his teeth. We left these juvenile *Sam Patches*, and returned to the town. (Sam Patch, an American peripatetic, who used to amuse himself and astonish his countrymen by leaping down the different falls in America. He leaped down a portion of the Niagara without injury; but one fine day, having taken a drop too much, he took a leap too much. He went down the Genassee Fall, and since that time he has not been seen or heard of.)

There is no part of the world, perhaps, where you have more difficulty in obtaining permission to be alone, and indulge in a reverie, than in America. The Americans are as gregarious as school-boys, and think it an incivility to leave you by yourself. Every thing is done in crowds, and among a crowd. They even prefer a double bed to a single one, and I have often had the offer to sleep with me made out of real kindness. You must go "east of sun-rise" (or west of sun-set) if you would have solitude.

I never was in a more meditative humour, more anxious to be left to my own dreamings, than when I ascended the railroad car with my companion to return to Jersey city; we were the only two in that division of the car, and my friend, who understood me, had the complaisance to go fast asleep. I made sure that, for an hour or two, I could indulge in my own castle-buildings, and allow my fleeting thoughts to pass over my brain, like the scud over the moon. At our first stoppage a third party stepped in and seated himself between us. He looked at my companion, who was fast asleep. He turned to me, and I turned away my head. Once more was I standing at the Falls of the Passaic; once more were the waters rolling down before me, the trees gracefully waving their boughs to the breeze, and the spray cooling my heated brain; my brain was, like the camera-obscura, filled with the pleasing images, which I watched as they passed before me so vividly portrayed, all in life and motion, when I was interrupted by—

"I was born in the very heart of Cheshire, sir."

Confound the fellow! The river, falls, foliage, all vanished at once; and I found myself sitting in a railroad-car (which I had been unconscious of), with a heavy lump of humanity by my side. I wished one of the largest Cheshire cheeses down his throat.

"Indeed!" replied I, not looking at the man.

"Yes, sir—in the very heart of Cheshire."

"Would you had staid there!" thought I, turning away to the window without replying.

"Will you oblige me with a pinch of your snuff, sir? I left my box at New York."

I gave him the box, and, when he had helped himself, laid it down on the vacant seat opposite to him, that he might not have to apply again, and fell back and shut my eyes, as a hint to him that I did not wish to enter into conversation. A pause ensued, and I had hopes; but they were delusive.

"I have been eighteen years in this country, sir."

"You appear to be quite *Americanised*!" thought I; but I made him no answer.

"I went up to Patterson, sir," continued he (now turning round to me, and speaking in my ear), "thinking that I could get to Philadelphia by that route, and found that I had made a mistake; so I have come back. I am *told* there are some pretty falls there, sir."

"Would you were beneath them!" thought I; but I could not help laughing at the idea of a man going to Patterson, and returning without seeing the falls! By this time he had awakened his companion, who, being American himself, and finding that there was to be no more sleep, took him up, in the American fashion, and put to him successively the following questions, all of which were answered without hesitation:— "What is your name? where are you from? where are you going? what is your profession? how many dollars have you made? have you a wife and children?" All these being duly responded to, he asked my companion who I might be, and was told that I was an operative artist, and one of the first cotton spinners in the country.

This communication procured for me considerable deference from our new acquaintance during the remainder of our journey. He observed in the ear of my companion, that he thought I knew a thing or two. In a country like America the Utilitarian will always command respect.

Volume One—Chapter Eight.

The 4th of July, the sixty-first anniversary of American independence!

Pop—pop—bang—pop—pop—bang—bang bang! Mercy on us! how fortunate it is that anniversaries come only once a year. Well, the Americans may have great reason to be proud of this day, and of the deeds of their forefathers, but why do they get so confoundedly drunk? why, on this day of independence, should they become so *dependent* upon posts and rails for support? The day is at last over; my head aches, but there will be many more aching heads tomorrow morning!

What a combination of vowels and consonants have been put together! what strings of tropes, metaphors, and allegories, have been used on this day! what varieties and gradations of eloquence! There are at least fifty thousand cities, towns, villages, and hamlets, spread over the surface of America—in each the Declaration of Independence has been read; in all one, and in some two or three, orations have been delivered, with as much gunpowder in them as in the squibs and crackers. But let me describe what I actually saw.

The commemoration commenced, if the day did not, on the evening of the 3rd, by the municipal police going round and pasting up placards, informing the citizens of New York, that all persons letting off fireworks would be taken into custody, which notice was immediately followed up by the little boys proving their independence of the authorities, by letting off squibs, crackers, and bombs; and cannons, made out of shin bones, which flew in the face of every passenger, in the exact ratio that the little boys flew in the face of the authorities. This continued the whole night, and thus was ushered in the great and glorious day, illumined by a bright and glaring sun (as if bespoken on purpose by the mayor and corporation), with the thermometer at 90 degrees in the shade. The first sight which met the eye after sunrise, was the precipitate escape, from a city visited with the plague of gunpowder, of respectable or timorous people in coaches, carriages, waggons, and every variety of vehicle. "My kingdom for a horse!" was the general cry of all those who could not stand fire. In the mean while, the whole atmosphere was filled with independence. Such was the quantity of American flags which were hoisted on board of the vessels, hung out of windows, or carried about by little boys, that you saw more stars at noon-day than ever could be counted on the brightest night. On each side of the whole length of Broadway, were ranged booths and stands, similar to those at an English fair, and on which were displayed small plates of oysters, with a fork stuck in the board opposite to each plate; clams sweltering in the hot sun; pineapples, boiled hams, pies, puddings, barley-sugar, and many other indescribables. But what was most remarkable, Broadway being three miles long, and the booths lining each side of it, in every booth there was a roast pig, large or small, as the centre attraction. Six miles of roast pig! and that in New York city alone; and roast pig in every other city, town, hamlet, and village, in the Union. What association can there be between roast pig and independence? Let it not be supposed that there was any deficiency in the very necessary articks of potation on this auspicious day: no! the booths were loaded with porter, ale, cyder, mead, brandy, wine, ginger-beer, pop, soda-water, whiskey, rum, punch, gin slings, cocktails, mint julips, besides many other compounds, to name which nothing but the luxuriance of American-English could invent a word. Certainly the preparations in the refreshment way were most imposing, and gave you some idea of what had to be gone through on this auspicious day. Martial music sounded from a dozen quarters at once; and as you turned your head, you tacked to the first bars of a march from one band, the concluding bars of Yankee Doodle from another. At last the troops of militia and volunteers, who had been gathering in the park and other squares, made their appearance, well dressed and well equipped, and, in honour of the day, marching as independently as they well could. I did not see them go through many manoeuvres, but there was one which they appeared to excel in, and that was grounding arms and eating pies. I found that the current went towards Castle Garden, and away I went with it. There the troops were all collected on the green, shaded by the trees, and the effect was very beautiful. The artillery and infantry were drawn up in a line pointing to the water. The officers in their regimental dresses and long white feathers, generals and aides-de-camp, colonels, commandants, majors, all galloping up and down in front of the line, —white horses and long tails appearing the most fashionable and correct. The crowds assembled were, as American crowds usually are, quiet and well behaved. I recognised many of my literary friends turned into generals, and flourishing their swords instead of their pens. The scene was very animating; the shipping at the wharfs were loaded with star-spangled banners; steamers paddling in every direction, were covered with flags; the whole beautiful Sound was alive with boats and sailing vessels, all flaunting with pennants and streamers. It was, as Ducrow would call it, "A Grand Military and Aquatic Spectacle."

Then the troops marched up into town again, and so did I follow them as I used to do the reviews in England, when a boy. All creation appeared to be independent on this day; some of the horses particularly so, for they would not keep "in no line not no how." Some preferred going sideways like crabs, others went backwards, some would not go at all, others went a great deal too fast, and not a few parted company with their riders, whom they kicked off just to shew their independence; but let them go which way they would, they could not avoid the squibs and crackers. And the women were in the same predicament: they might dance right, or dance left, it was only out of the frying-pan into the fire, for it was pop, pop; bang, bang; fiz, pop, bang, so that you literally trod upon gunpowder.

When the troops marched up Broadway, louder even than the music were to be heard the screams of delight from the children at the crowded windows on each side. "Ma! ma! there's pa!" "Oh! there's John." "Look at uncle on his big horse."

The troops did not march in very good order, because, independently of their not knowing how, there was a great deal of independence to contend with. At one time an omnibus and four would drive in and cut off the general and his staff from his division; at another, a cart would roll in and insist upon following close upon the band of music; so that it was a mixed procession— Generals, omnibus and four, music, cart-loads of bricks, troops, omnibus and pair, artillery, hackney-coach, etcetera. etcetera. Notwithstanding all this, they at last arrived at the City Hall, when those who were old enough heard the Declaration of Independence read for the sixty-first time; and then it was —"Begone, brave army, and don't kick up a row."

I was invited to dine with the mayor and corporation at the City Hall. We sat down in the Hall of Justice, and certainly, great justice was done to the dinner, which (as the wife says to her husband after a party, where the second course follows the first with unusual celerity) "went off remarkably well." The crackers popped outside, and the champagne popped in. The celerity of the Americans at a public dinner is very commendable; they speak only now and then; and the toasts follow so fast, that you have just time to empty your glass, before you are requested to fill again. Thus the arranged toasts went off rapidly, and after them, any one might withdraw. I waited till the thirteenth toast, the last on the paper, to wit, the ladies of America; and, having previously, in a speech from the recorder, bolted Bunker's Hill and New Orleans, I thought I might as well bolt myself, as I wished to see the fireworks, which were to be very splendid.

Unless you are an amateur, there is no occasion to go to the various places of public amusement where the fireworks are let off, for they are sent up every where in such quantities that you hardly know which way to turn your eyes. It is, however, advisable to go into some place of safety, for the little boys and the big boys have all got their supply of rockets, which they fire off in the streets—some running horizontally up the pavement, and sticking into the back of a passenger; and others mounting slantingdicularly and Paul-Prying into the bed-room windows on the third floor or attics, just to see how things are going on *there*. Look in any point of the compass, and you will see a shower of rockets in the sky: turn from New York to Jersey City, from Jersey City to Brooklyn, and shower is answered by shower on either side of the water. Hoboken repeats the signal: and thus it is carried on to the east, the west, the north, and the south, from Rhode Island to the Missouri, from the Canada frontier to the Gulf of Mexico. At the various gardens the combinations were very beautiful, and exceeded anything that I had witnessed in London or Paris. What with sea-serpents, giant rockets scaling heaven, Bengal lights, Chinese fires, Italian suns, fairy bowers, crowns of Jupiter, exeranthemums, Tartar temples, Vesta's diadems, magic circles, morning glories, stars of Colombia, and temples of liberty, all America was in a blaze; and, in addition to this mode of manifesting its joy, all America was tipsy.

There is something grand in the idea of a national intoxication. In this world, vices on a grand scale dilate into virtues; he who murders one man, is strung up with ignominy; but he who murders twenty thousand has a statue to his memory, and is handed down to posterity as a hero. A staggering individual is a laughable and, sometimes, a disgusting spectacle; but the whole of a vast continent reeling, offering a holocaust of its brains for mercies vouchsafed, is an appropriate tribute of gratitude for the rights of equality and the *levelling spirit* of their institutions.

Volume One—Chapter Nine.

Once more flying up the noble Hudson. After you have passed West Point, the highlands, through which the river has forced its passage, gradually diminish, and as the shore becomes level, so does the country become more fertile.

We passed the manor of Albany, as it is called, being a Dutch grant of land, now in the possession of one person, a Mr Van Rensalaer, and equal to many a German principality, being twenty miles by forty-eight miles square. Mr Van Rensalaer still retains the old title of Patroon. It is generally supposed in England that, in America, all property must be divided between the children at the decease of the parent. This is not the case. The entailing of estates was abolished by an act of Congress in 1788, but a man may will away his property entirely to his eldest son if he pleases. This is, however, seldom done; public opinion is too strong against it, and the Americans fear public opinion beyond the grave. Indeed, were a man so to act, the other claimants would probably appeal to have the will set aside upon the grounds of lunacy, and the sympathy of an American jury would decree in their favour.

As you ascend to Albany City, the banks of the river are very fertile and beautiful, and the river is spotted with many very picturesque little islands. The country seats, which fringe the whole line of shore, are all built in the same, and very bad, style. Every house or tenement, be it a palace or a cottage, has its porticos and pillars—a string of petty Parthenons which tire you by their uniformity and pretence.

I had intended to stop at Hudson, that I might proceed from thence to New Lebanon to visit the Shaking Quakers; but, as I discovered that there was a community of them not five miles from Troy, I, to avoid a fatiguing journey, left Albany, and continued on to that city.

Albany is one of the oldest Dutch settlements, and among its inhabitants are to be found many of the descendants of the Dutch aristocracy. Indeed, it may even now be considered as a Dutch city. It is the capital of the state of New York, with a population of nearly 30,000. Its commerce is very extensive, as it is here that the Erie canal communications with the Far West, as well as the Eastern States, debouche into the Hudson.

We have here a singular proof, not only of the rapidity with which cities rise in America, but also how superior energy will overcome every disadvantage. Little more than twenty years ago, Albany stood by itself, a large and populous city without a rival, but its population was chiefly Dutch. The Yankees from the Eastern States came down and settled themselves at Troy, not five miles distant, in opposition to them. It would be supposed that Albany could have crushed this city in its birth, but it could not, and Troy is now a beautiful city, with its mayor, its corporation, and a population of 20,000 souls, and divides the commerce with Albany, from which most of the eastern trade has been ravished. The inhabitants of Albany are termed Albanians, those of Troy, Trojans! In one feature these cities are very similar, being both crowded with lumber and pretty girls.

I went out to see the Shakers at Niskayuna. So much has already been said about their tenets that I shall not repeat them, further than to observe that all their goods are in common, and that, although the sexes mix together, they profess the vows of celibacy and chastity. Their lands are in excellent order, and they are said to be very rich. (I should be very sorry to take away the character of any community, but, as I was a little sceptical as to the possibility of the vow of chastity being observed under circumstances above alluded to, I made some inquiries, and having met with one who had seceded from the fraternity, I discovered that my opinion of human nature was correct, and the conduct of the Shakers not altogether so. I must not enter into details, as they would be unfit for publication.)

We were admitted into a long room on the ground-floors where the Shakers were seated on forms, the men opposite to the women, and apart from each other. The men were in their waistcoats and shirt-sleeves, twiddling their thumbs, and looking awfully puritanical. The women were attired in dresses of very light striped cotton, which hung about them like full dressing-gowns, and concealed all shape and proportions. A plain mob cap on their heads, and a thick muslin handkerchief in many folds over their shoulders, completed their attire. They each held in their hands a pocket-handkerchief as large as a towel, and of almost the same substance. But the appearance of the women was melancholy and unnatural; I say unnatural because it required to be accounted for. They had all the advantages of exercise and labour in the open air, good food, and good clothing; they were not overworked, for they are not required to work more than they please; and yet there was something so pallid, so unearthly in their complexions, that it gave you the idea that they had been taken up from their coffins a few hours after their decease: not a hue of health, not a vestige of colour in any cheek or lip;—one cadaverous yellow tinge prevailed. And yet there were to be seen many faces very beautiful, as far as regarded outline, but they were the features of the beautiful in death. The men, on the contrary, were ruddy, strong, and vigorous. Why, then, this difference between the sexes, where they each performed the same duties, where none were taxed beyond their strength, and all were well fed and clothed?

After a silence of ten minutes, one of the men of the community, evidently a coarse illiterate person, rose and addressed a few words to the spectators, requesting them not to laugh at what they saw, but to behave themselves properly, etcetera, and then he sat down.

One of the leaders then burst out into a hymn, to a jigging sort of tune, and all the others joined chorus. After the hymn was sung they all rose, put away the forms on which they had been seated, and stood in lines, eight in a row, men and women separate, facing each other, and about ten feet apart—the ranks of men being flanked by the boys, and those of the women by the girls. They commenced their dancing by advancing in rows, just about as far as profane people do in *L'été* when they dance quadrilles, and then retreated the same distance, all keeping regular time, and turning back to back after every third advance. The movement was rather quick, and they danced to their own singing of the following beautiful composition:—

Law,	law,		de	lawdel	law,
Law,		law,		de	law,
Law,	law,		de	lawdel	law,
Lawdel, lawdel, law—					

keeping time also with the hands as well as feet, the former raised up to the chest, and hanging down like the fore-paws of a dancing bear. After a quarter of an hour they sat down again, and the women made use of their large towel pocket-handkerchiefs to wipe off the perspiration. Another hymn was sung, and then the same person addressed the spectators, requesting them not to laugh, and inquiring if any of them felt a wish to be saved—adding, "Not one of you, I don't think." He looked round at all of us with the most ineffable contempt, and then sat down; and they sang another hymn, the burden of which was—

"Our   souls   are   saved,   and   we   are   free
From vice and all in-i-qui-ty."

which was a very comfortable delusion, at all events.

They then rose again, put away the forms as before, and danced in another fashion. Instead of *L'été*, it was *Grande ronde*. About ten men and women stood in two lines in the centre of the room, as a vocal band of music, while all the others, two and two, women first and men following, promenaded round, with a short quick step, to the tune chaunted in the centre. As they went round and round, shaking their paws up and down before them, the scene was very absurd, and I could have laughed had I not felt disgusted at such a degradation of rational and immortal beings. This dance lasted a long while, until the music turned to croaking, and the perspiration was abundant; they stopped at last, and then announced that their exercise was finished. I waited a little while after the main body had dispersed, to speak with one of the elders. "I will be with you directly," replied he, walking hastily away; but he never came back.

I never heard the principle upon which they dance. David danced before the ark; but it is to be presumed that David danced as well as he sung. At least he thought so; for when his wife Michal laughed at him, he made her conduct a ground of divorce.

Every community which works in common, and is provided for in the mass, must become *rich*, especially when it has no children to maintain. It is like receiving a person's labour in exchange for victuals and clothing only, and this is all I can perceive that can be said in favour of these people. Suffice it to say, I have a very bad opinion of them: and were I disposed to dilate on the subject, I should feel no inclination to treat them with the lenity shewn to them by other travellers.

From this mockery, I went to see what had a real tendency to make you feel religious—the Falls of the Mohawk, about three miles from Troy. Picturesque and beautiful as all falling water is, to describe it is extremely difficult, unless, indeed by a forced simile; the flow of language is too tame for the flow of water; but if the reader can imagine a ledge of black rocks, about sixty or seventy feet high, and that over this ledge was poured simultaneously the milk of some millions of cows, he will then have some idea of the beauty of the creaming Falls of the Mohawk, imbedded as they are in their wild and luxuriant scenery.

Close to the Falls, I perceived a few small wooden shealings, appearing, under the majestic trees which overshadowed them, more like dog-kennels than the habitations of men: they were tenanted by Irish emigrants, who had taken work at the new locks forming on the Erie canal. I went up to them. In a tenement about fourteen feet by ten, lived an Irishman, his wife, and family, and seven boys as he called them, young men from twenty to thirty years of age, who boarded with him. There was but one bed, on which slept the man, his wife, and family. Above the bed were some planks, extending half way the length of the shealing, and there slept the seven boys, without any mattress, or even straw, to lie upon. I entered into conversation with them: they complained bitterly of the times, saying that their pay was not 2 shillings 6 pence of our money per day, and that they could not live upon it. This was true, but the distress had been communicated to all parts, and they were fortunate in finding work at all, as most of the public works had been discontinued. I mentioned to them that the price of labour in Ohio, Illinois, and the West, was said to be two dollars a-day, and asked them, why they did not go there? They replied, that such were the price quoted, to induce people to go, but that they never could find it when they arrived; that the clearing of new lands was attended with ague and fever; and that if once down with these diseases there was no one to help them to rise again. I looked for the pig, and there he was, sure enough, under the bed.

Volume One—Chapter Ten.

Troy, like a modern academy, is classical, as well as commercial, having Mount Olympus on one side, and Mount Ida in its rear. The panorama from the summit of the latter is splendid. A few years back a portion of Mount Ida made a slip, and the avalanche destroyed several cottages and five or six individuals. The avalanche took place on a dark night and in a heavy snow storm. Two brick kilns were lighted at the time, and, as the mountain swept them away, the blaze of the disturbed fires called out the fire engines, otherwise more lives would have been lost. Houses, stables, and sheds, were all hurled away together. Horses, children, and women, rolled together in confusion. One child had a very strange escape. It had been forced out of its bed, and was found on the top of a huge mass of clay, weighing forty or fifty tons; he was crying, and asking who had put him there. Had all the inhabitants of the cottages been within, at least forty must have perished; but notwithstanding the severity of the weather, the day being Sunday, they had all gone to evening meeting, and thus, being good Christians, they were for once rewarded for it on this side of the grave.

As I surveyed the busy scene below me, the gentleman who accompanied me to the summit of the mountain, informed me that forty-three years ago his father was the first settler, and that then there was but his one hut in the place where now stood the splendid town.

But signs of the times were manifest here also. Commerce had stopped for the present, and a long line of canal boats was laid up for want of employment.

I remained two hours perched upon the top of the mountain. I should not have staid so long, perhaps, had they not brought me a basket of cherries, so that I could gratify more senses than one. I felt becomingly classical whilst sitting on the precise birth-place of Jupiter, attended by Pomona, with Troy at my feet, and Mount Olympus in the distance; but I was obliged to descend to lumber and gin-slings, and I set off for Albany, where I had an engagement, having been invited to attend at the examination of the young ladies at the seminary.

Here again is a rivalry between Albany and Troy, each of them glorying in possessing the largest seminary for the education of young ladies, who are sent from every State of the Union, to be finished off at one or the other of them. Here, and indeed in many other establishments, the young ladies now quitting it have diplomas given, to them, if they pass their examinations satisfactorily. They are educated upon a system which would satisfy even Miss Martineau, and prepared to exercise the rights of which she complains that women have been so unjustly deprived. Conceive three hundred modern Portias, who regularly take their degrees, and emerge from the portico of the seminary full of algebra, equality, and the theory of the constitution! The quantity and variety crammed into them is beyond all calculation. The examination takes place yearly, to prove to the parents that the preceptors have, done their duty, and is in itself very innocent, as it only causes the young ladies to blush a little.

This afternoon they were examined in algebra, and their performance was very creditable. Under a certain age girls are certainly much quicker than boys, and I presume would retain what they learnt if it were not for their subsequent duties in making puddings, and nursing babies. Yet there are affairs which must be performed by one sex or the other, and of what use can algebra and other abstruse matters be to a woman in her present state of domestic thraldom.

The theory of the American constitution was the next subject on which they were examined; by their replies, this appeared to be to them more abstruse than algebra: but the fact is, women are born tories, and admit no other than petticoat government as legitimate.

The next day we again repaired to the hall, and French was the language in which they were to be examined, and the examination afforded us much amusement.

The young ladies sat down in rows on one side of the room. In the centre, towards the end, was an easel, on which was placed a large black board on which they worked with chalk the questions in algebra, etcetera,—a towel hanging to it, that they might wipe out and correct. The French preceptor, an old Emigré Count, sat down with the examiners before the board, the visitors (chiefly composed of anxious papas and mammas) being seated on benches behind them. As it happened, I had taken my seat close to the examining board, and at some little distance from the other persons who were deputed or invited to attend. I don't knew how I came there. I believe I had come in too late; but there I was, within three feet of every young lady who came up to the board.

"Now, messieurs, have the kindness to ask any question you please," said the old Count. "Mademoiselle, you will have the goodness to step forward." A question was proposed in English, which the young lady had to write down in French. The very first went wrong: I perceived it, and without looking at her, pronounced the right word, so that she could hear it. She caught it, rubbed out the wrong word with the towel, and rectified it. This was carried on through the whole sentence, and then she retreated from the board that her work might be examined. "Very well, very well, indeed, Miss, c'est parfaitement bien;" and the young lady sat down blushing. Thus were they all called up, and one after another prompted by me; and the old Count was delighted at the success of his pupils.

Now, what amused me in this was the little bit of human nature; the *tact* displayed by the sex, which appears to be innate, and which never deserts them. Had I prompted a boy, he would most likely have turned his head round towards me, and thus have revealed what I was about; but not one of the whole class was guilty of such indiscretion. They heard me, rubbed out, corrected, waited for the word when they did not know it, but never by any look or sign made it appear that there was any understanding between us. Their eyes were constantly fixed on the board, and they appeared not to know that I was in the room. It was really beautiful. When the examination was over, I received a look from them all, half comic, half serious, which amply repaid me for my assistance.

As young ladies are assembled here from every State of the Union, it was a *fair* criterion of American beauty, and it must be acknowledged that the American women are the *prettiest* in the whole world.

Volume One—Chapter Eleven.

Saratoga Springs.—Watering places all over the world are much alike: they must be well filled with company, and full of bustle, and then they answer the purpose for which they are intended—a general muster, under the banner of folly, to drive care and common sense out of the field. Like assembly-rooms, unless lighted up and full of people, they look desolate and forlorn: so it was with Saratoga: a beautiful spot, beautiful hotels, and beautiful water; but all these beauties were thrown away, and the water ran away unheeded, because the place was empty. People's pockets were empty, and Saratoga was to let. The consequence was that I remained a week there, and should have remained much longer had I not been warned, by repeated arrivals, that the visitors were increasing, and that I should be no longer alone.

The weariness of solitude, as described by Alexander Selkirk and the Anti-Zimmermanns, can surely not be equal to the misery of never being alone; of feeling that your thoughts and ideas, rapidly accumulating, are in a state of chaos and confusion, and that you have not a moment to put them into any lucid order; of finding yourself, against your will, continually in society, bandied from one person to the other, to make the same bows, extend the same hand to be grasped, and reply to the same eternal questions; until, like a man borne down by sleep after long vigils, and at each moment roused to reply, you either are not aware of what you do say, or are dead beat into an unmeaning smile. Since I have been in this country, I have suffered this to such a degree as at last to become quite nervous on the subject; and I might reply in the words of the spirit summoned by Lochiel—

"Now   my   weary   lips   I   close;
Leave, oh! leave me to repose."

It would be a strange account, had it been possible to keep one, of the number of introductions which I have had since I came into this country. Mr A introduces Mr B and C, Mr B and C introduce Mr D, E, F, and G. Messrs D, E, F, and G introduce Messrs H, I, J, K, L, M, N, O, and so it goes on, *ad infinitum* during the whole of the day; and this to me who never could remember either a face or a name.

At introduction it is invariably the custom to shake hands; and thus you go on shaking hands here, there, and everywhere, and with everybody; for it is impossible to know who is who, in this land of equality.

But one shake of the hand will not do; if twenty times during the same day you meet a person to whom you have been introduced, the hand is every where extended with—"Well, captain, how do you find yourself by this time?" and, in their good-will, when they seize your hand, they follow the apothecary's advice—"When taken, to be well shaken." As for the constant query—"How do you like our country?"—that is natural enough. I should ask the same of an American in England, but to reply to it is not the less tedious. It is all well meant, all kindness, but it really requires fortitude and patience to endure it. Every one throws in his voluntary tribute of compliments and good-will, but the accumulated mass is too great for any one individual to bear. How I long for the ocean prairies, or the wild forests. Subsequently, I begged hard to be shut up for six months in the Penitentiary at Philadelphia, but Sammy Wood said it was against the regulations. He comforted me with a *tête-à-tête* dinner, which was so agreeable, that at the time I quite forgot I wished to be alone.

When I left Saratoga, I found no one, as I thought, in the car, who knew me; and I determined, if possible, they should, in the Indian phrase, *lose my trail*. I arrived at Schenectady, and was put down there. I amused myself until the train started for Utica, which was to be in a few hours, in walking about the engine-house, and examining the locomotives; and having satisfied myself, set out for a solitary walk in the country. There was no name on my luggage, and I had not given my name when I took my ticket for the railroad. "At last," said I to myself, "*I am incog.*" I had walked out of the engine-house, looked round the compass, and resolved in which direction I would bend my steps, when a young man came up to me, and very politely taking off his hat, said, "I believe I have the pleasure of speaking to Captain M——." Had he known my indignation when he mentioned my name, poor fellow! but there was no help for it, and I replied in the affirmative. After apologising, he introduced himself, and then requested the liberty of introducing his friend. "Well, if ever," thought I; and, "no never," followed afterwards as a matter of course, and as a matter of course his friend was introduced. It reminded me of old times, when, midshipmen at balls, we used to introduce each other to ladies we had none of us seen before in our lives. Well, there I was, between two overpowering civilities, but they meant it kindly, and I could not be angry. These were students of Schenectady College: would I like to see it? a beautiful location, not half a mile off. I requested to know if there was any thing to be seen there, as I did not like to take a hot walk for nothing, instead of the shady one I had proposed for myself. "Yes, there was Professor Nott"—I had of course heard of Professor Nott.—Professor Nott, who governed by moral influence and paternal sway, and who had written so largely on stones and anthracite coal. I had never before heard of moral influence, stones, or anthracite coal. Then there were more professors, and a cabinet of minerals— the last was an inducement, and I went.

I saw Professor Nott, but not the cabinet of minerals, for Professor Savage had the key. With Professor Nott I had rather a hot argument about anthracite coal, and then escaped before he was cool again. The students walked back with me to the hotel, and, with many apologies for leaving me, informed me that dinner was ready. I would not tax their politeness any longer, and they departed.

Schenectady College, like most of the buildings in America, was commenced on a grand scale, but has never been finished; the two wings are finished, and the centre is lithographed, which looks very imposing in the plate. There is a peculiarity in this college: it is called the Botany Bay, from its receiving young men who have been expelled from other colleges, and who are kept in order by moral influence and paternal sway, the only means certainly by which wild young men are to be reclaimed. Seriously speaking Professor Nott is a very clever man, and I suspect this college will turn out more clever men than any other in the Union. It differs from the other colleges in another point. It upholds no peculiar sect of religion, which almost all the rest do. For instance, Yule (Yale), William's Town, and Amherst Colleges, are under presbyterian influence; Washington episcopal; Cambridge, in Massachusets, unitarian.

There is one disadvantage generally attending railroads. Travellers proceed more rapidly, but they lose all the beauty of the country. Railroads of course run through the most level portions of the States; and the levels, except they happen to be on the banks of a river, are invariably uninteresting. The road from Schenectady to Utica is one of the exceptions to this rule: there is not perhaps a more beautiful variety of scenery to be found anywhere. You run the whole way through the lovely valley of the Mohawk, on the banks of the Mohawk river. It was really delightful, but the motion was so rapid that you lamented passing by so fast. The Utica railroad is one of the best in America; the eighty miles are performed in four hours and a-half, stoppages for taking in water, passengers, and refreshments, included. The locomotive was of great power, and as it snorted along with a train of carriages of half a mile long in tow, it threw out such showers of fire, that we were constantly in danger of conflagration. The weather was too warm to admit of the windows being closed, and the ladies, assisted by the gentlemen, were constantly employed in putting out the sparks which settled on their clothes—the first time I ever heard ladies complain of having too many *sparks* about them. As the evening closed in we actually were whirled along through a stream of fiery threads—a beautiful, although humble imitation of the tail of a comet.

I had not been recognised in the rail car, and I again flattered myself that I was unknown. I proceeded, on my arrival at Utica, to the hotel, and asking at the bar for a bed, the book was handed to me, and I was requested to write my name. Wherever you stop in America, they generally produce a book and demand your name, not on account of any police regulations, but merely because they will not allow secrets in America, and because they choose to know who you may be. Of course, you may frustrate this espionage by putting down any name you please; and I had the pen in my hand, and was just thinking whether I should be Mr Snooks or Mr Smith, when I received a slap on the shoulder, accompanied with—"Well, captain, how are you by this time?" In despair I let the pen drop out of my hand, and instead of my name I left on the book a large blot. It was an old acquaintance from Albany, and before I had been ten minutes in the hotel, I was recognised by at least ten more. The Americans are such locomotives themselves, that it is useless to attempt the incognito in any part except the west side of the Missisippi, or the Rocky Mountains. Once known at New York, and you are known every where, for in every place you will meet with some one whom you have met walking in Broadway.

A tremendous thunder-storm, with torrents of rain, prevented my leaving Utica for Trenton Falls until late in the afternoon. The roads, ploughed up by the rain, were any thing but democratic; there was no level in them; and we were jolted and shaken like peas in a rattle, until we were silent from absolute suffering.

I rose the next morning at four o'clock. There was a heavy fog in the air, and you could not distinguish more than one hundred yards before you. I followed the path pointed out to me the night before, through a forest of majestic trees, and descending a long flight of steps found myself below the Falls. The scene impressed you with awe—the waters roared through deep chasms, between two walls of rock, one hundred and fifty feet high, perpendicular on each side, and the width between the two varying from forty to fifty feet. The high rocks were of black carbonate of lime in perfectly horizontal strata, so equally divided that they appeared like solid masonry. For fifty or sixty feet above the rushing waters they were smooth and bare; above that line vegetation commenced with small bushes, until you arrived at their summits, which were crowned with splendid forest trees, some of them inclining over the chasm, as if they would peep into the abyss below and witness the wild tumult of the waters.

From the narrowness of the pass, the height of the rocks, and the superadded towering of the trees above, but a small portion of the heavens was to be seen, and this was not blue, but of a misty murky grey. The first sensation was that of dizziness and confusion, from the unusual absence of the sky above, and the dashing frantic speed of the angry boiling waters. The rocks on each side have been blasted so as to form a path by which you may walk up to the first fall; but this path was at times very narrow and you have to cling to the chain which is let into the rock. The heavy storm of the day before had swelled the torrent so that it rose nearly a foot above this path; and before I had proceeded far, I found that the flood swept between my legs with a force which would have taken some people off their feet. The rapids below the Falls are much grander than the Falls themselves; there was one down in a chasm between two riven rocks which it was painful to look long upon, and watch with what a deep plunge—what irresistible force—the waters dashed down and then returned to their own surface, as if struggling and out of breath. As I stood over them in their wild career, listening to their roaring as if in anger, and watching the madness of their speed, I felt a sensation of awe—an inward acknowledgment of the tremendous power of Nature; and, after a time, I departed with feelings of gladness to escape from thought which became painful when so near to danger.

I gained the lower falls, which now covered the whole width of the rock, which they seldom do except during the freshets. They were extraordinary from their variety. On the side where I stood, poured down a rapid column of water about one-half of the width of the fall; on the other, it was running over a clear thin stream, as gentle and amiable as water could be. That part of the fall reminded me of ladies' hair in flowing ringlets, and the one nearest me of the Lord Chancellor Eldon, in all the pomposity and frowning dignity of his full-bottomed wig. And then I thought of the lion and the lamb, not lying down, but falling down together; and then I thought that I was wet through, which was a fact; so I climbed up a ladder, and came to a wooden bridge above the fall, which conveyed me to the other side. The bridge posses over a staircase of little falls, sometimes diagonally, sometimes at right angles with the sites, and is very picturesque. On the other side you climb up a ladder of one hundred feet, and arrive at a little building with a portico, where travellers are refreshed. Here you have a view of all the upper falls, but these seem tame after witnessing the savage impetuosity of the rapids below. You ascend another ladder of one hundred feet, and you arrive at a path pointed out to you by the broad chips of the woodman's axe. Follow the chips and you will arrive four or five hundred feet above both the bridge and the level of the upper fall. This scene is splendid. The black perpendicular rocks on the other side; the succession of falls; the rapids roaring below; the forest trees rising to the clouds and spreading with their majestic boughs the vapour ascending from the falling waters; together with the occasional glimpses of the skies here and there—all this induces you to wander with your eyes from one point of view to another, never tiring with its beauty, wildness, and vastness: and, if you do not exclaim with the Mussulman, God is great! you *feel* it through every sense, and at every pulsation of the heart.

The mountain was still above me, and I continued my ascent; but the chips now disappeared, and, like Tom Thumb, I lost my way. I attempted to retreat, but in vain; I was no longer amongst forest trees, but in a maze of young mountain ash, from which I could not extricate myself: so I stood still to think what I should do. I recollected that the usual course of proceeding on such occasions, was either to sit down and cry, or attempt to get out of your scrape. Tom Thumb did both; but I had no time to indulge in the former luxury, so I pushed and pushed, till I pushed myself out of my scrape, and found myself in a more respectable part of the woods. I then stopped to take breath. I heard a rustling behind me, and made sure it was a panther:— it was a beautiful little palm squirrel, who came close to me, as if to say "Who are you?" I took off my hat and told him my name, when, very contemptuously, as I thought, he turned short round, cocked his tail over his back, and skipped away. "Free, but not enlightened," thought I; "hasn't a soul above nuts." I also beat a retreat, and on my arrival at the hotel, found that, although I had no guides to pay, Nature had made a very considerable levy upon my wardrobe: my boots were bursting, my trowsers torn to fragments, and my hat was spoilt; and, moreover, I sat shivering in the garments which remained. So I, in my turn, levied upon a cow that was milking, and having improved her juice very much by the addition of some rum, I sat down under the portico, and smoked the cigar of meditation.

The walls of the portico were, as usual, scribbled over by those who would obtain cheap celebrity. I always read these productions; they are pages of human life. The majority of the scribblers leave a name and nothing more: beyond that, some few of their productions are witty, some sententious, mostly gross. My thoughts, as I read over the rubbish, were happily expressed by the following distich which I came to:—

Les   Fenêtres   et   les   Murailles,
Sont le papier des Canailles.

A little farther on, I found the lie given to this remark by some philosophic Spaniard:

Amigo   quien   quiera   que   seas,   piensa   que   si   acqui
Pones   tu   nombre,   pronto   il   tiempo   lo   borrara
Escribe   lo   pues   en   il   libro   de   Dio   en   donde.
Permancera   eternamente—
            In Amigo.

Volume One—Chapter Twelve.

Returning to Utica, I fell in with a horse bridled and saddled, that was taking his way home without his master, every now and then cropping the grass at the road-side, and then walking on in a most independent manner. His master had given him a certificate of leave, by chalking in large letters on the saddle-flaps on each side, "*Let him go.*" This was a very primitive proceeding; but I am not quite sure that it could be ventured upon in Yorkshire, or in Virginia either, where they know a good horse, and are particularly careful of it. It is a fact, that wherever they breed horses they invariably learn to steal them.

Set off for Oswego in a canal boat; it was called a packet-boat because it did not carry merchandise, but was a very small affair, about fifty feet long by eight wide. The captain of her was, however, in his own opinion, no small affair; he puffed and swelled until he looked larger than his boat. This personage, as soon as we were under weigh, sat down in the narrow cabin, before a small table; sent for this writing-desk, which was about the size of street organ, and, like himself, no small affair; ordered a bell to be rung in our ears to summon the passengers; and, then, taking down the names of four or five people, received the enormous sum of ten dollars passage-money. He then locked his desk with a key large enough for a street-door, ordered his steward to remove it, and went on deck to walk just three feet and return again. After all, there is nothing like being a captain.

Although many of the boats are laid up, there is still considerable traffic on this canal. We passed Rome, a village of two thousand inhabitants, at which number it has for many years been nearly stationary. This branch of the canal is, of course, cut through the levels, and we passed through swamps and wild forests; here and there some few acres were cleared, and a log-house was erected, looking very solitary and forlorn, surrounded by the stumps of the trees which had been felled, and which now lay corded up on the banks of the canal, ready to be disposed of. Wild and dreary as the country is, the mass of forest is gradually receding, and occasionally some solitary tree is left standing, throwing out its wide arms, and appearing as if in lamentation at its separation from its companions, with whom for centuries it had been in close fellowship.

Extremes meet: as I looked down from the roof of the boat upon the giants of the forest, which had for so many centuries reared their heads undisturbed, but now lay prostrate before civilisation, the same feelings were conjured up in my mind as when I have, in my wanderings, surveyed such fragments of dismembered empires as the ruins of Carthage or of Rome. There the reign of Art was over, and Nature had resumed her sway—here Nature was deposed, and about to resign her throne to the usurper Art. By the bye, the mosquitoes of this district have reaped some benefit from the cutting of the canal here. Before these impervious forest retreats were thus pierced, they could not have tasted human blood; for ages it must have been unknown to them, even by tradition; and if they taxed all other boats on the canal as they did, ours, a *canal share* with them must be considerably above par, and highly profitable.

At five o'clock we arrived at Syracuse. I do detest these old names vamped up. Why do not the Americans take the Indian names? They need not be so very scrupulous about it; they have robbed the Indians of everything else.

After you pass Syracuse, the country wears a more populous and inviting appearance. Salina is a village built upon a salt spring, which has the greatest flow of water yet known, and this salt spring is the cause of the improved appearance of the country; the banks of the canal, for three miles, are lined with buildings for the boiling down of the salt water, which is supplied by a double row of wooden pipes. Boats are constantly employed up and down the canal, transporting wood for the supply of the furnaces. It is calculated that two hundred thousand cord of wood are required every year for the present produce; and as they estimate upon an average about sixty cord of wood per acre in these parts, those salt works are the means of yearly clearing away upwards of three thousand acres of land. Two million of bushels of salt are boiled down every year: it is packed in barrels, and transported by the canals and lakes to Canada, Michigan, Chicago, and the far West. When we reflect upon the number of people employed in the manufactories, and in cutting wood, and making barrels, and engaged on the lakes and canals in transporting the produce so many thousand miles, we must admire the spring to industry which has been created by this little, but bounteous, spring presented by nature.

The first sixty miles of this canal (I get on very slow with my description, but canal travelling is very slow), which is through a flat swampy forest, is without a lock; but after you pass Syracuse, you have to descend by locks to the Oswego river, and the same at every rapid of the river; in all, there is a fall of one hundred and sixty feet. Simple as locks are, I could not help reverting to the wild rapids at Trenton Falls, and reflecting upon how the ingenuity of man had so easily been able to overcome and control Nature! The locks did not detain us long—they never lose time in America. When the boat had entered the lock, and the gate was closed upon her, the water was let off with a rapidity which considerably affected her level, and her bows pointed downwards. I timed one lock with a fall of fifteen feet. From the time the gate was closed behind us until the lower one was opened for our egress, was exactly one minute and a quarter; and the boat sank down in the lock so rapidly as to give you the idea that she was scuttled and sinking.

The country round the Oswego is fertile and beautiful, and the river, with its islands, falls, and rapids, very picturesque. At one p.m. we arrived at the town of Oswego, on Lake Ontario; I was pleased with the journey, although, what with ducking to bridges, bites from mosquitoes, and the constant blowing of their unearthly horn with only one note, and which one must have been borrowed from the gamut of the infernal regions, I had had enough of it.

For the first time since my arrival in the country, no one—that is to say, on board the canal-boat—knew who I was. As we tracked above the Oswego river, I fell into conversation with a very agreeable person, who had joined us at Syracuse. We conversed the whole day, and I obtained much valuable information from him about the country: when we parted, he expressed a wish that we should meet again. He gave me his name and address, and when I gave my card in return, he looked at it, and then said, "I am most happy to make your acquaintance, sir; but I will confess that had I known with whom I had been conversing, I should not have *spoken so freely* upon certain points connected with the government and institutions of this country." This was American all over; they would conceal the truth, and then blame us because we do not find it out. I met him afterwards, but he never would enter into any detailed conversation with me.

Volume One—Chapter Thirteen.

Niagara Falls.—Perhaps the wisest, if not the best description of the Falls of Niagara, is in the simple ejaculation of Mrs Butler; for it is almost useless to attempt to describe when you feel that language fails; but if the falls cannot be described, the ideas which are conjured up in the mind, when we contemplate this wonderful combination of grandeur and beauty, are often worth recording. The lines of Mrs Sigourney, the American poetess, please me most.

Flow on for ever, in thy glorious robe
Of terror and of beauty; God hath set
His rainbow on thy forehead, and the cloud
Mantles around thy feet. And he doth give
Thy voice of thunder power to speak of him
Eternally—bidding the lip of man
Keep silence, and upon thy rocky altar pour
Incense of awe-struck praise.

When the Indian first looked upon the falls, he declared them to be the dwelling of the Great Spirit. The savage could not imagine that the Great Spirit dwelt also in the leaf which he bruised in his hand; but here it appealed to his senses in thunder and awful majesty, and he was compelled to acknowledge it.

The effects which the contemplation of these glorious waters produce, are of course very different, according to one's temperament and disposition. As I stood on the brink above the falls, continuing for a considerable time to watch the great mass of water tumbling, dancing, capering, and rushing wildly along, as if in a hurry to take the leap and, delighted at it, I could not help wishing that I too had been made of such stuff as would have enabled me to have joined it; with it to have rushed innocuously down the precipice; to have rolled uninjured into the deep unfathomable gulf below, or to have gambolled in the atmosphere of spray, which rose again in a dense cloud from its recesses. For about half an hour more I continued to watch the rolling waters, and then I felt a slight dizziness and a creeping sensation come over me—that sensation arising from strong excitement, and the same, probably, that occasions the bird to fall into the jaws of the snake. This is a feeling which, if too long indulged in, becomes irresistible, and occasions a craving desire to leap into the flood of rushing waters. It increased upon me every minute; and retreating from the brink, I turned my eyes to the surrounding foliage, until the effect of the excitement had passed away. I looked upon the waters a second time, and then my thoughts were directed into a very different channel. I wished myself a magician, that I might transport the falls to Italy, and pour their whole volume of waters into the crater of Mount Vesuvius; witness the terrible conflict between the contending elements, and create the largest steam-boiler that ever entered into the imagination of man.

I have no doubt that the opinion that these falls have receded a distance of seven miles is correct; but what time must have passed before even this tremendous power could have sawed away such a mass of solid rock! Within the memory of man it has receded but a few feet—changed but little. How many thousand years must these waters have been flowing and falling, unvarying in their career, and throwing up their sheets of spray to heaven.

It is impossible for either the eye or the mind to compass the whole mass of falling water; you cannot measure, cannot estimate its enormous volume; and this is the reason, perhaps, why travellers often express themselves disappointed by it. But fix your eye upon one portion—one falling and heaving wave out of the millions, as they turn over the edge of the rocks; watch, I say, this fragment for a few minutes, its regular time-beating motion never varying or changing; pursuing the laws of nature with a regularity never ceasing and never tiring; minute after minute; hour after hour; day after day; year after year, until time recedes into creation: then cast your eyes over the whole multitudinous mass which is, and has been, performing the same and coeval duty, and you feel its vastness! Still the majesty of the whole is far too great for the mind to compass—too stupendous for its limited powers of reception.

Sunday.—I had intended to have passed the whole day at the Falls; but an old gentleman whose acquaintance I had made in the steam boat on Lake Ontario, asked me to go to church; and as I felt he would be annoyed if I did not, I accompanied him to a Presbyterian meeting not far from the Falls, which sounded like distant thunder. The sermon was upon temperance—a favourite topic in America; and the minister rather quaintly observed, that "alcohol was not sealed by the hand of God." It was astonishing to me that he did not allude to the Falls, point out that the seal of God was there, and shew how feeble was the voice of man when compared to the thunder of the Almighty so close at hand. But the fact was, he had been accustomed to preach every Sunday with the Falls roaring in his ear, and (when the wind was in a certain quarter,) with the spray damping the leaves of his sermon: he therefore did not feel as we did, and, no doubt, thought his sermon better than that from the God of the elements.

Yes, it is through the elements that the Almighty has ever deigned to commune with man, or to execute his supreme will, whether it has been by the wild waters to destroy an impious race—by the fire hurled upon the doomed cities—by seas divided, that the chosen might pass through them—by the thunders on Sinai's Mount when his laws were given to man—by the pillar of fire or the gushing rock, or by the rushing of mighty winds. And it is still through the elements that the Almighty speaks to man, to warn, to terrify, to chasten; to raise him up to wonder, to praise, and adore. The forked and blinding lightning which, with the rapidity of thought, dissolves the union between the body and the soul; the pealing thunder, announcing that the bolt has sped; the fierce tornado, sweeping away everything in its career, like a besom of wrath; the howling storm; the mountain waves; the earth quaking, and yawning wide, in a second overthrowing the work and pride of centuries, and burying thousands in a living tomb; the fierce vomiting of the crater, pouring out its flames of liquid fire, and changing fertility to the arid rock: it is through these that the Deity still speaks to man; yet what can inspire more awe of him, more reverence, and more love, than the contemplation of thy falling waters, great Niagara!

Volume One—Chapter Fourteen.

Two gentlemen have left their cards, and will be happy to see me on my route; one lives at Batavia, the other at Pekin. I recollect going over the ferry to Brooklyn to visit the Commodore at the Navy Yard; I walked to where the omnibuses started from, to see if one was going my way. There were but two on the stand: one was bound to *Babylon*, the other to *Jericho*. Buffalo is one of the wonders of America. It is hardly to be credited that such a beautiful city could have risen up in the wilderness in so short a period. In the year 1814 it was burnt down, being then only a village; only one house was left standing, and now it is a city with twenty-five thousand inhabitants. The Americans are very judicious in planning their new towns; the streets are laid out so wide that there will never be any occasion to pull down to widen and improve, as we do in England. The city of Buffalo is remarkably well built; all the houses in the principal streets are lofty and substantial, and are either of brick or granite. The main street is wider, and the stores handsomer, than the majority of those in New York. It has five or six very fine churches, a handsome theatre, town-hall, and market, and three or four hotels, one of which is superior to most others in America; and to these we must add a fine stone pier, with a lighthouse, and a harbour full of shipping and magnificent steam-boats. It is almost incomprehensible, that all this should have been accomplished since the year 1814. And what has occasioned this springing up of a city in so short a time as to remind you of Aladdin's magic palace?—the Erie Canal, which here joins the Hudson River with the Lake, passing through the centre of the most populous and fertile States.

At present, however, the business of Buffalo, as well as of every other city, is nearly at a stand-still; the machinery of America is under repair, and until that repair is completed, the country will remain paralysed. America may just now be compared to one of her own steamboats, which, under too high pressure, has burst her boiler. Some of her passengers have (in a commercial point of view) been killed outright, others severely injured, and her progress has for a time been stopped: but she will soon be enabled to go a-head again as fast as ever, and will then probably pay a little more attention to her safety-valve.

I went out to the Indian reservation, granted to the remnant of the Seneca tribe of Indians, once a portion of the Mohawks, and all that now remains in the United States of the famed six nations. The chief of them (Red Jacket), lately dead, might be considered as the last of the Mohicans. I had some conversation with his daughter, who was very busily employed in the ornamenting of a pair of mocassins, and then visited the tomb, or rather the spot, where her father was buried, without name or record. This omission has since been repaired, and a tablet is now raised over his grave. It is creditable to the profession that the "poor player," as Shakespeare hath it, should be the foremost to pay tribute to worth. Cooke, the tragedian, was lying without a stone to mark his resting-place, when Kean came to America, found out the spot, and raised a handsome cenotaph to his memory; and it is to Mr Placide, one of the very best of American actors, that Red Jacket is indebted for the tablet which has been raised to rescue his narrow home from oblivion.

Red Jacket was a great chief and a great man, but, like most of the Indians, he could not resist the temptations of alcohol, and was during the latter part of his life very intemperate. When Red Jacket was sober, he was the proudest chief that ever walked, and never would communicate even with the highest of the American authorities but through his interpreter; but when intoxicated, he would speak English and French fluently, and then the proud Indian warrior, the most eloquent of his race, the last chief of the six nations, would demean himself by begging for a sixpence to buy more rum.

I must now revert to the singular causes by which, independent of others, such as locality, etcetera, Buffalo was so rapidly brought to a state of perfection—not like many other towns which, commencing with wooden houses, gradually supersede them by brick and stone. The person who was the cause of this unusual rise was a Mr Rathbun, who now lies incarcerated in a gaol of his own building. It was he who built all the hotels, churches, and other public edifices; in fact, every structure worthy of observation in the whole town was projected, contracted for, and executed by Mr Rathbun. His history is singular. Of quiet, unassuming manners, Quaker in his dress, moderate in all his expenses, (except in charity, wherein, assisted by an amiable wife, he was very liberal) he concealed under this apparent simplicity and goodness a mind capable of the vastest conceptions, united with the greatest powers of execution. He undertook contracts, and embarked in building speculations, to an amount almost incredible. Rathbun undertook every thing, and every thing undertaken by Rathbun was well done. Not only at Buffalo, but at Niagara and other places, he was engaged in raising vast buildings, when the great crash occurred, and Rathbun, with others, was unable to meet his liabilities. Then, for the first time, it was discovered that for more than five years he had been conniving at a system of forgery, to the amount of two millions of dollars: the forgery consisted in putting to his bills the names of responsible parties as indorsers, that they might be more current. It does not appear that he ever intended to defraud, for he took up all his notes as fast as they became due; and it was this extreme regularity on his part which prevented the discovery of his fraud for so unusually long a period. It is surmised, that had not the general failure taken place, he would have eventually withdrawn all these forged bills from the market, and have paid all his creditors, reserving for himself a handsome fortune. It is a singular event in the annals of forgery, that this should have been carried on undiscovered for so unprecedented a time. Mr Rathbun is to be tried as an accessory, as it was his brother who forged the names. As soon as it was discovered, the latter made his escape, and he is said to have died miserably in a hovel on the confines of Texas.

Embarked on board of the Sandusky, for Detroit. As we were steering clear of the pier, a small brig of about two hundred tons burthen was pointed out to me as having been the *flag-ship* of Commodore Barclay, in the action upon Lake Erie. The appearance of Buffalo from the Lake is very imposing. Stopped at Dunkirk to put some emigrants on shore. As they were landing, I watched them carefully counting over their little property, from the iron tea-kettle to the heavy chest. It was their whole fortune, and invaluable to them; the nest-egg by which, with industry, their children were to rise to affluence. They remained on the wharf as we shoved off, and no wonder that they seemed embarrassed and at a loss. There was the baby in the cradle, the young children holding fast to their mother's skirt, while the elder had seated themselves on a log, and watched the departure of the steam-vessel;—the bedding, cooking utensils, etcetera, all lying in confusion, and all to be housed before night. Weary did they look, and weary indeed they were, and most joyful would they be when they at last should gain their resting-place. It appears from the reports sent in, that upwards of 100,000 emigrants pass to the west every year by the route of the Lakes, of which it is estimated that about 30,000 are from Europe, the remainder migrating from the eastern States of the Union.

I may keep a log now.—5 AM Light breezes and clear weather, land trending from South to South South West. Five sail in the offing.

At 6 AM, ran into Grand River. Within these last two years, three towns have sprung up here, containing between them about three thousand inhabitants.

How little are they aware, in Europe, of the vastness and extent of commerce carried on in these inland seas whose coasts are now lined with flourishing towns and cities, and whose waters are ploughed by magnificent steam-boats, and hundreds of vessels laden with merchandise. Even the Americans themselves are not fully aware of the rising importance of these Lakes as connected with the West. Since the completion of the Ohio Canal, which enters the Lake Erie at Cleveland, that town has risen almost as rapidly as Buffalo. It is beautifully situated. It is about six years back that it may be said to have commenced its start, and it now contains more than ten thousand inhabitants. The buildings are upon the same scale as those of Buffalo, and it is conjectured with good reason, that it will become even a larger city than the other, as the ice breaks up here and the navigation is open in the spring, six weeks sooner than it is at Buffalo; abreast of which town the ice is driven down and collected, previous to its forcing its passage over the falls.

Erie, which was the American naval depôt during the war, has a fine bay, but it is now falling into insignificance: it has a population of about one thousand.

Sandusky is a fast-rising town, beautifully situated upon the verge of a small prairie; it is between Sandusky and Huron that the prairie lands commence. The bay of Sandusky is very picturesque, being studded with small verdant islands. On one of these are buried in the same grave all those who fell in the hard-fought battle of the Lakes, between Perry and Barclay, both of whom have since followed their companions.

Toledo is the next town of consequence on the Lake. It is situated at the mouth of the Miami River; and as a railroad has already been commenced across the isthmus, so as to avoid going round the whole peninsula of Michigan, it is fast rising into importance. Three years ago the land was purchased at a dollar and a-half per acre; now, it is selling for building lots at one hundred dollars per foot. They handed me a paper printed in this town called "The Toledo Blade;" a not inappropriate title, though rather a bold one for an editor to write up to, as his writings ought to be very *sharp*, and, at the same time, extremely *well-tempered.*

The American government have paid every attention to their inland waters. The harbours, light-houses, piers, etcetera, have all been built at the expense of government, and every precaution has been taken to make the navigation of the Lakes as safe as possible.

In speaking of the new towns rising so fast in America, I wish the reader to understand that, if he compares them with the country towns of the same population in England, he will not do them. In the smaller towns of England you can procure but little, and you have to send to London for any thing good: in the larger towns, such as Norwich, etcetera, you may procure most things; but, still, luxuries must usually be obtained from the metropolis. But in such places as Buffalo and Cleveland, every thing is to be had that you can procure at New York or Boston. In those two towns on Lake Erie are stores better furnished, and handsomer, than any shops at Norwich, in England; and you will find, in either of them, articles for which, at Norwich, you would be obliged to send to London. It is the same thing at almost every town in America with which communication is easy. Would you furnish a house in one of them, you will find every article of furniture—carpets, stoves, grates, marble chimney-pieces, pier-glasses, pianos, lamps, candelabra, glass, china, etcetera, in twice the quantity, and in greater variety, than at any provincial town in England.

This arises from the system of credit extended through every vein and artery of the country, and by which English goods are forced, as if with a force-pump, into every available dépôt in the Union; and thus, in a town so newly raised, that the stumps of the forest-trees are not only still surrounding the houses, but remain standing in the cellars, you will find every luxury that can be required. It may be asked what becomes of all these goods. It must be recollected that hundreds of new houses spring up every year in the towns, and that the surrounding country is populous and wealthy. In the farmhouses—mean-looking and often built of logs—is to be found not only comfort, but very often luxury.

Volume One—Chapter Fifteen.

The French never have succeeded as colonists, and their want of success can only be ascribed to an amiable want of energy. When located at any spot, if a Frenchman has enough, he seeks no more; and, instead of working as the Englishman or the American does, he will pass his time away, and spend his little surplus in social amusements. The town of Detroit was founded as early as the city of Philadelphia, but, favourably as it is situated, it never until lately rose to any thing more than, properly speaking, a large village. There is not a paved street in it, or even a foot-path for a pedestrian. In winter, in rainy weather, you are up to your knees in mud; in summer, invisible from dust: indeed, until lately, there was not a practicable road for thirty miles round Detroit. The muddy and impassable state of the streets has given rise to a very curious system of making morning or evening calls. A small one-horse cart is backed against the door of a house; the ladies dressed get into it, and seat themselves upon a buffalo skin at the bottom of it; they are carried to the residence of the party upon whom they wish to call; the cart is backed in again, and they are landed dry and clean. An old inhabitant of Detroit complained to me that people were now getting so proud, that many of them refused to visit in that way any longer. But owing to the rise of the other towns on the lake, the great increase of commerce, and Michigan having been admitted as a State into the Union, with Detroit as its capital, a large Eastern population has now poured into it, and Detroit will soon present an appearance very different from its present, and become one of the most flourishing cities of America. Within these last six years it has increased its population from two to ten thousand. The climate here is the very best in America, although the State itself is unhealthy. The land near the town is fertile. A railroad from Detroit already extends thirty miles through the State; and now that the work has commenced, it will be carried on with the usual energy of the Americans.

Left Detroit in the Michigan steam-vessel for Mackinaw; passed through the Lake St. Clair, and entered Lake Huron; stopped at a solitary wharf to take in wood, and met there with a specimen of American politeness or (if you please) independence in the gentleman who cut down and sold it. Without any assignable motive, he called out to me, "You are a damned fool of an Englishman;" for which, I suppose, I ought to have been very much obliged to him.

Miss Martineau has not been too lavish in her praises of Mackinaw. It has the appearance of a fairy isle floating on the water, which is so pure and transparent that you may see down to almost any depth; and the air above is as pure as the water, so that you feel invigorated as you breathe it. The first reminiscence brought to my mind after I had landed, was the description by Walter Scott of the island and residence of Magnus Troil and his daughters Minna and Brenda, in the novel of the "Pirate."

The low buildings, long stores, and out-houses full of nets, barrels, masts, sails, and cordage; the abundance of fish lying about; the rafters of the houses laden with dried and smoked meat; and the full and jolly proportions of most of the inhabitants, who would have rivalled Scott's worthy in height and obesity, immediately struck my eye; and I might have imagined myself transported to the Shetland isle, had it not been for the lodges of the Indians on the beach, and the Indians themselves either running about, or lying stripped in the porches before the whisky stores.

I inquired of one of the islanders, why all the white residents were generally such large portly men, which they are at a very early age; he replied, "We have good air, good water, and what we eat agrees with us." This was very conclusive.

I enquired of another, if people lived to a good old age in the island; his reply was quite American—"I guess they do; if people want to die, they can't die here—they're obliged to go elsewhere."

Wandering among the Indian lodges (wigwams is a term not used now-a-days), I heard a sort of flute played in one of them, and I entered. The young Indian who was blowing on it, handed it to me. It was an imperfect instrument, something between a flute and a clarionet, but the sound which it gave out was soft and musical. An islander informed me that it was the only sort of musical instrument which the Northern tribes possessed, and that it was played upon by the young men only when they were *in love*. I suspected at first that he was bantering me, but I afterwards found that what he said was true. The young Indian must have been very deeply smitten, for he continued to play all day and all night, during the time that I was there.

"If music be the food of love, play on."

Started in a birch canoe for Sault St. Marie, a small town built under the rapids of that name, which pour out a portion of the waters of Lake Superior. Two American gentlemen, one a member of Congress, and the other belonging to the American Fur Company, were of the party. Our crew consisted of five Canadian half-breeds—a mixture between the Indian and the white, which spoils both. It was a lovely morning; not a breath of air stirred the wide expanse of the Huron, as far as the eye could scan; and the canoe, as it floated along side of the landing-place, appeared as if it were poised in the air, so light did it float, and so clear and transparent are these northern waters. We started, and in two hours arrived at Goose Island, unpoetical in its name, but in itself full of beauty. As you stand on the beach, you can look down through the water on to the shelving bottom, bright with its variety of pebbles, and trace it almost as far off as if it had not been covered with water at all. The island was small, but gay as the gayest of parterres, covered with the sweet wild rose in full bloom (certainly the most fragrant rose in the world), blue campanellos, yellow exeranthemums, and white ox-eyed daisies. Underneath there was a perfect carpet of strawberries, ripe, and inviting you to eat them, which we did, while our Canadian brutes swallowed long strings of raw salt pork. And yet, in two months hence, this lovely little spot will be but one mass of snow —a mound rising above to serve as a guide to the chilled traveller who would find his way over the frozen expanse of the wide Huron Lake.

As soon as our Canadians had filled themselves to repletion with raw pork, we continued our route that we might cross the lake and gain the detour, or point which forms the entrance of the river St. Marie, before it was dark. We arrived a little before sunset, when we landed, put up our light boat, and bivouacked for the night. As soon as we put our feet on shore, we were assailed by the mosquitoes in myriads. They congregated from all quarters in such numbers, that you could only see as if through a black veil, and you could not speak without having your mouth filled with them. But in ten minutes we had a large fire, made, not of logs or branches, but of a dozen small trees. The wind eddied, and the flame and smoke, as they rose in masses, whirled about the mosquitoes right and left, and in every quarter of the compass, until they were fairly beaten off to a respectable distance. We supped upon lake-trout and fried ham; and rolling ourselves up in our Mackinaw blankets, we were soon fast asleep.

There was no occasion to call us the next morning. The Canadians were still snoring, and had let the fires go down. The mosquitoes, taking advantage of this neglect, had forced their way into the tent, and sounded the reveillé in our ears with their petty trumpets; following up the summons with the pricking of pins, as the fairies of Queen Mab are reported to have done to lazy housemaids. We kicked up our half-breeds, who gave us our breakfast, stowed away the usual quantity of raw pork, and once more did we float on the water in a piece of birch bark. The heat of the sun was oppressive, and we were broiled; but we dipped our hands in the clear cool stream as we skimmed along, listening to the whistling of the solitary loon as it paddled away from us, or watching the serrated back of the sturgeon, as he rolled lazily over and showed above the water. Now and then we stopped, and the silence of the desert was broken by the report of our fowling-pieces, and a pigeon or two was added to our larder. At noon a breeze sprung up, and we hoisted our sail, and the Canadians who had paddled dropped asleep as we glided quietly along under the guidance of the "timonier."

After you have passed through the river St. Clair, and entered the Huron lake, the fertility of the country gradually disappears. Here and there indeed, especially on the Canadian side, a spot more rich than the soil in general is shewn by the large growth of the timber; but the northern part of the Lake Huron shores is certainly little fit for cultivation. The spruce fir now begins to be plentiful; for, until you come to the upper end of the lake, they are scarce, although very abundant in Upper Canada. The country wears the same appearance all the way up to the Sault St. Marie, shewing maple and black poplar intermingled with fir: the oak but rarely appearing. The whole lake from Mackinaw to the Detour is studded with islands. A large one at the entrance of the river is called St. Joseph's. The Hudson Bay Company had a station there, which is now abandoned, and the island has been purchased, or granted, to an English officer, who has partly settled it. It is said to be the best land in this region, but still hardly fit for cultivation. It was late before our arrival at the Sault, and we were obliged to have recourse to our paddles, for the wind had died away. As the sun went down, we observed a very curious effect from the refraction of tints, the water changing to a bright violet every time that it was disturbed by the paddles. I have witnessed something like this just after sunset on the Lake of Geneva.

We landed at dusk, much fatigued; but the Aurora Borealis flashed in the heavens, spreading out like a vast plume of ostrich feathers across the sky, every minute changing its beautiful and fanciful forms. Tired as we were, we watched it for hours before we could make up our minds to go to bed.

Volume One—Chapter Sixteen.

Sault St. Marie—Our landlord is a very strange being. It appears that he has been annoyed by some traveller, who has published a work in which he has found fault with the accommodations at Sault St. Marie, and spoken very disrespectfully of our host's beds and bed-furniture. I have never read the work, but I am so well aware how frequently travellers fill up their pages with fleas, and "such small gear," that I presume the one in question was short of matter to furnish out his book; yet it was neither just nor liberal on his part to expect at Sault St. Marie, where, perhaps, not five travellers arrive in the course of a year, the same accommodations as at New York. The bedsteads certainly were a little rickety, but every thing was very clean and comfortable. The house was not an inn, nor, indeed, did it pretend to be one, but the fare was good and well cooked, and you were waited upon by the host's two pretty modest daughters—not only pretty, but well-informed girls; and, considering that this village is the Ultima Thule of this portion of America, I think that a traveller might have been very well content with things as they were. In two instances, I found in the log-houses of this village complete editions of Lord Byron's works.

Sault St. Marie contains, perhaps, fifty houses, mostly built of logs, and has a palisade put up to repel any attack of the Indians.

There are two companies of soldiers quartered here. The rapids from which the village takes its name are just above it; they are not strong or dangerous, and the canoes descend them twenty times a day. At the foot of the rapids the men are constantly employed in taking the white fish in scoop nets, as they attempt to force their way up into Lake Superior. The majority of the inhabitants here are half-breeds. It is remarkable that the females generally improve, and the males degenerate, from the admixture of blood. Indian wives are here preferred to white, and perhaps with reason—they make the best wives for poor men; they labour hard, never complain, and a day of severe toil is amply recompensed by a smile from their lord and master in the evening. They are always faithful and devoted, and very sparing of their talk, all which qualities are considered as recommendations in this part of the world.

It is remarkable, that although the Americans treat the negro with contumely, they have a respect for the red Indian: a well-educated half-bred Indian is not debarred from entering into society; indeed, they are generally received with great attention. The daughter of a celebrated Indian chief brings heraldry into the family, for the Indians are as proud of their descent (and with good reason) as we, in Europe, are of ours. The Randolph family in Virginia still boast of their descent from Pocahontas, the heroine of one of the most remarkable romances in real life which was ever heard of.

The whole of this region appears to be incapable of cultivation, and must remain in its present state, perhaps, for centuries to come. The chief produce is from the lakes; trout and white fish are caught in large quantities, salted down, and sent to the west and south. At Mackinaw alone they cure about two thousand barrels, which sell for ten dollars the barrel; at the Sault, about the same quantity; and on Lake Superior, at the station of the American Fur Company, they have commenced the fishing, to lessen the expenses of the establishment, and they now salt down about four thousand barrels; but this traffic is still in its infancy, and will become more profitable as the west becomes more populous. Be it here observed that, although the Canadians have the same rights and the same capabilities of fishing, I do not believe that one barrel is cured on the Canadian side. As the American fish is prohibited in England, it might really become an article of exportation from the Canadas to a considerable amount.

There is another source of profit, which is the collecting of the maple sugar; and this staple, if I may use the term, is rapidly increasing. At an average, the full grown maple-tree will yield about five pounds of sugar each tapping, and, if carefully treated, will last forty years. All the State of Michigan is supplied from this quarter with this sugar, which is good in quality, and refines well. At Mackinaw they receive about three hundred thousand pounds every year. It may be collected in any quantity from their vast wildernesses of forests, and although the notion may appear strange, it is not impossible that one day the Northern sugar may supersede that of the Tropics. The island of St. Joseph, which I have mentioned, is covered with large maple trees, and they make a great quantity upon that spot alone.

I was amused by a reply given me by an American in office here. I asked how much his office was worth, and his answer was six hundred dollars, besides*stealings*. This was, at all events, frank and honest; in England the word would have been softened down to perquisites. I afterwards found that it was a common expression in the States to say a place was worth so much besides cheatage.

In all this country, from Mackinaw to the Sault, hay is very scarce; and, during the short summer season, the people go twenty or thirty miles in their canoes to any known patch of prairie or grass land to collect it. Nevertheless, they are very often obliged, during the winter, to feed their cattle upon fish, and, strange to say, they acquire a taste for it. You will see the horses and cows disputing for the offal; and our landlord told me that he has often witnessed a particular horse wait very quietly while they were landing the fish from the canoes, watch his opportunity, dart in, steal one, and *run away with it in his mouth*.

A mutiny among our lazzaroni of half-breeds, they refuse to work today, because they are tired, they say, and we are obliged to procure others. Carried our canoe over the pasturage into the canal, and in five minutes were on the vast inland sea of Lake Superior. The waters of this lake are, if possible, more transparent than those of the Huron, or rather the variety and bright colours of the pebbles and agates which lie at the bottom, make them appear so. The appearance of the coast, and the growth of timber, are much the same as on Lake Huron, until you arrive at Gros Cape, a bold promontory, about three hundred feet high. We ascended this cape, to have a full view of the expanse of water: this was a severe task, as it was nearly perpendicular, and we were forced to cling from tree to tree to make the ascent. In addition to this difficulty, we were unremittingly pursued by the mosquitoes, which blinded us so as to impede our progress, being moreover assisted in their malevolent attacks by a sort of sand-fly, that made triangular incisions behind our ears, exactly like a small leech bite, from which the blood trickled down two or three inches as soon as the little wretch let go his hold. This variety of stinging made us almost mad, and we descended quite exhausted, the blood trickling down our faces and necks. We threw off our clothes, and plunged into the lake; the water was too cold; the agates at the bottom cut our feet severely, and thus were we phlebotomised from head to foot.

There is a singular geological feature at this cape; you do not perceive it until you have forced your way through a belt of firs, which grow at the bottom and screen it from sight. It is a ravine in which the rocks are pouring down from the top to the bottom, all so equal in size, and so arranged, as to wear the appearance of a cascade of stones; and when, half blinded by the mosquitoes, you look upon them, they appear as if they are actually in motion, and falling down in one continued stream. We embarked again, and after an hour's paddling landed upon a small island, where was the tomb of an Indian chief or warrior. It was in a beautiful spot, surrounded by the wild rose, blue peas, and campanellas. The kinnakinnee, or weed which the Indians smoke as tobacco, grew plentifully about it. The mound of earth was surrounded by a low palisade, about four feet wide and seven feet long, and at the head of it was the warrior's pole, with eagle feathers, and notches denoting the number of scalps he had taken from the enemy.

The Hudson Bay and American Fur Companies both have stations on Lake Superior, on their respective sides of the lake, and the Americans have a small schooner which navigates it. There is one question which the traveller cannot help asking himself as he surveys the vast mass of water, into which so many rivers pour their contributions, which is—In what manner is all this accumulation of water carried off? Except by a very small evaporation in the summer time, and the outlet at Sault St. Marie, where the water which escapes is not much more than equal to two or three of the rivers which feed the lake, there is no apparent means by which the water is carried off. The only conclusion that can be arrived at is, that when the lake rises above a certain height, as the soil around is sandy and porous, the surplus waters find their way through it; and such I believe to be the case.

We saw no bears. They do not come down to the shores, (or travel, as they term it here,) until the huckleberries are ripe. We were told that a month later there would be plenty of them. It is an ascertained fact, that the bears from this region migrate to the west every autumn, but it is not known when they return. They come down to the eastern shores of the Lakes Superior and Huron, swim the lakes and rivers from island to island, never deviating from their course, till they pass through by Wisconsin to the Missisippi. Nothing stops them; the sight of a canoe will not prevent their taking the water; and the Indians in the River St. Marie have been known to kill fifteen in one day. It is singular that the bears on the other side of the Missisippi are said to migrate to the east, exactly in the contrary direction. Perhaps the Missisippi is their fashionable watering-place.

A gathering storm induced us to return, instead of continuing our progress on the lake. A birch canoe in a gale of wind on Lake Superior, would not be a very insurable risk. On our return, we found our half-breeds very penitent, for had we not taken them back, they would have stood a good chance of wintering there. But we had had advice as to the treatment of these lazy gluttonous scoundrels, who swallowed long pieces of raw pork the whole of the day, and towards evening were, from repletion, hanging their heads over the sides of the canoe and quite ill. They had been regaled with pork and whisky going up; we gave them salt fish and a broomstick by way of variety on their return, and they behaved very well under the latter fare.

We started again down with the stream, and the first night took up our quarters on a prairie spot, where they had been making hay, which was lying in cocks about us. To have a soft bed we carried quantities into our tent, forgetting that we disturbed the mosquitoes who had gone to bed in the hay. We smoked the tent to drive them out again; but in smoking the tent we set fire to the hay, and it ended in a conflagration. We were burnt out, and had to re-pitch our tent.

I was sauntering by the side of the river when I heard a rustling in the grass, and perceived a garter snake, an elegant and harmless little creature, about a foot and a half long. It had a small toad in its mouth, which it had seized by the head: but it was much too large for the snake to swallow, without leisure and preparation. I was amused at the precaution, I may say invention of the toad, to prevent its being swallowed: it had inflated itself, till it was as round as a bladder, and upon this, issue was joined—the snake would not let go, the toad would not be swallowed. I lifted up the snake by the tail and threw them three or four yards into the river. The snake rose to the surface, as majestic as the great sea serpent in miniature, carrying his head well out of the water, with the toad still in his mouth, reminding me of Caesar with his Commentaries. He landed close to my feet; I threw him in again, and this time he let go the toad, which remained floating and inanimate an the water; but after a time he discharged his superfluous gas, and made for the shore; while the snake, to avoid me, swam away down with the current.

The next morning it blew hard, and as we opened upon Lake Huron, we had to encounter a heavy sea; fortunately, the wind was fair for the island of Mackinaw, or we might have been delayed for some days. As soon as we were in the Lake we made sail, having fifty-six miles to run before it was dark. The gale increased, but the canoe flew over the water, skimming it like a sea bird. It was beautiful, but not quite so pleasant, to watch it, as, upon the least carelessness on the part of the helmsman, it would immediately have filled. As it was, we shipped some heavy seas, but the blankets at the bottom being saturated, gave us the extra ballast which we required. Before we were clear of the islands, we were joined by a whole fleet of Indian canoes, with their dirty blankets spread to the storm, running, as we were, for Mackinaw, being on their return from Maniton Islands, where they had congregated to receive presents from the Governor of Upper Canada. Their canoes were, most of them, smaller than ours, which had been built for speed, but they were much higher in the gunnel. It was interesting to behold so many hundreds of beings trusting themselves to such fragile conveyances, in a heavy gale and running sea; but the harder it blew, the faster we went; and at last, much to my satisfaction, we found ourselves in smooth water again, alongside of the landing wharf at Mackinaw. I had had some wish to see a freshwater gale of wind, but in a birch canoe I never wish to try the experiment again.

Volume One—Chapter Seventeen.

Mackinaw.—I mentioned that, in my trip to Lake Superior, I was accompanied by a gentleman attached to the American Fur Company, who have a station at this island. I was amusing myself in their establishment, superintending the unpacking and cleaning of about forty or fifty bales of skins, and during the time collected the following information. It is an average computation of the furs obtained every year, and the value of each to the American Fur Company. The Hudson Bay Company are supposed to average about the same quantity, or rather more; and they have a larger proportion of valuable furs, such as beaver and sable, but they have few deer and no buffalo. When we consider how sterile and unfit for cultivation are these wild northern regions, it certainly appears better that they should remain as they are:—

Skins.		Average value.
Deer, four	15	45 cents per

varieties	0,000	lb.
Buffalo	35,000	5 dollars per skin
Elk	200	
Beaver	15,000	4.5 dollars per lb.
Musk Rat	500,000	12 cents per skin
Otters	5,000	6.5 dollars per skin
	2,500	2 do.
Martin or Sable	12,000	2 do. or more
Mink	10,000	

Silver and Black Fox	15	
Crop Fox	100	4 dollars per skin
Red Fox	3,000	1 do.
Grey Fox	1,000	1.5 do.
Prairie Fox	5,000	.5 do.
Bears	4,000	4.5 do.
Lynx	500	2.5 do.
Wild Cat	2,000	2.5 do.
Racoon	70,000	.5 do.
Wolves	12,000	.5 do.

Wolverein	50	2.5 do.
Panthers	50	
Badgers	250	.25 do.

besides skunks, ground-hogs, hares, and many others. These are priced at the lowest: in proportion as the skins are finer, so do they yield higher profit. The two companies may be said to receive, between them, skins yearly to the amount of from two to three millions of dollars.

Fable apropos to the subject.

A hare and a fox met one day on the vast prairie, and after a long conversation, they prepared to start upon their several routes. The hare, pleased with the fox, lamented that they would in all probability separate for ever. "No, no," replied the fox, "we shall meet again, never fear." "Where?" inquired his companion. "In the *hatter's shop*, to be sure," rejoined the fox, tripping lightly away.

Detroit.—There are some pleasant people in this town, and the society is quite equal to that of the eastern cities. From the constant change and transition which take place in this country, go where you will you are sure to fall in with a certain portion of intelligent, educated people. This is not the case in the remoter portions of the Old Continent, where every thing is settled, and generation succeeds generation, as in some obscure country town. But in America, where all is new, and the country has to be peopled from the other parts, there is a proportion of intelligence and education transplanted with the inferior classes, either from the Eastern States or from the Old World, in whatever quarter you may happen to find yourself.

Left my friends at Detroit with regret, and returned to Buffalo. There is a marked difference between the behaviour of the lower people of the eastern cities and those whom you fall in with in this town: they are much less civil in their behaviour here; indeed, they appear to think rudeness a proof of independence. I went to the theatre, and the behaviour of the majority of the company just reminded me of the Portsmouth and Plymouth theatres. I had forgotten that Buffalo was a fresh-water sea-port town.

Returning to Niagara, I took possession of the roof of the rail-coach, that I might enjoy the prospect. I had not travelled three miles before I perceived a strong smell of burning; at last the pocket of my coat, which was of cotton, burst out into flames, a spark having found its way into it: fortunately (not being insured) there was no property on the premises.

When the celebrated Colonel David Crocket first saw a locomotive, with the train smoking along the rail-road, he exclaimed, as it flew past him, "Hell in harness, by the 'tarnel!"

I may, in juxtaposition with this, mention an Indian idea. Nothing surprised the Indians so much at first, as the percussion for guns: they thought them the *ne plus ultra* of invention: when, therefore, an Indian was first shewn a locomotive, he reflected a little while, and then said, "I see—*percussion.*"

There is a beautiful island, dividing the Falls of Niagara, called Goat Island: they have thrown a bridge across the rapids, so that you can now go over. A mill has already been erected there, which is a great pity; it is a contemptible disfigurement of nature's grandest work.

At the head of the island, which is surrounded by the rapids, exactly where the waters divide to run on each side of it, there is a small triangular portion of still or slack water. I perceived this, and went in to bathe. The line of the current on each side of it is plainly marked, and runs at the speed of nine or ten miles an hour; if you put your hand or foot a little way outside this line, they are immediately borne away by its force; if you went into it yourself, nothing could prevent your going down the falls. As I returned, I observed an ugly snake in my path, and I killed it. An American, who came up, exclaimed, "I reckon that's a *copper-head*, stranger! I never knew that they were in this island." I found out that I had killed a snake quite as venomous, if not more so, than a rattlesnake.

One never tires with these falls; indeed, it takes a week at least to find out all their varieties and beauties. There are some sweet spots on Goat Island, where you can meditate and be alone.

I witnessed, during my short stay here, that indifference to the destruction of life, so very remarkable in this country. The rail-car crushed the head of a child of about seven years old, as it was going into the engine-house; the other children ran to the father, a blacksmith, who was at work at his forge close by, crying out, "Father, Billy killed." The man put down his hammer, walked leisurely to where the boy lay, in a pool of his own blood, took up the body, and returned with it under his arm to his house. In a short time, the hammer rang upon the anvil as before.

The game of nine-pins is a favourite game in America, and very superior to what it is in England. In America, the ground is always covered properly over, and the balls are rolled upon a wooden floor, as correctly levelled as a billiard table. The ladies join in the game, which here becomes an agreeable and not too fatiguing (an) exercise. I was very fond of frequenting their alleys, not only for the exercise, but because, among the various ways of estimating character, I had made up my mind that there was none more likely to be correct, than the estimate formed by the manner in which people roll the balls, especially the ladies. There were some very delightful specimens of American females when I was this time at Niagara. We sauntered about the falls and wood in the day time, or else played at nine-pins; in the evening we looked at the moon, spouted verses, and drank mint juleps. But all that was too pleasant to last long: I felt that I had not come to America to play at nine-pins; so I tore myself away, and within the next twenty-four hours found myself at Toronto, in Upper Canada.

Toronto, which is the present capital and seat of government of Upper Canada, is, from its want of spires and steeples, by no means an imposing town, as you view it on entering the harbour. The harbour itself is landlocked, and when deepened will be very good. A great deal of money has been expended by the English government upon the Canadian provinces, but not very wisely. The Rideau and Willend canals are splendid works; they have nothing to compare with them in the United States; but they are too much in advance of the country, and will be of but little use for a long period, if the provinces do not go a-head faster than they do now. One half the money spent in making good roads through the provinces would have done more good, and would have much increased the value of property. The proposed rail-road from Hamilton to Detroit would be of greater importance; and if more money is to be expended on Upper Canada, it cannot be better disposed of than in this undertaking.

The minute you put your foot on shore, you feel that you are no longer in the United States; you are at once struck with the difference between the English and the American population, systems, and ideas. On the other side of the Lake you have much more apparent property, but much less real solidity and security. The houses and stores at Toronto are not to be compared with those of the American towns opposite. But the Englishman has built according to his means—the American, according to his expectations. The hotels and inns at Toronto are very bad; at Buffalo they are splendid: for the Englishman travels little; the American is ever on the move. The private houses of Toronto are built, according to the English taste and desire of exclusiveness, away from the road, and are embowered in trees; the American, let his house be ever so large, or his plot of ground however extensive, builds within a few feet of the road, that he may see and know what is going on. You do not perceive the bustle, the energy, and activity at Toronto, that you do at Buffalo, nor the profusion of articles in the stores; but it should be remembered that the Americans procure their articles upon credit, whilst at Toronto they proceed more cautiously. The Englishman builds his house and furnishes his store according to his means and fair expectations of being able to meet his acceptances. If an American has money sufficient to build a two-story house, he will raise it up to four stories on speculation. We must not, on one side, be dazzled with the effects of the credit system in America, nor yet be too hasty in condemning it. It certainly is the occasion of much over-speculation; but if the parties who speculate are ruined, provided the money has been laid out, as it usually is in America, upon real property—such as wharfs, houses, etcetera.—a new country becomes a gainer, as the improvements are made and remain, although they fall into other hands. And it should be further pointed out, that the Americans are justified in their speculations from the fact, that property improved rises so fast in value, that they are soon able to meet all claims and realise a handsome profit. They speculate on the future; but the future with them is not distant as it is with us, ten years in America being, as I have before observed, equal to a century in Europe: they are therefore warranted in so speculating. The property in Buffalo is now worth one hundred times what it was when the first speculators commenced; for as the country and cities become peopled, and the communication becomes easy, so does the value of every thing increase.

Why, then, does not Toronto vie with Buffalo? Because the Canadas cannot obtain the credit which is given to the United States, and of which Buffalo has her portion. America has returns to make to England in her cotton crops: Canada has nothing; for her timber would be nothing, if it were not protected. She cannot, therefore, obtain credit as America does. What, then, do the Canadas require, in order to become prosperous? Capital!

I must not, however, omit to inform my readers that at Toronto I received a letter from a "Brother Author," who was polite enough to send me several specimens of his poetry; stating the remarkable fact, that he had never written a verse until he was past forty-five years of age; and that, as to the unfair accusation of his having plagiarised from Byron, it was not true, for he never had read Byron in his life. Having put the reader in possession of these facts, I shall now select one of his printed poems for his gratification:—

From   the   Regard   the   Author   has   for   the
Ladies   ***of***   ***Toronto***,
He   presents   them   with   the   following
Ode.
To the Ladies of the City of Toronto.

1.

How   famed   is   our   city
For   the   beauty   and   talents
Of   our   ladies,   that's   pretty
And *chaste* in   their *sentiments*.

2.

The   ladies   of   Toronto
Are   fine,   noble,   and   charming,
And   are   a   great   memento
To   all,   most   fascinating.

3.

Our   ladies   are   the   best   kind,
Of   all   others   the   most   fine;
In   their   manners   and   their   minds
Most   refined   and *genuine*.

4.

We   are   proud   of   our   ladies,
For   they   are   superior
To   all   other   beauties
And   others   are   inferior.

5.

How   favoured   is   our   land
To   be   honoured   with   the   fair,
That   is   so   majestic   grand!
And   to   please   them   is   our   care.

6.

Who   would   not   choose   them   before
All   others   that's   to   be   found,
And   think   of   others   no   more?
Their   like   is   not   in   the   world   round.

Volume One—Chapter Eighteen.

Through Lake Ontario to Montreal, by rail road to Lake Champlain, and then by steamboat to Burlington.

Burlington is a pretty county town on the border of the Lake Champlain; there is a large establishment for the education of boys kept here by the Bishop of Vermont, a clever man: it is said to be well conducted, and one of the best in the Union. The bishop's salary, as bishop, is only five hundred dollars; as a preacher of the established church he receives seven hundred; whilst as a schoolmaster his revenue becomes very handsome. The bishop is just now in bad odour with the *majority*, for having published some very sensible objections to the Revivals and Temperance Societies.

Plattsburg.—This was the scene of an American triumph. I was talking with a States officer, who was present during the whole affair, and was much amused with his description of it. There appeared to be some fatality attending almost all our attacks upon America during the last war; and it should be remarked, that whenever the Americans entered upon our territory, they met with similar defeat. Much allowance must at course be made for ignorance of the country, and of the strength and disposition of the enemy's force; but certainly there was no excuse for the indecision shewn by the British general, with such a force as he had under his command.

Now that the real facts are known, one hardly knows whether to laugh or feel indignant. The person from whom I had the information is of undoubted respectability. At the time that our general advanced with an army of 7,000 Peninsular troops, there were but 1,000 militia at Plattsburg, those ordered out from the interior of the State not having arrived. It is true that there were 2,000 of the Vermont militia at Burlington opposite to Plattsburg, but when they were sent for, they refused to go there; they were alarmed at the preponderating force of the British, and they stood upon their State rights— i.e., militia raised in a State are not bound to leave it, being raised for the defence of that State alone. The small force at Plattsburg hardly knew whether to retreat or not; they expected large reinforcements under General McCoomb, but did not know when they would come. At last it was proposed and agreed to that they should spread themselves and keep up an incessant firing, but out of distance, so as to make the British believe they had a much larger force than they really possessed; and on this judicious plan they acted, and succeeded.

In the mean time, the British general was anxious for the assistance of the squadron on the lakes, under Commodore Downie, and pressed him to the attack of the American squadron then off Plattsburg. Some sharp remarks from the General proved fatal to our cause by water. Downie, stung by his insinuations, rushed inconsiderately into a *close* engagement. Now, Commodore Downie's vessels had all long guns. McDonough's vessels had only carronades. Had, therefore, Downie not thrown away this advantage, by engaging at close quarters, there is fair reason to suppose that the victory would have been ours, as he could have chosen his distance, and the fire of the American vessels would have been comparatively harmless; but he ran down close to McDonough's fleet, and engaged them broadside to broadside, and then the carronades of the Americans, being of heavy calibre, threw the advantage on their side. Downie was killed by the wind of a shot a few minutes after the commencement of the action. Still it was the hardest contested action of the war; Pring being well worthy to take Downie's place.

It was impossible to have done more on either side; and the gentleman who gave me this information added, that McDonough told him that so nicely balanced were the chances, that he took out his watch just before the British colours were hauled down, and observed, "If they hold out ten minutes more, it will be more than, I am afraid, we can do." As soon as the victory was decided on the part of the Americans, the British general commenced his retreat, and was followed by this handful of militia. In a day or two afterwards, General McCoomb came up, and a large force was poured in from all quarters.

There was something very similar and quite as ridiculous in the affair at Sackett's harbour. Our forces advancing would have cut off some hundreds of the American militia, who were *really* retreating, but by a road which led in such a direction as for a time to make the English commandant suppose that they were intending to take him in flank. This made him imagine that they must be advancing in large numbers, when, the fact was, they were running away from his superior force. He made a retreat; upon ascertaining which, the Americans turned back and followed him, harassing his rear.

I was told, at Baltimore, that had the English advanced, the American militia was quite ready to run away, not having the idea of opposing themselves to trained soldiers. It really was very absurd; but in many instances during the war, which have come to my knowledge, it was exactly this,—"If you don't run, I will; but if you will, I won't!"

The name given by the French to Vermont, designates the features of the country, which is composed of small mountains, covered with verdure to their summits; but the land is by no means good.

At the bottoms, on the banks of the rivers, the alluvial soil is rich, and, generally speaking, the land in this State admits of cultivation about half-way up the mountains; after which, it is fit for nothing but sheep-walks, or to grow small timber upon. I have travelled much in the Eastern States, and have been surprised to find how very small a portion of all of them is under cultivation, considering how long they have been settled; nor will there be more of the land taken up, I presume, for a long period; that is to say, not until the West is so over-peopled that a reflux is compelled to fall back into the Eastern States, and the crowded masses, like the Gulf-stream, find vent to the northward and eastward.

Set off by coach, long before day-light. There is something very gratifying when once you *are up*, in finding yourself up before the sun; you can repeat to yourself, "How doth the little busy bee," with such satisfaction. Some few stars still twinkled in the sky, winking like the eyelids of tired sentinels, but soon they were relieved, one after another, by the light of morning.

It was still dark when we started, and off we went, up hill and down hill— short steep *pitches*, as they term them here—at a furious rate. There was no level ground; it was all undulating, and very trying to the springs. But an American driver stops at nothing; he will flog away with six horses in hand; and it is wonderful how few accidents happen: but it is very fatiguing, and one hundred miles of American travelling by stage, is equal to four hundred in England.

There is much amusement to be extracted from the drivers of these stages, if you will take your seat with them on the front, which few Americans do, as they prefer the inside. One of the drivers, soon after we had changed our team, called out to the off-leader, as he flanked her with his whip. "Go along, you *no-tongued* crittur!"

"Why *no-tongued*?" enquired I.

"Well, I reckon she has no tongue, having bitten it off herself, I was going to say—but it wasn't exactly that, neither."

"How was it, then?"

"Well now, the fact is, that she is awful ugly," (ill-tempered); "she bites like a badger, and kicks up as high as the church-steeple. She's an almighty crittur to handle. I was trying to hitch her under-jaw like, with the halter, but she worretted so, that I could only hitch her tongue: she ran back, the end of the halter was fast to the ring, and so she left her tongue in the hitch—that's a *fact*!"

"I wonder it did not kill her; didn't she bleed very much? How does she contrive to eat her corn?"

"Well, now, she bled pretty considerable—but not to speak off. I did keep her *one day* in the stable, because I thought she might feel *queer*; since that she has worked in the team every day; and she'll eat her peck of corn with any horse in the stable. But her tongue is out, that's certain—so *she'll tell no more lies*!"

Not the least doubting my friend's veracity I, nevertheless, took an opportunity, when we changed, of ascertaining the fact; and her tongue was *half* of it out, that *is* the fact.

When we stopped, we had to shift the luggage to another coach. The driver, who was a slight man, was, for some time, looking rather puzzled at the trunks which lay on the road, and which he had to put on the coach: he tried to lift one of the largest, let it down again, and then beckoned to me:—

"I say, captain, them four large trunks be rather overmuch for me; but I guess you can master them, so just lift them up on the hind board for me."

I complied; and as I had to lift them as high as my head, they required all my strength.

"Thank ye, captain; don't trouble yourself any more, the rest be all right, and I can manage them myself."

The Americans never refuse to assist each other in such difficulties as this. In a young country they must assist each other, if they wish to be assisted themselves—and there always will be a mutual dependence. If a man is in a *fix* in America, every one stops to assist him, and expects the same for himself.

Bellows Falls, a beautiful, romantic spot on the Connecticut River, which separates the States of New Hampshire and Vermont. The masses of rocks through which the river forces its way at the Falls, are very grand and imposing; and the surrounding hills, rich with the autumnal tints, rivet the eye. On these masses of rocks are many faces, cut out by the tribe of Pequod Indians, who formerly used to fish in their waters. Being informed that there was to be a militia muster, I resolved to attend it.

The militia service is not in good odour with the Americans just now. Formerly, when they did try to do as well as they could, the scene was absurd enough; but now they do all they can to make it ridiculous. In this muster there were three or four companies, well equipped; but the major part of the men were what they call here *flood-wood*, that is, of all sizes and heights—a term suggested by the pieces of wood borne down by the freshets of the river, and which are of all sorts, sizes, and lengths. But not only were the men of all sorts and sizes, but the uniforms also, some of which were the most extraordinary I ever beheld, and not unlike the calico dresses worn by the tumblers and vaulters at an English fair. As for the exercise, they either did not, or would not, know any thing about it; indeed, as they are now mustered but once a year, it cannot be expected that they should; but as they faced every way, and made mistakes on purpose, it is evident, from their consistent pertinacity in being wrong, that they did know something. When they marched off single file, quick time, they were one half of them dancing in and out of the ranks to the lively tune which was played—the only instance I saw of their keeping time. But the most amusing part of the ceremony was the speech made by the brigade major, whose patience had certainly been tried, and who wished to impress his countrymen with the importance of the militia. He ordered them to form a hollow square. They formed a circle, proving that if they could not square the circle, at all events they could circle the square, which is coming very near to it. The major found himself, on his white horse, in an arena about as large as that in which Mr Ducrow performs at Astley's. He then commenced a sort of perambulating equestrian speech, riding round and round the circle, with his cocked hat in his hand. As the arena was large, and he constantly turned his head as he spoke to those nearest to him in the circle, it was only when he came to within a few yards of you, that you could distinguish what he was saying; and of course the auditors at the other point were in the same predicament. However, he divided his speech out in portions very equally, and those which came to my share were as follows:

"Yes, gentlemen—the president, senate, and house of representatives, and all others ... you militia, the bones and muscle of the land, and by whom ... Eagle of America shall ruffle her wings, will ever dart ... those days so glorious, when our gallant forefathers ... terrible effect of the use of ardent spirits, and shewing ... Temperance societies, the full benefits of which, I am ... Star-spangled banner, ever victorious, blazing like...."

The last word I heard was *glory*; but his audience being very impatient for their dinner, cried out loudly for it—preferring it to the mouthfuls of eloquence which fell to their share, but did not stay their stomach. Altogether it was a scene of much fun and good-humour.

Stopped at the pretty village of Charlestown, celebrated for the defence it made during the French war. There is here, running by the river side, a turnpike road, which gave great offence to the American citizens of this State: they declared that to pay toll was *monarchical*, as they always assert every thing to be which taxes their pockets. So, one fine night, they assembled with a hawser and a team or two of horses, made the hawser fast to the house at the gate, dragged it down to the river, and sent it floating down the stream, with the gate and board of tolls in company with it.

Progressing in the stage, I had a very amusing specimen of the ruling passion of the country—the spirit of barter, which is communicated to the females, as well as to the boys. I will stop for a moment, however, to say, that I heard of an American, who had two sons, and he declared that they were so clever at barter, that he locked them both up together in a room, without a cent in their pockets, and that before they had *swopped* for an hour, they had each gained two dollars a piece. But now for my fellow-passengers—both young, both good-looking, and both ladies, and evidently were total strangers to each other. One had a pretty pink silk bonnet, very fine for travelling; the other, an indifferent plush one. The young lady in the plush, eyed the pink bonnet for some time: at last *Plush* observed in a drawling half-indifferent way:

"That's rather a pretty bonnet of your's, miss."

"Why yes, I calculate it's rather smart," replied Pink.

After a pause and closer survey.—"You wouldn't have any objection to part with it, miss?"

"Well now, I don't know but I might; I have worn it but three days, I reckon."

"Oh, my! I should have reckoned that you carried it longer—perhaps it rained on them three days."

"I've a notion it didn't rain, not one.—It's not the only bonnet I have, miss."

"Well now, I should not mind an exchange, and paying you the *balance*."

"That's an awful thing that you have on, miss!"

"I rather think not, but that's as may be.—Come, miss, what will you take?"

"Why I don't know,—what will you give?"

"I reckon you'll know best when you answer my question."

"Well then, I shouldn't like less than five dollars."

"Five dollars and my bonnet! I reckon two would be nearer the mark—but it's of no consequence."

"None in the least, miss, only I know the value of my bonnet.—We'll say no more about it."

"Just so, miss."

A pause and silence for half a minute, when Miss Plush, looks out of the window, and says, as if talking to herself, "I shouldn't mind giving four dollars, but no more." She then fell back in her seat, when Miss Pink, put her head out of the window, and said:— "I shouldn't refuse four dollars after all, if it was offered," and then she fell back to her former position.

"Did you think of taking four dollars, miss?"

"Well! I don't care, I've plenty of bonnets at home."

"Well," replied Plush, taking out her purse, and offering her the money.

"What bank is this, miss?"

"Oh, all's right there, Safety Fund, I calculate."

The two ladies exchange bonnets, and Pink pockets the balance.

I may here just as well mention the custom of *whittling*, which is so common in the Eastern States. It is a habit, arising from the natural restlessness of the American when he is not employed, of cutting a piece of stick, or any thing else, with his knife. Some are so wedded to it from long custom, that if they have not a piece of stick to cut, they will whittle the backs of the chairs, or any thing within their reach. A yankee shewn into a room to await the arrival of another, has been known to whittle away nearly the whole of the mantle-piece. Lawyers in court whittle away at the table before them; and judges will cut through their own bench. In some courts, they put sticks before noted whittlers to save the furniture. The Down-Easters, as the yankees are termed generally, whittle when they are making a bargain, as it fills up the pauses, gives them time for reflection, and moreover, prevents any examination of the countenance—for in bargaining, like in the game of brag, the countenance is carefully watched, as an index to the wishes. I was once witness to a bargain made between two respectable yankees, who wished to agree about a farm, and in which whittling was resorted to.

They sat down on a log of wood, about, three or four feet apart from each other, with their faces turned opposite ways—that is, one had his legs on one side of the log with his face to the East, and the other his legs on the other side with his face to the West. One had a piece of soft wood, and was sawing it with his penknife; the other had an unbarked hiccory stick which he was peeling for a walking-stick. The reader will perceive a strong analogy between this bargain and that in the stage between the two ladies.

"Well, good morning—and about this farm?"

"I don't know; what will you take?"

"What will you give?"

Silence, and whittle away.

"Well, I should think two thousand dollars, a heap of money for this farm."

"I've a notion it will never go for three thousand, any how."

"There's a fine farm, and cheaper, on the North side."

"But where's the sun to ripen the corn?"

"Sun shines on all alike."

"Not exactly through a Vermont hill, I reckon. The driver offered me as much as I say, if I recollect right."

"Money not always to be depended upon. Money not always forthcoming!"

"I reckon, I shall make an elegant 'backy stopper of this piece of sycamore."

Silence for a few moments. Knives hard at work.

"I've a notion this is as pretty a hiccory stick as ever came out of a wood."

"I shouldn't mind two thousand five hundred dollars, and time given."

"It couldn't be more than six months then, if it goes at that price."

(Pause.)

"Well, that might suit me."

"What do you say, then?"

"Suppose it must be so."

"It's a bargain then," rising up; "come let's liquor on it."

Volume One—Chapter Nineteen.

The farmers on the banks of the Connecticut river are the richest in the Eastern States. The majestic growth of the timber certified that the soil is generally good, although the crops were off the ground. They grow here a large quantity of what is called the broom corn: the stalk and leaves are similar to the maize or Indian corn, but, instead of the ear, it throws out, at top and on the sides, spiky plumes on which seed is carried. These plumes are cut off, and furnish the brooms and whisks of the country; it is said to be a very profitable crop. At Brattleboro' we stopped at an inn kept by one of the State representatives, and, as may be supposed, had very bad fare in consequence, the man being above his business. We changed horses at Bloody Brook, so termed in consequence of a massacre of the settlers by the Indians. But there are twenty Bloody Brooks in America, all records of similar catastrophes.

Whether the Blue laws of Connecticut are supposed to be still in force I know not, but I could not discover that they had ever been repealed. At present there is no theatre in Connecticut, nor does anybody venture to propose one. The proprietors of one of the equestrian studs made their appearance at the confines of the State, and intimated that they wished to perform, but were given to understand that their horses would be confiscated if they entered the State. The consequence is that Connecticut is the dullest, most disagreeable State in the Union; and, if I am to believe the Americans themselves, so far from the morals of the community being kept uncontaminated by this rigour, the very reverse is the case—especially as respects the college students, who are in the secret practice of more vice than is to be found in any other establishment of the kind in the Union. But even if I had not been so informed by creditable people, I should have decided in my own mind that such was the case. Human nature is everywhere the same.

It may be interesting to make a few extracts from a copy of the records and of the Blue laws which I have in my possession, as it will show that if these laws were still in force how hard they would now bear upon the American community. In the extracts from the records which follow I have altered a word or two, so as to render them fitter for perusal, but the sense remains the same:

"(13.) If any childe or children above sixteene yeares old, and of suffitient understanding, shall curse or smite their naturall father or mother, hee or they shall bee *put to death*; unless it can be sufficiently testified that the parents have been very unchristianly negligent in the education of such children, or so provoke them by extreme and cruell correction that they have been forced thereunto to preserve themselves from death, maiming.—Exo., xxi., 17. Levit., xx. Ex., xxi., 15.

"(14.) If any man have a stubborne and rebellious sonne of sufficient yeares and understanding, viz., sixteene yeares of age, which will not obey the voice of his father or the voice of his mother, and that when they have chastened him will not hearken unto them, then may his father and mother, being his naturall parents, lay hold on him, and bring him to the magistrates assembled in courte, and testifie unto them that their sonne is stubborne and rebellious, and will not obey theire voice and chastisement, but lives in sundry notorious crimes— such a sonne shall bee *put to death*.—Deut., xxi, 20, 21.

"(*Lyinge*.) That every person of the age of discretion, which is accounted fourteene yeares, who shall wittingly and willingly make, or publish, any lye which may be pernicious to the publique weal, or tending to the dammage or injury of any perticular person, to deceive and abuse the people with false news or reportes, and the same duly prooved in any courte, or before any one magistrate, who hath hereby power granted to heare and determine all offences against this lawe, such person shall bee fyned—for the first offence, ten shillings, or if the party bee unable to pay the same, then to be sett in the stocks so long as the said courte or magistrate shall appointe, in some open place, not exceeding three houres; for the second offence in that kinde, whereof any shall bee legally convicted, the summe of twenty shillings, or be whipped upon the naked body, not exceeding twenty stripes; and for the third offence that way, forty shillings, or if the party be unable to pay, then to be whipped with more stripes, not exceeding thirtye; and if yet any shall offend in like kinde, and be legally convicted thereof, such person, male or female, shall bee fyned ten shillings at a time more than formerly, or if the party so offending bee unable to pay, then to be whipped with five or six stripes more then formerly, not exceeding forty at any time.

"(*Ministers' Meintenance.*)—Whereas the most considerable persons in the land came into these partes of America, that they might enjoye Christe in his ordinances without disturbance; and whereas, amongst many other pretious meanes, the ordinances have beene, and are, dispensed amongst us, with much purity and power, they tooke it into their serious consideration, that a due meintenance, according to God, might bee provided and settled, both for the present and future, for the encouragement of the ministers' work therein; and doe order, that those who are taught in the word, in the severall plantations, bee called together, that every man voluntarily sett downe what he is willing to allow to that end and use; and if any man refuse to pay a meete proportion, that then hee bee rated by authority in some just and equal way; and if after this, any man withhold or delay due payment, the civill power to be exercised as in other just debts.

"(*Profane Swearing.*)—That if any person within this jurisdiction shall sweare rashly and vainely, either by the holy name of God, or any other oath, and shall sinfully and wickedly curse any, hee shall forfeitt to the common treasure, for every such severe offence, ten shillings: and it shall be in the power of any magistrate, by warrant to the constable, to call such persons before him, and uppon just proofe to pass a sentence, and levye the said penalty, according to the usual order of justice; and if such persons bee not able, or shall utterly refuse to pay the aforesaid fyne, hee shall bee committed to the stocks, there to continue, not exceeding three hours, and not less than one houre.

"(*Tobacko.*)—That no person under the age of twenty-one years, nor any other that hath not already accustomed himselfe to the use therof, shall take any tobacko, untill hee hath brought a certificate under the hands of some who are approved for knowledge and skill in phisick, that it is usefull for him, and allso that he hath received a lycense from the courte, for the same.

"*It is ordered*—That no man within this colonye, shall take any tobacko publiquely, in the streett, highwayes or any barne, yardes, or uppon training dayes, in any open places, under the penalty of sixpence for each offence against this order," etcetera, etcetera.

Among the records we have some curious specimens:—

"At a Court, held May 1, 1660.

"Jacob M Murline and Sarah Tuttle being called, appeared, concerning whom the governor declared, that the business for which they were warned to this Court, he had heard in private at his house, which he related thus:— On the day that John Potter was married, Sarah Tuttle went to Mistress Murline's house for some thredd; Mistress Murline bid her go to her daughters in the other roome, where she felle into speeche of John Potter and his wife, that they were both lame; upon which Sarah Tuttle said, how very awkward it would be. Whereupon Jacob came in, and tooke up, or tooke away her gloves. Sarah desired him to give her the gloves, to which he answered, he would do so if she would give him a kysse; upon which they sat down together, his arme being about her waiste, and her arme upon his shoulder, or about his neck, and *he* kissed her, and *she* kissed him, or they kissed one another, continuing in this posture about half an hour, as Marian and Susan testified, which Marian, now in Court, affirmed to be so.

"Mistress Murline, now in Court, said that she heard Sarah say, how very awkward it would be; but it was matter of sorrow and shame unto her.

"Jacob was asked what he had to say to these things; to which he answered, that he was in the other roome, and when he heard Sarah speak those words, he went in, when shee having let fall her gloves, he tooke them up, and she asked him for them; he told her he would, if she would kisse him. Further said, hee took her by the hand, and they both sat down upon a chest, but whether his arme were about her waiste, and her arme upon his shoulder, or about his neck, he knows not, for he never thought of it since, till Mr Raymond told him of it at Mannatos, for which he was blamed, and told he had not layde it to heart as he ought. But Sarah Tuttle replied, that shee did not kysse him. Mr Tuttle replied, that Marian hath denied it, and he doth not looke upon her as a competent witness. Thomas Tuttle said, that he asked Marian if his sister kyssed Jacob, and she said not. Moses Mansfield testified, that he told Jacob Murline that he heard Sarah kyssed him, but he denied it. But Jacob graunted not what Moses testified.

"Mr Tuttle pleaded that Jacob had endeavoured to steal away his daughter's affections. But Sarah being asked, if Jacob had inveigled her, she said no. Thomas Tuttle said, that he came to their house two or three times before he went to Holland, and they two were together, and to what end he came he knows not, unless it were to inveigle her: and their mother warned Sarah not to keep company with him: and to the same purpose spake Jonathan Tuttle. But Jacob denied that he came to their house with any such intendment, nor did it appear so to the Court.

"The governor told Sarah that her miscarriage is the greatest, that a virgin should be so bold in the presence of others, to carry it as she had done, and to speake suche corrupt words; most of the things charged against her being acknowledged by herself, though that about kyssing is denied, yet the *thing* is proved.

"Sarah professed that she was sorry that she had carried it so sinfully and foolishly, which she saw to be hateful: she hoped God would help her to carry it better for time to come.

"The governor also told Jacob that his carriage hath been very evil and sinful, so to carry it towards her, and to make such a light matter of it as not to think of it, (as he exprest) doth greatly aggravate; and for Marian, who was a married woman, to suffer her brother and a man's daughter to sit almost half an hour in such a way as they have related, was a very great evil. She was told that she should have showed her indignation against it, and have told her mother, that Sarah might have been shut out of doors. Mrs Murline was told, that she, hearing such words, should not have suffered it. Mrs Tuttle and Mrs Murline being asked if they had any more to say, they said, no.

"Whereupon the Court declared, that we have heard in the publique ministry, that it is a thing to be lamented, that young people should have their meetings, to the corrupting of themselves and one another. As for Sarah Tuttle, her miscarriages are very great, that she should utter so corrupt a speeche as she did, concerning the persons to be married; and that she should carry it in such a wanton, uncivil, immodest, and lacivious manner as hath been proved. And for Jacob, his carriage hath been very corrupt and sinful, such as brings reproach upon the family and place.

"The sentence, therefore, concerning them is, that they shall pay either of them as a fine, twenty shillings to the treasurer."

"Isaiah, Captain Turner's man, fined 5 pounds for being drunk on the Lord's-day.

"William Broomfield, Mr Malbon's man, was set in the stocks, for profaning the Lord's-day, and stealing wine from his master, which he drunk and gave to others.

"John Fenner, accused for being drunke with strong waters, was acquitted, it appearing to be of infirmity, and occasioned by the extremity of the cold.

"Mr Moulend, accused of being drunke, but not clearly proved, was respited."

Here comes a very disorderly reprobate, called Will Harding.

"1st of 1st month, 1643.

"John Lawrence and Valentine, servants to Mr Malbon, for imbezilling their master's goods, and keeping disorderly night meetings with Will Harding, a lewd and disorderly person, plotting with him to carry their master's daughters to the farmes in the night, concealing divers dalliances; all which they confessed, and were whipped.

"Ruth Acie, a covenant-servant to Mr Malbon, for stubornes, lyeing, stealing from her mistress, and yielding to dalliance with Will Harding, was *whipped*.

"Martha Malbon, for consenting to goe in the night to the farmes, with Will Harding, to a venison feast; for stealing things from her parents, and dalliance with the said Harding, was *whipped*.

"Goodman Hunt and his wife, for keeping the councells of the said Will Harding, *bakeing him a pastry and plum cakes*, and keeping company with him on the Lord's-day; and she suffering Harding to kisse her, they being only admitted to sojourn in this plantation upon their good behaviour, was ordered to be sent out of this towne within one month after the date hereof."

Will Harding, however, appears to have met with his deserts.

"Dec. 3rd, 1651.

"Will Harding, being convicted of a great deal of base carriage with divers yonge girls, together with enticing and corrupting divers men-servants in this plantation, haunting with them at night meetings and junketings, etcetera, was sentenced to be *severely* whipped, and fined 5 pounds to Mr Malbon, and 5 pounds to Will Andrews, whose famylyes and daughters he hath so much wronged; and presently to depart the plantation."

Thus winds up the *disgraceful* end of our Colonial Don Juan of 1643.

The articles of the Blue laws, which I have extracted, are from a portion which appears to have been drawn up more in detail; but, generally, they are much more pithy and concise, as the following examples will show:—

"No. 13. No food and lodgings shall be allowed a Quaker, Adamite, or other heretic.

"No. 14. If any person turns Quaker, he shall be banished, and not suffered to return, on pain of death."

I was walking in Philadelphia, when I perceived the name of Buffum, Hatter. Wishing to ascertain whether it was an English name or not, I went in, and entered into conversation with Mr Buffum, who was dressed as what is termed a wet Quaker. He told me that his was an English name, and that his ancestor had been banished from Salem for a heinous crime—which was, as the sentence worded it, for being a damned Quaker. The reason why Quakers were banished by the Puritans, was because they would not; go out to *shoot the Indians*! To continue:—

"No. 17. No one shall *run* of a Sabbath-day, or walk in his garden or elsewhere, except reverently to and from church.

"No. 18. No one shall travel, cook victuals, make beds, sweep houses, cut hair or shave on Sabbath-day.

"No. 19. No husband shall kiss his wife, and no mother shall kiss her child upon the Sabbath day.

"No. 31. No one shall read Common Prayer, keep Christmas or saints'-day, make mince-pies, dance, or play on any instrument of music, except the drum, the trumpet, and the jews-harp."

I do not know any thing that disgusts me so much as *cant*. Even now we continually hear, in the American public orations, about the *stern virtues* of the pilgrim fathers. *Stern*, indeed! The fact is, that these pilgrim fathers were fanatics and bigots, without charity or mercy, wanting in the very *essence* of Christianity. Witness their conduct to the Indians when they thirsted for their territory. After the death (murder, we may well call it) of Alexander, the brother of the celebrated Philip, the latter prepared for war. "And now," says a reverend historian of the times, "war was begun by a fierce nation of Indians upon an *honest, harmless* Christian generation of English, who might very truly have said to the aggressors, as it was said of old unto the Ammonites, 'I have not sinned against thee; but thou doest me wrong to war against me.'" Fanaticism alone—deep, incurable fanaticism—could have induced such a remark. Well may it be said, "We deceive ourselves, and the truth is not in us."

And when the war was brought to a close by the death of the noble-minded, high-spirited Philip; when the *Christians* had slaked their revenge in his blood, exposed his head in triumph on a pike, and captured his helpless innocent child of nine years old; would it be credited, that there was council held to put this child to death, and that the clergy were summoned to give their opinion? And the clergy *quoted Scripture*, that the *child must die*! Dr Increase Mather compared it with the child of Hadid, and recommended, with his brother apostles, that it be murdered. But these pious men were overruled; and, with many others, it was sent to the Bermudas, and sold as a slave. *Stern virtues*!! Call them rather diabolical vices. God of Heaven! when shall we learn to call things by their right names? The next time Governor Everett is called up for an oration at Bloody Brook, let him not talk quite so much of the virtues of the pilgrim fathers.

This reminds me of a *duty* towards this gentleman, which I have great pleasure in performing. Every one who is acquainted with him must acknowledge his amiable manners, and his high classical attainments and power of eloquence. His orations and speeches are printed, and are among the best specimens of American talent. Miss Martineau, in her work upon America, states that she went up to hear the orator at Bloody Brook; and, in two pages of very coarse, unmeasured language, states "that all her *sympathies* were baffled, and that she was deeply disgusted;" that the orator "offered them shreds of tawdry sentiment, without the intermixture of one sound thought or simple and natural feeling, simply and naturally expressed." I have the Address of Governor Everett before me. To insert the whole of it would be inconvenient; but I do most unequivocally deny this, as I must, I am afraid, to many of Miss Martineau's assertions. To prove, in this one instance alone, the very contrary to what she states, I will merely quote the peroration of Governor Everett's Address:—

"Yon simple monument shall rise a renewed memorial of their names on this sacred spot, where the young, the brave, the patriotic, poured out their life-blood in defence of that heritage which has descended to us. We this day solemnly bring our tribute of gratitude. Ages shall pass away; the majestic tree which overshadows us shall wither and sink before the blast, and we who are now gathered beneath it shall mingle with the honoured dust we eulogise; but the 'Flowers of Essex' shall bloom in undying remembrance; and, with every century, these rites of commemoration shall be repeated, as the lapse of time shall continually develope, in rich abundance, the fruits of what was done and suffered by our forefathers!"

I can, however, give the reader a key to Miss Martineau's praise or condemnation of every person mentioned in her two works: you have but to ask the question, "Is he, or is he not, an abolitionist?"

Governor Everett is *not*.

Volume One—Chapter Twenty.

Montreal, next to Quebec, is the oldest looking and most aristocratic city in all North America. Lofty houses, with narrow streets, prove antiquity. After Quebec and Montreal, New Orleans is said to take the next rank, all three of them having been built by the French. It is pleasant to look upon any structure in this new hemisphere which bears the mark of time upon it. The ruins of Fort Putnam are one of the curiosities of America.

Montreal is all alive—mustering here, drilling there, galloping every where; and, moreover, Montreal is knee-deep in snow, and the thermometer below zero. Every hour brings fresh intelligence of the movements of the rebels, or patriots—the last term is doubtful, yet it may be correct. When they first opened the theatre at Botany Bay, Barrington spoke the prologue, which ended with these two lines:—

"True *Patriots* we,   for   be   it   understood,
We left our country, for our country's good."

In this view of the case, some of them, it is hoped, will turn out patriots before they die, if they have not been made so already.

Every hour comes in some poor wretch, who, for refusing to join the insurgents, has been made a beggar; his cattle, sheep, and pigs driven away; his fodder, his barns, his house, all that he possessed, now reduced to ashes. The cold-blooded, heartless murder of Lieutenant Weir has, however, sufficiently raised the choler of the troops, without any further enormities on the part of the insurgents being requisite to that end: when an English soldier swears to shew no mercy, he generally keeps his word. Of all wars, a civil war is the most cruel, the most unrelenting, and the most exterminating; and deep indeed must be the responsibility of those, who, by their words or their actions, have contrived to set countryman against countryman, neighbour against neighbour, and very often brother against brother, and father against child.

On the morning of the — the ice on the branch of the Ottawa river, which we had to cross, being considered sufficiently strong to bear the weight of the artillery, the whole force marched out, under the command of Sir John Colborne in person, to reduce the insurgents, who had fortified themselves at St. Eustache and St. Benoit, two towns of some magnitude in the district of Bois Brulé. The snow, as I before observed, lay very deep; but by the time we started, the road had been well beaten down by the multitudes which had preceded us.

The effect of the whole line of troops, in their fur caps and great-coats, with the trains of artillery, ammunition, and baggage-waggons, as they wound along the snow-white road, was very beautiful. It is astonishing how much more numerous the force, and how much larger the men and horses appeared to be, from the strong contrast of their colours with the wide expanse of snow.

As we passed one of the branches of the Ottawa, one of the ammunition-waggons falling through the ice, the horses were immediately all but choaked by the drivers—a precaution which was novel to me, and a singular method of saving their lives: but such was the case: the air within them, rarified by heat, inflated their bodies like balloons, and they floated high on the water. In this state they were easily disengaged from their traces, and hauled out upon the ice; the cords which had nearly strangled them were then removed, and, in a few minutes, they recovered sufficiently to be led to the shore.

Let it not be supposed that I am about to write a regular dispatch. I went out with the troops, but was of about as much use as the fifth wheel of a coach; with the exception, that as I rode one of Sir John Colborne's horses, I was, perhaps, so far supplying the place of a groom who was better employed.

The town of St. Eustache is very prettily situated on the high banks of the river, the most remarkable object being the Catholic church, a very large massive building, raised about two hundred yards from the river side, upon a commanding situation. This church the insurgents had turned into a fortress, and perhaps, for a fortress "*d'occasion,*" there never was one so well calculated for a vigorous defence, it being flanked by two long stone-built houses, and protected in the rear by several lines of high and strong palisades, running down into the river. The troops halted about three hundred yards from the town, to reconnoitre; the artillery were drawn up and opened their fire, but chiefly with a view that the enemy, by returning the fire, might demonstrate their force and position. These being ascertained, orders were given by Sir John Colborne, so that in a short time the whole town would be invested by the troops. The insurgents perceiving this, many of them escaped, some through the town, others by the frozen river. Those who crossed on the ice were chased by the volunteer dragoons, and the slipping and tumbling of the pursued and the pursuers, afforded as much merriment as interest; so true it is, that any thing ludicrous will make one laugh, in opposition to the feelings of sympathy, anxiety, and fear. Some of the runaways were cut down, and many more taken prisoners.

As soon as that portion of the troops which had entered the town, and marched up the main street towards the church, arrived within half-musket shot, they were received with a smart volley, which was fired from the large windows of the church, and which wounded a few of the men. The soldiers were then ordered to make their approaches under cover of the houses; and the artillery being brought up, commenced firing upon the church: but the walls of the building were much too solid for the shot to make any impression, and had the insurgents stood firm they certainly might have given a great deal of trouble, and probably have occasioned a severe loss of men; but they became alarmed, and fired one of the houses which abutted upon and flanked the church,—this they did with the view of escaping under cover of the smoke. In a few minutes the church itself was obscured by the volumes of smoke thrown out; and at the same time that the insurgents were escaping, the troops marched up and surrounded the church. The poor wretches attempted to get away, either singly or by twos and threes; but the moment they appeared a volley was discharged, and they fell. Every attempt was made by the officers to make prisoners, but with indifferent success; indeed, such was the exasperation of the troops at the murder of Lieut. Weir, that it was a service of danger to attempt to save the life of one of these poor deluded creatures. The fire from the house soon communicated to the church. Chenier, the leader, with ten others, the remnant of the insurgents who were in the church, rushed out; there was one tremendous volley, and all was over.

By this time many other parts of the town were on fire, and there was every prospect of the whole of it being burnt down, leaving no quarters for the soldiers to protect them during the night. The attention of everybody was therefore turned to prevent the progress of the flames. Some houses were pulled down, so as to cut off the communication with the houses in the centre of the town, and in these houses the troops were billeted off. The insurgents had removed their families, and most of their valuables and furniture, before our arrival; but in one house were the commissariat stores, consisting of the carcases of all the cattle, sheep, pigs, etcetera, which they had taken from the loyal farmers; there was a very large supply, and the soldiers were soon cooking in all directions. The roll was called, men mustered, and order established.

The night was bitterly cold: the sky was clear, and the moon near to her full: houses were still burning in every direction, but they were as mere satellites to the lofty church, which was now one blaze of fire, and throwing out volumes of smoke, which passed over the face of the bright moon, and gave to her a lurid reddish tinge, as if she too had assisted in these deeds of blood. The distant fires scattered over the whole landscape, which was one snow-wreath; the whirling of the smoke from the houses which were burning close to us, and which, from the melting of the snow, were surrounded by pools of water, reflecting the fierce yellow flames, mingled with the pale beams of the bright moon—this, altogether, presented a beautiful, novel, yet melancholy panorama. I thought it might represent, in miniature, the burning of Moscow.

About midnight, when all was quiet, I walked up to the church, in company with one of Sir John Colborne's aides-de-camp: the roof had fallen, and the flames had subsided for want of further aliment. As we passed by a house which had just taken fire we heard a cry, and, on going up, found a poor wounded Canadian, utterly incapable of moving, whom the flames had just reached; in a few minutes he would have been burned alive: we dragged him out, and gave him in charge of the soldiers, who carried him to the hospital.

But what was this compared to the scene which presented itself in the church! But a few weeks back, crowds were there, kneeling in adoration and prayer; I could fancy the Catholic priests in their splendid stoles, the altar, its candlesticks and ornaments, the solemn music, the incense, and all that, by appealing to the senses, is so favourable to the cause of religion with the ignorant and uneducated; and what did I now behold?—nothing but the bare and blackened walls, the glowing beams and rafters, and the window-frames which the flames still licked and flickered through. The floor had been burnt to cinders, and upon and between the sleepers on which the floor had been laid, were scattered the remains of human creatures, injured in various degrees, or destroyed by the fire; some with merely the clothes burnt off, leaving the naked body; some burnt to a deep brown tinge; others so far consumed that the viscera were exposed; while here and there the blackened ribs and vertebra were all that the fierce flames had spared.

Not only inside of the church, but without its walls, was the same revolting spectacle. In the remains of the small building used as a receptacle for the coffins previous to interment, were several bodies, heaped one upon another, and still burning, the trestles which had once supported the coffins serving as fuel; and further off were bodies still unscathed by fire, but frozen hard by the severity of the weather.

I could not help thinking, as I stood contemplating this melancholy scene of destruction, bloodshed, and sacrilege, that if Mr Hume or Mr Roebuck had been by my side, they might have repented their inflammatory and liberal opinions, as here they beheld the frightful effects of them.

Volume One—Chapter Twenty One.

Crossing the river St. Lawrence at this season of the year is not very pleasant, as you must force your passage through the large masses of ice, and are occasionally fixed among them; so that you are swept down the current along with them. Such was our case for about a quarter of an hour, and, in consequence, we landed about three miles lower down than we had intended. The next day the navigation of the river, such as it was, was stopped, and in eight and forty hours heavy waggons and carts were passing over where we had floated across.

My course lay through what were termed the *excited* districts; I had promised to pass through them, and supply the folks at Montreal with any information I could collect. The weather was bitterly cold, and all communication was carried on by sleighs, a very pleasant mode of travelling when the roads are smooth, but rather fatiguing when they are uneven, as the sleigh then jumps from hill to hill, like an oyster-shell thrown by a boy to skim the surface of the water. To defend myself from the cold, I had put on, over my coat, and under my cloak, a wadded black silk dressing-gown; I thought nothing of it at the time, but I afterwards discovered that I was supposed to be one of the rebel priests escaping from justice.

Although still in the English dominions, I had not been over on the opposite side more than a quarter of an hour before I perceived that it would be just as well to hold my tongue; and my adherence to this resolution, together with my supposed canonicals, were the cause of not a word being addressed to me by my fellow-travellers. They presumed that I spoke French only, which they did not, and I listened in silence to all that passed.

It is strange how easily the American people are excited, and when excited, they will hesitate at nothing. The coach (for it was the stage-coach although represented by an open sleigh), stopped at every town, large or small, every body eager to tell and to receive the news. I always got out to warm myself at the stove in the bar, and heard all the remarks made upon what I do really believe were the most absurd and extravagant lies ever circulated—lies which the very people who uttered them knew to be such, but which produced the momentary effect intended. They were even put into the newspapers, and circulated every where; and when the truth was discovered, they still remained uncontradicted, except by a general remark that such was the Tory version of the matter, and of course was false. The majority of those who travelled with me were Americans who had crossed the St. Lawrence in the same boat, and who must, therefore, have known well the whole circumstances attending the expedition against St. Eustache; but, to my surprise, at every place where we stopped they declared that there had been a battle between the insurgents and the King's troops, in which the insurgents had been victorious; that Sir John Colborne had been compelled to retreat to Montreal; that they had themselves seen the troops come back (which was true), and that Montreal was barricaded (which was also true) to prevent the insurgents from marching in. I never said one word; I listened to the exultations—to the declarations of some that they should go and join the patriots, etcetera. One man amused me by saying —"I've a great mind to go, but what I want is a good general to take the command; I want a Julius Caesar, or a Bonaparte, or a Washington—then I'll go."

I stopped for some hours at St. Alban's. I was recommended to go to an inn, the landlord of which was said not to be of the democratic party, for the other two inns were the resort of the Sympathisers,—and in these, consequently, scenes of great excitement took place. The landlord put into my hand a newspaper, published that day, containing a series of resolutions, founded upon such falsehoods that I thought it might be advantageous to refute them. I asked the landlord whether I could see the editor of the paper; he replied that the party lived next door; and I requested that he would send for him, telling him that I could give him information relative to the affair of St. Eustache.

I had been shewn into a large sitting-room on the ground-floor, which I presumed was a private room, when the editor of the newspaper, attracted by the message I had sent him, came in. I then pointed to the resolutions passed at the meeting, and asked him whether he would allow me to answer them in his paper. His reply was, "Certainly; that his paper was open to all."

"Well, then, call in an hour, and I will by that time prove to you that they can only be excused or accounted for by the parties who framed them being totally ignorant of the whole affair."

He went away, but did not return at the time requested. It was not until late in the evening that he came; and, avoiding the question of the resolutions, begged that I would give him the information relative to St. Eustache. As I presumed that, like most other editors in the United States, he dared not put in anything which would displease his subscribers, I said no more on that subject, but commenced dictating to him, while he wrote the particulars attending the St. Eustache affair. I was standing by the stove, giving the editor this information, when the door of the room opened, and in walked seven or eight people, who, without speaking, took chairs; in a minute, another party of about the same number was ushered into the room by the landlord, who, I thought, gave me a significant look. I felt surprised at what I thought an intrusion, as I had considered my room to be private; however, I appeared to take no notice of it, and continued dictating to the editor. The door opened again and again, and more chairs were brought in for the accommodation of the parties who entered, until at last the room was so full that I had but just room to walk round the stove. Not a person said a word; they listened to what I was dictating to the editor, and I observed that they all looked rather fierce; but whether this was a public meeting, or what was to be the end of it, I had no idea. At last, when I had finished, the editor took up his papers and left the room, in which I suppose there might have been from one hundred to a hundred and fifty persons assembled. As soon as the door closed, one of them struck his thick stick on the floor (they most of them had sticks), and gave a loud "Hem!"

"I believe, sir, that you are Captain M—."

"Yes," replied I, "that is my name."

"We are informed, sir, by the gentleman who has just gone out, that you have asserted that our resolutions of yesterday could only be excused or accounted for from our total ignorance." Here he struck his stick again upon the floor, and paused.

"Oh!" thinks I to myself, "the editor has informed against me!"

"Now, sir," continued the spokesman, "we are come to be enlightened; we wish you to prove to us that we are totally ignorant; you will oblige us by an explanation of your assertion."

He was again silent. (Thinks I to myself, I'm in for it now, and if I get away without a broken head, or something worse, I am fortunate; however, here goes.) Whereupon, without troubling the reader with what I did say, I will only observe, that I thought the best plan was to gain time by going back as far as I could. I therefore commenced my oration at the period; when the Canadas were surrendered to the English; remarking upon the system which had been acted upon by our government from that time up to the present; proving, as well as I could, that the Canadians had nothing to complain of, and that if England had treated her other American colonies as well, there never would have been a declaration of independence, etcetera. etcetera. Having spoken for about an hour, and observing a little impatience on the part of some of my company, I stopped. Upon which, one rose and said, that there were several points not fully explained, referring to them one after another, whereupon "the honourable member rose to explain,"—and was again silent. Another then spoke, requesting information as to points not referred to by me. I replied, and fortunately had an opportunity of paying the Americans a just compliment; in gratitude for which their features relaxed considerably. Perceiving this, I ventured to introduce a story or two, which made them laugh. After this, the day was my own; for I consider the Americans, when not excited (which they too often are), as a very good-tempered people: at all events, they won't break your head for making them laugh; at least, such I found was the case. We now entered freely into conversation; some went away, others remained, and the affair ended by many of them shaking hands with me, and our taking a drink at the bar.

I must say, that the first appearances of this meeting were not at all pleasant; but I was rightly served for my own want of caution, in so publicly stating, that the free and enlightened citizens of St. Alban's were very ignorant, and for opposing public opinion at a time when the greatest excitement prevailed. I have mentioned this circumstance, as it threws a great deal of light upon the character of the Yankee or American of the Eastern States. They would not suffer opposition to the majority to pass unnoticed (who, in England, would have cared what a stranger may have expressed as his opinion); but, at the same time, they gave me a patient hearing, to knew whether I could shew cause for what I said. Had I refused this, I might have been very roughly handled; but as I defended my observations, although they were not complimentary to them, they gave me fair play. They were evidently much excited when they came into the room, but they gradually cooled down until convinced of the truth of my assertions; and then all animosity was over. The landlord said to me afterwards, "I reckon you got out of that uncommon well, captain." I perfectly agreed with him, and made a resolution to hold my tongue until I arrived at New York.

The next day, as I was proceeding on my journey, I fell in with General Brown, celebrated for running away so fast at the commencement of the fight at St. Charles. He had a very fine pair of mustachios. We both warmed our toes at the same stove in solemn silence.

Sunday, at Burlington.—The young ladies are dressing up the church with festoons, and garlands of evergreens for the celebration of Christmas, and have pressed me into the service. Last Sunday I was meditating over the blackened walls of the church at St. Eustache, and the roasted corpses lying within its precincts; now I am in another church, weaving laurel and cypress, in company with some of the prettiest creatures in creation. As the copy-book says, *variety is charming*.

Volume One—Chapter Twenty Two.

Philadelphia is certainly, in appearance, the most wealthy and imposing city in the Union. It is well built, and ornamented with magnificent public edifices of white marble; indeed there is a great show of this material throughout the whole of the town, all the flights of steps to the doors, door-lintels, and window-sills, being very generally composed of this material. The exterior of the houses, as well as the side pavement, are kept remarkably clean; and there is no intermixture of commerce, as there is at New York, the bustle of business being confined to the Quays, and one or two streets adjoining the river side.

The first idea which strikes you when you arrive at Philadelphia, is that it is Sunday: every thing is so quiet, and there are so few people stirring; but by the time that you have paraded half a dozen streets, you come to a conclusion that it must be Saturday, as that day is, generally speaking, a washing-day. Philadelphia is so admirably supplied with water from the Schuykill water-works, that every house has it laid on from the attic to the basement; and all day long they wash windows, door, marble step, and pavements in front of the houses. Indeed, they have so much water, that they can afford to be very liberal to passers-by. One minute you have a shower-bath from a negress, who is throwing water at the windows on the first floor; and the next you have to hop over a stream across the pavement, occasioned by some black fellow, who, rather than go for a broom to sweep away any small portion of dust collected before his master's door, brings out the leather hose, attached to the hydrants, as they term them here, and fizzes away with it till the stream has forced the dust into the gutter.

Of course, fire has no chance in this city. Indeed, the two elements appear to have arranged that matter between them; fire has the ascendant in New York, while water reigns in Philadelphia. If a fire does break out here, the housekeepers have not the fear of being *burnt* to death before them; for the water is poured on in such torrents, that the furniture is washed out of the windows, and all that they have to look out for, is to escape from being drowned.

The public institutions, such as libraries, museums, and the private cabinets of Philadelphia, are certainly very superior to those of any other city or town in America, Boston not excepted. Every thing that is undertaken in this city is well done; no expense is spared, although they are not so rapid in their movements as at New York: indeed the affluence and ease pervading the place, with the general cultivation which invariably attend them, are evident to a stranger.

Philadelphia has claimed for herself the title of the most aristocratic city in the Union. If she refers to the aristocracy of wealth, I think she is justified; but if she would say the aristocracy of family, which is much more thought of by the few who can claim it, she must be content to divide that with Boston, Baltimore, Charlestown, and the other cities which can date as far back as herself. One thing is certain, that in no city is there so much fuss made about lineage and descent; in no city are there so many cliques and sets in society, who keep apart from each other; and it is very often difficult to ascertain the grounds of their distinctions. One family will live at No. 1, and another at No. 2 in the same street, both have similar establishments, both keep their carriages, both be well educated, and both may talk of their grandfathers and grandmothers; and yet No. 1 will tell you that No. 2 is nobody, and you must not visit there; and when you enquire why? there is no other answer, but that they are not of the right sort. As long as a portion are rich and a portion are poor, there is a line of demarcation easy to be drawn, even in a democracy; but in Philadelphia, where there are so many in affluent circumstances, that line has been effaced, and they now seek an imaginary one, like the equinoctial, which none can be permitted to pass without going through the ceremonies of perfect ablution. This social contest, as may be supposed, is carried on among those who have no real pretensions; but there are many old and well-connected families in Philadelphia, whose claims are universally, although perhaps unwillingly, acknowledged.

I doubt if the claims of Boston to be the most scientific city in the Union, can be now established. I met a greater number of scientific men in Philadelphia than I did in Boston; and certainly the public and private collections in the former city are much superior. The collection of shells and minerals belonging to Mr Lee, who is well known as an author and a naturalist, is certainly the most interesting I saw in the States, and I passed two days in examining it: it must have cost him much trouble and research.

The Girard College, when finished, will be a most splendid building. It is, however, as they have now planned it, incorrect, according to the rules of architecture, in the number of columns on the sides in proportion to those in front. This is a great pity; perhaps the plan will be re-considered, as there is plenty of time to correct it, as well as money to defray the extra expense.

The water-works at Schuykill are well worth a visit, not only for their beauty, but their simplicity. The whole of the river Schuykill is dammed up, and forms a huge water-power, which forces up the supply of water for the use of the city. As I presume that river has a god as well as others, I can imagine his indignation, not only at his waters being diverted from his channel, but at being himself obliged to do all the work for the benefit of his tyrannical masters.

I have said that the museums of Philadelphia are far superior to most in the States; but I may just as well here observe, that, as in many other things, a great improvement is necessary before they are such as they ought to be. There is not only in these museums, but in all that I have ever entered in the United States, a want of taste and discrimination, of that correct feeling which characterises the real lovers of science, and knowledge of what is worthy of being collected. They are such collections as would be made by school-boys and school-girls, not those of erudite professors and scientific men. Side by side with the most interesting and valuable specimens, such as the fossil mammoth, etcetera, you have the greatest puerilities and absurdities in the world—such as a cherry-stone formed into a basket, a fragment of the boiler of the Moselle steamer, and Heaven knows what besides. Then you invariably have a large collection of daubs, called portraits, of eminent personages, one-half of whom a stranger never heard of—but that is national vanity; and lastly, I do not recollect to have seen a museum that had not a considerable portion of its space occupied by most execrable wax-work, in which the sleeping beauty (a sad misnomer) generally figures very conspicuously. In some, they have models of celebrated criminals in the act of committing a murder, with the very hatchet or the very knife: or such trophies as the bonnet worn by Mrs — when she was killed by her husband; or the shirt, with the blood of his wife on it, worn by Jack Sprat, or whoever he might be, when he committed the bloody deed. The most favourite subject, after the sleeping beauty in the wax-work, is General Jackson, with the battle of New Orleans in the distance. Now all these things are very well in their places: exhibit wax-work as much as you please—it amuses and interests children; but the present collections in the museums remind you of American society—a chaotic mass, in which you occasionally meet what is valuable and interesting, but of which the larger proportion is pretence.

It was not until I had been some time in Philadelphia that I became convinced how very superior the free coloured people were in intelligence and education, to what, from my knowledge of them in our West-India Islands, I had ever imagined them capable of. Not that I mean to imply that they will ever attain to the same powers of intellect as the white man, for I really believe that the race are not formed for it by the Almighty. I do not mean to say that there *never* will be great men among the African race, but that such instances will always be very *rare*, compared to the numbers produced among the white. But this is certain, that in Philadelphia the free coloured people are a very respectable class, and, in my opinion, quite as intelligent as the more humble of the free whites. I have been quite surprised to see them take out their pencils, write down and calculate with quickness and precision, and in every other point shew great intelligence and keenness.

In this city they are both numerous and wealthy. The most extravagant funeral I saw in Philadelphia was that of a black; the coaches were very numerous, as well as the pedestrians, who were all well dressed, and behaving with the utmost decorum. They were preceded by a black clergyman, dressed in his full black silk canonicals. He did look very odd, I must confess.

Singular is the degree of contempt and dislike in which the free blacks are held in all the free States of America. They are deprived of their rights as citizens; and the white pauper, who holds out his hand for charity (and there is no want of beggars in Philadelphia), will turn away from a negro, or coloured man, with disdain. It is the same thing in the Eastern States, notwithstanding their religious professions. In fact, in the United States, a negro, from his colour, and I believe his colour alone, is a degraded being. Is not this extraordinary, in a land which professes universal liberty, equality, and the rights of man? In England this is not the case. In private society no one objects to sit in company with a man of colour, provided he has the necessary education and respectability. Nor, indeed, is it the case in the Slave States, where I have frequently seen a lady in a public conveyance with her negress sitting by her, and no objection has been raised by the other parties in the coach; but in the Free States a man of colour is not admitted into a stage coach; and in all other public places, such as theatres, churches, etcetera, there is always a portion divided off for the negro population, that they may not be mixed up with the whites. When I first landed at New York, I had a specimen of this feeling. Fastened by a rope yarn to the rudder chains of a vessel next in the tier, at the wharf to which the packet had hauled in, I perceived the body of a black man, turning over and over with the ripple of the waves. I was looking at it, when a lad came up: probably his curiosity was excited by my eyes being fixed in that direction. He looked, and perceiving the object, turned away with disdain, saying, "Oh, it's only a nigger."

And all the Free States in America respond to the observation, "It's only a nigger." (See note 1.) At the time that I was at Philadelphia a curious cause was decided. A coloured man of the name of James Fortin, who was, I believe, a sailmaker by profession, but at all events a person not only of the highest respectability, but said to be worth 150,000 dollars, appealed because he was not permitted to vote at elections, and claimed his right as a free citizen. The cause was tried, and the verdict, a very lengthy one, was given by the judge against him, I have not that verdict in my possession; but I have the opinion of the Supreme Court on one which was given before, and I here insert it as a curiosity. It is a remarkable feature in the tyranny and injustice of this case, that although James Fortin was not considered white enough (he is, I believe, a mulatto) to *vote* as a citizen, he has always been quite white enough to be *taxed* as one, and has to pay his proportion, (which, from the extent of his business, is no trifle) of all the rates and assessments considered requisite for the support of the poor, and improving and beautifying that city, of which he is declared not to be a citizen.

Although the decision of the Supreme Court enters into a lengthened detail, yet as it is very acute and argumentative, and touches upon several other points equally anomalous to the boasted freedom of the American institutions, I wish the reader would peruse it carefully, as it will amply repay him for his trouble; and it is that he *may* read it, that I have not inserted it in an Appendix.

The question arose upon a writ of error to the judgment of the Common Pleas of Luzerne county, in an action by Wm. Fogg, a negro, against Hiram Hobbs, inspector, and Levi Baldwin and others, judges of the election, for refusing his vote. In the Court below the plaintiff recovered. The Supreme Court being of opinion that a negro has not a right to vote under the present constitution, reversed the judgment.

"Respectfully, Fred. Watts.

"Wm. Fogg *versus* Hiram Hobbs and others.

"The opinion of the Court was delivered by Gibson, CJ.

"This record raises, a second time, the only question on a phrase in the Constitution which has occurred since its adoption; and, however partisans may have disputed the clearness and precision of phraseology, we have often been called upon to enforce its limitations of legislative power; but the business of interpretation was incidental, and the difficulty was not in the diction, but in the uncertainty of the act to which it was to be applied. I have said a question on the meaning of a phrase has arisen a second time. It would be more accurate to say the *same* question has arisen the second time. About the year 1795, as I have it from James Gibson, Esquire, of the Philadelphia bar, the very point before us was ruled by the High Court of Errors and Appeals against the right of negro suffrage. Mr Gibson declined an invitation to be concerned in the argument, and therefore has no memorandum of the cause to direct us to the record. I have had the office searched for it; but the papers had fallen into such disorder as to preclude a hope of its discovery. Most of them were imperfect, and many were lost or misplaced. But Mr Gibson's remembrance of the decision is perfect, and entitled to full confidence. That the case was not reported, is probably owing to the fact that the judges gave no reasons; and the omission is the more to be regretted, as a report of it would have put the question at rest, and prevented much unpleasant excitement. Still, the judgment is not the less authoritative as a precedent. Standing as the court of last resort, that tribunal bore the name relation to this court that the Supreme Court does to the Common Pleas; and as its authority could not be questioned then, it cannot be questioned now. The point, therefore, is not open to discussion on original grounds.

"But the omission of the judges renders it proper to show that their decision was founded in the true principles of the constitution. In the first section of the third article it is declared, that 'in elections by the citizens, every *freeman* of the age of twenty-one years, having resided in the State two years before the election, and having within that time paid *a state or county tax*,' shall enjoy the rights of an elector. Now, the argument of those who assert the claim of the coloured population is, that a negro is a *man*; and when not held to involuntary service, that he is free, consequently that he is a *freeman*; and if a freeman in the common acceptation of the term, then a freeman in every acceptation of it. This pithy and syllogistic sentence comprises the whole argument, which, however elaborated, perpetually goes back to the point from which it started. The fallacy of it is its assumption that the term 'freedom' signifies nothing but exemption from involuntary service; and that it has not a legal signification more specific. The freedom of a municipal corporation, or body politic, implies fellowship and participation, of corporate rights; but an inhabitant of an incorporated place, who is neither servant nor slave, though bound by its laws, may be no freeman in respect to its government. It has indeed been affirmed by text writers, that habitance, paying scot and lot, give an incidental right to corporate freedom; but the courts have refused to acknowledge it, even when the charter seemed to imply it; and when not derived from prescription or grant, it has been deemed a qualification merely, and not a title. (*Wilcox*, chap. iii. p. 456.) Let it not be said that the legal meaning of the word freeman is peculiar to British corporations, and that we have it not in the charters and constitutions of Pennsylvania. The laws agreed upon in England in May 1682, use the word in this specific sense, and even furnish a definition of it: 'Every inhabitant of the said province that is, or shall be, a purchaser of one hundred acres of land or upwards, his heirs or assigns, and every person who shall have paid his passage, and shall have taken up one hundred acres of land, at a penny an acre, and have cultivated ten acres thereof; and every person that hath been a servant or bondsman, and is free by his service, that shall have taken up his fifty acres of land, and shall have cultivated twenty thereof; and every inhabitant, artificer, or other resident in the said province, that pays scot and lot to the government, *shall be deemed and accounted a **freeman** of the said province*; and every such person shall be capable of electing, or being elected, representatives of the people in provincial council, or general assembly of the said province.' Now, why this minute and elaborate detail? Had it been intended that all but servants and slaves should be freemen to every intent, it had been easier and more natural to say so. But it was not intended. It was foreseen that there would be inhabitants, neither planters nor taxable, who, though free as the winds, might be unsafe depositories of popular power; and the design was, to admit no man to the freedom of the province who had not a stake in it. That the clause which relates to freedom by service was not intended for manumitted slaves is evident, from the fact that there were none; and it regarded not slavery, but limited servitude expired by efflux of time. At that time, certainly, the case of a manumitted slave, or of his free-born progeny, was not contemplated as one to be provided for in the founder's scheme of policy: I have quoted the passage, however, to show that the word freeman was applied in a peculiar sense to the political compact of our ancestors, resting like a corporation, on a charter from the crown; and exactly as it was applied to bodies politic at home. In entire consonance, it was declared in the Act of Union, given at Chester in the same year, that strangers and foreigners holding land 'according to the law of a freeman,' and promising obedience to the proprietary, as well as allegiance to the crown, 'shall be held and reputed freemen of the province and counties aforesaid;' and it was further declared, that when a foreigner 'shall make his request to the governor of the province *for the aforesaid freedom*, the same person shall be *admitted* on the conditions herein expressed, paying twenty shillings sterling, and no more:'—modes of expression peculiarly appropriate to corporate fellowship. The word in the same sense pervades the charter of privileges, the act of settlement, and the act of naturalisation, in the preamble to the last of which it was said, that some of the inhabitants were 'foreigners and not freemen, according to the acceptation of the laws of England;' it held its place also in the legislative style of enactment down to the adoption of the present constitution; after which, the words 'by and with the advice and consent of the freemen,' were left out, and the present style substituted. Thus, till the instant when the phrase on which the question turns was penned, the term freeman had a peculiar and specific sense, being used like the term citizen, which supplanted it, to denote one who had a voice in public affairs. The citizens were denominated freemen even in the constitution of 1776; and under the present constitution, the word, though dropped in the style, was used in legislative acts, convertible with electors, so late as the year 1798, when it grew into disuse. In an act passed the 4th of April in that year for the establishment of certain election districts, it was, for the first time, used indiscriminately with that word; since when it has been entirely disused. Now, it will not be pretended, that the legislature meant to have it inferred, that every one not a freeman within the purview, should be deemed a slave; and how can a convergent intent be collected from the same word in the constitution, that every one not a slave is to be accounted an elector? Except for the word citizen, which stands in the context also as a term of qualification, an affirmance of these propositions would extend the right of suffrage to aliens; and to admit of any exception to the argument, its force being derived from the supposed universality of the term, would destroy it. Once concede that there may be a freeman in one sense of it, who is not so in another, and the whole ground is surrendered. In what sense, then, must the convention of 1790 be supposed to have used the term? questionless in that which it had acquired by use in public acts and legal proceedings, for the reason that a dubious statute is to be expounded by usage. 'The meaning of things spoken and written, must be as hath been constantly received.' (Vaugh. 169.) On this principle, it is difficult to discover how the word freeman, as used in previous public acts, could have been meant to comprehend a coloured race: as well might it be supposed, that the declaration of universal and unalienable freedom in both our constitutions was meant to comprehend it. Nothing was ever more comprehensively predicted, and a practical enforcement of it would have liberated every slave in the State; yet mitigated slavery long continued to exist among us, in derogation of it. Rules of interpretation demand a strictly verbal construction of nothing but a penal statute; and a constitution is to be construed still more liberally than even a remedial one, because a convention legislating for masses, can do little more than mark an outline of fundamental principles, leaving the interior gyrations and details to be filled up by ordinary legislation. 'Conventions intended to regulate the conduct of nations,' said Chief Justice Tilghman, in the Farmers' Bank versus Smith, 3 Sergt. and Rawl. 69, 'are not to be construed like articles of agreement at the common law. It is of little importance to the public, whether a tract of land belongs to A or B. In deciding these titles, strict rules of construction may be adhered to; and it is best that they should be adhered to, though sometimes at the expense of justice. But where multitudes are to be affected by the construction of an amendment, great regard is to be paid to the spirit and intention.' What better key to these, than the tone of antecedent legislation discoverable in the application of the disputed terms.

"But in addition to interpretation from usage, this antecedent legislation furnishes other proofs that no coloured race was party to our social compact. As was justly remarked by President Fox, in the matter of the late contested election, our ancestors settled the province as a community of white men, and the blacks were introduced into it as a race of slaves, whence an unconquerable prejudice of caste, which has come down to our day, insomuch that a suspicion of taint still has the unjust effect of sinking the subject of it below the common level. Consistently with this prejudice, is it to be credited that parity of rank would be allowed to such a race? Let the question be answered by the statute of 1726, which denominated it an idle and a slothful people; which directed the magistrates to bind out free negroes for laziness or vagrancy; which forbade them to harbour Indian or mulatto slaves, on pain of punishment by fine, or to deal with negro slaves, on pain of stripes; which annexed to the interdict of marriage with a white, the penalty of reduction to slavery; which punished them for tippling with stripes, and even a white person with servitude for intermarriage with a negro. If freemen, in a political sense, were subjects of these cruel and degrading oppressions, what must have been the lot of their brethren in bondage? It is also true, that degrading conditions were sometimes assigned to white men, but never as members of a caste. Insolvent debtors, to indicate the worst of them, are compelled to make satisfaction by servitude; but that was borrowed from a kindred, and still less rational, principle of the common law. This act of 1726, however, remained in force, till it was repealed by the Emancipating Act of 1789; and it is irrational to believe, that the progress of liberal sentiments was so rapid in the next ten years,—as to produce a determination in the convention of 1790 to raise this depressed race to the level of the white one. If such were its purpose, it is strange that the word chosen to effect it should have been the very one chosen by the convention of 1776 to designate a white elector. 'Every freeman,' it is said, (chap. 2, sect. 6,) 'of the full age of twenty-one years, having resided in this State for the space of one whole year before the day of election, and paid taxes during that time, shall enjoy the rights of an elector.' Now, if the word freeman were not potent enough to admit a free negro to suffrage under the first constitution, it is difficult to discern a degree of magic in the intervening plan of emancipation sufficient to give it potency, in the apprehension of the convention, under the second.

"The only thing in the history of the convention which casts a doubt upon the intent, is the fact, that the word *white* was prefixed to the word freeman in the report of the committee, and *subsequently struck* out—probably because it was thought superfluous, or still more probably, because it was feared that respectable men of dark complexion would often be insulted at the polls, by objections to their colour. I have heard it said, that Mr Gallatin sustained his motion to strike out on the latter ground. Whatever the motive, the disseverence is insufficient to wrap the interpretation of a word of such settled and determinate meaning as the one which remained. A legislative body speaks to the judiciary, only through its final act, and expresses its will in the words of it; and though their meaning may be influenced by the sense in which they have usually been applied to extrinsic matters, we cannot receive an explanation of them from what has been moved or said in debate. The place of a judge is his forum—not the legislative hall. Were he even disposed to pry into the motives of the members, it would be impossible for him to ascertain them; and, in attempting to discover the ground on which the conclusion was obtained, it is not probable that a member of the majority could indicate any that was common to all; previous prepositions are merged in the act of consummation, and the interpreter of it must look to that alone.

"I have thought it fair to treat the question as it stands affected by our own municipal regulations, without illustration from those of other States, where the condition of the race has been still less favoured. Yet it is proper to say, that the second section of the fourth article of the Federal Constitution presents an obstacle to the political freedom of the negro, which seems to be insuperable. It is to be remembered that citizenship, as well as freedom, is a constitutional qualification; and how it could be conferred, so as to overbear the laws, imposing countless disabilities on him in other States, is a problem of difficult solution. In this aspect, the question becomes one, not of intention, but of power; so doubtful, as to forbid the exercise of it. Every man must lament the necessity of the disabilities; but slavery is to be dealt with by those whose existence depends on the skill with which it is treated. Considerations of mere humanity, however, belong to a class with which, as judges, we have nothing to do; and, interpreting the constitution in the spirit of our own institutions, we are bound to pronounce that men of colour are destitute of title to the elective franchise: their blood, however, may become so diluted in successive descent, as to lose its distinctive character; and then both policy and justice require that previous disabilities should cease. By the amended constitution of North Carolina, no free negro, mulatto, or free person of mixed blood, descended from negro ancestors to the fourth generation inclusive, *though one ancestor of each generation may have been a white person*, shall vote for the legislature. I regret to say, no similar regulation, for practical purposes, has been attempted here; in consequence of which, every case of disputed colour must be determined by no particular rule, but by the discretion of the judges; and thus a great constitutional right, even under the proposed amendments of the constitution, will be left the sport of caprice. In conclusion, we are of opinion the court erred in directing that the plaintiff could have his action against the defendant for the rejection of his vote. Judgment reversed."

It will be observed by those who have had patience to read through so long a legal document, that reference is made to the unjust prejudice against any taint of the African blood. There is an existing proof of the truth of this remark, in the case of one of the most distinguished members of the House of Representatives. This gentleman has some children who are not of pure blood; but, to his honour, he has done his duty by them, he has educated them, and received them into his house as his acknowledged daughters. What is the consequence? Why, it is considered that by so doing he has outraged society; and whenever they want to raise a cry against him, this is the charge, and very injurious it is to his popularity,—"that he has done his duty as a father and a Christian."

"Captain Marryat, we are a very moral people!"

The laws of the State relative to the intermarriage of the whites with the coloured population are also referred to. A case of this kind took place at New York when I was there; and as soon as the ceremony was over, the husband, I believe it was, but either the husband or the wife, was seized by the mob, and put under the pump for half an hour. At Boston, similar modes of expressing public opinion have been adopted, notwithstanding that that city is the stronghold of the abolitionists.

It also refers to the white slavery, which was not abolished until the year 1789. Previous to that period, a man who arrived out, from the old continent, and could not pay his passage, was put up to auction for the amount of his debt, and was compelled to serve until he had worked it out with the purchaser. But not only for the debt of passage-money, but for other debts, a white man was put up to auction, and sold to the best bidder. They tell a curious story, for the truth of which I cannot vouch, of a lawyer, a very clever but dissipated and extravagant man, who, having contracted large debts and escaped to New Jersey, was taken and put up to auction; a keen Yankee purchased him, and took him regularly round to all the circuits to plead causes, and made a very considerable sum out of him before his time expired.

I have observed that Mr Fortin, the coloured man, was considered quite white enough to pay taxes. It is usually considered in this country, that by going to America you avoid taxation, but such is not the case. The municipal taxes are not very light. I could not obtain any very satisfactory estimates from the other cities, but I gained thus much from Philadelphia.

The assessments are on property.

City Tax, 70 cents upon the 100 dollars valuation.

County Tax, 65 cents upon ditto.

Poor's Rate, 40 cents.

Taxes on Horses, 1 dollar each.

Taxes on Dogs, half a dollar each.

Poll Tax, from a quarter dollar to 4 dollars each person.

It is singular that such a tax as the *poll* tax, that which created the insurrection of Wat Tyler in England, should have forced its way into a democracy. In the collection of their taxes, they are quite as summary as they are in England. This is the notice:

"You are hereby informed, that your property is included in a list of delinquents now preparing, and will be advertised and sold for the assessments due thereon. (This being the last call.)

"Your immediate attention will save the costs of advertising, sale, etcetera.

"— Collector.

"Collector's Office, Number 1, State of —."

It is a strange fact, and one which must have attracted the reader's notice, that there should be a poor's rate in America, where there is work for every body; and still stranger that there should be one in the city of Philadelphia, in which, perhaps, there are more beneficent and charitable institutions than in any city in the world of the same population: notwithstanding this there are many mendicants in the street. All this arises from the advantage taken of an unwise philanthropy in the first place, many people preferring to live upon alms in preference to labour; and next from the state of destitution to which many of the emigrants are reduced after their arrival, and before they can obtain employment. Indeed, not only Philadelphia, but Baltimore and New York, are equally charged for the support of these people—the two first by legal enactment, the latter by voluntary subscription. And it is much to the credit of the inhabitants of all these cities that the charge is paid cheerfully, and that an appeal is never made in vain.

But let the Americans beware: the poor rate at present is trifling—40 cents in the 100 dollars, or about 1.75 pence in the pound; but they must recollect, that they were not more in England about half a century back, and see to what they have risen now! It is the principle which is bad. There are now in Philadelphia more than 1,500 paupers, who live entirely upon the public, but who, if relief had not been continued to them, would, in all probability, by this time, have found their way to where their labour is required. The Philadelphians are proverbially generous and charitable; but they should remember that in thus yielding to the dictates of their hearts, they are sowing the seeds of what will prove a bitter curse to their posterity. See note 2.

Note 1. "On the whole, I cannot help considering it a mistake to suppose that slavery has been abolished in the Northern States of the Union. It is true, indeed, that in these States the power of compulsory labour no longer exists; and that one human being within their limits can no longer claim property in the thews and sinews of another. But is this all that is implied in the boon of freedom? if the word mean anything, it must mean the enjoyment of equal rights, and the unfettered exercise in each individual of such powers and faculties as God has given. In this true meaning of the word, it may be safely asserted that this poor degraded class are still slaves—they are subject to the most grinding and humiliating of all slaveries, that of universal and unconquerable prejudice. The whip, indeed, has been removed from the back of the negro; but the chains are still upon his limbs, and he bears the brand of degradation on his forehead. What is it but the mere abuse of language to call him *free*, who is tyrannically deprived of all the motives to exertion which animate other men? The law, in truth, has left him in that most pitiable of all conditions—*a masterless slave*."—*Hamilton's Men and Manners in America*.

Note 2. Miss Martineau, who is not always wrong, in her remarks upon pauperism in the United States, observes:— "The amount, altogether, is far from commensurate with the charity of the community; and it is to be hoped that the curse of a legal charity will be avoided in a country where it certainly cannot become necessary within any assignable time. I was grieved to see the magnificent Pauper Asylum near Philadelphia, made to accommodate, luxuriously, 1,200 persons; and to have its arrangements pointed out to me, as yielding more comforts to the inmates than the labourer could secure at home by any degree of industry and prudence."

Volume Two—Chapter One.

Washington. Here are assembled from every State in the Union what ought to be the collected talent, intelligence, and high principle of a free and enlightened nation. Of talent and intelligence there is a very fair supply, but principle is not so much in demand; and in everything, and everywhere, by the demand the supply is always regulated.

Everybody knows that *Washington* has a Capitol; but the misfortune is that the Capitol wants a city. There it stands, reminding you of a general without an army, only surrounded and followed by a parcel of ragged little dirty boys, for such is the appearance of the dirty, straggling, ill-built houses which lie at the foot of it.

Washington, notwithstanding, is an agreeable city, full of pleasant clever people, who come there to amuse and be amused; and you observe in the company (although you occasionally meet some very queer importations from the Western settlements) much more *usage du monde* and continental ease than in any other parts of the State. A large portion of those who come up for the meeting of Congress, as well as of the residents, having travelled, and thereby gained more respect for other nations, are consequently not so conceited about their own country as are the majority of other Americans.

If anything were required to make Washington a more agreeable place than it is at all times, the arrival and subsequent conduct of Mr Fox as British Ambassador would be sufficient. His marked attention to all Americans of respectability: his *empressement* in returning the calls of English gentlemen who may happen to arrive, his open house; his munificent allowance dedicated wholly to the giving of fêtes and dinner parties as his Sovereign's representative; and, above all, his excessive urbanity, can never be forgotten by those who have ever visited the Capitol.

The Chamber of the House of Representatives is a fine room, and taking the average of the orations delivered there, it possesses this one great merit—*you cannot hear in it*. Were I to make a comparison between the members of our House of Commons and those of the House of Representatives, I should say that the latter had certainly real advantages. In the first place; the members of the American Senate and House of Representatives are paid, not only their travelling expenses to and fro, but eight dollars a day during the sitting of Congress. Out of these allowances many save money, and those who do not, are at all events enabled to bring their families up to Washington for a little amusement. In the next place, they are so comfortably accommodated in the house, every man having his own well-stuffed arm-chair, and before him his desk, with his papers and notes! Then they are supplied with everything, even to pen-knives with their names engraved on them—each knife having two pen-blades, one whittling blade, and a fourth to clean their nails with, showing on the part of the government, a paternal regard for their cleanliness as well as convenience. Moreover, they never work at night, and do very little during the day.

It is astonishing how little work they get through in a session at Washington: this is owing to every member thinking himself obliged to make two or three speeches, not for the good of the nation, but for the benefit of his constituents. These speeches are printed and sent to them, to prove that their member makes some noise in the house. The subject upon which he speaks is of little consequence, compared to the sentiments expressed. It must be full of eagles, star-spangled banners, sovereign people, clap-trap, flattery, and humbug. I have said that very little business is done in these houses; but this is caused not only by their long-winded speeches about nothing, but by the fact that both parties (in this respect laudably following the example of the old country) are chiefly occupied, the one with the paramount and vital consideration of keeping in, and the other with that of getting in,—thus allowing the business of the nation, (which after all is not very important, unless such a trump as the Treasury Bill turns up,) to become a very secondary consideration.

And yet there are principle and patriotism among the members of the legislature, and the more to be appreciated from their rarity. Like the seeds of beautiful flowers, which, when cast upon a manure-heap, spring up in greater luxuriance and beauty, and yield a sweeter perfume from the rankness which surrounds them, so do these virtues show with more grace and attractiveness from the hot-bed of corruption in which they have been engendered. But there has been a sad falling-off in America since the last war, which brought in the democratic party with General Jackson. America, if she would wish her present institutions to continue, must avoid war; the best security for her present form of government existing another half century, is a state of tranquillity and peace; but of that hereafter. As for the party at present in power, all I can say in its favour is, that there are three clever gentlemen in it —Mr Van Buren, Mr Poinsett, and Mr Forsyth. There may be more, but I know so little of them, that I must be excused if I do not name them, which otherwise I should have had great pleasure in doing.

Mr Van Buren is a very gentleman-like, intelligent man; very proud of talking over his visit to England, and the English with whom he was acquainted. It is remarkable that, although at the head of the democratic party, Mr Van Buren has taken a step striking at the very roots of their boasted equality, and one on which General Jackson did not venture—i.e. he has prevented the mobocracy from intruding themselves at his levées. The police are now stationed at the door, to prevent the intrusion of any improper person. A few years ago, a fellow would drive his cart, or hackney coach, up to the door; walk into the saloon in all his dirt, and force his way to the president, that he might shake him by the one hand; whilst he flourished his whip in the other. The revolting scenes which took place when refreshments were handed round, the injury done to the furniture, and the disgust of the ladies, may be well imagined. Mr Van Buren deserves great credit for this step, for it was a bold one; but I must not praise him too much, or he may lose his next election.

The best lounge at Washington is the library of the Capitol, but the books are certainly not very well treated. I saw a copy of Audubon's Ornithology, and many other valuable works, in a very dilapidated state, but this must be the case when the library is open to all, and there are so many juvenile visitors. Still it is much better than locking it up, for only the bindings to be looked at. It is not a library for show, but for use, and is a great comfort and amusement.

There are three things in great request amongst Americans of all classes,— male, I mean,—to wit, oysters, spirits, and tobacco. The first and third are not prohibited by Act of Congress and may be sold in the Capitol, but spirituous liquors may not. I wondered how the members could get on without them, but upon this point I was soon enlightened. Below the basement of the building is an oyster shop and refectory. The refectory has been permitted by Congress upon the express stipulation that no spirituous liquors should be sold there, but law-makers are too often law-breakers all over the world. You go there and ask for pale sherry, and they hand you gin; brown sherry, and it is brandy; madeira, whisky; and thus do these potent, grave, and reverend signors evade their own laws, beneath the very hall wherein they were passed in solemn conclave.

It appears that tobacco is considered very properly as an article of fashion. At a store close to the hotel, the board outside informs you that among fashionable requisites to be found there, are gentlemen's shirts, collars, gloves, silk handkerchiefs, and the best chewing tobacco. But not only at Washington but at other large towns I have seen at silk-mercers and hosiers this notice stuck up in the window—"*Dulcissimus* chewing tobacco." So prevalent is the habit of chewing, and so little, from long custom, do the ladies care about it, that I have been told that many young ladies in the South carry, in their work-boxes, etcetera, pigtail, nicely ornamented with gold and coloured papers; and when their swains are at fault administer to their wants, thus meriting their affections by such endearing solicitude.

I was rather amused in the Senate at hearing the claims of parties who had suffered during the last war, and had hitherto not received any redress, discussed for adjudication. One man's claim, for instance, was for a cow, value thirty dollars, eaten up, of course, by the Britishers. It would naturally be supposed that such claims were unworthy of the attention of such a body as the Senate, or, when brought forward, would have been allowed without comment: but it was not so. The member who saves the public money always finds favour in the eyes of the people, and therefore every member tries to save as much as he can, except when he is himself a party concerned. And there was as much arguing and objecting, and discussion of the merits of this man's claim, as there would be in the English House of Commons at passing the Navy Estimates. Eventually he lost it. The claims of the Fulton family were also brought forward, when I was present, in the House of Representatives. Fulton was certainly the father of steam-navigation in America, and to his exertions and intelligence America may consider herself in a great degree indebted for her present prosperity. It once required six or seven months to ascend the Mississippi, a passage which is now performed in fifteen days. Had it not been for Fulton's genius, the West would still have remained a wild desert, and the now flourishing cotton-growing States would not yet have yielded the crops which are the staple of the Union. The claim of his surviving relatives was a mere nothing, in comparison with the debt of gratitude owing to that great man: yet member after member rose to oppose it with all the ingenuity of argument. One asserted that the merit of the invention did not belong to Fulton; another, that even if it did, his relatives certainly could found no claim upon it; a third rose and declared that he would prove that, so far from the government owing money to Fulton, Fulton was in debt to the government. And thus did they go on, showing to their constituents how great was their consideration for the public money, and to the world (if another proof were required) how little gratitude is to be found in a democracy. The bill was thrown out, and the race of Fultons left to the chance of starving, for anything that the American nation seemed to care to the contrary. Whitney, the inventor of the gin for clearing the cotton of its seeds (perhaps the next greatest boon ever given to America), was treated in the same way. And yet, on talking over the question, there were few of the members who did not individually acknowledge the justice of their claims, and the duty of the State to attend to them: but the *majority* would not have permitted it, and when they went back to their constituents to be re-elected, it would have been urged against them that they had voted away the public money, and they would have had the difficult task of proving that the interests of the *majority*, and of the majority alone, had regulated their conduct in Congress.

There was one event of exciting interest which occurred during my short stay at Washington, and which engrossed the minds of every individual: the fatal duel between Mr Graves and Mr Cilley. Not only the duel itself, but what took place after it, was to me, as a stranger, a subject for grave reflection.

Notice of Mr Cilley's decease having been formally given to the House, it adjourned for a day or two, as a mark of respect, and a day was appointed for the funeral.

The coffin containing the body was brought into the House of Representatives, and there lay in state, as it were. The members of Senate and the Supreme Court were summoned to attend, whilst an eulogium was passed on the merits and virtues of the deceased by the surviving representative of the State of Maine: the funeral sermon was delivered by one clergyman, and an exhortation by another, after which the coffin was carried out to be placed in the hearse. The following printed order of the procession was distributed, that it might be rigidly attended to by the members of the two Houses and the Supreme Court:—

Order of Arrangements for the Funeral of The Hon. Jonathan Cilley, Late a Representative in Congress, from the State of Maine.

The Committee of Arrangement, Pall-bearers, and Mourners, will attend at the late residence of the deceased, at Mr Birth's, in third-street, at 11 o'clock AM, Tuesday, February 27th; at which time the remains will be removed, in charge of the Committee of Arrangements, attended by the Serjeant-at-arms of the House of Representatives, to the hall of the House.

At 12 o'clock, meridian, funeral service will be performed in the hall of the House of Representatives, and immediately after the procession will move to the place of interment, in the following order,—

The Chaplains of both Houses.

Committee of Arrangement, viz:

Mr Evans, of Maine.

Mr Atherton, of NH. Mr Coles, of Va.

Mr Conner, of NC. Mr Johnson, of La.

Mr Whittlesey, of Ohio, Mr Fillmore, of NV.

Pall-bearers, viz:

Mr Thomas, of Maryland. Mr Campbell, of SC.

Mr Williams, of NH. Mr White, of Indiana.

Mr Ogle, of Pennsylvania. Mr Martin, of Ala.

The Family and Friends of the deceased.

The Members of the House of Representatives, and Senators from Maine, as Mourners.

The Serjeant-at-Arms of the House of Representatives.

The House of Representatives, preceded by their Speaker and Clerk.

The Serjeant-at-Arms of the Senate.

The Senate of the United States, preceded by the Vice President and their Secretary.

The President of the United States.

The Heads of Departments.

Judges of the Supreme Court, and its Officers.

Foreign Ministers.

Citizens and Strangers.

February, 26th, 1838.

The burial-ground being at some distance, carriages were provided for the whole of the company, and the procession even then was more than half a mile long. I walked there to witness the whole proceeding; but when the body had been deposited in the vault, I found, on my return, a vacant seat in one of the carriages, in which were two Americans, who went under the head of "Citizens." They were very much inclined to be communicative. One of them observed of the clergyman, who, in his exhortation, had expressed himself very forcibly against the practice of duelling:—

"Well, I reckon that chaplain won't be 'lected next year, and sarve him right too; he did pitch it in rather too strong for the members; that last flourish of his was enough to raise all their danders."

To the other, who was a more staid sort of personage, I put the question, how long did he think this tragical event, and the severe observations on duelling, would stop the practice.

"Well, I reckon three days, or thereabouts," replied the man.

I am afraid that the man is not far out in his calculation. Virginia. Mississippi, Louisiana, and now Congress, as respects the district of Columbia, in which Washington is built, have all passed severe laws against the practice of duelling, which is universal; but they are no more than dead letters. The spirit of their institutions is adverse to such laws; and duelling always has been, and always will be, one of the evils of democracy. I have, I believe, before observed, that in many points a young nation is, in all its faults, very like to a young individual; and this is one in which the comparison holds good. But there are other causes for, and other incentives to this practice, besides the false idea that it is a proof of courage. Slander and detraction are the inseparable evils of a democracy; and as neither public nor private characters are spared, and the law is impotent to protect them, men have no other resource than to defend their reputations with their lives, or to deter the defamer by the risk which he must incur.

And where political animosities are carried to such a length as they are in this exciting climate, there is no time given for coolness and reflection. Indeed, for one American who would attempt to prevent a duel, there are ten who would urge the parties on to the conflict. I recollect a gentleman introducing me to the son of another gentleman who was present. The lad, who was about fourteen, I should think, shortly after left the room; and then the gentleman told me, before the boy's father, that the lad was one of the right sort, having already fought, and wounded his man; and the father smiled complacently at this tribute to the character of his son. The majority of the editors of the newspapers in America are constantly practising with the pistol, that they may be ready when called upon, and are most of them very good shots. In fact, they could not well refuse to fight, being all of them colonels, majors, or generals —"*tam Marte quam Mercurio*." But the worst feature in the American system of duelling is, that they do not go out, as we do in this country, to satisfy honour, but with the determination to kill. Independently of general practice, immediately after a challenge has been given and received, each party practises as much as he can.

And now let us examine into the particulars of this duel between Mr Graves and Mr Cilley. It was well known that Mr Graves had hardly ever fired a rifle in his life. Mr Cilley, on the contrary, was an excellent rifle-shot, constantly in practice: it was well known, also, that he intended to fix a quarrel upon one of the southern members, as he had publicly said he would. He brought his rifle down to Washington with him; he practised with it almost every day, and more regularly so after he had sent the challenge, and it had been accepted. It so happened that, contrary to the expectations of all parties, Mr Cilley, instead of Mr Graves, was the party who fell; but surely, if ever there was a man who *premeditated murder*, it was Mr Cilley. I state this, not with the wish to assail Mr Cilley's character, as I believe that almost any other American would have done the same thing; for whatever license society will give, that will every man take, and moreover, from habit, will not consider it as wrong.

But my reason for pointing out all this is to show that society must be in a very loose state, and the standard of morality must be indeed low in a nation, when a man who has fallen in such a manner, a man who, had he killed Mr Graves, would, according to the laws of our country, have been condemned and executed for murder, (inasmuch as from his practising after the challenge was given, it would have proved *malice prepense*, on his part) should now, because he falls in the attempt, have *honours paid to his remains*, much *greater* than we paid to those of *Nelson*, when he fell so nobly in his country's cause. The chief magistrate of England, which is the king, did not follow Nelson to the grave; while the chief magistrate of the United States (attended by the Supreme Court and judges, the Senate, the Representatives) does honour to the remains of one who, if Providence had not checked him in his career, would have been considered as a cold-blooded murderer.

And yet the Americans are continually dinning into my ears—Captain Marryat, we are a very moral people! Again, I repeat, the Americans are the happiest people in the world in their own delusions. If they wish to be a moral people, the government must show them some better example than that of paying those honours to vice and immorality which are only due to honour and to virtue.

Legislation on Duelling.—The legislature of Mississippi has prohibited duelling, and the parties implicated, in any instance, are declared to be ineligible to office. The act also imposes a fine of not less than three hundred dollars, and not more than one thousand, and an imprisonment of not less than six months: and in case of the death of one of the parties, the survivor is to be held chargeable with the payment of the debts of his antagonist. The estate of the party who falls in the combat is to be exonerated from such debts until the surviving party be first prosecuted to insolvency. The seconds are made subject to incapacity to hold office, fine, and imprisonment.

Anti-Duelling Bill.

The bill, as it passed the senate, is in the following words:—

A Bill to prohibit the giving or accepting, within the District of Columbia, of a Challenge to fight a Duel, and for the punishment thereof.

Be it enacted by the Senate and House of Representatives of the United States of America, in Congress assembled, That if any person shall, in the district of Columbia, challenge another to fight a duel, or shall send or deliver any written or verbal message purporting or intending to be such challenge, or shall accept any such challenge or message, or shall knowingly carry or deliver any such challenge or message, or shall knowingly carry or deliver an acceptance of such challenge or message to fight a duel in or out of said district, and such duel shall be fought in or out of said district; and if either of the parties thereto shall be slain or mortally wounded in such duel, the surviving party to such duel, and every person carrying or delivering such challenge or message, or acceptance of such challenge or message as aforesaid, and all others aiding and abetting therein, shall be deemed guilty of felony, and upon conviction thereof; in any court competent to the trial thereof, in the said district, shall be punished by imprisonment and confinement to hard labour in the penitentiary for a term not exceeding ten years, nor less than five years, in the discretion of the court.

Sec. 2. And be it further enacted, that if any person shall give or send, or cause to be given or sent, to any person in the district of Columbia, any challenge to fight a duel, or to engage in single combat with any deadly or dangerous instrument or weapon whatever, or shall be the bearer of any such challenge, every person so giving or sending, or causing to be given or sent, or accepting such challenge, or being the bearer thereof, and every person aiding or abetting in the giving, sending, or accepting such challenge, shall be deemed guilty of a high crime and misdemeanor, and on conviction thereof in any court competent to try the same, in the said district, shall be punished by imprisonment and confinement to hard labour in the penitentiary, for a term not exceeding ten years, nor less than five years, in the discretion of the court.

Sec. 3. And be it further enacted, that if any person shall assault, strike, beat, or wound, or cause to be assaulted, stricken, beaten, or wounded, any person in the district of Columbia for declining or refusing to accept any challenge to fight a duel, or to engage in single combat with any deadly or dangerous instrument or weapon whatever, or shall, post or publish, or cause to be posted or published, any writing charging any such person so declining or refusing to accept any such challenge to be a coward, or using any other opprobrious or injurious language therein, tending to deride and disgrace such person, for so offending, on conviction thereof in any court competent to trial thereof in said district, shall be punished by confinement to hard labour in the penitentiary for a term not exceeding seven years, nor less than three years, in the discretion of the court.

Sec. 4. And be it further enacted, that in addition to the oath now to be prescribed by law to be administered to the grand jury in the district of Columbia, they shall be sworn faithfully and impartially to inquire into, and true presentment make of, all offences against this act.

Volume Two—Chapter Two.

I have been for some time journeying through the province of Upper Canada, and, on the whole, I consider it the finest portion of all North America. In America every degree of longitude which you proceed west, is equal to a degree of latitude to the southward in increasing the mildness of the temperature. Upper Canada, which is not so far west as to sever you from the civilised world, has every possible advantage of navigation, and is at the same time, from being nearly surrounded by water, much milder than the American States to the southward of it. Every thing grows well and flourishes in Upper Canada; even tobacco, which requires a very warm atmosphere. The land of this province is excellent, but it is a hard land to clear, the timber being very close and of a very large size. A certain proof of the value of the land of Upper Canada is, that there are already so many Americans who have settled there. Most of them had originally emigrated to establish themselves in the neighbouring state of Michigan; but the greater part of that state is at present so unhealthy from swamps, and the people suffer so much from fever and agues, that the emigrants have fallen back upon Upper Canada, which (a very small portion of it excepted) is the most healthy portion of North America. I have before observed, that the Rideau and Welland canals, splendid works as they are, are too much in advance of the country: and had the Government spent one-half the money in opening communications and making good roads, the province would have been much more benefited. In the United States you have a singular proof of the advantages of communication; in the old continent, towns and villages rise up first, and the communications, are made afterwards; in the United States, the roads are made first, and when made, towns and villages make their appearance on each side of them, just as the birds drop down for their aliment upon the fresh furrows made across the fallow by the plough.

From Hamilton, on Lake Ontario, to Bradford, the country is very beautifully broken and undulating, occasionally precipitate and hilly. You pass through forests of splendid timber, chiefly fir, but of a size which is surprising. Here are masts for "tall admirals," so lofty that you could not well perceive a squirrel, or even a large animal, if upon one of the topmast boughs. The pine forests are diversified by the oak; you sometimes pass through six or seven miles of the first description of timber, which gradually changes, until you have six or seven miles of forest composed entirely of oak. The road is repairing and levelling, preparatory to its being macadamised—certainly not before it was required, for it is at present execrable throughout the whole province. Every mile or so you descend into a hollow, at the bottom of which is what they term a *mud hole*, that is, a certain quantity of water and mud, which is of a depth unknown, but which you must fathom by passing through it. To give an Englishman an idea of the roads is not easy; I can only say that it is very possible for a horse to be drowned in one of the *ruts*, and for a pair of them to disappear, waggon and all, in a *mud hole*.

At Bradford, on Grand River, are located some remnants of the Mohawk tribe of Indians; they are more than demi-civilised; they till their farms, and have plenty of horses and cattle. A smart looking Indian drove into town, when I was there, in a waggon with a pair of good horses; in the waggon were some daughters of one of their chiefs; they were very richly dressed after their own fashion, their petticoats and leggings being worked with beads to the height of two feet from the bottom, and in very good taste; and they wore beaver hats and feathers of a pattern which used formerly to be much in vogue with the ladies of the seamen at Plymouth and Portsmouth.

From Bradford to London the roads are *comparatively* good; the country rises, and the plain is nearly one hundred feet above the level of the river Thames, a beautifully wide stream, whose two branches join at the site of this town. The land here is considered to be the finest in the whole province, and the country the most healthy.

From London to Chatham the roads are really *awful*. I had the pleasure of tumbling over head and ears into a mud hole, at about twelve o'clock at night; the horses were with difficulty saved, and the waggon remained *fixed* for upwards of three hours, during which we laboured hard, and were refreshed with plentiful showers of rain.

Chatham, on the river Thames, is at present a sad dirty hole; but, as the country rises, will be a place of great importance. From Chatham I embarked in the steam-boat, and went down the Thames into Lake St. Clair, and from thence to Sandwich, having passed through the finest country, the most beautiful land, and about the most infamous roads that are to be met with in all America.

Within these last seven or eight years the lakes have risen; many hypotheses have been offered to account for this change. I do not coincide with any of the opinions which I have heard, yet, at the same time, it is but fair to acknowledge that I can offer none of my own. It is quite a mystery. The consequence of this rising of the waters is, that some of the finest farms at the month of the river Thames and on Lake St. Clair, occupied by the old Canadian settlers, are, and have been for two or three years under water. These Canadians have not removed; they are waiting for the water to subside; their houses stand in the lake, the basements being under water, and they occupy the first floors with their families, communicating by boats. As they cannot cultivate their land, they shoot and fish. Several miles on each side of the mouth of the river Thames the water is studded with these houses, which have, as may be supposed, a very forlorn appearance, especially as the top rail of the fences is generally above water, marking out the fields which are now tenanted by fish instead of cattle.

Went out with a party into the bush, as it is termed, to see some land which had been purchased. Part of the road was up to the saddle-flaps under water, from the rise of the lakes. We soon entered the woods, not so thickly growing but that our horses could pass through them, had it not been for the obstacles below our feet. At every third step a tree lay across the path, forming, by its obstruction to the drainage, a pool of water; but the Canadian horses are so accustomed to this that they very coolly walked over them, although some were two feet in diameter. They never attempted to jump, but deliberately put one foot over and the other—with equal dexterity avoiding the stumps and sunken logs concealed under water. An English horse would have been foundered before he had proceeded fifty yards. Sometimes we would be for miles wading through swamps; at others the land rose, and then it was clear and dry, and we could gallop under the oak trees.

We continued till noon before we could arrive at the land in question, forcing our way through the woods, and guided by the blazing of the trees. *Blazing* is cutting off a portion of the bark of the trees on both sides of the road with an axe, and these marks, which will remain for many years, serve as a guide. If lost in the woods you have but to look out for a blaze, and by following it you are certain to arrive at some inhabited place. We found the land at last, which was high, dry, and covered with large oak trees. A herd of deer bounded past us as we approached the river, which ran through it; and we could perceive the flocks of wild turkeys at a distance, running almost as fast as the deer. The river was choked by trees which had fallen across its bed, damming up its stream, and spreading it over the land; but the scene was very beautiful and wild, and I could not help fancying what a pretty spot it would one day be, when it should be cleared, and farm-houses built on the banks of the river.

On our way we called upon a man who had been in the hush but a year or so; he had a wife and six children. He was young and healthy, and although he had been used to a life of *literary* idleness, he had made up his mind to the change, and taken up the axe—a thing very few people can do. I never saw a person apparently more cheerful and contented. He had already cleared away about fifteen acres, and had procured a summer crop from off a portion of it the year before! having no other assistance than his two boys, one thirteen and the other fourteen years old, healthy, but not powerfully built lads. When we called upon him, he was busied in burning the felled timber, and planting Indian corn. One of his boys was fencing-in the ground. I went with the man into his log-hut, which was large and convenient, and found his wife working at her needle, and three little girls all as busy as bees; the eldest of these girls was not twelve years old, yet she cooked, baked, washed, and, with the assistance of her two little sisters, did all that was required for the household. After a short repose, we went out again into the clearing, when one of my friends asked him how he got on with his axe? "Pretty well," replied he, laughing; "I'll show you." He led us to where a button-wood tree was lying; the trunk was at least ninety feet long, and the diameter where it had been cut through between five and six feet; it was an enormous tree. "And did you cut that down yourself?" enquired my companion, who was an old settler. "Not quite; but I cut through the north half while my two boys cut through the south; we did it between us." This was really astonishing, for if these two lads could cut through half the tree, it is evident that they could have cut it down altogether. We had here a proof of how useful children can be made at an early age.

We promised to call upon him on our return; which we did. We found him sitting with his wife in his log-house; it was five o'clock in the afternoon; he told us "work was over now, and that the children had gone into the bush to play." They had all worked from five o'clock in the morning, and had since learnt their lessons. We heard their laughter ringing in the woods at a distance.

Now this is rather a remarkable instance among settlers, as I shall hereafter explain. Had this man been a bachelor, he would have been, in all probability, a drunkard; but, with his family, he was a happy, contented, and thriving man. We parted with him, and arrived at Windsor, opposite Detroit, very tired, having been, with little exception, fourteen hours in the saddle.

I took cold, and was laid up with a fever. I mention this, not as any thing interesting to the reader, but merely to show what you may expect when you travel in these countries. I had been in bed three days, when my landlady came into the room. "Well, captain, how do you find yourself by this time?" "Oh, I am a little better, thank you," replied I. "Well, I am glad of it, because I want to whitewash your room; for if the coloured man stops to do it to-morrow, he'll be for charging us another quarter of a dollar." "But I am not able to leave my room." "Well, then, I'll speak to him; I dare say he won't mind your being in bed while he whitewashes."

I have often remarked the strange effects of intoxication, and the different manner in which persons are affected with liquor. When I was on the road from London to Chatham, a man who was very much intoxicated got into the waggon, and sat beside me. As people in that state generally are, he was excessively familiar; and although jerked off with no small degree of violence, would continue, until we arrived at the inn where we were to sup, to attempt to lay his head upon my shoulder.

As soon as we arrived, supper was announced. At first he refused to take any, but on the artful landlady bawling in his ear, that all *gentlemen* supped when they arrived, he hesitated to consider (which certainly was not at all necessary) whether he was not bound to take some. Another very important remark of the hostess, which was, that he would have nothing to eat until the next morning, it being then eleven o'clock at night, decided him, and he staggered in, observing, "Nothing to eat till next morning! well, I never thought of that." He sat down opposite to me, at the same table. It appeared as if his *vision was inverted* by the quantity of liquor which he had taken; everything close to him on the table he considered to be out of his reach, whilst everything at a distance he attempted to lay hold of. He sat up as erect as he could, balancing himself so as not to appear *canned*, and fixing his eyes upon me, said, "Sir, I'll trouble you—for some fried ham." Now the ham was in the dish next to him, and altogether out of my reach; I told him so. "Sir," said he again, "as a gentleman, I ask you to give me some of that fried ham." Amused with the curious demand, I rose from my chair, went round to him and helped him. "Shall I give you a potato," said I, the potatoes being at my end of the table, and I not wishing to rise again. "No, Sir," replied he, "I can help myself to them." He made a dash at them, but did not reach them; then made another, and another, till he lost his balance, and lay down upon his plate; this time he gained the potatoes, helped himself, and commenced eating. After a few minutes he again fixed his eyes upon me. "Sir, I'll trouble you—for the pickles." They were actually under his nose, and I pointed them out to him. "I believe, Sir, I asked you for the pickles," repeated he, after a time. "Well, there they are," replied I, wishing to see what he would do. "Sir, are you a gentleman—as a gentleman—I ask you as a gentleman, for them 'ere pickles." It was impossible to resist this appeal, so I rose and helped him. I was now convinced that his vision was somehow or another inverted, and to prove it, when he asked me for the salt, which was within his reach, I removed it farther off. "Thank ye, Sir," said he, sprawling over the table after it. The circumstance, absurd as it was, was really a subject for the investigation of Dr Brewster.

At Windsor, which is directly opposite to Detroit, where the river is about half a mile across, are stores of English goods, sent there entirely for the supply of the Americans, by smugglers. There is also a row of tailor shops, for cloth is a very dear article in America, and costs nearly double the price it does in the English provinces. The Americans go over there, and are measured for a suit of clothes which, when ready, they put on, and cross back to Detroit with their old clothes in a bundle. The smuggling is already very extensive, and will, of course, increase as the Western country becomes more populous.

Near Windsor and Sandwich are several villages of free blacks, probably the major portion of them having been assisted in their escape by the Abolitionists. They are not very good neighbours from their propensity to thieving, which either is innate, or, as Miss Martineau would have it, is the effect of slavery. I shall not dispute that point; but it is certain that they are most inveterately hostile to the Americans, and will fight to the last, from the dread of being again subjected to their former masters. They are an excellent frontier population; and in the last troubles they proved how valuable they would become, in case their services were more seriously required.

Volume Two—Chapter Three.

Once more on board of the Michigan, one of the best vessels on Lake Erie; as usual, full of emigrants, chiefly Irish. It is impossible not to feel compassion for these poor people, wearied as they are with confinement and suffering, and yet they do compose occasionally about as laughable a group as can well be conceived. In the first place, they bring out with them from Ireland, articles which no other people would consider worth the carriage. I saw one Irish woman who had old tin tea pots; there was but one spout among the whole, and I believe not one bottom really sound and good. And then their costumes, more particularly the fitting out of the children, who are not troubled with any extra supply of clothes at any time! I have witnessed the seat of an old pair of corduroy trowsers transformed into a sort of bonnet for a laughing fair-haired girl. But what amused me more was the very reverse of this arrangement; a boy's father had just put a patch upon the hinder part of his son's trousers; and cloth not being at hand, he had, as an expedient for stopping the gap, inserted a piece of an old straw bonnet; in so doing he had not taken the precaution to put the smooth side of the plait inwards, and, in consequence, young Teddy when he first sat down felt rather uncomfortable. "What's the matter wid ye, Teddy; what makes ye wriggle about in that way? Sit aisy, man; sure enough, havn't ye a strait-bottomed chair to sit down upon all the rest of your journey, which is more than your father ever had before you?" And then their turning in for the night! A single bed will contain one adult and four little ones at one end, and another adult and two half-grown at the other. But they are all packed away so snug and close, and not one venturing to move, there appears to be room for all.

We stopped half an hour at Mackinaw to take in wood, and then started for Green Bay, in the Wisconsin territory. Green Bay is a military station; it is a pretty little place, with soil as rich as garden mould. The Fox river debouches here, but the navigation is checked a few miles above the town by the rapids, which have been dammed up into a water power; yet there is no doubt that as soon as the whole of the Wisconsin lands are offered for sale by the American Government, the river will be made navigable up to its meeting with the Wisconsin, which falls into the Mississippi. There is only a portage of a mile and a half between the two, through which a canal will be cut, and then there will be another junction between the lakes and the Far West. It was my original intention to have taken the usual route by Chicago and Galena to St. Louis, but I fell in with Major F—, with whom I had been previously acquainted, who informed me that he was about to send a detachment of troops from Green Bay to Fort Winnebago, across Wisconsin territory. As this afforded me an opportunity of seeing the country, which seldom occurs, I availed myself of an offer to join the party. The detachment consisted of about one hundred recruits, nearly the whole of them Canada patriots, as they are usually called, who, having failed in taking the provinces from John Bull, were fain to accept the shilling from uncle Sam.

Major F— accompanied us to pay the troops at the fort, and we therefore had five waggons with us, loaded with a considerable quantity of bread and pork, and not quite so large a proportion of specie, the latter not having as yet become plentiful again in the United States. We set off, and marched fifteen miles in about half a day, passing through the settlement Des Peres, which is situated at the rapids of the Fox river. Formerly they were called the Rapids des Peres, from a Jesuit college which had been established there by the French. Our course lay along the banks of the Fox river, a beautiful swift stream pouring down between high ridges, covered with fine oak timber.

The American Government have disposed of all the land on the banks of this river and the Lake Winnebago, and consequently it is well settled; but the Winnebago territory in Wisconsin, lately purchased of the Winnebago Indians, and comprising all the prairie land and rich mineral country from Galena to Mineral Point, is not yet offered for sale: when it is, it will be eagerly purchased; and the American Government, as it only paid the Indians at the rate of one cent and a fraction per acre, will make an enormous profit by the speculation. Well may the Indians be said, like Esau, to part with their birthright for a mess of pottage; but, in truth, they are *compelled* to sell—the purchase-money being a mere subterfuge, by which it may *appear* as if their lands were not wrested from them, although, in fact, it is.

On the second day we continued our march along the banks of the Fox river, which, as we advanced, continued to be well settled, and would have been more so, if some of the best land had not fallen, as usual, into the hands of speculators, who, aware of its value, hold out that they may obtain a high price for it. The country through which we passed was undulating, consisting of a succession of ridges, covered with oaks of a large size, but not growing close as in a forest; you could gallop your horse through any part of it. The tracks of deer were frequent, but we saw but one herd of fifteen, and that was at a distance. We now left the banks of the river, and cut across the country to Fond du Lac, at the bottom of Lake Winnebago, of which we had had already an occasional glimpse through the openings of the forest. The deer were too wild to allow of our getting near them; so I was obliged to content myself with shooting wood pigeons, which were very plentiful.

On the night of the third day we encamped upon a very high ridge; as usual studded with oak trees. The term used here to distinguish this variety of timber land from the impervious woods is *oak openings*. I never saw a more beautiful view than that which was afforded us from our encampment. From the high ground upon which our tents were pitched, we looked down to the left, upon a prairie flat and level as a billiard-table, extending, as far as the eye could scan, one rich surface of unrivalled green. To the right the prairie gradually changed to oak openings, and then to a thick forest, the topmost boughs and heads of which were level with our tents. Beyond them was the whole broad expanse of the Winnebago lake, smooth and reflecting like a mirror the brilliant tints of the setting sun, which disappeared, leaving a portion of his glory behind him; while the moon in her ascent, with the dark portion of her disk as clearly defined as that which was lighted, gradually increased in brilliancy, and the stars twinkled in the clear sky. We watched the features of the landscape gradually fading from our sight, until nothing was left but broad masses partially lighted up by the young moon.

Nor was the foreground less picturesque: the spreading oaks, the tents of the soldiers, the waggons drawn up with the horses tethered, all lighted up by the blaze of our large fires. Now, when I say our large fires, I mean the *large* fires of *America*, consisting of three or four oak trees, containing a load of wood each, besides many large boughs and branches, altogether forming a fire some twenty or thirty feet long, with flames flickering up twice as high as one's head. At a certain distance from this blazing pile you may perceive what in another situation would be considered as a large coffee-pot (before this huge fire it makes a very diminutive appearance). It is placed over some embers drawn out from the mass, which would have soon burnt up coffee-pot and coffee all together; and at a still more respectful distance you may perceive small rods, not above four or five feet long, bifurcated at the smaller end, and fixed by the larger in the ground, so as to hang towards the huge fire, at an angle of forty degrees, like so many tiny fishing-rods. These rods have at their bifurcated ends a piece of pork or ham, or of bread, or perhaps of venison, for we bought some, not having shot any: they are all private property, as each party cooks for himself. Seeing these rods at some distance, you might almost imagine that they were the fishing-rods of little imps bobbing for salamanders in the fiery furnace.

In the mean time, while the meat is cooking and the coffee is boiling, the brandy and whisky are severely taxed, as we lie upon our cloaks and buffalo skins at the front of our tents. There certainly is a charm in this wild sort of life, which wins upon people the more they practise it; nor can it be wondered at: our wants are in reality so few and so easily satisfied, without the restraint of form and ceremony. How often, in my wanderings, have I felt the truth of Shakespeare's lines in "As You Like It."

"Now,   my   co-mates   and   partners   in   exile,
Hath   not   old   custom   made   this   life   more   sweet
Than   that   of   painted   pomp?   Are   not   these   woods
More   free   from   peril   than   the   envious   court?
Here   feel   we   but   the   penalty   of   Adam—
The seasons' difference."

On the fourth day we descended, crossed the wide prairie, and arrived at the Fond du Lac, where we again fell in with the Fox river, which runs through the Winnebago lake. The roads through the forests had been very bad, and the men and horses showed signs of fatigue; but we had now passed through all the thickly wooded country, and had entered into the prairie country, extending to Fort Winnebago, and which was beautiful beyond concoction. Its features alone can be described; but its effects can only be felt by being seen. The prairies here are not very large, seldom being above six or seven miles in length or breadth; generally speaking, they lie in gentle undulating flats, and the ridges and hills between them are composed of oak openings. To form an idea of these oak openings, imagine an inland country covered with splendid trees, about as thickly planted as in our English parks; in fact, it is English park scenery, Nature having here spontaneously produced what it has been the care and labour of centuries in our own country to effect. Sometimes the prairie will rise and extend along the hills, and assume an undulating appearance, like the long swell of the ocean; it is then called rolling prairie.

Often, when I looked down upon some fifteen or twenty thousand acres of these prairies, full of rich grass, without one animal, tame or wild, to be seen, I would fancy what thousands of cattle will, in a few years, be luxuriating in those pastures, which, since the herds of buffalo have retreated from them, are now useless, and throwing up each year a fresh crop, to seed and to die unheeded.

On our way we had fallen in with a young Frenchman, who had purchased some land at Fond du Lac, and was proceeding there in company with an American, whom he had hired to settle on it. I now parted company with him; he had gone out with me in my shooting excursions, and talked of nothing but his purchase: it had water; it had a waterfall; it had, in fact, everything that he could desire; but he thought that, after two years, he would go home and get a wife: a Paradise without an Eve would be no Paradise at all.

The price of labour is, as may be supposed, very high in this part of the country. Hiring by the year, you find a man in food, board, and washing, and pay him three hundred dollars per annum (about 70 pounds English.)

The last night that we bivouacked out was the only unfortunate one. We had been all comfortably settled for the night, and fast asleep, when a sudden storm came on, accompanied with such torrents of rain as would have washed us out of our tents, if they had not been already blown down by the violence of the gale. Had we had any warning, we should have provided against it; as it was, we made up huge fires, which defied the rain; and thus we remained till day-light, the rain pouring on us, while the heat of the fire drying us almost as fast as we got wet, each man threw up a column of steam from his still saturating and still heated garments. Every night we encamped where there was a run of water, and plenty of dead timber for our fires; and thus did we go on, emptying our waggons daily of the bread and pork, and filling up the vacancies left by the removal of the empty casks with the sick and lame, until at last we arrived at Fort Winnebago.

Volume Two—Chapter Four.

We had not to arrive at the fort to receive a welcome, for when we were still distant about seven miles, the officers of the garrison, who had notice of our coming, made their appearance on horseback, bringing a britchska and grey horses for our accommodation. Those who were not on duty (and I was one) accepted the invitation, and we drove in upon a road which, indeed, for the last thirty miles, had been as level as the best in England. The carriage was followed by pointers, hounds, and a variety of dogs, who were off duty like ourselves, and who appeared quite as much delighted with their run as we were tired with ours. The medical officer attached to the fort, an old friend and correspondent of Mr Lee of Philadelphia, received me with all kindness, and immediately installed me into one of the rooms in the hospital.

Fort Winnebago is situated between the Fox and Wisconsin rivers at the portage, the two rivers being about a mile and a-half apart; the Fox river running east, and giving its waters to Lake Michigan at Green Bay, while the Wisconsin turns to the west, and runs into the Mississippi at Prairie du Chien. The fort is merely a square of barracks, connected together with palisades, to protect it from the Indians; and it is hardly sufficiently strong for even that purpose. It is beautifully situated, and when the country fills up will become a place of importance. Most of the officers are unmarried, and live a very quiet, and secluded, but not unpleasant life. I stayed there two days, much pleased with the society and the kindness shown to me; but an opportunity of descending the Wisconsin to Prairie du Chien, in a keel-boat, having presented itself, I availed myself of an invitation to join the party, instead of proceeding by land to Galena, as had been my original intention.

The boat had been towed up the Wisconsin with a cargo of flour for the garrison; and a portion of the officers having been ordered down to Prairie du Chien, they had obtained this large boat to transport themselves, families, furniture, and horses, all at once, down to their destination. The boat was about one hundred and twenty feet long, covered in to the height of six feet above the gunnel, and very much in appearance like the Noah's Ark given to children, excepting that the roof was flat. It was an unwieldy craft, and, to manage it, it required at least twenty-five men with poles and long sweeps; but the army gentlemen had decided that, as we were to go down with the stream, six men with short oars would be sufficient—a very great mistake. In every other respect she was badly found, as we term it at sea, having but one old piece of rope to hang on with, and one axe. Our freight consisted of furniture stowed forward and aft, with a horse and cow. In a cabin in the centre we had a lady and five children, one maid and two officers. Our crew was composed of six soldiers, a servant, and a French *half bred* to pilot us down the river. All Winnebago came out to see us start; and as soon as the rope was cast off, away we went down with the strong current at the rate of five miles an hour. The river passed through forests of oak, the large limbs of which hung from fifteen to twenty feet over the banks on each side; sometimes whole trees lay prostrate in the stream, held by their roots still partially remaining in the ground, while their trunks and branches offering resistance to the swift current, created a succession of small masses of froth, which floated away on the dark green water.

We had not proceeded far, before we found that it was impossible to manage such a large and cumbrous vessel with our few hands; we were almost at the mercy of the current, which appeared to increase in rapidity every minute; however, by exertion and good management, we contrived to keep in the middle of the stream until the wind sprung up and drove us on to the southern bank of the river, and then all was cracking and tearing away of the wood-work, breaking of limbs from the projecting trees, the snapping, cracking, screaming, hallooing, and confusion. As fast as we cleared ourselves of one tree, the current bore us down upon another; as soon as we were clear above water, we were foul and entangled below. It was a pretty general average; but, what was worse than all a snag had intercepted and unshipped our rudder, and we were floating away from it, as it still remained fixed upon the sunken tree. We had no boat with us, not oven a *dug-out*—(a canoe made out of the trunk of a tree)—so one of the men climbed on shore by the limbs of an oak, and went back to disengage it. He did so, but not being able to resist the force of the stream, down he and the rudder came together—his only chance of salvation being that of our catching him as he came past us. This we fortunately succeeded in effecting; and then hanging on by our old piece of rope to the banks of the river, after an hour's delay we contrived to re-ship our rudder, and proceeded on our voyage, which was a continuation of the same eventful history. Every half hour we found ourselves wedged in between the spreading limbs of the oaks, and were obliged to have recourse to the axe to clear ourselves: and on every occasion we lost a further portion of the frame-work of our boat, either from the roof, the sides, or by the tearing away of the stancheons themselves.

A little before sunset, we were again swept on to the bank with such force as to draw the pintles of our rudder. This finished us for the day: before it could be replaced, it was time to make fast for the night; so there we lay, holding by our rotten piece of rope, which cracked and strained to such a degree, as inclined us to speculate upon where we might find ourselves in the morning. However, we could not help ourselves, so we landed, made a large fire, and cooked our victuals; not, however, venturing to wander away far, on account of the rattle-snakes, which here abounded. Perhaps there is no portion of America in which the rattle-snakes are so large and so numerous as in Wisconsin. There are two varieties: the black rattle-snake, that frequents marshy spots, and renders it rather dangerous to shoot snipes and ducks; and the yellow, which takes up its abode in the rocks and dry places. Dr F— told me that he had killed, inside of the fort Winnebago, one of the latter species, between seven and eight feet long. The rattle-snake, although its poison is so fatal, is in fact not a very dangerous animal, and people are seldom bitten by it. This arises from two causes: first, that it invariably gives you notice of its presence by its rattle; and secondly, that it always coils itself up like a watch-spring before it strikes, and then darts forward only about its own length. Where they are common, the people generally carry with them a vial of ammonia, which, if instantly applied to the bite, will at least prevent death. The copper-head is a snake of a much more dangerous nature, from its giving no warning, and its poison being equally active.

This river has been very appropriately named by the Indians the 'Stream of the Thousand Isles,' as it is studded with them; indeed, every quarter of a mile you find one or two in its channel. The scenery is fine, as the river runs through high ridges, covered with oak to their summits; sometimes these ridges are backed by higher cliffs and mountains, which halfway up are of a verdant green, and above that present horizontal strata of calcareous rock of rich grey tints, having, at a distance, very much the appearance of the dilapidated castles on the Rhine.

The scenery, though not so grand as the highlands of the Hudson, is more diversified and beautiful. The river was very full, and the current occasionally so rapid, as to leave a foam as it swept by any projecting point. We had, now that the river widened, sand banks to contend with, which required all the exertions of our insufficient crew.

On the second morning, I was very much annoyed at our having left without providing ourselves with a boat, for at the grey of dawn, we discovered that some deer had taken the river close to us, and were in midstream. Had we had a boat, we might have procured a good supply of venison. We cast off again and resumed our voyage; and without any serious accident we arrived at the shot-tower, where we remained for the night. Finding a shot-tower in such a lone wilderness as this, gives you some idea of the enterprise of the Americans; but the Galena, or lead district, commences here, on the south bank of the Wisconsin. The smelting is carried on about twelve miles inland, and the lead is brought here, made into shot, and then sent down the river to the Mississippi, by which, and its tributary streams, it is supplied to all America, west of the Alleghanies. The people were all at work when we arrived. The general distress had even affected the demand for shot, which was now considerably reduced.

On the third day we had the good fortune to have no wind, and consequently made rapid progress, without much further damage. We passed a small settlement called the English prairie—for the prairies were now occasionally mixed up with the mountain scenery. Here there was a smelting-house and a steam saw-mill.

The *diggings*, as they term the places where the lead is found (for they do not mine, but dig down from the surface,) were about sixteen miles distant. We continued our course for about twenty miles lower down, when we wound up our day's work by getting into a more serious *fix* among the trees, and eventually losing our only *axe*, which fell overboard into deep water. All Noah's Ark was in dismay, for we did not know what might happen, or what the next day might bring forth. Fortunately, it was not necessary to cut wood for firing. During the whole of this trip I was much amused with our pilot, who, fully aware of the dangers of the river, was also equally conscious that there were not sufficient means on board to avoid them; when, therefore, we were set upon a sand-bank, or pressed by the wind on the sunken trees, he always whistled; that was all he could do, and in proportion as the danger became more imminent, so did he whistle the louder, until the affair was decided by a bump or a crash, and then he was silent.

On the ensuing day we had nothing but misfortunes. We were continually twisted and twirled about, sometimes with our bows, sometimes with our stern foremost, and as often with our broadside to the stream. We were whirled against one bank, and, as soon as we were clear of that we were thrown upon the other. Having no axe to cut away, we were obliged to use our hands. Again our rudder was unshipped, and with great difficulty replaced. By this time we had lost nearly the half of the upper works of the boat, one portion after another having been torn off by the limbs of the trees as the impetuous current drove us along. To add to our difficulties, a strong wind rose against the current, and the boat became quite unmanageable. About noon, when we had gained only seven miles, the wind abated, and two Menonnomie Indians, in a *dug-out*, came alongside of us; and as it was doubtful whether we should arrive at the mouth of the river on that night, or be left upon a sand-bank, I got into the canoe with them, to go down to the landing-place, and from thence to cross over to Prairie du Chien, to inform the officers of the garrison of our condition, and obtain assistance. The canoe would exactly hold three, and no more; but we paddled swiftly down the stream, and we soon lost sight of the Noah's Ark. Independently of the canoe being so small, she had lost a large portion of her stem, so that at the least ripple of the water she took it in, and threatened us with a swim; and she was so very narrow, that the least motion would have destroyed her equilibrium and upset her. One Indian sat in the bow, the other in the stern, whilst I was doubled up in the middle. We had given the Indians some bread and pork, and after paddling about half an hour, they stopped to eat. Now, the Indian at the bow had the pork, while the one at the stern had the bread; any attempt to move, so as to hand the eatables to each other, must have upset us; so this was their plan of communication:— The one in the bow cut off a slice of pork, and putting it into the lid of a saucepan which he had with him, and floating it alongside of the canoe, gave it a sufficient momentum to make it swim to the stern, when the other took possession of it. He in the stern then cut off a piece of bread, and sent it back in return by the same conveyance. I had a flask of whisky, but they would not trust that by the same perilous little conveyance; so I had to lean forward very steadily, and hand it to the foremost, and, when he returned it to me, to lean backwards to give it the other, with whom it remained till we landed, for I could not regain it. After about an hour's more paddling, we arrived safely at the landing-place. I had some trouble to get a horse, and was obliged to go out to the fields where the men were ploughing. In doing so, I passed two or three very large snakes. At last I was mounted somehow, but without stirrups, and set off for Prairie du Chien. After riding about four miles, I had passed the mountain, and I suddenly came upon the prairie (on which were feeding several herd of cattle and horses), with the fort in the distance, and the wide waters of the Upper Mississippi flowing beyond it. I crossed the prairie, found my way into the fort, stated the situation of our party, and requested assistance. This was immediately dispatched, but on their arrival at the landing-place, they found that the keel-boat had arrived at the ferry without further difficulty. Before sunset the carriages returned with the whole party, who were comfortably accommodated in the barracks—a sufficient number of men being left with the boat to bring it round to the Mississippi, a distance of about twelve miles.

Volume Two—Chapter Five.

Prairie du Chiens is a beautiful meadow, about eight miles long by two broad, situated at the confluence of the Wisconsin and the Mississippi; it is backed with high bluffs, such as I have before described, verdant two-thirds of the way up, and crowned with rocky summits. The bluffs, as I must call them, for I know not what other name to give them, rise very abruptly, often in a sugar-loaf form, from the flat lands, and have a very striking appearance; as you look up to them, their peculiar formation and vivid green sides, contrasting with their blue and grey summits, give them the appearance of a succession of ramparts investing the prairie. The fort at the prairie, which is named Fort Crawford, is, like most other American outposts, a mere inclosure, intended to repel the attacks of Indians; but it is large and commodious, and the quarters of the officers are excellent; it is, moreover, built of stone, which is not the case with Fort Winnebago, or Fort Howard at Green Bay. The Upper Mississippi is here a beautiful clear blue stream, intersected with verdant islands, and very different in appearance from the Lower Mississippi, after it has been joined by the Missouri. The opposite shore is composed of high cliffs, covered with timber, which, not only in form, but in tint and colour, remind you very much of Glover's landscapes of the mountainous parts of Scotland and Wales.

I made one or two excursions to examine the ancient mounds which are scattered all over this district, and which have excited much speculation as to their origin; some supposing them to have been fortifications, others the burial-places of the Indians. That they have lately been used by the Indians as burial-places there is no doubt; but I suspect they were not originally raised for that purpose. A Mr Taylor has written an article in one of the periodicals, stating his opinion that they were the burial-places of chiefs; and to prove it, he asserts that some of them are thrown up in imitation of the figure of the animal which was the heraldic distinction of the chief whose remains they contain, such as the beaver, elk, etcetera. He has given drawings of some of them. That the Indians have their heraldic distinctions, their *totems*, as they call them, I know to be a fact; as I have seen the fur trader's books, containing the receipts of the chiefs, with their crests drawn by themselves, and very correctly too; but it required more imagination than I possess to make out the form of any animal in the mounds. I should rather suppose the mounds to be the remains of tenements, sometimes fortified, sometimes not, which were formerly built of mud or earth, as is still the custom in the northern portion of the Sioux country. Desertion and time have crumbled them into these mounds, which are generally to be found in a commanding situation, or in a string, as if constructed for mutual defence. On Rock River there is a long line of wall, now below the surface, which extends for a considerable distance, and is supposed to be the remains of a city built by a former race, probably the Mexican, who long since retreated before the northern race of Indians. I cannot recollect the name which has been given to it. I had not time to visit this spot; but an officer showed me some pieces of what they called the brick which composes the wall. Brick it is not—no right angles have been discovered, so far as I could learn; it appears rather as if a wall had been raised of clay, and then exposed to the action of fire, as portions of it are strongly vitrified, and others are merely hard clay. But admitting my surmises to be correct, still there is evident proof that this country was formerly peopled by a nation whose habits were very different, and in all appearance more civilised, than those of the races which were found here: and this is all that can be satisfactorily sustained. As, however, it is well substantiated that a race similar to the Mexican formerly existed on these prairie lands, the whole question may perhaps be solved by the following extract from Irving's Conquest of Florida:—

"The village of Onachili resembles most of the Indian villages of Florida. The natives always endeavoured to build upon high ground, not least to erect the house of their cacique, or chief, upon an eminence. As the country was very level and high places seldom to be found, they constructed artificial mounds of earth, capable of containing from ten to twenty houses; there resided the chief, his family, and attendants. At the foot of the hill was a square, according to the size of the village, round which were the houses of the leaders and most distinguished inhabitants."

I consider the Wisconsin territory as the finest portion of North America, not only from its soil, but its climate. The air is pure, and the winters, although severe, are dry and bracing; very different from, and more healthy than, those of the Eastern States. At Prairie du Chien every one dwelt upon the beauty of the winter, indeed they appeared to prefer it to the other seasons. The country is, as I have described it in my route from Green Bay, alternate prairie, oak openings, and forest; and the same may be said of the other side of the Mississippi, now distinguished as the district of Ioway. Limestone quarries abound; indeed, the whole of this beautiful and fertile region appears as if nature had so arranged it that man should have all difficulties cleared from before him, and have but little to do but to take possession and enjoy. There is no clearing of timber requisite; on the contrary, you have just as much as you can desire, whether for use or ornament. Prairies of fine rich grass, upon which cattle fatten in three or four months, lay spread in every direction. The soil is so fertile that you have but to turn it up to make it yield grain to any extent; and the climate is healthy, at the same time that there is more than sufficient sun in the summer and autumn to bring every crop to perfection. Land carriage is hardly required from the numerous rivers and streams which pour their waters from every direction into the Upper Mississippi. Add to all this, that the Western lands possess an inexhaustible supply of minerals, only a few feet under the surface of their rich soil—a singular and wonderful provision, as, in general, where minerals are found below, the soil above is usually arid and ungrateful. The mineral country is to the south of the Wisconsin river—at least nothing has at present been discovered north of it; but the northern part is still in the possession of the Winnebago Indians, who are waiting for the fulfilment of the treaty before they surrender it, and at present will permit no white settler to enter it. It is said that the other portions of the Wisconsin territory will come into the market this year; at present, with the exception of the Fox river and Winnebago Lake settlements, and that of Prairie du Chien, at the confluence of the two rivers Wisconsin and Mississippi, there is hardly a log-house in the whole district. The greatest annoyance at present in this western country is the quantity and variety of snakes; it is hardly safe to land upon some parts of the Wisconsin river banks, and they certainly offer a great impediment to the excursions of geologist and botanist; you are obliged to look right and left as you walk, and as for putting your hand into a hole, you would be almost certain to receive a very unwished-for and unpleasant shake to welcome you.

I ought here to explain an American law relative to what is termed squatting, that is, taking possession of land belonging to government and cultivating it: such was the custom of the back-woodsmen, and, for want of this law, it often happened that after they had cultivated a farm, the land would be applied for and purchased by some speculator, who would forcibly eject the occupant, and take possession of the improved property. A back-woodsman was not to be trifled with, and the consequences very commonly were that the new proprietor was found some fine morning with a rifle-bullet through his head. To prevent this unjust spoliation on the one part, and summary revenge on the other, a law has been passed, by which any person having taken possession of land belonging to the States Government shall, as soon as the lands have been surveyed and come into the market, have the right of purchasing the quarter section, or one hundred and sixty acres round him. Many thousands are settled in this way all over the new Western States, and this pre-emption right is one of the few laws in Western America strictly adhered to. A singular proof of this occurred the other day at Galena. The government had made regulations with the diggers and smelters on the government lands for a percentage on the lead raised, as a government tax; and they erected a large stone building to warehouse their portion, which was paid in lead. As soon as the government had finished it, a man stepped forward and proved his right of pre-emption on the land upon which the building was erected, and it was decided against the government, although the land was actually government land!

Volume Two—Chapter Six.

(This chapter incomplete at end) I remained a week at Prairie du Chien, and left my kind entertainers with regret; but an opportunity offering of going up to St. Peters in a steam-boat, with General Atkinson, who was on a tour of inspection, I could not neglect so favourable a chance. St. Peters is situated at the confluence of the St. Peters River with the Upper Mississippi, about seven miles below the Falls of St. Anthony, where the River Mississippi becomes no longer navigable; and here, removed many hundred miles from civilisation, the Americans have an outpost called fort Snelling, and the American Fur Company an establishment. The country to the north is occupied by the Chippeway tribe of Indians; that to the east by the Winnebagos, and that to the west by the powerful tribe of Sioux or Dacotahs, who range over the whole prairie territory between the Mississippi and Missouri rivers.

The river here is so constantly divided by numerous islands, that its great width is not discernible: it seldom has less than two or three channels, often more: it courses through a succession of bold bluffs, rising sometimes perpendicularly, and always abruptly from the banks or flat land, occasionally diversified by the prairies, which descend to the edge of the stream. These bluffs are similar to those I have described in the Wisconsin river and Prairie do Chien, but are on a grander scale, and are surmounted by horizontal layers of limestone rock. The islands are all covered with small timber and brushwood, and in the spring, before the leaves have burst out, and the freshets come down, the river rises so as to cover the whole of them, and then you behold the width and magnificence of this vast stream. On the second day we arrived at Lake Pepin, which is little more than an expansion of the river, or rather a portion of it, without islands. On the third, we made fast to the wharf, abreast of the American Fur Company's Factory, a short distance below the mouth of the River St. Peters. Fort Snelling is about a mile from the factory, and is situated on a steep promontory, in a commanding position; it is built of stone, and may be considered as impregnable to any attempt which the Indians might make, provided that it has a sufficient garrison. Behind it is a splendid prairie, running back for many miles.

The Falls of St. Anthony are not very imposing, although not devoid of beauty. You cannot see the whole of the falls at one view, as they are divided, like those of Niagara, by a large island, about one third of the distance from the eastern shore. The river which, as we ascended, poured through a bed below the strata of calcareous rock, now rises above the limestone formation; and the large masses of this rock, which at the falls have been thrown down in wild confusion over a width of from two hundred to two hundred and fifty yards, have a very picturesque effect. The falls themselves, I do not think, are more than from thirty to thirty-five feet high; but, with rapids above and below them, the descent of the river is said to be more than one hundred feet. Like those of Niagara, these falls have constantly receded, and are still receding.

Here for the first time, I consider that I have seen the Indians in their primitive state; for till now all that I had fallen in with have been debased by intercourse with the whites, and the use of spirituous liquors. The Winnebagos at Prairie du Chien were almost always in a state of intoxication, as were the other tribes at Mackinaw, and on the Lakes. The Winnebagos are considered the dirtiest race of Indians, and with the worst qualities: they were formerly designated by the French, *Puans*, a term sufficiently explanatory. When I was at Prairie du Chien, a circumstance which had occurred there in the previous winter was narrated to me. In many points of manners and customs the red men have a strong analogy with the Jewish tribes: among others, an eye for an eye, and a tooth for a tooth, is most strictly adhered to. If an Indian of one tribe is killed by an Indian of another, the murderer is demanded, and must either be given up, or his life must be taken by his own tribe: if not, a feud between the two nations would be the inevitable result. It appeared that a young Menonnomie, in a drunken fray, had killed a Winnebago, and the culprit was demanded by the head men of the Winnebago tribe. A council was held; and instead of the Menonnomie, the chiefs of the tribe offered them whisky. The Winnebagos could not resist the temptation; and it was agreed that ten gallons of whisky should be produced by the Menonnomies, to be drunk by all parties over the grave of the deceased. The squaws of the Menonnomie tribe had to dig the grave, as is the custom,—a task of no little labour, as the ground was frozen hard several feet below the surface.

The body was laid in the grave; the mother of the deceased, with the rest of the Winnebago squaws, howling over it, and denouncing vengeance against the murderer; but in a short time the whisky made its appearance, and they all set to, to drink. In an hour they were all the best friends in the world, and all very drunk. The old squaw mother was hugging the murderer of her son; and it was a scene of intoxication which, in the end, left the majority of the parties assembled, for a time, quite as dead as the man in the grave. Such are the effects of whisky upon these people, who have been destroyed much more rapidly by spirituous liquors than by all the wars which they have engaged in against the whites.

The Sioux are a large band, and are divided into six or seven different tribes; they are said to amount to from 27,000 to 30,000. They are, or have been, constantly at war with the Chippeways to the north of them, and with Saucs and Foxes, a small but very warlike band, residing to the south of them, abreast of Des Moines River. The Sioux have fixed habitations as well as tents; their tents are large and commodious, made of buffalo skins dressed without the hair, and very often handsomely painted on the outside. I went out about nine miles to visit a Sioux village on the borders of a small lake. Their lodges were built cottage-fashion, of small fir-poles, erected stockade-wise, and covered inside and out with bark; the roof also of bark with a hole in the centre for the smoke to escape through. I entered one of these lodges: the interior was surrounded by a continued bed-place round three of the sides, about three feet from the floor, and on the platform was a quantity of buffalo skins and pillows; the fire was in the centre, and their luggage was stowed away under the bed-places. It was very neat and clean; the Sioux generally are, indeed, particularly so, compared with the other tribes of Indians. A missionary resides at this village and has paid great attention to the small band under his care. Their patches of Indian corn were clean and well tilled; and although, from demi-civilisation, the people have lost much of their native grandeur, still they are a fine race, and well disposed. But the majority of the Sioux tribe remain in their native state: they are *Horse*Indians, as those who live on the prairies are termed; and although many of them have rifles, the majority still adhere to the use of the bow and arrows, both in their war parties and in the chase of the buffalo.

During the time that I passed here, there were several games of ball played between different bands, and for considerable stakes; one was played, on the prairie close to the house of the Indian agent. The Indian game of ball is somewhat similar to the game of golf in Scotland, with this difference, that the sticks used by the Indians have a small network racket at the end, in which they catch the ball and run away with it, as far as they are permitted, towards the goal, before they throw it in that direction. It is one of the most exciting games in the world, and requires the greatest activity and address. It is, moreover, rendered celebrated in American History from the circumstance that it was used as a stratagem by the renowned leader of the northern tribes, Pontiac, to surprise in one day all the English forts on and near to the lakes, a short time after the Canadas had been surrendered to the British. At Mackinaw they succeeded, and put the whole garrison to the sword, as they did at one or two smaller posts; but at Detroit they were foiled by the plan having been revealed by one of the squaws.

Pontiac's plan was as follows. Pretending the greatest good-will and friendship, a game of ball was proposed to be played, on the same day, at all the different outposts, for the amusement of the garrisons. The interest taken in the game would, of course, call out a proportion of the officers and men to witness it. The squaws were stationed close to the gates of the fort, with the rifles of the Indians cut short, concealed under their blankets. The ball was, as if by accident, thrown into the fort; the Indians, as usual, were to rush in crowds after it; by this means they were to enter the fort, receiving their rifles from their squaws as they hurried in, and then slaughter the weakened and unprepared garrisons. Fortunately, Detroit, the most important post, and against which Pontiac headed the stratagem in person, was saved by the previous information given by the squaw; not that she had any intention to betray him, but the commanding officer having employed her to make him several pairs of moccasins out of an elk skin, desiring her to take the remainder of the skin for the same purpose; this she refused, saying it was of no use, as he would never see it again. This remark excited his suspicions, and led to the discovery.

The game played before the fort when I was present lasted nearly two hours, during which I had a good opportunity of estimating the agility of the Indians, who displayed a great deal of mirth and humour at the same time. But the most curious effect produced was by the circumstance, that having divested themselves of all their garments except their middle clothing, they had all of them fastened behind them a horse's tail; and as they swept by, in their chase of the ball, with their tails streaming to the wind, I really almost made up my mind that such an appendage was rather an improvement to a man's figure than otherwise.

While I was there a band of Sioux from the *Lac qui parle*, (so named from a remarkable echo there,) distant about two hundred and thirty miles from Port Snelling, headed by Monsieur Rainville, came down on a visit to the American Fur Company's factory. Monsieur Rainville, (or *de* Rainville, as he told me was his real name,) is, he asserts, descended from one of the best families is France, which formerly settled in Canada. He is a half-breed, his father being a Frenchman, and his mother a Sioux; his wife is also a Sioux, so that his family are three-quarters red. He had been residing many years with the Sioux tribes, trafficking with them for peltry, and has been very judicious in his treatment of them, not interfering with their pursuits of hunting; he has, moreover, to a certain degree civilised them, and ob

(This chapter is 2 or 3 pages incomplete.)

Volume Two—Chapter Seven.

(This chapter is 2 or 3 pages incomplete) my wrist that he might not escape during the night, and tried to go to sleep. I rose before daylight on Monday morning, and found that my father had discovered that I had employed the Sabbath in looking for a dog; and in consequence, as he was a very strict man, I received a severe caning. On these memorable occasions, he always used to hold me by the wrist with one hand, while he chastised me with the other. I found the best plan was to run round him as fast as I could, which obliged my father to turn round after me with the stick, and then in a short time he left off; not because he thought I had enough, but because he became so giddy that he could not stand. A greater punishment, however, was threatened—that of not being permitted to go to the bear-hunt, which was to take place on that day; but I pleaded hard, and asked my father how he would have liked it, if he had been prevented from going to the battle of B— (where he had very much distinguished himself). This was taking the old man on his weak side, and I was, at last, permitted to be present. Then there arose another difficulty. I was thought too little to carry a gun, which I had provided; but a neighbour, who had witnessed my anxiety, took my part, said that he would be answerable for me, and that I should not quit his side; so at last all was settled to my satisfaction. As for the caning, I thought nothing at all of that.

"We set off and before we reached the mill, we passed a hollow; the dog barked furiously, and I let him go. After a time I heard a noise in a bush. 'Did you not hear?' said I to my neighbour.—'Yes,' replied he; 'but I also heard a rustling on the bank this way. Do you look out sharp in that direction, whilst I look out in this.' He had hardly said so, and I had not turned my head, when out came the old she-bear, in the direction where my neighbour had been watching, and sat upon her hind legs in a clear place. My friend levelled his gun; to my delight he had forgotten to cock it. While he was cocking it, the bear dropped down on her fore legs, and I fired; the ball passed through her chest into her shoulder. She was at that time on the brink of a shelving quarry of sharp stone, down which she retreated. I halloo'd for the dog, and followed, slipping and tumbling after her, for I was mad at the idea of her escaping me. Down we went together, the dog following; when we arrived at the bottom, the dog seized her. She was so weak that she supported herself against a rock; at last she rolled on her back, hogging the dog in her fore paws. This was a terrible source of alarm to me. I caught the dog by the tail, pulling at it as hard as I could to release him, crying out, although no one was near me, 'Save the dog—save the dog—or I'll have to pay ten dollars.' But, fortunately, the bear, although she held the dog fast, had not sufficient strength left to kill it. Other people now came up; my own musket was down the bear's throat, where, in my anxiety, I had thrust it; one of them handed me his, and I shot the bear through the head. Even then, so fearful was I of losing my prey, that I seized a large stone and beat the animal on the head till I was exhausted. Then I had my triumph. The Pratts had only killed bear-cubs; I had killed a full-grown bear. I was, as you may suppose, also carried home upon the animal's back; and from that day, was pointed out as a bear-hunter."

Secondly. "I was once buffalo hunting in Arkansas. I was on a strong well-trained horse, pursuing a bull, when we arrived at a rent or crack in the prairie, so wide, that it was necessary for the animals to leap it. The bull went over first, and I, on the horse, following it close, rose on my stirrups, craning a little, that I might perceive the width of the rent. At that moment the bull turned round to charge; the horse, perceiving it, and knowing his work, immediately wheeled also. This sudden change of motion threw me off my saddle, and I remained hanging by the side of the horse, with my leg over his neck: there I was, hanging on only by my leg, with my head downwards below the horse's belly. The bull rushed on to the charge, ranging up to the flank of the horse on the side where I was dangling, and the horse was so encumbered by my weight in that awkward position, that each moment the bull gained upon him. At last my strength failed me; I felt that I could hold on but a few seconds longer; the head of the bull was close to me, and the steam from his nostrils blew into my face. I gave myself up for lost; all the prayer I could possibly call to mind at the time was, the first two lines of a hymn I used to repeat as a child:— 'Lord now I lay me down to sleep,' and that I repeated two or three times, when, fortunately, the horse wheeled short round, evaded the bull, and leaped the gap. The bull was at fault; the jolt of the leap, after nearly dropping me into the gap, threw me up so high, that I gained the neck of my horse, and eventually my saddle. I then thought of my rifle, and found that I had held it grasped in my hand during the whole time. I wheeled my horse and resumed the chase, and in a minute the bull was dead at my horse's feet."

Thirdly. "I was riding out one day in Arkansas, and it so happened I had not my rifle with me, nor indeed a weapon of any description, not even my jack-knife. As I came upon the skirts of a prairie, near a small copse, a buck started out, and dashed away as if much alarmed. I thought it was my sudden appearance which had alarmed him; I stopped my horse to look after him, and turning my eyes afterwards in the direction from whence it had started, I perceived, as I thought, on a small mound of earth raised by an animal called a gopher, just the head of the doe, her body concealed by the high grass. I had no arms, but it occurred to me, that if I could contrive to crawl up very softly, the high grass might conceal my approach, and I should be able to spring upon her and secure her by main strength. 'If I can manage this,' said I to myself, 'it will be something to talk about.' I tied my horse to a tree, and commenced crawling very softly on my hands and knees towards the gopher hill; I arrived close to it, and the doe had not started; I rose gently with both hands ready for a grab, and prepared to spring, slowly raising my head that I might get a sight of the animal. It appeared that the animal was equally inquisitive, and wished to gain a sight of me, and it slowly raised its head from the grass as I did mine. Imagine what was my surprise and consternation, to find that, instead of a doe, I was face to face with a large male panther. It was this brute which had so scared the buck, and now equally scared me. There I was, at hardly one yard's distance from him, without arms of any description, and almost in the paws of the panther. I knew that my only chance was keeping my eyes fixed steadfastly on his, and not moving hand or foot; the least motion to retreat would have been his signal to spring: so there I was, as white as a sheet, with my eyes fixed on him. Luckily he did not know what was passing within me. For some seconds the animal met my gaze, and I began to give myself up for lost. 'Tis time for you to go, thought I, or I am gone: will you never go? At last, the animal blinked, and then his eyes opened like balls of fire; I remained fascinated as it were; he blinked again, turned his head a very little, then turned round and went away at a light canter. Imagine the relief. I hastened back to my horse, and away also went I at a light canter, and with a lighter heart, grateful to Heaven for having preserved me."

Volume Two—Chapter Eight.

The band of warriors attached to Monsieur Rainville have set up their war-tent close to the factory, and have entertained us with a variety of dances. Their dresses are very beautiful, and the people, who have been accustomed to witness these exhibitions for years, say that they have never seen any thing equal to them before, I was very anxious to obtain one of them, and applied to Mr Rainville to effect my purpose; but it required all his influence to induce them to part with it, and they had many arguments and debates among themselves before they could make up their minds to consent to do so. I was the more anxious about it, as I had seen Mr Catlin's splendid exhibition, and I knew that he had not one in his possession. The dress in question consisted of a sort of kilt of fine skins, ornamented with beautiful porcupine quill-work, and eagle's feathers; garters of animals' tails, worn at their ankles, head-dress of eagle's feathers and ermine's tails, etcetera. They made little objection to part with any portions of the dress except the kilt; at last they had a meeting of the whole band, as the dress was not the property of any one individual; and I was informed that the warriors would come and have a *talk* with me.

I received them at the factory's new house, in my room, which was large, and held them all. One came and presented me with a pair of garters; another with a portion of the head-dress; another with moccasins; at last, the kilt or girdle was handed to me. M. Rainville sat by as interpreter. He who had presented me with the kilt or girdle spoke for half a minute, and then stopped while what he said was being interpreted.

"You are an Englishman, and a warrior in your own country. You cross the great waters as fast as we can our prairies. We recollect the English, and we like them; they used us well. The rifles and blankets which they gave us, according to promise, were of good quality: not like the American goods; their rifles are bad, and their blankets are thin. The English keep their word, and they live in our memory."

"Ho!" replied I; which is as much as to say, I understand what you have said, and you may proceed.

"You have asked for the dress which we wear when we dance; we have never parted with one as yet; they belong to the band of warriors; when one who has worn a dress goes to the land of spirits, we hold a council, to see who is most worthy to put it on in his place. We value them highly; and we tell you so not to enhance their value, but to prove what we will do for an English warrior."

"Ho!" says I.

"An American, in the fort, has tried hard to obtain this dress from us; he offered us two barrels of flour, and other things. You know that we have no game, and we are hungry; but if he had offered twelve barrels of flour, we would not have parted with them. (This was true.) But our father, Rainville, has spoken; and we have pleasure in giving them to an English warrior. I have spoken."

"Ho!" says I; upon which the Indian took his seat with the other; and it was my turn to speak. I was very near beginning, "Unaccustomed as I am to public speaking;" but I knew that such an acknowledgment would in their estimation, have very much lessened my value as a warrior; for, like the Duke of Wellington, one must be as valuable in the council as in the field, to come up to their notions of excellence. So I rose, and said—

"I receive with great pleasure the dress which you have given me.—I know that you do not like to part with it, and that you have refused the American at the fort, and I therefore value it the more. I shall never look upon it, when I am on the other side of the great waters, without thinking of my friends the Sioux; and I will tell my nation that you gave them to me because I was an English warrior, and because you liked the English."

"Ho!" grunted the whole conclave, after this was interpreted.

"I am very glad that you do not forget the English, and that you say they kept their word, and that their rifles and blankets were good. I know that the blankets of the Americans are thin and cold. (I did not think it worth while to say that they were all made in England.) We have buried the hatchet now; but should the tomahawk be raised again between the Americans and the English, you must not take part with the Americans."

"Ho!" said they.

"In the Fur Company's store you will find many things acceptable to you. I leave Mr Rainville to select for you what you wish; and beg you will receive them in return for the present which you have made me."

"Ho!" said they; and thus ended my first Indian council.

It is remarkable that the Sioux have no expression to signify, "I thank you," although other Indians have. When they receive a present, they always say, *Wash tay*: it is good.

Of all the tribes I believe the Sioux to be the most inimical to the Americans. They have no hesitation in openly declaring so; and it must be acknowledged that it is not without just grounds. During the time that I was at St. Peters, a council was held at the Indian agent's. It appears that the American Government, in its paternal care for the Indians, had decided that at any *strike* taking place between tribes of Indians near to the confines, no war should take place in consequence: that is to say, that should any Indians of one tribe attack or kill any Indians belonging to another, that instead of the tribes going to war, they should apply for and receive redress from the American Government. Some time back, a party of Chippeways came down to a trader's house, about half a mile from Port Snelling. Being almost hereditary enemies of the Sioux, they were fired at, at night, by some of the young men of the Sioux village close by, and two of the Chippeways were wounded. In conformity with the intimation received, and the law laid down by the American Government, and promulgated by the Indian agent, the Chippeways applied for redress. It was granted—four Sioux were taken and shot. This summary justice was expected to produce the best effects, and, had it been followed up, it might have prevented bloodshed: but, since the above occurrence, some Chippeways came down, and meeting a party of Sioux, were received kindly into their lodges; they returned this hospitality by treacherously murdering eleven of the Sioux, while they were asleep. This time the Sioux brought forward their complaint. "You tell us not to go to war; we will not; you shot four of our people for wounding two Chippeways; now do us justice against the Chippeways, who have murdered eleven of our Sioux." As yet no justice has been done to the Sioux. The fact is, that the Chippeways live a long way off; and there are not sufficient men to garrison the fort, still less to send a party out to capture the Chippeways; and the Sioux are, as may well be supposed, indignant at this partial proceeding.

I was at the council, and heard all the speeches made by the Sioux chiefs on the occasion. They were some of them very eloquent, and occasionally very severe; and the reply of the Indian agent must have rendered the American Government very contemptible in the eyes of the Indians—not that the agent was so much in fault as was the American Government, which, by not taking proper measures to put their promises and agreements into force, had left their officer in such a position. First, the Indian agent said, that the wounding of the two Chippeways took place close to the fort, and that it was on account of the insult offered to the *American flag* that it was so promptly punished—a very different explanation, and quite at variance with the principle laid down by the American Government. The Indians replied; and the agent then said, that they had not sufficient troops to defend the fort, and, therefore, could not send out a party; an admission very unwise to make, although strictly true. The Indians again replied; and then the agent said wait a little till we hear from Washington, and then, if you have no redress, you are brave men, you have arms in your hands, and your enemies are before you. This was worse than all, for it implied the inability or the indifference of the American Government to do them justice, and told them, after that government had distinctly declared that they should fight no longer, but receive redress from it, that they now might do what the government had forbidden them to do, and that they had no other chance of redress. The result of this council was very unsatisfactory. The Indian chiefs declared that they were ashamed to look their people in the lace, and walked solemnly away.

To make this matter still worse, after I left St. Peters, I read in the St. Louis Gazette a report of some Chippeways having come down, and that, in consequence of the advice given by the Indian agent, the Sioux had taken the law into their own hands and murdered some of the Chippeways; and that although they had never received redress for the murder of their own people, some of the Sioux were again taken and executed.

The arms of the Sioux are the rifle, tomahawk, and bow; they carry spears more for parade than use. Their bows are not more than three feet long, but their execution with them is surprising. A Sioux, when on horseback chasing the buffalo, will drive his arrow which is about eighteen inches long, with such force that the barb shall appear on the opposite side of the animal. And one of their greatest chiefs, *Wanataw*, has been known to kill two buffaloes with one arrow, it having passed through the first of the animals, and mortally wounded the second on the other side of it. I was about two hundred yards from the fort, and asked a Sioux if he could send his arrow into one of the apertures for air, which were near the foundation, and about three inches wide. It appeared more like a thread from where we stood. He took his bow, and apparently with a most careless aim he threw the arrow right into it.

The men are tall and straight, and very finely made, with the exception of their arms, which are too small. The arms of the squaws, who do all the labour, are much more muscular. One day, as I was on the prairie, I witnessed the effect of custom upon these people. A Sioux was coming up without perceiving me; his squaw followed very heavily laden, and to assist her he had himself a large package on his shoulder. As soon as they perceived me, he dropped his burden, and it was taken up by the squaw and added to what she had already. If a woman wishes to upbraid another, the severest thing she can say is, "You let your husband carry burthens."

Volume Two—Chapter Nine.

Left St. Peters. Taking the two varieties in the mass, the Indians must be acknowledged the most perfect gentlemen in America, particularly in their deportment. It was with regret that I parted with my friends in the fort, my kind host, Mr Sibley, and my noble-minded warrior Sioux. I could have remained at St. Peters for a year with pleasure, and could only regret that life was so short, and the Mississippi so long.

There is, however, one serious drawback in all America to life in the woods, or life in cities, or every other kind of life; which is the manner, go where you will, in which you are pestered by the mosquitoes. Strangers are not the only sufferers; those who are born and die in the country are equally tormented, and it is slap, slap, slap, all day and all night long, for these animals bite through everything less thick than a buffalo's skin. As we ascended the river they attacked us on the crown of the head—a very unusual thing,—and raised swellings as large as pigeons' eggs. I must have immolated at least five hundred of them upon my bump of benevolence. Whatever people may think, I feel that no one can be very imaginative where these animals are so eternally tormenting them. You meditate under the shady boughs of some forest-king (slap knee, slap cheek), and farewell to anything like concentration of thought; you ponder on the sailing moon (clap again, right and left, above, below), always unpleasantly interrupted. It won't do at all: you are teased and phlebotomised out of all poetry and patience.

It is midnight, the darkness is intense, not even a star in the heavens above, and the steamboat appears as if it were gliding through a current of ink, with black masses rising just perceptible on either side of it; no sound except the reiterated note of the "Whip poor Will," answered by the loud coughing of the high-pressure engine. Who, of those in existence fifty years ago, would have contemplated that these vast and still untenanted solitudes would have had their silence invaded by such an unearthly sound? a sound which ever gives you the idea of vitality. It is this appearance of breathing which makes the high-pressure engine the nearest approach to creation which was ever attained by the ingenuity of man. It appears to have respiration, and that short, quick respiration occasioned by exertion; its internal operations are performed as correctly and as mechanically as are our own; it is as easily put out of order and rendered useless as we are; and like us, it can only continue its powers of motion by being well supplied with aliment.

Ran up Fever River to Galena, the present emporium of the Mineral Country. There is an unpleasant feeling connected with the name of this river; it is, in fact, one of the American translations. It was originally called Fève, or Bean River, by the French, and this they have construed into Fever. The Mineral district comprehends a tract of country running about one hundred miles North and South, and fifty miles East and West, from the River Wisconsin to about twenty miles south of Galena. It was purchased by the American Government about fifteen years ago, the northern portion from the Winnebagos, and the southern from the Sioux and Fox Indians. The Indians used to work the diggings to a small extent, bringing the lead which they obtained to exchange with the traders. As may be supposed, they raised but little, the whole work of digging and smelting being carried on by the squaws. After the land was surveyed a portion of it was sold, but when the minerals made their appearance the fact was notified by the surveyors to the government, and the remaining portions were withdrawn from the market. A licence was granted to speculators to dig the ore and smelt it, upon condition of their paying to the government a percentage on the mineral obtained. Those who found a good vein had permission to work it for forty yards square on condition that they carried the ore to a licensed smelter. This occasioned a new class of people to spring up in this speculative country, namely, *finders*, who would search all over the country for what they called a good*prospect*, that is, every appearance on the surface of a good vein of metal. This when found they would sell to others, who would turn *diggers*; and as soon as these finders had spent their money, they would range over the whole country to find another *prospect* which they might dispose of. But although it was at first supposed that the government had retained all the mineral portion of the district in its own hands, it was soon discovered that nearly the whole country was one continued lead mine, and that there was an equal supply of mineral to be obtained from those portions which had been disposed of. Lead was found not only in the mountains and ravines, but under the surface of the wide prairies. As the lands sold by government had not to pay a percentage for the lead raised from them, those who worked upon the government lands refused to pay any longer, asserting that it was not *legal*. The superintendent of government soon found that his office was a sinecure, as all attempt at *coercion* in that half-civilised country would have been not only useless but dangerous. The government have gone to law with their tenants, but that is of no avail, for a verdict against the latter would not induce them to pay. The cause was not attempted to be tried at Galena, for the government knew what the decision of the jury would have been, but it is contested at Vandalia. It is three years since the mines have paid any percentage, and the government are now advised to sell all their reserved lands, and thus get rid of the business. How weak must that government be when it is compelled to submit to such a gross violation of all justice. The quantity of mineral found does not appear to affect the quality of the soil, which is as fine here, if not finer, than in those portions of Wisconsin where the mineral is not so plentiful. The quantity of lead annually smelted is said to amount to from 18,000,000 to 20,000,000 lbs. Galena is a small town, picturesquely situated on the banks of the river, but very dirty.

Ioway, the new district opposite to Wisconsin, on the western banks of the Mississippi, has, in all probability, a large proportion of metal under its surface. When it was in the possession of the Sioux Indians, they used to obtain from it a considerable portion of lead, which they brought down to barter; and I am inclined to think, that to the north of the Wisconsin river, they will find no want of minerals, even as high up as Lake Superior, where they have already discovered masses of native copper weighing many *tons*: and on the west side of the river, as you proceed south, you arrive at the iron mines, or rather mountains of iron, in the Missouri.

After you proceed south of Prairie du Chien, the features of the Mississippi river gradually change; the bluffs decrease in number and in height, until you descend to Rock Island, below which point they are rarely to be met with. The country on each side now is chiefly composed of variegated rolling prairies, with a less proportion of timber. To describe these prairies would be difficult; that is, to describe the effect of them upon a stranger: I have found myself lost, as it were; and indeed sometimes, although on horseback, have lost myself, having only the sun for my guide. Look round in every quarter of the compass, and there you are as if on the ocean—not a landmark, not a vestige of any thing human but yourself. Instead of sky and water, it is one vast field, bounded only by the horizon, its surface gently undulating like the waves of the ocean; and as the wind (which always blows fresh on the prairies) bows down the heads of the high grass, it gives you the idea of a running swell. Every three or four weeks there is a succession of beautiful flowers, giving a variety of tints to the whole map, which die away and are succeeded by others equally beautiful; and in the spring, the strawberries are in such profusion, that you have but to sit down wherever you may happen to be, and eat as long as you please.

We stopped at Alton, in the State of Missouri, to put on shore three thousand pigs of lead. This town has been rendered notorious by the murder—for murder it was, although it was brought on by his own intemperate conduct—of Mr Lovejoy, who is now raised to the dignity of a martyr by the abolitionists. Alton is a well-built town, of stone, and, from its locality, must increase; it is, however, spoilt by the erection of a penitentiary with huge walls, on a most central and commanding situation. I read a sign put out by a small eating-house, and which was very characteristic of the country—

"Stranger, here's your chicken fixings."

Four miles below Alton, the Missouri joins its waters with the Mississippi; and the change which takes place at the mingling of the two streams is very remarkable—the clear pellucid current of the upper Mississippi being completely extinguished by the foul mud of the other turbid and impetuous river. It was a great mistake of the first explorers, when they called the western branch, at the meeting of the two rivers, the Missouri, and the eastern the Mississippi: the western branch, or the Missouri, is really the Mississippi, and should have been so designated: it is the longest and farthest navigable of the two branches, and therefore is the main river.

The Falls of St. Anthony put an end to the navigation of the eastern branch, or present upper Missouri, about nine hundred miles above St. Louis; while the western branch, or present Missouri, is navigable above St. Louis for more than one thousand two hundred miles.

The waters of the present upper Mississippi are clear and beautiful; it is a swift, but not an angry stream, full of beauty and freshness, and fertilising as it sweeps along; while the Missouri is the same impetuous, discoloured, devastating current as the Mississippi continues to be after its junction—like it, constantly sweeping down forests of trees in its wild course, overflowing, inundating, and destroying, and exciting awe and fear.

As soon as you arrive at St. Louis, you feel that you are on the great waters of Mississippi. St. Louis is a well-built town, now containing about twenty thousand inhabitants, and situated on a hill shelving down to the river. The population increases daily; the river a-breast of the town is crowded with steamboats, lying in two or three tiers, and ready to start up or down, or to the many tributary navigable rivers which pour their waters into the Mississippi.

In point of heat, St. Louis certainly approaches the nearest to the Black Hole of Calcutta of any city that I have sojourned in. The lower part of the town is badly drained, and very filthy. The flies, on a moderate calculation, are in many parts fifty to the square inch. I wonder that they have not a contagious disease here during the whole summer; it is, however, indebted to heavy rains for its occasional purification. They have not the yellow-fever here; but during the autumn they have one which, under another name, is almost as fatal—the bilious congestive fever. I found sleep almost impossible from the sultriness of the air, and used to remain at the open window for the greater part of the night. I did not expect that the muddy Mississippi would be able to reflect the silver light of the moon; yet it did, and the effect was very beautiful. Truly it may be said of this river, as it is of many ladies, that it is a candle-light beauty. There is another serious evil to which strangers who sojourn here are subject—the violent effects of the waters of the Mississippi upon those who are not used to them. The suburbs of the town are very pretty; and a few miles behind it you are again in a charming prairie country, full of game, large and small. Large and small are only so by comparison. An American was asked what game they had in his district? and his reply was, "Why, we've plenty of *baar* (bear) and deer, but no *large* game to count on."

There is one great luxury in America, which is the quantity of clear pure ice which is to be obtained wherever you are, even in the hottest seasons, and ice-creams are universal and very cheap. I went into an establishment where they vended this and other articles of refreshment, when about a dozen black swarthy fellows, employed at the iron-foundry close at hand, with their dirty shirt-sleeves tucked up, and without their coats and waistcoats, came in, and sitting down, called for ice-creams. Miss Martineau says in her work, "Happy is the country where factory-girls can carry parasols, and pig-drivers wear spectacles." She might have added, and the sons of Vulcan eat ice-creams. I thought at the time what the ladies, who stop in their carriages at Gunter's, would have said, had they behold these Cyclops with their bare sinewy arms, blackened with heat and smoke, refreshing themselves with such luxuries; but it must be remembered that *porter* is much the dearer article. Still the working classes all over America can command not only all necessary comforts, but many luxuries; for labour is dear and they are very well paid. The Americans will point this out and say, behold the effects of our institutions; and they fully believe that such is the case. Government has, however, nothing to do with it; it is the result of circumstances. When two years' exertion will procure a clever mechanic an independence, the effects will be the same, whether they labour under a democratic or a monarchical form of government.

Bear cubs (I mean the black bear) are caught and brought down to the cities on this side of the river, to be fattened for the table. I saw one at Alton about a year old, which the owner told me was to be killed the next day, having been bespoken for the feast of the 4th of July. I have eaten old bear, which I dislike; but they say that the cub is very good. I also saw here a very fine specimen of the grizzly bear (Ursus Horridus of Linnaeus). It was about two years old, and although not so tall, it must have weighed quite as much as a good-sized bullock. Its width of shoulder and apparent strength were enormous, and they have never yet been tamed: Mr Van Amburgh would be puzzled to handle one of them. The Indians reckon the slaying of one of these animals as a much greater feat than killing a man, and the proudest ornament they can wear is a necklace of the grizzly bear's claws.

I for myself, must confess, that I had rather be attacked by, and take my chance with, three men than by one of these animals, as they are seldom killed by the first or even the second bullet. It requires numbers to overcome them. The largest lion, or Bengal tiger, would stand but a poor chance, if opposed to one of these animals full grown. One of the gentlemen employed by the Fur Company told me, that he once saw a grizzly bear attack a bull buffalo, and that, at the first seizure, he tore one of the ribs of the buffalo out of his side, and eventually carried away the whole carcass, without much apparent effort. They are only to be found in the rocky mountains, and valleys between them, when the game is plentiful.

Visited the museum. There were once five large alligators to be seen alive in this museum; but they are now all dead. One demands our sympathy, as there was something Roman in his fate. Unable to support such a life of confinement, and preferring death to the loss of liberty, he committed suicide by throwing himself out of a three-storey-high window. He was taken up from the pavement the next morning; the vital spark had fled, as the papers say, and, I believe, his remains were decently interred.

The other four, never having been taught in their youth the hymn, "Birds in their little nests agree," fought so desperately, that one by one they all died of their wounds. They were very large, being from seventeen to twenty-one feet long. One, as a memorial, remains preserved in the museum, and to make him look more poetical, he has a stuffed negro in his mouth.

Volume Two—Chapter Ten.

Thank Heaven I have escaped from St. Louis; during the time that I remained in that city, I was, day and night, so melting away, that I expected, like some of the immortal half-breeds of Jupiter, to become a tributary stream to the Mississippi.

As you descend the river the land through which it flows becomes more level and flat, while the size of the forest trees increases; the log houses of the squatters, erected on the banks under their trunks, appear, in contrast with their size, more like dog-kennels than the habitations of men. The lianes, or creeping plants, now become plentiful, and embrace almost every tree, rising often to the height of fifty or sixty feet, and encircling them with the apparent force of the boa-constrictor. Most of them are poisonous; indeed, it is from these creeping parasites that the Indians, both in North and South America, obtain the most deadly venom. Strange that these plants, in their appearances and their habits so similar to the serpent tribe, should be endowed with the same peculiar attributes, and thus become their parallels in the vegetable kingdom—each carrying sudden death in their respective juices. I hate the Mississippi, and as I look down upon its wild and filthy waters, boiling and eddying, and reflect how uncertain is travelling in this region of high-pressure, and disregard of social rights, I cannot help feeling a disgust at the idea of perishing in such a vile sewer, to be buried in mud, and perhaps to be rooted out again by some pig-nosed alligator.

Right glad was I when we turned into the stream of the Ohio, and I found myself on its purer waters. The Ohio is a splendid river, running westward from the chain of Alleghany mountains into the Mississippi, dividing the States of Illinois, Indiana, and Ohio on its northern bank from Kentucky, and Virginia on its south; the northern being free, and the southern slave States. We stopped at the month of the Cumberland river, where we took in passengers. Among others were a slave-dealer and a runaway negro whom he had captured. He was secured by a heavy chain, and followed his master, who, as soon as he arrived on the upper deck, made him fast with a large padlock to one of the stancheons.

Here he remained looking wistfully at the northern shore, where every one was free, but occasionally glancing his eye on the southern, which had condemned him to toil for others, I had never seen a slave-dealer, and scrutinised this one severely. His most remarkable feature was his eye; it was large but not projecting, clear as crystal, and eternally in motion. I could not help imagining, as he turned it right and left from one to the other of the passengers, that he was calculating what price he could obtain for them in the market. The negro had run away about seven months before, and not having a pass, he had been secured in goal until the return of his master, who had been on a journey with a string of slaves, to the State of Arkansas: he was about to be sold to pay expenses, when his master saw the advertisement and claimed him. As may be supposed, a strong feeling exists on the opposite shores of the river as to slavery and freedom. The Abolitionists used to assist the slaves to escape, and send them off to Canada; even now many do escape; but this has been rendered more difficult by a system which has latterly been put in practice by a set of miscreants living on the free side of the river. These would go to the slave states opposite, and persuade the negroes to run away, promising to conceal them until they could send them off to Canada; for a free state is bound to give up a slave when claimed. Instead of sending them away, they would wait until the reward was offered by the masters for the apprehension of the slaves, and then return them, receiving their infamous guerdon. The slaves, aware of this practice, now seldom attempt to escape.

Louisville is the largest city in Kentucky; the country about is very rich, and every thing vegetable springs up with a luxuriance which is surprising. It is situated at the falls of the Ohio, which are only navigable during the freshets; there is no river in America which has such a rise and fall as the Ohio, sometimes rising to sixty feet in the spring; but this is very rare, the general average being about forty feet. The French named it La Belle Riviere: it is a very grand stream, running through hills covered with fine timber and underwood; but a very small portion is as yet cleared by the settlers. At the time that I was at Louisville the water was lower than it had been remembered for years, and you could walk for miles over the bed of the river, a calcareous deposite full of interesting fossils; but the mineralogist and geologist have as much to perform in America as the agriculturist.

Arrived at Cincinnati. How rapid has been the advance of this western country. In 1803, deer-skin at the value of forty cents per pound, were a legal tender; and if offered instead of money could not be refused—even by a lawyer. Not fifty years ago, the woods which towered where Cincinnati is now built, resounded only to the cry of the wild animals of the forest, or the rifle of the Shawnee Indian; now Cincinnati contains a population of 40,000 inhabitants. It is a beautiful, well built, clean town, reminding you more of Philadelphia than any other city in the Union. Situated on a hill on the banks of the Ohio, it is surrounded by a circular phalanx of other hills; so that look up and down the streets, whichever way you will, your eye reposes upon verdure and forest trees in the distance. The streets have a row of trees on each side, near the curb-stone; and most of the houses have a small frontage, filled with luxuriant flowering shrubs, of which the Althea Frutex is the most abundant. It is, properly speaking, a Yankee city, the majority of its inhabitants coming from the East; but they have intermarried, and blended with the Kentuckians of the opposite shore, a circumstance which is advantageous to the character of both.

There are, however, a large number of Dutch and German settlers here; they say 10,000. They are not much liked by the Americans but have great influence, as may be conceived when it is stated that, when a motion was brought forward, in the Municipal Court, for the city regulations to be printed in German as well as English, it was lost by one vote only.

I was told a singular fact, which will prove how rapidly the value of land rises in this country as it becomes peopled. Fifty-six years ago, the major part of the land upon which the city of Cincinnati stands, and which is now worth many millions of dollars, was *swapped* away by the owner of it for a pony!! The man who made this unfortunate bargain is now alive, and living in or near Cincinnati.

Cincinnati is the pork-shop of the Union; and in the autumnal, and early winter months, the way they kill pigs here is, to use a Yankee phrase, *quite a caution*. Almost all the hogs fed in the oak forests of Ohio, Kentucky, and Western Virginia, are driven into this city, and some establishments kill as many as fifteen hundred a day; at least so I am told. They are despatched in a way quite surprising; and a pig is killed upon the same principle as a pin is made,—by division, or, more properly speaking, by combination of labour. The hogs confined in a large pen are driven into a smaller one; one man knocks them on the head with a sledge hammer, and then cuts their throats; two more pull away the carcase, when it is raised by two others, who tumble it into a tub of scalding water. His bristles are removed in about a minute and a half by another party; when the next duty is to fix a stretcher between his legs. It is then hoisted up by two other people, cut open, and disembowelled; and in three minutes and a half from the time that the hog was grunting in his obesity, he has only to get cold before he is again packed up, and reunited in a barrel to travel all over the world. By the by, we laugh at the notion of pork and molasses. In the first place, the American pork is far superior to any that we ever have salted down; and, in the next, it eats uncommonly well with molasses. I have tasted it, and *"it is a fact."* After all, why should we eat currant jelly with venison, and not allow the Americans the humble imitation of pork and molasses?

Mrs Trollope's bazaar raises its head in a very imposing manner: it is composed of many varieties of architecture; but I think the order under which it must be classed is the *preposterous*. They call it Trollope's folly; and it is remarkable how a shrewd woman like Mrs Trollope should have committed such an error. A bazaar like an English bazaar is only to be supported in a city which has arrived at the acme of luxury; where there are hundreds of people willing to be employed for a trifle; hundreds who will work at trifles, for want of better employment; and thousands who will spend money on trifles, merely to pass away their time. Now, in America, in the first place, there is no one who makes trifles; no one who will devote their time, as sellers of the articles unless well compensated; and no one who will be induced, either by fashion or idleness, to give a halfpenny more for a thing than it is worth. In consequence, nothing was sent to Mrs Trollope's bazaar. She had to furnish it from the shops, and had to pay very high salaries to the young women who attended; and the people of Cincinnati, aware that the same articles were to be purchased at the stores for less money, preferred going to the stores. No wonder then that it was a failure. It is now used as a dancing academy, and occasionally as an assembly-room.

Whatever the society of Cincinnati may have been at the time that Mrs Trollope resided there, I cannot pretend to say; probably some change may have taken place in it; but at present it is as good as any in the Union, and infinitely more agreeable than in some other cities, as in it there is a mixture of the southern frankness of character. A lady, who had long resided at Cincinnati, told me that they were not angry with Mrs Trollope for having described the society which she saw, but for having asserted that that was the best society; and she further remarked,—"It is fair to us that it should be understood that when Mrs Trollope came here, she was quite unknown, except inasmuch as that she was a married woman, travelling without her husband. In a small society, as ours was, it was not surprising, therefore, that we should be cautious about receiving a lady who, in our opinion was offending against *les bienséances*. Observe, *we do not accuse Mrs Trollope of any impropriety*; but you must be aware how necessary it is, in this country, to be regardful of appearances, and how afraid every one is of their neighbour. Mrs Trollope then took a cottage on the hill, and used to come down to the city to market, and attend to the erection of her bazaar. I have now told you all that we know about her, and the reason why she did not receive those attentions, the omission of which caused her indignation." I think it but fair that the lady's explanation should be given, as Mrs Trollope is considered to have been very severe and very unjust by the inhabitants of Cincinnati.

The fact is, that Mrs Trollope's representation of the manners and custom of Cincinnati, at the period when she wrote, was probably more correct than the present inhabitants of the city will allow: that it would be a libel upon the Cincinnatians of the present day is certain; whether it was one at the time she wrote, and the city was, comparatively speaking, in its infancy, is quite another affair. However, one thing is certain, which is, that the Americans have quite forgiven Mrs Trollope, and if she were again to cross the water, I think she would be well received. Her book made them laugh, though at their own expense; and the Americans, although appearances are certainly very much against it, are really, at the bottom, a very good tempered people.

The heat has been this year very remarkable all over the Western country, and the drought equally uncommon, the thermometer standing from 100 degrees to 106 degrees, in the shade, every where from St. Peters to New Orleans. It is very dangerous to drink iced water, and many have died from yielding to the temptation. One young man came into the bar of the hotel where I resided, drank a glass of water, and fell down dead at the porch. This reminds me of an ingenious plan put in practice by a fellow who had drunk every cent out of his pocket, and was as thirsty as ever. The best remedy, in case of a person being taken ill from drinking cold water, is to pour brandy down his throat immediately. Aware of this, the fellow used to go to one of the pumps, pump away, and pretend to drink water in large quantities; he would then fall down by the pump, as if he had been taken suddenly ill; out would run people from every house, with brandy, and pour it down his throat till even he had had enough; he would then pretend gradually to recover, thank them for their kindness, and walk away. When he required another dose, he would perform the same farce at another pump; and this he continued to do for some time, before his trick was discovered.

I had two good specimens of democracy during my stay in this city. I sent for a tailor to take my measure for a coat, and he returned for answer, that such a proceeding was not *republican*, and that I must *go to him*.

A young lady, with whom I was acquainted, was married during the time I was there, and the marriage-party went a short tour. On their return, when but a few miles from the city, they ordered the driver of the carriage to put his horses to, that they might proceed; he replied that he would take them no further. On inquiring the cause of his refusal, he said that he had not been treated as a gentleman; that they had had private meals every day, and had not asked him to the table; that they had used him very ill, and that he would drive no more. Things appear to be fast verging to the year 1920, or thereabouts, as described by Theodore Hook. A duchess wishing for a drive, the old mare sends an answer from the stable, that "She'll be d—d if she'll go out today."

Left Cincinnati, in a very small steam-boat, for Guyandotte, on my way to the Virginia Springs. I have often heard the expression of "Hell afloat" applied to very uncomfortable ships in the service, but this metaphor ought to have been reserved for a small high-pressure steamboat in the summer months in America; the sun darting his fierce rays down upon the roof above you, which is only half-inch plank, and rendering it so hot that you quickly remove your hand if, by chance, you put it there; the deck beneath your feet so heated by the furnaces below that you cannot walk with slippers; you are panting and exhausted between these two fires, without a breath of air to cool your forehead. Go forward, and the chimneys radiate a heat which is even more intolerable. Go—but there is no where to go, except overboard, and then you lose your passage. It is, really, a fiery furnace, and, day or night, it is in vain to seek a cool retreat. As we proceeded up the river, things became worse. We had not proceeded more than twenty miles, when a larger steamboat, which had started an hour before us, was discovered aground on a bar, which, from the low state of the river, she could not pass. After a parley between the captains, we went alongside and took out all her passengers, amounting to upward of a hundred, being more than we were on board of our own vessel. But they behaved like pirates, and treated us just as if we had been a captured vessel. Dinner was just ready; they sat down and took possession of it, leaving us to wait till the table was replenished. A young Englishman had just taken his seat by me, when a very queer-looking man came up to him and begged that he would give up his place to a *lady*. Aware of the custom of the country, he immediately resigned his seat, and went to look for another. When the lady took her seat by me I involuntarily drew my chair to a more respectful distance, there being something so particularly uninviting in her ladyship's appearance. On our arrival at Maysville, this lady, with her gentleman, told the captain that they were sorry they had not a cent wherewith to defray the expenses of their passage. Their luggage had been landed before this declaration was made, but it was immediately ordered on board again by the captain; and as, of course, they would not part with their goods and chattels, they remained on board of the boat. The captain took them to the river about twenty miles further, and then landed them on the bank, with their luggage, to find their way back to Maysville how they could. This is the usual punishment for such trial-practices; but, after all, it is only the punishment of delay, as they would hail the first boat which came down the river, make out a piteous tale of ill-treatment, be received on board, and landed at their destination.

This reminds me of a clever trick played by a Yankee pedlar upon one of the captains of the steamboats running from New York to Albany on the Hudson river. The Yankee was fully aware of this custom of putting people on shore who attempted to gain a passage for nothing, and his destination was to a place called Poughkeepsie, about halfway between New York and Albany. He, therefore, waited very quietly until he was within a mile or two of Poughkeepsie, and then went up to the captain.—"Well, now, Captain, I like to do things on the square, that's a fact;—I might have said nothing to you, and run up all the way to Albany—and to Albany I must go on most particular business—that's a fact; but I thought it more honourable-like to tell you at once—I hav'nt got a cent in my pocket; I've been unfortunate; but, by the 'tarnal I'll pay you my passage-money as soon as I get it. You see I tell you now, that you may'nt say that I cheat you; for pay you I will as soon as I can, that's a fact." The captain, indignant, as usual, at being tricked, called him certain names, swore a small quantity, and as soon as he arrived at Poughkeepsie, as a punishment put him ashore at the very place the keen Yankee wished to be landed at.

The Ohio river becomes much more rapid as you ascend. Abreast of Guyandotte, where we landed, the current was so strong that it was very difficult for men to wade across it, and the steamboats running against the stream could not gain more than a mile in the course of half an hour.

On board of this steamboat was a negro woman, very neatly dressed, with a very good-looking negro child, about nine months old, in her arms. It was of the darkest ebony in colour, and its dress rather surprised me. It was a chali frock, of a neat fawn coloured pattern, with fine muslin trousers edged with Valenciennes lace at the bottom; and very pretty did its little tiny black feet look, relieved by these expensive unnecessaries. I did not inquire who the young gentleman was; but I thought what pleasure the sight of him would have given Miss Martineau, who, as I have before observed, exclaims, "Happy is the country where factory-girls carry parasols, and pig-drivers wear spectacles." How much more happy must be that country where a little black boy, of nine months old, wears Valenciennes lace at the bottom of his trousers! It is, however a question of figures, and may be solved, not by the rule of three, but by the rule of five, which follows it in the arithmetic-book.

If a pig-driver	produces so much	a little black boy

with spectacles	happiness,	Valenciennes lace.

I leave Miss Martineau to make the calculation.

Volume Two—Chapter Eleven.

There is extreme beauty in the Ohio river. As may be supposed, where the rise and fall are so great the banks are very steep; and, now that the water is low, it appears deeply embedded in the wild forest scenery through which it flows. The whole stream is alive with small fresh-water turtle, who play on the surface of its clear water; while the more beautiful varieties of the butterfly tribe cross over from one side to the other, from the slave States to the free—their liberty, at all events, not being interfered with as, on the free side, it would be thought absurd to catch what would not produce a cent; while, on the slaves', their idleness and their indifference to them are their security.

Set off, one of nine, in a stage-coach, for the Blue Sulphur springs. The country, which is very picturesque, has been already described. It is one continuation of rising ground, through mountains covered with trees and verdure. Nature is excessively fond of drapery in America. I have never yet fallen in with a naked rock. She clothes every thing; and although you may occasionally meet with a slight nudity, it is no more than the exposure of the neck or the bare feet of the mountain-nymph. This ridge of the Alleghanies is very steep; but you have no distinct view as you climb up, not even at the Hawk's Nest, where you merely peep down into the ravine below. You are jammed up in the forests through which you pass nearly the whole of the way; and it was delightful to arrive at any level, and fall in with the houses and well-tilled fields of the Virginian farmers, exhibiting every proof of prosperity and ease. The heat was dreadful; two horses fell dead, and I thought that many others would have died, for two of the wheels were defective, and the labour of the poor animals, in dragging us constantly up hill, was most severe.

The indifference of the proprietors of public conveyances in America as to the safety of their passengers, can only be accounted for by the extreme indifference of the passengers themselves, and the independent feeling shewn by every class, who, whatever may be their profession, will never acknowledge themselves to be what we term the servants of the public. Here was an instance. The coach we were put into was defective in two of its wheels, and could only be repaired at Louisburg, about a hundred miles distant. Instead of sending it on to that town empty, as would have been done by our coach proprietors, and providing another (as they had plenty), for the passengers; instead of this, in order to save the extra trouble and expense, they risked the lives of the passengers on a road with a precipice on one side of it for at least four-fifths of the way. One of the wheels would not hold the grease, and creaked most ominously during the whole journey; and we were obliged to stop and pour water on it continually. The box and irons of the other were loose, and before we were half way it came off, and we were obliged to stop and get out. But the Americans are never at a loss when they are in a *fix*. The passengers borrowed an axe; in a short time wedges were cut from one of the trees at the road-side, and the wheel was so well repaired that it lasted us the remainder of our journey.

Our road for some time lay through the valley of Kenawha, through which runs the river of that name—a strong, clear stream. It is hemmed in by mountains on each side of it; and here, perhaps, is presented the most curious varieties of mineral produce that ever were combined in one locality. The river runs over a bed of horizontal calcareous strata, and by perforating this strata about forty or fifty feet below the level of the river, you arrive at salt-springs, the waters of which are pumped up by small steam-engines, and boiled down into salt in buildings erected on the river's banks. The mountains which hem in the river are one mass of coal; a gallery is opened at that part of the foot of the mountain most convenient to the buildings, and the coal is thrown down by shoots or small railways. Here you have coal for your fuel; salt water under fresh; and as soon as the salt is put into the barrels (which are also made from the mountain timber), the river is all ready to transplant them down to Ohio. But there is another great curiosity in this valley: these beds of coal have produced springs, as they are termed, of carburetted hydrogen gas, which run along the banks of the river close to the water's-edge. The negroes take advantage of these springs when they come down at night to wash clothes; they set fire to the springs, which yield them sufficient light for their work. The one which I examined was dry, and the gas bubbled up through the sand. By kicking the sand about, so as to make communications after I had lighted the gas, I obtained a very large flame, which I left burning.

The heat, as we ascended, was excessive, and the passengers availed themselves of every spring, with the exception of those just described, that they fell in with on the route. We drank of every variety of water excepting pure water—sometimes iron, sometimes sulphur; and, indeed, every kind of chalybeate, for every rill was impregnated in some way or another. At last, it occurred to me that there were such things as chemical affinities, and that there was no saying what changes might take place by the admixture of such a variety of metals and gases, so drank no more. I did not like, however, to interfere with the happiness of others, so I did not communicate my ideas to my fellow-passengers, who continued drinking during the whole day; and as I afterwards found out, did not sleep very well that night; they were, moreover, very sparing in the use of them the next day.

There are a great variety of springs already discovered on these mountains, and probably there will be a great many more. Already they have the blue, the white, and the red sulphur springs; the sweet and the salt; the warm and the hot, all of which have their several virtues; but the greatest virtue of all these mineral springs is, as in England and every where else, that they occasion people to live regularly, to be moderate in the use of wine, and to dwell in a pure and wholesome air. They always remind me of the eastern story of the Dervish, who, being sent for by a king who had injured his health by continual indulgence, gave him a racket-ball, which he informed the king possessed wonderful medicinal virtues; with this ball his majesty was to play at racket two or three hours every day with his courtiers. The exercise it induced, which was the only medicinal virtue the ball possessed, restored the king to health. So it is with all watering places; it is not so much the use of the water, as the abstinence from what is pernicious, together with exercise and early hours, which effect the majority of cures.

We arrived first at the blue sulphur springs, and I remained there for one day to get rid of the dust of travelling. They have a very excellent hotel there, with a ball room, which is open till eleven o'clock every night; the scenery is very pretty, and the company was good—as indeed is the company at all these springs, for they are too distant, and the travelling too expensive for every body to get there. But the blue sulphur are not fashionable, and the consequence was, we were not crowded, and were very comfortable. People who cannot get accommodated at the white sulphur, remain here until they can, the distance between those being only twenty-two miles.

The only springs which are fashionable are the white sulphur, and as these springs are a feature in American society, I shall describe them more particularly.

They are situated in a small valley, many hundred feet above the level of the sea, and are of about fifteen or twenty acres in area, surrounded by small hills, covered with foliage to their summits: at one end of the Valley is the hotel, with the large dining-room for all the visitors. Close to the hotel, but in another building, in the ballroom, and a little below the hotel on the other side, is the spring itself; but beautiful as is the whole scenery, the great charm of this watering place is, the way in which those live who visit it. The rises of the hills which surround the valley are covered with little cottages, log-houses, and other picturesque buildings, sometimes in rows, and ornamented with verandahs, without a second storey above; or kitchen below. Some are very elegant and more commodious than the rest, having been built by gentlemen who have the right given to them by the company to whom the springs belong, of occupying themselves when there, but not of preventing others from taking possession of them in their absence. The dinners and other meals are, generally speaking, bad; not that there is not a plentiful supply, but that it is so difficult to supply seven hundred people sitting down in one room. In the morning, they all turn out from their little burrows, meet in the public walks, and go down to the spring before breakfast; during the forenoon, when it is too warm, they remain at home; after dinner, they ride out or pay visits, and then end the day, either at the ball-room or in little societies among one another. There is no want of handsome equipages, many four in hand (Virginny long tails) and every accommodation for these equipages. The crowd is very great, and it is astonishing what inconvenience people will submit to, rather than not be accommodated somehow or another. Every cabin is like a rabbit burrow. In the one next to where I was lodged, in a room about fourteen feet square, and partitioned off as well as it could be, there slept a gentleman and his wife, his sister and brother, and a female servant. I am not sure that the nigger was not under the bed—at all events, the young sister told me that it was not at all pleasant.

There is a sort of major-domo here who regulates every department: his word is law, and his fiat immoveable, and he presumes not a little upon his power; a circumstance not to be surprised at, as he is as much courted and is as despotic as all the lady patronesses of Almacks rolled into one. He is called the Metternich of the mountains. No one is allowed accommodation at these springs who is not known, and generally speaking, only those favourites who travel in their private carriages. It is at this place that you feel how excessively aristocratical and exclusive the Americans would be, and indeed will be, in spite of their institutions. Spa, in its palmiest days, when princes had to sleep in their carriages at the doors of the hotels, was not more in vogue than are these white sulphur springs with the *élite* of the United States. And it is here, and here only, in the States, that you do meet with what may be fairly considered as select society, for at Washington there is a great mixture. Of course, all the celebrated belles of the different States are to be met with here, as well as all the large fortunes, nor is there a scarcity of pretty and wealthy widows. The president, Mrs Caton, the mother of Lady Wellesley, Lady Strafford, and Lady Caermarthen, the daughter of Carrol, of Carroltown, one of the real aristocracy of America, and a signer of the Declaration of Independence, and all the first old Virginian and Carolina families, many of them descendants of the old cavaliers, were at the springs when I arrived there; and I certainly must say that I never was at any watering-place in England where the company was so good and so select as at the Virginia springs in America.

I passed many pleasant days at this beautiful spot, and was almost as unwilling to leave it as I was to part with the Sioux Indians at St. Peters. Refinement and simplicity are equally charming. I was introduced to a very beautiful girl here, whom I should not have mentioned so particularly, had it not been that she was the first and only lady in America that I observed to *whittle*. She was sitting one fine morning on a wooden bench, surrounded by admirers, and as she carved away her seat with her pen-knife, so did she cut deep into the hearts of those who listened to her lively conversation.

There are, as may be supposed, a large number of negro servants here attending their masters and mistresses. I have often been amused, not only here, but during my residence in Kentucky, at the high-sounding Christian names which have been given to them. "Byron, tell Ada to come here directly." "Now, *Telemachus*, if you don't leave *Calypso* alone, you'll get a taste of the *cow-hide*."

Among others, attracted to the springs professionally, was a very clever German painter, who, like all Germans, had a very correct ear for music. He had painted a kitchen-dance in Old Virginia, and in the picture he had introduced all the well-known coloured people in the place; among the rest were the band of musicians, but I observed that one man was missing. "Why did you not put him in?" inquired I. "Why, Sir, I could not put him in; it was impossible; he never *plays in tune*. Why, if I put him in, Sir, he would spoil the *harmony* of my whole picture!"

I asked this artist how he got on in America. He replied, "But so-so: the Americans in general do not estimate genius. They come to me and ask what I want for my pictures, and I tell them. Then they say, 'How long did it take you to paint it?' I answer, 'So many days.' Well, then they calculate and say, 'If it took you only so many days, you ask so many dollars a day for your work; you ask a great deal too much; you ought to be content with so much per day, and I will give you that.' So that, thought I, invention and years of study go for nothing with these people. There is only one way to dispose of a picture in America, and that is, to raffle it; the Americans will then run the chance of getting it. If you do not like to part with your pictures in that way, you must paint portraits; people will purchase their own faces all over the world: the worst of it is, that in this country, they will purchase nothing else."

During my stay here, I was told of one of the most remarkable instances that perhaps ever occurred, of the discovery of a fact by the party from whom it was of the utmost importance to conceal it—a very pretty interesting young widow. She had married a promising young man, to whom she was tenderly attached, and who, a few months after the marriage, unfortunately fell in a duel. Aware that the knowledge of the cause of her husband's death would render the blow still more severe to her, (the ball having passed through the eye into his brain, and there being no evident gun-shot wound,) her relations informed her that he had been thrown from his horse, and killed by the fall. She believed them. She was living in the country, when, about nine months after her widowhood, her brother rode down to see her, and as soon as he arrived went into his room to shave and dress. The window of his room, which was on the ground-floor, looked out upon the garden, and it being summer time, it was open. He tore off a portion of an old newspaper to wipe his razor. The breeze caught it, and carried it away into the garden until it stopped at the feet of his sister, who happened to be walking. Mechanically she took up the fragment, and perceiving her husband's name upon it, she read it. It contained a full account of the duel in which he lost his life! The shock she received was so great that it unsettled her mind for nearly two years. She had but just recovered, and for the first time re-appeared in public, when she was pointed out to me.

Returning to Guyandotte, one of the travellers wished to see the view from the Hawk's Nest, or rather wished to be able to say that he had seen it. We passed the spot when it was quite dark, but he persisted in going there, and, to help his vision, borrowed one of the coach-lamps from the driver. He returned, and declared that with the assistance of the lamp he had had a very excellent view, down a precipice of several hundred feet. His bird's-eye view by candle-light must have been very extensive. After all, it is but to be able to say that they had been, to such a place, or have seen such a thing, that, more than any real taste for it, induces the majority of the world to incur the trouble and fatigue of travelling.

Volume Two—Chapter Twelve.

I was informed that a camp-meeting was to be held about seven miles from Cincinnati, and, anxious to verify the accounts I had heard of them, I availed myself of this opportunity of deciding for myself. We proceeded about five miles on the high road, and then diverged by a cross-road until we arrived at a steep conical hill, crowned with splendid forest trees without underwood; the trees being sufficiently apart to admit of wagons and other vehicles to pass in every direction. The camp was raised upon the summit of this hill, a piece of table-land comprising many acres. About an acre and a half was surrounded on the four sides by cabins built up of rough boards; the whole area in the centre was fitted up with planks, laid about a foot from the ground, as seats. At one end, but not close to the cabins, was a raised stand, which served as a pulpit for the preachers, one of them praying, while five or six others sat down behind him on benches. There was ingress to the area by the four corners; the whole of it was shaded by vast forest trees, which ran up to the height of fifty or sixty feet without throwing out a branch; and to the trunks of these trees were fixed lamps in every direction, for the continuance of service by night. Outside the area, which may be designated as the church, were hundreds of tents pitched in every quarter, their snowy whiteness contrasting beautifully with the deep verdure and gloom of the forest. These were the temporary habitations of those who had come many miles to attend the meeting, and who remained there from the commencement until it concluded—usually, a period of from ten to twelve days, but often much longer. The tents were furnished with every article necessary for cooking; mattresses to sleep upon, etcetera; some of them even had bedsteads and chests of drawers, which had been brought in the wagons in which the people in this country usually travel. At a farther distance were all the wagons and other vehicles which had conveyed the people to the meeting, whilst hundreds of horses were tethered under the trees, and plentifully provided with forage. Such were the general outlines of a most interesting and beautiful scene.

Where, indeed, could so magnificent a temple to the Lord be raised as on this lofty hill, crowned as it was with such majestic verdure. Compared with these giants of the forest, the cabins and tents of the multitude appeared as insignificant and contemptible as almost would man himself in the presence of the Deity. Many generations of men must have been mowed down before the arrival of these enormous trees to their present state of maturity; and at the time they sent forth their first shoots, probably were not on the whole of this continent, now teeming with millions, as many white men as are now assembled on this field. I walked about for some time surveying the panorama, when I returned to the area, and took my seat upon a bench. In one quarter the coloured population had collected themselves; their tents appeared to be better furnished and better supplied with comforts than most of those belonging to the whites. I put my head into one of the tents, and discovered a sable damsel lying on a bed and singing hymns in a loud voice.

The major portion of those not in the area were cooking the dinners. Fires were burning in every direction, pots boiling, chickens roasting, hams seething; indeed there appeared to be no want of creature comforts.

But the trumpet sounded, as in days of yore, as a signal that the service was about to recommence and I went into the area and took my seat. One of the preachers rose and gave out a hymn, which was sung by the congregation, amounting to about seven or eight hundred. After the singing of the hymn was concluded he commenced an extempore sermon: it was good, sound doctrine, and, although Methodism of the mildest tone, and divested of its bitterness of denunciation, as indeed is generally the case with Methodism in America. I heard nothing which could be offensive to any other sect, or which could be considered objectionable by the most orthodox, and I began to doubt whether such scenes as had been described to me did really take place at these meetings. A prayer followed, and after about two hours the congregation were dismissed to their dinners, being first informed that the service would recommence at two o'clock at the sound of the trumpet. In front of the pulpit there was a space railed off; and strewed with straw, which I was told was the *Anxious seat*, and on which sat those who were touched by their consciences or the discourse of the preacher; but, although there were several sitting on it, I did not perceive any emotion on the part of the occupants: they were attentive, but nothing more.

When I first examined the area, I saw a very large tent at one corner of it, probably fifty feet long, by twenty wide. It was open at the end, and, being full of straw, I concluded it was used as a sleeping-place for those who had not provided themselves with separate accommodation. About an hour after the service was over, perceiving many people directing their steps toward it, I followed them. On one side of the tent were about twenty females, mostly young, squatted down on the straw; on the other a few men; in the centre was a long form, against which were some other men kneeling, with their faces covered with their hands, as if occupied in prayer. Gradually the numbers increased, girl after girl dropped down upon the straw on the one side, and men on the other. At last an elderly man gave out a hymn, which was sung with peculiar energy; then another knelt down in the centre, and commenced a prayer, shutting his eyes (as I observed most clergymen in the United States do when they pray) and raising his hands above his head; then another burst out into a prayer, and another followed him; then their voices became all confused together; and then were heard the more silvery tones of woman's supplication. As the din increased so did their enthusiasm; handkerchiefs were raised to bright eyes, and sobs were intermingled with prayers and ejaculations. It became a scene of Babel; more than twenty men and women were crying out at the highest pitch of their voices, and trying apparently to be heard above the others. Every minute the excitement increased; some wrung their hands and called for mercy; some tore their hair; boys laid down crying bitterly, with their heads buried in the straw; there was sobbing almost to suffocation, and hysterics and deep agony. One young man clung to the form, crying, "Satan tears at me, but I would hold fast. Help—help, he drags me down!" It was a scene of horrible agony and despair; and, when it was at its height, one of the preachers came in, and raising his voice high above the tumult, intreated the Lord to receive into his fold those who now repented and would fain return. Another of the ministers knelt down by some young men, whose faces were covered up, and who appeared to be almost in a state of frenzy; and putting his hands upon them, poured forth an energetic prayer, well calculated to work upon their over excited feelings. Groans, ejaculations, broken sobs, frantic motions, and convulsions succeeded; some fell on their backs with their eyes closed, waving their hands with a slow motion, and crying out—"Glory, glory, glory!" I quitted the spot, and hastened away into the forest, for the sight was too painful, too melancholy. Its sincerity could not be doubted, but it was the effect of over-excitement, not of sober reasoning. Could such violence of feeling have been produced had each party retired to commune alone? most surely not. It was a fever created by collision and contact, of the same nature as that which stimulates a mob to deeds of blood and horror.

Gregarious animals are by nature inoffensive. The cruel and the savage live apart, and in solitude; but the gregarious, upheld and stimulated by each other, become formidable. So it is with man.

I was told that the scene would be much more interesting and exciting after the lamps were lighted; but I had seen quite enough of it. It was too serious to laugh at, and I felt that it was not for me to condemn. "Cry aloud, and spare not," was the exhortation of the preacher and certainly, if heaven was only to be taken by storm, he was a proper leader for his congregation.

Whatever may be the opinion of the reader as to the meeting which I have described, it is certain that nothing could be more laudable than the intention by which these meetings were originated. At the first settling of the country the people were widely scattered, and the truths of the Gospel, owing to the scarcity of preachers, but seldom heard. It was to remedy this unavoidable evil that they agreed, like the Christians in earlier times, to collect together from all quarters, and pass many days in meditation and prayer, "exhorting one another —comforting one another." Even now it is not uncommon for the settlers in Indians and Illinois to travel one hundred miles in their wagons to attend one of these meetings,—meetings which are now too often sullied by fanaticism on the one hand, and on the other by the levity and infidelity of those who go not to pray, but to scoff; or to indulge in the licentiousness which, it is said, but too often follows, when night has thrown her veil over the scene.

Volume Two—Chapter Thirteen.

Lexington, the capital of the State, is embosomed in the very heart of the vale of Kentucky. This vale was the favourite hunting-ground of the Indians; and a fairer country for the chase could not well be imagined than this rolling, well-wooded, luxuriant valley, extending from hill to hill, from dale to dale, for so many long miles. No wonder that the Indians fought so hard to retain, or the Virginians to acquire it; nor was it until much blood had saturated the ground, many reeking scalps had been torn from the head, and many a mother and her children murdered at their hearths, that the contest was relinquished. So severe were the struggles, that the ground obtained the name of the "Bloody Ground." But the strife is over; the red man has been exterminated, and peace and plenty now reign over this smiling country. It is indeed a beautiful and bounteous land; on the whole, the most eligible in the Union. The valley is seven hundred and fifty feet above the level of the sea, and, therefore, not so subject to fevers as the States of Indiana and Illinois, and indeed that portion of its own state which borders on the Mississippi. But all the rest of the Kentucky land is by no means equal in richness of soil to that of this valley. There are about ninety counties in the State, of which about thirty are of rich land; but four of them, namely, Fayette, Bourbon, Scotts, and Woodford, are the finest. The whole of these four counties are held by large proprietors, who graze and breed stock to a very great extent, supplying the whole of the Western States with the best description of every kind of cattle. Cattle-shows are held every year, and high prizes awarded to the owners of the finest beasts which are there produced. The State of Kentucky, as well as Virginia, is in fact an agricultural and grazing State; the pasture is very rich, and studded with oak and other timber, as in the manner I have described in Ioway and Wisconsin. The staples of Kentucky are hemp and mules; the latter are in such demand for the south that they can hardly produce them fast enough for the market. The minimum price of a three-year old mule is about eighty dollars; the maximum usually one hundred and sixty dollars, or thirty-five pounds, but they often fetch much higher prices. I saw a pair in harness, well matched, and about seventeen hands high, for which they refused one thousand dollars—upwards of two hundred pounds.

The cattle-show took place when I was at Lexington. That of horned beasts I was too late for; but the second day I went to the exhibition of thorough-bred horses. The premiums were for the best two-year old, yearlings, and colts, and many of them were very fine animals. The third day was for the exhibition of mules; which, on account of size there being a great desideratum, are bred only from mares; the full-grown averaged from fifteen to sixteen hands high, but they have often been known to be seventeen hands high. I had seen them quite as large in a nobleman's carriage in the south of Spain; but then they were considered rare, and of great value. After all the other varieties of age had made their appearance, and the judges had given their decision, the mules foaled down this year were to be examined. As they were still sucking, it was necessary that the brood mares should be led into the enclosed paddock, where the animals were inspected, that the foals might be induced to follow; as soon as they were all in the enclosure the mares were sent out, leaving all the foals by themselves. At first they commenced a concert of wailing after their mothers, and then turned their lamentations into indignation and revenge upon each other. Such a ridiculous scene of kicking took place as I never before witnessed, about thirty of them being most sedulously engaged in the occupation, all at the same time. I never saw such ill-behaved mules; it was quite impossible for the judges to decide upon the prize, for you could see nothing but heels in the air; it was rap, rap, rap, incessantly against one another's sides, until they were all turned out, and the show was over. I rather think the prize must, in this instance, have been awarded to the one that kicked highest.

The fourth day was for the exhibition of jackasses, of two-year and one-year, and for foals, and jennies also; this sight was to me one of peculiar interest. Accustomed as we are in England to value a jackass at thirty shillings, we look down upon them with contempt; but here the case is reversed: you look up at them with surprise and admiration. Several were shown standing fifteen hands high, with head and ears in proportion; the breed has been obtained from the Maltese jackass, crossed by those of Spain and the south of France. Those imported seldom average more than fourteen hands high; but the Kentuckians, by great attention and care, have raised them up to fifteen hands, and sometimes even to sixteen.

But the price paid for these splendid animals, for such they really were, will prove how much they are in request. Warrior, a jackass of great celebrity, sold for 5,000 dollars, upwards of 1,000 pounds sterling. Half of another jackass, Benjamin by name, was sold for 2,500 dollars. At the show I asked a gentleman what he wanted for a very beautiful female ass, only one year old; he said that he could have 1,000 dollars, 250 pounds for her, but that he had refused that sum. For a two-year old jack, shown during the exhibition, they asked 3000 dollars, more than 600 pounds. I never felt such respect for donkeys before; but the fact is, that mule-breeding is so lucrative, that there is no price which a very large donkey will not command.

I afterwards went to a cattle sale a few miles out of the town. Don Juan, a two-year old bull, Durham breed, fetched 1,075 dollars; an imported Durham cow, with her calf, 985 dollars. Before I arrived, a bull and cow fetched 1,300 dollars each of them, about 280 pounds. The cause of this is, that the demand for good stock, now that the Western States are filling up, becomes so great that they cannot be produced fast enough. Mr Clay, who resides near Lexington, is one of the best breeders in the State, which is much indebted to him for the fine stock which he has imported from England.

Another sale took place, which I attended, and I quote the prices:— Yearling bull, 1,000 dollars; ditto heifer, 1,500. Cows, of full Durham blood, but bred in Kentucky, 1,245 dollars; ditto, 1,235 dollars. Imported cow and calf, 2,100 dollars.

It must be considered, that although a good Durham cow will not cost more than twenty guineas perhaps, in England, the expenses of transport are very great, and they generally stand it to the importers, about 600 dollars, before they arrive at the State of Kentucky.

But to prove that the Kentuckians are fully justified in giving the prices they do, I will shew what was the profit made upon an old cow before she was sold for 400 dollars. I had a statement from her proprietor, who had her in his possession for nine years. She was a full-bred cow, and during the time that he had held her in his possession, she had cleared him 15,000 dollars by the sale of her progeny: As follows:—

Years.	Calves	Second	Third		Fourth

		d		
		Generation	Generation	Generation
1	1			
2	1			
3	1	1		
4	1	1		
5	1	1	1	
6	1	1	1	
7	1	1	1	1
8	1	1	1	1
9	1	1	1	1

	9	7	5	3

Total, 24

averaging 625 dollars a head, which is by no means a large price, as the two cows, which sold at the sale for 1,245, and 1,235 dollars, were a part of her issue.

Lexington is a very pretty town, with very pleasant society, and afforded me great relief after the unpleasant sojourn I had had at Louisville. Conversing one day with Mr Clay, I had another instance given me of the mischief which the conduct of Miss Martineau has entailed upon all those English who may happen to visit America. Mr Clay observed that Miss Martineau had remained with him for some time, and that during her stay, she had professed very different, or at least more modified opinions on the subject of slavery, than those she has expressed in her book: so much so, that one day, having read a letter from Boston cautioning her against being cajoled by the hospitality and pleasant society of the Western States, she handed it to him, saying, "They want to make a regular abolitionist of me." "When her work came out," continued Mr Clay, "although I read but very little of it, I turned to this subject so important with us, and I must say I was a little surprised to find that she had so changed her opinions." The fact is, Miss Martineau appears to have been what the Kentuckians call, "playing 'possum." I have met with some of the Southern ladies whose conversations on slavery are said, or supposed, to have been those printed by Miss Martineau, and they deny that they are correct. That the Southern ladies are very apt to express great horror at living too long a time at the plantations, is very certain; not, however, because they expect to be murdered in their beds by the slaves, as they tell their husbands, but because they are anxious to spend more of their time at the cities, where they can enjoy more luxury and amusement than can be procured at the plantations.

Every body rides in Virginia and Kentucky, master, man, woman, and slave, and they all ride well: it is quite as common to meet a woman on horseback as a man, and it is a pretty sight in their States to walk by the Church doors and see them all arrive. The Churches have stables, or rather sheds, built close to them, for the accommodation of the cattle.

Elopements in these States are all made on horseback. The goal to be obtained is to cross to the other side of the Ohio. The consequence is that it is a regular steeple-chase; the young couple clearing everything, father and brothers following. Whether it is that, having the choice, the young people are the best mounted, I know not, but the runaways are seldom overtaken. One couple crossed the Ohio when I was at Cincinnati, and had just time to tie the noose before their pursuers arrived.

At Lexington, on Sunday, there is not a carriage or horse to be obtained by a white man for any consideration, they having all been regularly engaged for that day by the negro slaves, who go out in every direction. Where they get the money I do not know; but certain it is, that it is always produced when required. I was waiting at the counter of a sort of pastry-cook's, when three negro lads, about twelve or fourteen years old, came in, and, in a most authoritative tone, ordered three glasses of soda-water.

Returned to Louisville.

Volume Two—Chapter Fourteen.

There is one great inconvenience in American travelling, arising from the uncertainty of river navigation. Excepting the Lower Mississippi and the Hudson, and not always the latter, the communication by water is obstructed during a considerable portion of the year, by ice in the winter, or a deficiency of water in the dry season. This has been a remarkable season for heat and drought; and thousands of people remain in the States of Ohio, Virginia, and Kentucky, who are most anxious to return home. It must be understood, that during the unhealthy season in the southern States on the Mississippi, the planters, cotton-growers, slave holders, store-keepers, and indeed almost every class, excepting the slaves and overseers, migrate to the northward, to escape the yellow fever, and spend a portion of their gains in amusement.

They go to Cincinnati and the towns of Ohio, to the Lakes occasionally, but principally to the cities and watering places of Virginia and Kentucky, more especially Louisville, where I now am; and Louisville, being also the sort of general rendezvous for departure south, is now crammed with southern people. The steam boats cannot run, for the river is almost dry; and I (as well as others) have been detained much longer on the banks of the Ohio than was my intention. There is land-carriage certainly, but the heat of the weather is so overpowering that even the Southerns dread it; and in consequence of this extreme heat the sickness in these western States has been much greater than usual. Even Kentucky, especially that part which borders on the Mississippi, which, generally speaking, is healthy, is now suffering under malignant fevers. I may here remark, that the two States, Illinois and Indiana, and the western portions of Kentucky and Tennessee, are very unhealthy; not a year passes without a great mortality from the bilious congestive fever, a variety of the yellow fever, and the ague; more especially Illinois and Indiana, with the western portion of Ohio, which is equally flat with the other two States. The two States of Indiana and Illinois lie, as it were, at the bottom of the western basin; the soil is wonderfully rich, but the drainage is insufficient, as may be seen from the sluggishness with which these rivers flow. Many and many thousands of poor Irish emigrants, and settlers also, have been struck down by disease, never to rise again, in these rich but unhealthy States; to which, stimulated by the works published by land-speculators, thousands and thousands every year repair, and, notwithstanding the annual expenditure of life, rapidly increase the population. I had made up my mind to travel by land-carriage to St. Louis, Missouri, through the States of Indiana and Illinois, but two American gentlemen, who had just arrived by that route, succeeded in dissuading me. They had come over on horseback. They described the disease and mortality as dreadful. That sometimes, when they wished to put up their horses at seven or eight o'clock in the evening, they were compelled to travel on till twelve or one o'clock before they could gain admittance, some portion in every house suffering under the bilious fever, tertian ague, or flux. They described the scene as quite appalling. At some houses there was not one person able to rise and attend upon the others; all were dying or dead and to increase the misery of their situations, the springs had dried up, and in many places they could not procure water except by sending many miles. A friend of mine, who had been on a mission through the portion of Kentucky and Tennessee bordering on them Mississippi, made a very similar statement. He was not refused to remain where he stopped, but he could procure no assistance, and everywhere ran the risk of contagion. He said that some of the people were obliged to send their negroes with a waggon upwards of fifteen miles to wash their clothes.

That this has been a very unhealthy season is certain, but still, from all the information I could obtain, there is a great mortality every year in the districts I have pointed out; and such indeed must be the case, from the miasma created every fall of the year in these rich alluvial soils, some portions of which have been worked for fifty years without the assistance of manure, and still yield abundant crops. It will be a long while before the drainage necessary to render them healthy can be accomplished. The sickly appearance of the inhabitants establishes but too well the facts related to me; and yet, strange to say, it would appear to be a provision of Providence, that a remarkable fecundity on the part of the women in the more healthy portions of their Western States, should meet the annual expenditure of life. Three children at a birth are more common here than twins are in England; and they, generally speaking, are all reared up. There have been many instances of even four.

The western valley of America, of which the Mississippi may be considered as the common drain, must, from the surprising depth of the alluvial soil, have been (ages back) wholly under water, and, perhaps, by some convulsion raised up. What insects are we in our own estimation when we meditate upon such stupendous changes.

Since I have been in these States, I have been surprised at the stream of emigration which appears to flow from North Carolina to Indiana, Illinois, and Missouri. Every hour you meet with a caravan of emigrants from that sterile but healthy state. Every night the banks of the Ohio are lighted up with their fires, where they have bivouacked previously to crossing the river; but they are not like the poor German or Irish settlers: they are well prepared, and have nothing to do, apparently, but to sit down upon their land. These caravans consist of two or three covered wagons, full of women and children, furniture, and other necessaries, each drawn by a team of horses; brood mares, with foals by their sides, following; half a dozen or more cows, flanked on each side by the men, with their long rifles on their shoulders; sometimes a boy or two, or a half-grown girl on horseback. Occasionally they wear an appearance of more refinement and cultivation, as well as wealth, the principals travelling in a sort of worn-out old carriage, the remains of the competence of former days.

I often surmised, as they travelled cheerfully along, saluting me as they passed by, whether they would not repent their decision, and sigh for their pine barrens and heath, after they had discovered that with fertility they had to encounter such disease and mortality.

I have often heard it asserted by Englishmen, that America has no coal. There never was a greater mistake: she has an abundance, and of the very finest that ever was seen. At Wheeling and Pittsburg, and on all the borders of the Ohio river above Guyandotte, they have an inexhaustible supply, equal to the very best offered to the London market. All the spurs of the Alleghany range appear to be one mass of coal. In the Eastern States the coal is of a different quality, although there is some very tolerable. The anthracite is bad, throwing out a strong sulphureous gas. The fact is that wood is at present cheaper than coal, and therefore the latter is not in demand. An American told me one day, that a company had been working a coal mine in an Eastern State, which proved to be of a very bad quality; they had sent some to an influential person as a present, requesting him to give his opinion of it, as that would be important to them. After a certain time he forwarded to them a certificate couched in such terms as these:— "I do hereby certify that I have tried the coal sent me by the company at —, and it is my decided opinion, that when the general conflagration of the world shall take place, any man who will take his position on that *coal-mine* will certainly be the *last man* who will be *burnt*."

I had to travel by coach for six days and nights, to arrive at Baltimore. As it may be supposed, I was not a little tired before my journey was half over; I therefore was glad when the coach stopped for a few hours, to throw off my coat, and lie down on a bed. At one town, where I had stopped, I had been reposing more than two hours when my door was opened—but this was too common a circumstance for me to think any thing of it; the people would come into my room whether I was in bed or out of bed, dressed or not dressed, and if I expostulated, they would reply, "Never mind, *we* don't care, Captain." On this occasion I called out, "Well, what do you want?"

"Are you Captain M—?" said the person walking up to the bed where I was lying.

"Yes, I am," replied I.

"Well, I reckon I wouldn't allow you to go through our town without seeing you any how. Of all the humans, you're the one I most wish to see."

I told him I was highly flattered.

"Well now," said he, giving a jump, and coming down right upon the bed in his great coat, "I'll just tell you; I said to the chap at the bar, 'Ain't the Captain in your house?' 'Yes,' says he. 'Then where is he?' says I. 'Oh,' says he, 'he's gone into his own room, and locked himself up; he's a d—d aristocrat, and won't drink at the bar with other gentlemen.' So, thought I, I've read M—'s works, and I'll be swamped if he is an aristocrat, and by the 'tarnal I'll go up and see; so here I am, and you're no aristocrat."

"I should think not," replied I, moving my feet away, which he was half sitting on.

"Oh, don't move; never mind me, Captain, I'm quite comfortable. And how do you find yourself by this time?"

"Very tired indeed," replied I.

"I suspicion as much. Now, d'ye see, I left four or five good fellows down below who wish to see you; I said I'd go up first, and come down to them. The fact is, Captain, we don't like you should pass through our town without showing you a little American hospitality."

So saying, he slid off the bed, and went out of the room. In a minute he returned, bringing with him four or five others, all of whom he introduced by name, and reseated himself on my bed, while the others took chairs.

"Now, gentlemen," said he, "as I was telling the Captain, we wish to show him a little American hospitality; what shall it be, gentlemen; what d'ye say—a bottle of Madeira?"

An immediate answer not being returned, he continued:

"Yes, gentlemen, a bottle of Madeira; at my expense, gentlemen, recollect that; now ring the bell."

"I shall be most happy to take a glass of wine with you," observed I, "but in my own room the wine must be at *my* expense."

"At *your* expense, Captain; well, if it must be, I don't care; at *your* expense then, Captain, if you say so; only, you see, we must show you a little American hospitality, as I said to them all down below; didn't I, gentlemen?"

The wine was ordered, and it ended in my hospitable friends drinking three bottles, and then they all shook hands with me, declaring how happy they should be if I came to the town again, allowed them to show me a little more American hospitality.

There was something so very ridiculous in this event, that I cannot help narrating it; but let it not be supposed, for a moment, that I intend it as a sarcasm upon American hospitality in general. There certainly are conditions usually attached to their hospitality, if you wish to profit by it to any extent; and one is, that you do not venture to find fault with themselves, their manners, or their institutions.

Note—That a guest, partaking of their hospitality, should give his opinions unasked, and find fault, would be in very bad taste, to say the least of it. But the fault in America is, that you are compelled to give an opinion, and you cannot escape by a doubtful reply: as the American said to me in Philadelphia, "I wish a*categorical* answer." Thus, should you not agree with them, you are placed upon the horns of a dilemma: either you must affront the company, or sacrifice truth.

End of Diary.

Volume Three—Chapter One.

Remarks—Language.

The Americans boldly assert that they speak better English than we do, and I was rather surprised not to find a statistical table to that effect in Mr Carey's publication. What I believe the Americans would imply by the above assertion is that you may travel through all the United States and find less difficulty in understanding or being understood, than in some of the counties of England, such as Cornwall, Devonshire, Lancashire and Suffolk. So far they are correct; but it is remarkable how very debased the language has become in a short period in America. There are few provincial dialects in England much less intelligible than the following. A Yankee girl, who wished to hire herself out, was asked if the had any followers or sweethearts? After a little hesitation, she replied, "Well, now, can't exactly say; I bees a sorter courted and a sorter not; reckon more a sorter yes than a sorter no." In many points the Americans have to a certain degree obtained that equality which they profess; and, as respects their language, it certainly is the case. If their lower classes are more intelligible than ours, it is equally true that the higher classes do not speak the language so purely or so classically as it is spoken among the well educated English. The peculiar dialect of the English counties is kept up because we are a settled country; the people who are born in a county live in it, and die in it, transmitting their sites of labour or of amusement to their descendants, generation after generation, without change: consequently, the provincialisms of the language become equally hereditary. Now, in America, they have a dictionary containing many thousands of words, which, with us, are either obsolete or are provincialisms, or are words necessarily invented by the Americans. When the people of England emigrated to the states, they came from every county in England, and each county brought its provincialisms with it. These were admitted into the general stock; and were since all collected and bound up by one Mr Webster. With the exception of a few words coined for local uses (such as *snags* and *sawyers*, on the Mississippi,) I do not recollect a word which I have not traced to be either a provincialism of some English county, or else to be obsolete English. There are a few from the Dutch, such as *stoup*, for the porch of a door, etcetera. I was once talking with an American about Webster's dictionary, and he observed, "Well now, sir, I understand it's the only one used in the Court of St. James, by the king, queen, and princesses, and that by royal order."

The upper class of the Americans do not, however, speak or pronounce English according to our standard; they appear to have no exact rule to guide them, probably from the want of any intimate knowledge of Greek or Latin. You seldom hear a derivation from the Greek pronounced correctly, the accent being generally laid upon the wrong syllable. In fact, every one appears to be independent, and pronounces just as he pleases.

But it is not for me to decide the very momentous question, as to which nation speaks the best English. The Americans generally improve upon the inventions of others; probably they may have improved upon our language.

I recollect some one observing how very superior the German language was to the English, from their possessing so many compound substantives and adjectives; whereupon his friend replied, that it was just as easy for us to possess them in England if we pleased, and gave us as an example an observation made by his old dame at Eaton, who declared that young Paulet was, without any exception, the most *good-for-nothing-est*, the most *provoking-people-est*, and the most *poke-about-every-corner-est* boy she had ever had charge of in her life.

Assuming this principle of improvement to be correct, it must be acknowledged that the Americans have added considerably to our dictionary; but, as I have before observed, this being a point of too much delicacy for me to decide upon, I shall just submit to the reader the occasional variations, or improvements, as they may be, which met my ears during my residence in America, as also the idiomatic peculiarities, and having so done, I must leave him to decide for himself.

I recollect once talking with one of the first men in America, who was narrating to me the advantages which might have accrued to him if he had followed up a certain speculation, when he said, "Sir, if I had done so, I should not only have *doubled* and *trebled*, but I should have *fourbled* and *fivebled* my money."

One of the members of congress once said, "What the honourable gentleman has just asserted I consider as *catamount* to a denial;"—(catamount is the term given to a panther or lynx.)

"I presume," replied his opponent, "that the honourable gentleman means *tantamount*."

"No, sir, I do not mean *tantamount*; I am not so ignorant of our language, not to be aware that catamount and tantamount are anonymous."

The Americans dwell upon their words when they speak—a custom arising, I presume, from their cautious, calculating habits; and they have always more or less of a nasal twang. I once said to a lady, "Why do you drawl out your words in that way?"

"Well," replied she, "I'd drawl all the way from Maine to Georgia, rather than *clip* my words as you English people do."

Many English words are used in a very different sense from that which we attach to them; for instance: a *clever* person in America means an amiable, good-tempered person, and the Americans make the distinction by saying, I mean English clever.

Our *clever* is represented by the word *smart*.

The verb *to admire* is also used in the East, instead of the verb *to like*.

"Have you ever been at Paris?"

"No; but I should *admire* to go."

A Yankee description of a clever woman:—

"Well, now, she'll walk right into you, and talk to you like a book;" or, as I have heard them say, "she'll talk you out of sight."

The word ugly is used for cross, ill-tempered. "I did feel so *ugly* when he said that."

Bad is used in an odd sense: it is employed for awkward, uncomfortable: sorry:—

"I did feel so *bad* when I read that"—awkward.

"I have felt quite *bad* about it ever since"—uncomfortable.

"She was so *bad*, I thought she would cry"—sorry.

And as bad is tantamount to not *good*, I have heard a lady say, "I don't feel *at all good* this morning."

Mean is occasionally used for ashamed.

"I never felt so mean in my life."

The word handsome is oddly used.

"We reckon this very handsome scenery, sir," said an American to me, pointing to the landscape.

"I consider him very truthful," is another expression.

"He stimulates too much."

"He dissipates awfully."

And they are very fond of using the noun as a verb, as—"I *suspicion* that's a fact."

"I *opinion* quite the contrary."

The word *considerable* is in considerable demand in the United States. In a work in which the letters of the party had been given to the public as specimens of good style and polite literature, it is used as follows:—

"My dear sister, I have taken up the pen early this morning, as I intend to write *considerable*." (Life and Remains of Charles Pont.)

The word great is oddly used for fine, splendid.

"She's the *greatest* gal in the whole Union."

But there is one word which we must surrender up to the Americans as their *very own*, as the children say. I will quote a passage from one of their papers:—

"The editor of the *Philadelphia Gazette* is wrong in calling absquatiated a Kentucky *phrase* (he may well say phrase instead of *word*.) It may prevail there, but its origin was in South Carolina, where it was a few years since regularly derived from the Latin, as we can prove from undoubted authority. By the way, there is a little *corruption* is the word as the *Gazette* uses it, *absquatalized* is the true reading."

Certainly a word worth quarrelling about!

"Are you cold, miss?" said I to a young lady, who pulled the shawl closer over her shoulders.

"*Some*," was the reply.

The English *what*? implying that you did not hear what was said to you, is changed in America to the word *how*?

"I reckon," "I calculate," "I guess," are all used as the common English phrase, "I suppose." Each term is said to be peculiar to different states, but I found them used everywhere, one as often as the other. *I opine*, is not so common.

A specimen of Yankee dialect and conversation:—

"Well now, I'll tell you—you know Marble Head?"

"Guess I do."

"Well, then, you know Sally Hackett."

"No, indeed."

"Not know Sally Hackett? Why she lives at Marble Head."

"Guess I don't."

"You don't mean to say that?"

"Yes, indeed."

"And you really don't know Sally Hackett?"

"No, indeed."

"I guess you've heard talk of her?"

"No, indeed."

"Well, that's considerable odd. Now, I'll tell you—Ephraim Bagg, he that has the farm three miles from Marble Head—just as—but now, are you sure you don't know Sally Hackett?"

"No, indeed."

"Well, he's a pretty substantial man, and no mistake. He has got a heart as big as an ox, and everything else in proportion, I've a notion. He loves Sal, the worst kind; and if she gets up there, she'll think she has got to Palestine (Paradise); ain't she a screamer? I were thinking of Sal myself, for I feel lonesome, and when I am thrown into my store promiscuous alone, I can tell you I have the blues, the worst kind, no mistake—I can tell you that. I always feel a kind o' queer when I sees Sal, but when I meet any of the other gals I am as calm and cool as the milky way," etcetera, etcetera.

The verb "to fix" is universal. It means to do anything.

"Shall I *fix* your coat or your breakfast first?" That is—"Shall I brush your coat, or *get ready* your breakfast first!"

Right away, for immediately or at once, is very general.

"Shall I fix it right away?"—i.e. "Shall I do it immediately?"

In the West, when you stop at an inn, they say—

"What will you have? Brown meal and common doings, or white wheat and chicken *fixings*;"—that is, "Will you have pork and brown bread, or white bread and fried chicken?"

Also, "Will you have a *feed* or a *check*?"—A dinner, or a luncheon?

In *full blast*—something in the extreme.

"When she came to meeting, with her yellow hat and feathers, wasn't she *in fall blast?*"

But for more specimens of genuine Yankee, I must refer the reader to Sam Slick and Major Downing, and shall now proceed to some farther peculiarities.

There are two syllables—um, hu—which are very generally used by the Americans as a sort of reply, intimating that they are attentive, and that the party may proceed with his narrative; but, by inflection and intonation, these two syllables are made to express dissent or assent, surprise, disdain, and (like Lord Burleigh's nod in the play) a great deal more. The reason why these two syllables have been selected is, that they can be pronounced without the trouble of opening your mouth, and you may be in a state of listlessness and repose while others talk. I myself found them very convenient at times, and gradually got into the habit of using them.

The Americans are very local in their phrases, and borrow their similes very much from the nature of their occupations and pursuits. If you ask a Virginian or Kentuckian where he was born, he will invariably tell you that he was *raised* in such a county—the term applied to horses, and, in breeding states, to men also.

When a man is tipsy (spirits being made from grain), they generally say he is *corned*.

In the West, where steam-navigation is so abundant, when they ask you to drink they say, "Stranger, will you take in wood?"—the vessels taking in wood as fuel to keep the steam up, and the person taking in spirits to keep *his* steam up.

The roads in the country being cut through woods, and the stumps of the trees left standing, the carriages are often brought up by them. Hence the expression of, "Well, I am *stumped* this time."

I heard a young man, a farmer in Vermont, say, when talking about another having gained the heart of a pretty girl, "Well, how he contrived to *fork* into her young affections, I can't tell; but I've a mind to *put my whole team on*, and see if I can't run him off the road."

The old phrase of "straining at a gnat, and swallowing a camel," is, in the Eastern states, rendered "straining at a *gate*, and swallowing a *saw-mill*."

To strike means to attack. "The Indians have struck on the frontier,"—"A rattle-snake *struck* at me."

To make tracks—to walk away. "Well, now, I shall make tracks;"—from foot-tracks in the snow.

Clear out, quit, and put—all mean "be off." "Captain, now, you *hush* or *put*"—that is, "Either hold your tongue, or be off." Also, "Will you shut, mister?"—i.e. will you shut your mouth? i.e. hold your tongue?

"Curl up"—to be angry—from the panther and other animals when angry raising their hair. "Rise my dandee up," from the human hair; and a nasty idea. "Wrathy" is another common expression. Also, "Savage as a meat-axe."

Here are two real American words:—

"Sloping"—for slinking away.

"Splunging," like a porpoise.

The word "enthusiasm," in the south, is changed to "entuzzy-muzzy."

In the Western states, where the racoon is plentiful, they use the abbreviation 'coon when speaking of people. When at New York, I went into a hair-dresser's shop to have my hair cut; there were two young men front the west—one under the barber's hands, the other standing by him.

"I say," said the one who was having his hair cut, "I hear Captain is in the country."

"Yes;" replied the other, "so they say; I should like to see the 'coon."

"I'm a *gone 'coon*" implies "I am distressed—*or* ruined—*or* lost." I once asked the origin of this expression, and was very gravely told as follows:—

"There is a Captain Martin Scott (already mentioned in the Diary) in the United States Army who is a remarkable shot with a rifle. He was raised, I believe, in Vermont. His fame was so considerable through the state, that even the animals were aware of it. He went out one morning with his rifle, and spying a racoon upon the upper branches of a high tree, brought his gun up to his shoulder; when the racoon perceiving it, raised his paw for a parley. 'I beg your pardon, mister,' said the racoon, very politely; 'but may I ask you if your name is Scott?'—'Yes,' replied the captain.—'*Martin* Scott?' continued the racoon—'Yes,' replied the captain—'*Captain* Martin Scott?' still continued the animal.—'Yes,' replied the captain, 'Captain Martin Scott?'—'Oh! then,' says the animal, 'I may just as well come down, for I'm a *gone 'coon.*'"

But one of the strangest perversions of the meaning of a word which I ever heard of is in Kentucky, where sometimes the word *nasty* is used for *nice*. For instance: at a rustic dance in that state a Kentuckian said to an acquaintance of mine, in reply to his asking the name of a very fine girl, "That's my sister, stranger; and I flatter myself that she shows the *nastiest* ankle in all Kentuck"—*Unde derivatur*, from the constant rifle-practice in that state, a good shot or a pretty shot is termed also a nasty shot, because it would make a *nasty* wound: *ergo*, a nice or pretty ankle becomes a *nasty* one.

The term for all baggage, especially in the south or west, is "plunder." This has been derived from the buccaneers, who for so long a time infested the bayores and creeks near the mouth of the Mississippi, and whose luggage was probably very correctly so designated.

I must not omit a specimen of American criticism.

"Well, Abel, what d'ye think of our native genus, Mister Forrest?"

"Well, I don't go much to theatricals, that's a fact; but I do think *he piled the agony up a little too high* in that last scene."

The gamblers on the Mississippi use a very refined phrase for "cheating"—"playing the advantages over him."

But, as may be supposed, the principal terms used are those which are borrowed from trade and commerce.

The rest, or remainder, is usually termed the balance.

"Put some of those apples into a dish, and the *balance* into the storeroom."

When a person has made a mistake, or is out in his calculation, they say, "You missed a figure that time."

In a skirmish last war, the fire from the British was very severe, and the men in the American ranks were falling fast, when one of the soldiers stepped up to the commanding officer and said, "Colonel, don't you think that we might compromise this affair?" "Well, I reckon I should have no objection to *submit it to arbitration* myself," replied the colonel.

Even the thieves must be commercial in their ideas. One rogue meeting another, asked him what he had done that morning; "Not much," was the reply, "I've only *realised* this umbrella."

This reminds me of a conversation between a man and his wife, which was overheard by the party who repeated it to me. It appears that the lady was economically inclined, and in cutting out some shirts for her husband, resolved that they should not descend much lower than his hip; as thereby so much linen would be saved. The husband expostulated, but in vain. She pointed out to him that it would improve his figure, and make his nether garments set much better; in a word, that long shirt-tails were quite unnecessary; and she wound up her arguments by observing that linen was a very expensive article, and that she could not see what on earth was the reason that people should stuff so much *capital* into their pantaloons.

There is sometimes in the American metaphors, an energy which is very remarkable.

"Well, I reckon, that from his teeth to his toe-nail, there's not a human of a more conquering nature than General Jackson."

One *gentleman* said to me, "I wish I had all hell boiled down to a pint, just to pour down your throat."

It is a great pity that the Americans have not adhered more to the Indian names, which are euphonous, and very often musical; but, so far from it, they appear to have had a pleasure in dismissing them altogether. There is a river running into Lake Champlain, near Burlington, formerly called by the Indians the Winooski; but this name has been superseded by the settlers, who, by way of improvement, have designated it the Onion river. The Americans have ransacked scripture, and ancient and modern history, to supply themselves with names, yet, notwithstanding, there appears to be a strange lack of taste in their selection. On the route to Lake Ontario you pass towns with such names as Manlius, Sempronius, Titus, Cato, and then you come to *Butternuts*. Looking over the catalogue of cities, towns, villages, rivers, and creeks in the different states in the Union, I find the following repetitions:—

Of towns, etcetera, named after distinguished individuals, there are:—

Washingtons	43	Carroll	16

		s	
Jacksons	41	Adamses	18
Jeffersons	32	Bolivars	8
Franklins	41	Clintons	19
Madisons	26	Waynes	14
Mo	25	C	6

nroes		asses	
Perrys	22	Clays	4
Fayettes	14	Fultons	17
Hamiltons	13		

Of other towns, etcetera, there are:—

Columbus	27	Libertys	14
Cen	14	S	24

tre Villes		alems	
Fair fiel ds	17	Onions	28
Ath ens es	10	Muds	8
Ro mes	4	Little Muds	1
Cro oke ds	22	Muddies	11
Litt les	20	San	39

		d y s	
Longs	18		

In colours they have:—

Clears	13	Greens	16
Blacks	33	Whites	15
Blues	8	Yellows	10
Vermilions	14		

Named after trees:—

Cedars	25	Laurels	14
Cypresses	12	Pines	18

After animals:—

Beavers	23	Foxes	12
Buffaloes	21	Otters	13

Bulls	9	Racoons	11
Deers	13	Wolfs	16
Dogs	9	Bears	12
Elks	11	Bear's Rump	1

After birds, etcetera:—

Gooses	10	Fishes	7
Du	8	Tur	12

cks		keys	
Eagles	8	Swans	15
Pigeons	10	Pikes	20

The consequence of these repetitions is, that if you do not put the name of the state, and often of the county in the state in which the town you refer to may be, your letter may journey all over the Union, and perhaps, after all, never arrive at its place of destination.

The states have already accommodated each other with nicknames, as per example:—

Illinois people are termed	Suckers
Missouri	Pukes
Michigan	Wolverines
Indiana	Hoosiers

Kentucky	Corn Crackers
Ohio	Buckeyes, etcetera

The names of persons are also very strange; and some of them are, at all events, obsolete in England, even if they ever existed there. Many of them are said to be French or Dutch names Americanised. But they appear still more odd to us from the high sounding Christian names prefixed to them; as, for instance: Philo Doolittle, Populorum Hightower, Preserved Fish, Asa Peabody, Alonzo Lilly, Alceus Wolf, etcetera. I was told by a gentleman that Doolittle was originally from the French Do l'hotel; Peabody from Pibaudiere; Bunker from Bon Coeur; that Mr Ezekial Bumpus is a descendant of Monsieur Bon Pas, etcetera, all which is very possible.

Every one who is acquainted with Washington Irving must know that, being very sensitive himself, he is one of the last men in the world to do anything to annoy another. In his selection of names for his writings, he was cautious in avoiding such as might be known; so that, when he called his old schoolmaster Ichabod Crane, he thought himself safe from the risk of giving offence. Shortly afterward a friend of his called upon him, accompanied by a stranger whom he introduced as Major Crane; Irving started at the name; "Major Ichabod Crane," continued his friend, much to the horror of Washington Irving.

I was told that a merchant went down to New Orleans with one Christian name, and came back, after a lapse of years, with another. His name was John Flint. The French at New Orleans translated his surname, and called him Pierre Fusée—on his return the Pierre stuck to him, and rendered into English as Peter, and he was called Peter Flint ever afterward.

People may change their names in the United States by application to Congress. They have a story hardly worth relating, although considered a good one in America, having been told me by a member of congress. A Mr Whitepimple, having risen in the world, was persuaded by his wife to change his name, and applied for permission accordingly. The clerk of the office inquired of him what other name he would have, and he being very indifferent about it himself, replied carelessly, as he walked away, "Oh, anything;" whereupon the clerk enrolled him as Mr *Thing*. Time passed on, and he had a numerous family, who found the new name not much more agreeable than the old one, for there was Miss Sally Thing, Miss Dolly Thing, the old Things, and all the little Things; and worst of all, the eldest son being christened Robert, went by the name of Thingum Bob.

There were, and I believe still are, two lawyers in partnership in New York, with the peculiarly happy names of Catchem and Chetum. People laughed at seeing these two names in juxtaposition over the door; so the lawyers thought it advisable to separate them by the insertion of their Christian names. Mr Catchem's Christian name was Isaac, Mr Chetum's Uriah. A new board was ordered, but when sent to the painter, it was found to be too short to admit the Christian names at full length. The painter, therefore, put in only the initials before the surnames, which made the matter still worse than before, for there now appeared—

"I Catchem and U Chetum."

I cannot conclude this chapter without adverting to one or two points peculiar to the Americans. They wish, in everything, to improve upon the Old Country, as they call us, and affect to be excessively refined in their language and ideas: but they forget that very often in the covering, and the covering only, consists the indecency; and that, to use the old aphorism—"Very nice people are people with very nasty ideas."

They object to everything nude in statuary. When I was at the house of Governor Everett, at Boston, I observed a fine cast of the Apollo Belvidere; but in compliance with general opinion, it was hung with drapery, although Governor Everett himself is a gentleman of refined mind and high classical attainments, and quite above such ridiculous sensitiveness. In language it is the same thing. There are certain words which are never used in America, but an absurd substitute is employed. I cannot particularise them after this preface, lest I should be accused of indelicacy myself. I may, however, state one little circumstance which will fully prove the correctness of what I say.

When at Niagara Falls I was escorting a young lady with whom I was on friendly terms. She had been standing on a piece of rock, the better to view the scene, when she slipped down, and was evidently hurt by the fall: she had, in fact, grazed her shin. As she limped a little in walking home, I said, "Did you hurt your leg much?" She turned from me, evidently much shocked, or much offended,—and not being aware that I had committed any very heinous offence, I begged to know what was the reason of her displeasure. After some hesitation, she said that as she knew me well, she would tell me that the word *leg* was never mentioned before ladies. I apologised for my want of refinement, which was attributable to having been accustomed only to *English* society; and added, that as such articles must occasionally be referred to, even in the most polite circles in America, perhaps she would inform me by what name I might mention them without shocking the company. Her reply was, that the word *limb* was used; "nay," continued she, "I am not so particular as some people are, for I know those who always say limb of a table, or limb of a piano-forte."

There the conversation dropped; but a few months afterwards I was obliged to acknowledge that the young lady was correct when she asserted that some people were more particular than even she was.

I was requested by a lady to escort her to a seminary for young ladies, and on being ushered into the reception-room, conceive my astonishment at beholding a square piano-forte with four *limbs*. However, that the ladies who visited their daughters might feel in its full force the extreme delicacy (see note at end of chapter) of the mistress of the establishment, and her care to preserve in their utmost purity the ideas of the young ladies under her charge, she had dressed all these four limbs in modest little trousers, with frills at the bottom of them!

"An English lady, who had long kept a fashionable boarding-school in one of the Atlantic cities, told me that one of her earliest cares with every new-comer, was to endeavour to substitute real delicacy for that affected precision of manner. Among many anecdotes, she told me of a young lady about fourteen, who, on entering the receiving-room, where she only expected to see a lady who had inquired for her, and finding a young man with her, put her hands before her eyes and ran out of the room again, screaming 'A man, a man, a man!' On another occasion, one of the young ladies in going up stairs to the drawing-room, unfortunately met a boy of fourteen coming down, and her feelings were so violently agitated, that she stopped, panting and sobbing, nor would she pass on till the boy had swung himself up on the upper bannisters, to leave the passage free."—*Mrs Trollope's Domestic Manners of the Americans*.

Volume Three—Chapter Two.

Remarks—Credit.

In the state of New York they have abolished imprisonment for debt; this abolition however, only holds good between the citizens of that state, as no one state in the Union can interfere with the rights of another. A stranger, therefore, can imprison a New Yorker, and a New Yorker can imprison a stranger, but the citizens of New York cannot incarcerate one another. Now although the unprincipled may, and do occasionally take advantage of this enactment, yet the effects of it are generally good, as character becomes more valuable. Without character, there will be no credit—and without credit no commercial man can rise in this city. I was once in a store where the widow who kept it complained to me that a person who owed her a considerable sum of money would not pay her, and aware that she had no redress, I asked her how she would obtain her money. Her reply was—"Oh, I shall eventually get my money, for I will *shame* him out of it by exposure."

The Americans, probably from being such great speculators, and aware of the uncertainty attending their commerce, are very lenient towards debtors. If a man proves that he cannot pay, he is seldom interfered with, but allowed to recommence business. This is not only Christians like, but wise. A man thrown into prison is not likely to find the means of paying his debts; but if allowed his liberty and the means of earning a subsistence, he may eventually be more fortunate, and the creditors have a chance of being ultimately paid. This, to my knowledge, has often been the case after the release had been signed, and the creditors had no farther legal claim upon the bankrupt. England has not yet made up her mind to the abolition of imprisonment for debt, but from what I have learnt in this city, I have no hesitation in saying, that it would work well for the morals of the community, and that more debts would eventually be paid, than are paid under the present system. Another circumstance which requires to be pointed out when we would examine into the character of the New York commercial community, is, the difference between their bankrupt-laws and those of England. Here there is no law to compel a bankrupt to produce his books; every man may be his own assignee, and has the power of giving preference to one creditor over another; that is to say, he may repay those who have lent him money in the hope of preventing his becoming a bankrupt, and all other debts of a like description. He may also turn over his affairs to an assignee of his own selection, who then pays the debts as he pleases. A bankrupt is also permitted to collect his own debts.

The English bankrupt laws were introduced, but after one year's trial they were discontinued, as it was found they were attended with so much difficulty, and, what is of more importance to Americans, with so much loss of time. Again, in America, if a person wishes to become a special partner (a sleeping partner) in any concern, he may do so to any extent he pleases, upon advertising the same, and is responsible for no more than the sum he invests, although the house should fail for ten times the amount.

Here is an advertisement of special partnership.

"Co-partnership. Notice is hereby given, that a limited partnership hath been entered into by Lambert Morange, DN Morange, and Samah Solomon, of the city of New York, merchants, in pursuance of the provisions of the revised statutes of the city of New York. The general nature of the business of said co-partnership is the manufacturing and selling of fur and silk hats. The said Lambert Morange is the special partner, and as such, hath contributed the sum of ten thousand dollars in cash to the common stock: the said DN Morange and Samah Solomon are the general partners; and the said business is to be conducted under the name and firm of DN Morange and Solomon; said co-partnership is to commence on the 14th day of March, 1837, and to expire on the 14th March, 1840.

"March 14th, 1837. L. Morange. D.N. Morange. Samah Solomon."

That this loose state of the bankrupt law may be, and has been a cause of much dishonesty, is true, but at the same it is the cause of the flourishing state of the community. The bee can always work; indeed the bankrupt-laws themselves provide for a man's not starving. In the city the bankrupt's household furniture is sacred, that his family may not be beggars; and in case of the bankruptcy of a farmer, he is permitted, not only to retain the furniture of his cottage, but even his plough, with a proportion of his team, his kine and sheep, are reserved for him, that he may still be able to support his family. Surely this is much preferable to the English system under which the furniture is dragged away, the hearth made desolate, and the children left to starve, because their father has been unfortunate. Is it not better that a little villainy should escape punishment, than that such cruelty should be in daily practice? I say a little villainy, for if a man becomes bankrupt in New York, it is pretty well known whether he has dealt fairly with his creditors, or has made a fraudulent bankruptcy: and if so, his character is gone, and with it his credit, and without credit he never can rise again in that city, but must remove to some other place.

In England, character will procure to a bankrupt a certificate, but in New York it will leave him the means of re-commencing business. In England, it is a disgrace to be a bankrupt; in America, it is only a misfortune; but this distinction arises from the boldness of the speculations carried on by the Americans in their commercial transactions, and owing to which the highest and most influential, as well as the smaller capitalists, are constantly in a state of jeopardy. I do not believe that there is anywhere a class of merchants more honourable than those of New York. The notorious Colonel Chartres said that he would give 20,000 pounds for a character, because he would have made 100,000 pounds by it. I shall not here enter into the question, whether it is by a similar conviction, or by moral rectitude of feeling, that the merchants of New York are actuated; it is sufficient that it is their interest to be honest, and that they are so. I state the case in this way, because I do not intend to admit that the honesty of the merchants is any proof of the morality of a nation; and I think I am borne out in my opinion by their conduct in the late state of difficulty, and the strenuous exertions made by them to pay to the uttermost farthing, sacrificing at times twenty per cent—in order to be enabled to remit money to their London and Liverpool correspondents, and fulfil their engagements with them.

That there is a great deal of roguery going on in this city is undeniable, much more, perhaps, than (taking into consideration the difference between the populations) in the good city of London. But it should be borne in mind that New York has become, as it were, the Alsatia of the whole continent of Europe. Every scoundrel who has swindled, forged, or robbed in England, or elsewhere, makes his escape to New York. Every pickpocket, who is too well known to the English police, takes refuge here. In this city they all concentrate; and it is a hard thing for the New York merchants, that the stream of society, which otherwise might gradually become more pure, should be thus poisoned by the continual inpourings of the continental dregs, and that they should be made to share in the obloquy of those who are outcasts from the society of the old world.

America exists at present upon credit. If the credit of her merchants were destroyed she would be checked in her rapid advance. But this system of credit, which is necessarily reciprocal, is nevertheless acted upon with all possible caution. Many are the plans which the large New York importers have been compelled to resort to, to ascertain whether their customers from the interior could be trusted or not. Agents have been despatched to learn the characters, standing, and means of the country dealers who are their correspondents, and who purchase their goods; for the whole of the transactions are upon credit, and a book of reference as to people's responsibility is to be found in many of the mercantile houses of New York.

Willing as I am to do justice to the New York merchants, I cannot, however, permit Mr Carey's remarks upon credit to pass unnoticed. Had he said nothing I should have said no more; but, as he asserts that the security of property and credit in America is greater than in England, I must, in defence of my country, make a few observations.

At the commencement of his article Mr Carey says,—

"In England confidence is *almost* universal. The banker credits the manufacturer and the farmer. They are willing to give credit to the merchant, because they have confidence that he will pay them. He gives credit to the shopkeeper, who, in his turn, gives credit to the labourer.

"Immense masses of property change owners without examination; confidence thus producing a great saving of labour. Orders to a vast extent are given, with a certainty that they will be executed with perfect good faith; and this system is continued year after year, proving that the confidence was deserved."

Now, after this admission what more can be required? Confidence proves security of property, and should any change take place so as to render the security doubtful, confidence would immediately cease. It is, therefore, rather bold of Mr Carey, after such an admission, to attempt to prove that the security of property is greater in America than in England; yet, nevertheless, such is his assertion.

Mr Carey bases his calculation, first upon the losses sustained by the banks of England, in comparison with those sustained by the banks of Massachusetts. Here, as in almost every other argument, Mr Carey selects one state—a state, *par excellence*, superior to all the others of the Union; a pattern state, in fact—as representing *all* America against *all* England. He admits that, as you go south or west, the complexion of things is altered; but notwithstanding this admission, he still argues upon this one state only, and consequently upon false premises. But allowing that he proved that the losses of all the banks in America were less than the losses of all the banks in England, he would still prove nothing, or if he did prove anything, it would be against himself. Why are the losses of the American banks less? Simply because they trust less. There is not that confidence in America that there is in England, and the want of confidence proves the want of security of property.

The next comparison which Mr Carey makes is between the failures of the banks of the two countries; and in this argument he takes most of the states in the Union into his calculation, and he winds up by observing (in italics) that —"From the first institution of banks in America to the year 1837, the failures have been less by about one-fourth, than those of England in the three years of 1814, 15, and 16; and the amount of loss sustained by the public bears, probably, a still smaller proportion to the amount of business transactions."

Now, all this proves nothing, except that the banks of America are more careful in discounting than our own, and that by running less risk they lose less money. But from it Mr Carey draws this strange conclusion:—

"Individuals in Great Britain enjoy as high a degree of *credit* as can possibly exist, but *confidence* is more universal in the United States."

Credit is the result of *confidence*; and if, as appears to be the case, the American confidence in each other will not procure credit, it is a very useless compliment passed between them. It is simply this—"I am certain that you are a very honest man, but notwithstanding I will not lend you a shilling." Indeed. Mr Carey contradicts himself, for, two pages farther on, he says:—"The existence of the credit system is evidence of mutual confidence."

I should like Mr Carey to answer one question.

What would have been the amount of the failures of the banks of America in 1836, if they had not suspended cash payments? It is very easy to carry on the banking business when, in defiance of their charters, the banks will give you nothing but their paper, and refuse you specie. Banks which will not pay bullion for their own notes are not very likely to fail, except in their covenant with the public. But it is of little use for Mr Carey to assert on the one hand, or for me to deny on the other. Every nation makes its own character with the rest of the world, and it is by other nations that the question between us must be decided. The question is then, "Is the credit of America better than that of England, in the intercourse of the two countries with each other, and with foreign nations?" Let the commercial world decide.

Volume Three—Chapter Three.

Remarks—Penitentiaries, etcetera.

Although, during my residence in the cities of the United States, I visited most of the public institutions, I have not referred to them at the time in my Diary, as they have been so often described by preceding travellers? I shall now, however, make a few remarks upon the penitentiary system.

I think it was Wilkes who said, that the very worst use to which you could put a man was to hang him; and such appears to be the opinion in America. That hanging does not prevent crime, where people are driven into it by misery and want, I believe; but it does prevent crime where people commit it merely from an unrestrained indulgence of their passions. This has been satisfactorily proved in the United States. At one time the murders in the city of New Orleans were just as frequent as in all the states contiguous to the Mississippi; but the population of the city determined to put an end to such scenes of outrage. The population of New Orleans is very different from that of the southern states in general, being composed of Americans from the eastern states, English merchants, and French creoles. Vigorous laws and an efficient police were established; and one of the southern planters, of good family and connexions, having committed a murder, was tried and condemned. To avoid the gallows, he committed suicide in prison. This system having been rigorously followed up, New Orleans has become perhaps the *safest* city in the Union; and now, not even a brawl is heard in those streets where, a few years back, murders occurred every hour of the day.

In another chapter I shall enter more fully into this question: at present I shall only say that there is a great unwillingness to take away life in America, and it is this aversion to capital punishment which has directed the attention of the American community to the penitentiary system. Several varieties of this species of punishment have been resorted to, more or less severe. The most rigid—that of solitary confinement in dark cells, and without labour—was found too great an infliction, as, in many cases, it unsettled the reason, and ended in confirmed lunacy. Confinement, with the boon of light, but without employment, was productive of no good effect; the culprit sank into a state of apathy and indifference. After a certain time, day and night passed away unheeded, from the want of a healthy tone to the mind. The prisoners were no longer lunatics, but they were little better than brute animals.

Neither do I consider the present system, as practised at Sing Sing, the state prison of New York, as tending to *reform* the offenders; it punishes them severely, but that is all. Where corporal punishment is resorted to, there always will be feelings of vindictiveness; and all the bad passions must be allowed to repose before the better can gain the ascendant.

The best system that is acted upon in the Penitentiary at Philadelphia, where there is solitary confinement, but with labour and exercise. Mr Samuel Wood, who superintends this establishment, is a person admirably calculated for his task, and I do not think that any arrangements could be better, or the establishment in more excellent hands. But my object was, not so much to view the prison and witness the economy of it, as to examine the prisoners themselves, and hear what their opinions were. The surgeon may explain the operation, but the patient who has undergone it is the proper person to apply to, if you wish to know the degree and nature of the pain inflicted. I requested, therefore, and obtained permission, to visit a portion of the prisoners without a third party being present to prevent their being communicative; selecting some who had been in but a short time, others who had been there for years, and referring also to the books, as to the nature and degree of their offence. I ought to state that I re-examined almost the whole of the parties about six months afterward, and the results of the two examinations are now given. I did not take their names, but registered them in my notes as No. 1, 2, 3, etcetera.

No. 1—a man who had been sentenced to twelve years' imprisonment for the murder of his wife. He had been bred up as a butcher. (I have observed that when the use of the knife is habitual, the flinching which men naturally feel at the idea of driving it into a fellow-creature, is overcome; and a man who is accustomed to dissect the still palpitating carcasses of animals, has very little compunction in resorting to the knife in the event of collision with his own race.) This fellow looked a butcher; his face and head were all animal; he was by no means intelligent. He was working at a loom, and had already been confined for seven years and a half. He said that, after the first six months of his confinement, he had lost all reckoning of time, and had not cared to think about it until lately, when he inquired, and was told how long he had been locked up. Now that he had discovered that more than half his time had passed away, it occupied his whole thoughts, and sometimes he felt very impatient.

Mr Wood told me afterwards that this feeling, when the expiration of the sentence was very near at hand, sometimes amounted to agony.

This man had denied the murder of his wife, and still persisted in the denial, although there was no doubt of his having committed the crime. Of course, in this instance there was no repentance; and the Penitentiary was thrown away upon him, farther than that, for twelve years, he could not contaminate society.

No. 2—sentenced to four years' imprisonment for forgery; his time was nearly expired. This was a very intelligent man; by profession he had been a schoolmaster. He had been in prison before for the same offence.

His opinion as to the Penitentiary was, that it could do no harm, and might do much good. The fault of the system was one which could not well be remedied, which was, that there was degradation attached to it. Could punishment undergone for crime be viewed in the same way as repentance was by the Almighty, and a man, after suffering for his fault, re-appear in the world with clean hands, and be admitted into society as before, it would be attended with the very best effects; but there was no working out the degradation. When he was released from his former imprisonment, he had been obliged to fly from the place where he was known. He was pursued by the harshness of the world, not only in himself, but in his children. No one would allow that his punishment had wiped away his crime, and this was the reason why people, inclined to be honest, were driven again into guilt. Not only would the world not encourage them, but it would not permit them to become honest; the finger of scorn was pointed wherever they were known, or found out, and the punishment after release was infinitely greater than that of the prison itself.

Miss Martineau observes, "I was favoured with the confidence of a great number of the prisoners in the Philadelphia Penitentiary, where absolute seclusion is the principle of punishment. Every one of these prisoners (none of them being aware of the existence of any other) told me that he was under obligations to those who had charge of him for treating him 'with respect.'"

No 3—a very intelligent, but not educated man: imprisoned three years for stealing. He had only been a few months in the penitentiary, but had been confined for ten years in Sing Sing prison for picking pockets. I asked him his opinion as to the difference of treatment in the two establishments. He replied, "In Sing Sing the punishment is corporal—here it is more mental. In Sing Sing there was little chance of a person's reformation, as the treatment was harsh and brutal, and the feelings of the prisoners were those of indignation and resentment."

Their whole time was occupied in trying how they could deceive their keepers, and communicate with each other by every variety of stratagem. Here a man was left to his own reflections, and at the same time he was treated like a *man*. Here he was his own tormentor; at Sing Sing he was tormented by others. A man was sent to Sing Sing for doing wrong to others; when there, he was quite as much wronged himself. Two wrongs never made a right. Again, at Sing Sing they all worked in company, and knew each other; when they met again, after they were discharged, they enticed one another to do wrong again. He was convinced that no man left Sing Sing a better man than he went in. He here felt very often that he could become better—perhaps he might. At all events his mind was calm, and he had no feelings of resentment for his treatment. He had now leisure and quiet for self-examination, if he chose to avail himself of it. At Sing Sing there was great injustice and no redress. The infirm man was put to equal labour with the robust, and punished if he did not perform as much. The flogging was very severe at Sing Sing. He once ventured to express his opinion that such was the case, and (to prove the contrary he supposed) they awarded him eighty-seven lashes for the information.

That many of this man's observations, in the parallel drawn between the two establishments, are correct, must be conceded; but still some of his assertions must be taken with due reservation, as it is evident that he had no very pleasant reminiscences of his ten years' geological studies in Sing Sing.

No. 4—an Irishman; very acute. He had been imprisoned seven years for burglary, and his time would expire in a month. He had been confined also in Walnut-street prison, Philadelphia, for two years previous to his coming here. He said that it was almost impossible for any man to reform in that prison, although some few did. He had served many years in the United States navy. He declared that his propensity to theft was only strong upon him when under the influence of liquor, or tobacco, which latter had the same effect upon him as spirits. He thought that he was reformed now; the reason why he thought so was, that he now liked work, and had learnt a profession in the prison, which he never had before. He considered himself a good workman, as he could make a pair of shoes in a day. He cannot now bear the smell of liquor or tobacco. (This observation must have been from imagination, as he had no opportunity in the Penitentiary of testing his dislike.) He ascribed all his crimes to ardent spirits. He was fearful of only one thing: his time was just out, and where was he to go? If known to have been in the prison, he would never find work. He knew a fact which had occurred, which would prove that he had just grounds for his fear. A tailor, who had been confined in Walnut-street prison with him, had been released as soon as his time was up. He was an excellent workman, and resolved for the future to be honest. He obtained employment from a master tailor in Philadelphia, and in three months was made foreman. One of the inspectors of Walnut-street prison came in for clothes, and his friend was called down to take the measures. The inspector recognised him, and as soon as he left the shop told his master that he had been in the Walnut-street prison. The man was in consequence immediately discharged. He could obtain no more work, and in a few months afterwards found his way back again to Walnut-street prison for a fresh offence.

No. 5—a fine intelligent Yankee, very bold in bearing. He was in the penitentiary under a false name, being well connected had been brought up as an architect and surveyor, and was imprisoned for having counterfeit bank notes in his possession. This fellow was a regular lawyer, and very amusing; it appeared as if nothing could subdue his elasticity of spirit. He said that he did not think that he should be better for his incarceration; on the contrary, that it would produce very bad effects. "I am punished," said he, "not for having passed counterfeit notes, but for having them in my possession. The facts are, I had lost all my money by gambling; and then the gamblers, to make me amends, gave me some of their counterfeit notes, which they always have by them. I do not say that I should not have uttered them; I believe that in my distress I should have done so; but I had not exactly made up my mind. At all events, *I had not* passed them when, from information given, I was taken up. This is certain, that not having passed them, it is very possible for a man to have forged notes in his possession without being aware of it; but this was not considered by my judges, although it ought to have been, as I had never been brought up before; and I have now been sentenced to exactly the same term of imprisonment as those who were convicted of passing them. Now, this I consider as unfair; my punishment is too severe for my offence, and that always does harm—it creates a vindictive feeling, and a desire to revenge yourself for the injustice done to you.

"Now, sir," continued he, "I should have no objection to compromise; if they would reduce my punishment one-half, I would acknowledge the justice of it, and turn honest when I go out again; but, if I am confined here for three years, why, it is my opinion, that I shall revenge myself upon society as soon as I am turned loose again." This was said in a very cheerful, playful manner, as he stood up before his loom. A more energetic expression, a keener grey eye, I never met with. There was evidently great daring of soul in this man.

No 6—had only been confined six weeks; his offence was stealing pigs, and his companion in the crime had been sent here with him. He declared that he was innocent, and that he had been committed by false swearing. There is no country in the world where there is so much perjury as in the United States, if I am to believe the Americans themselves; but Mr Wood told me that he was present at the trial, and that there was no doubt of their guilt. This man was cheerful and contented; he was working at the loom, and had already become skilful. All whom I had seen up to the present had employment of some sort or other, and should have passed over this man, as I had done some others, if it had not been for the contrast between him and his companion.

No. 7—His companion or accomplice. In consequence of the little demand for the penitentiary manufactures this man had no employment. The first thing he told me was that he had nothing to do, and was very miserable. He earnestly requested me to ask for employment for him. He cried bitterly while he spoke, was quite unmanned and depressed, and complained that he had not been permitted to hear from his wife and children. The want of employment appeared to have completely prostrated this man; although confined but six weeks, he had already lost the time, and inquired of me the day of the week and the month.

No. 8—was at large. He had been appointed apothecary to the prison; of course he was not strictly confined, and was in a comfortable room. He was a shrewd man, and evidently well educated; he had been reduced to beggary by his excesses, and being too proud to work, he had not been too proud to commit forgery. I had a long conversation with him, and he made some sensible remarks upon the treatment of prisoners, and the importance of delegating the charge of prisoners to competent persons. His remarks also upon American juries were very severe, and, as I subsequently ascertained, but too true.

No. 9—a young woman about nineteen, confined for larceny; in other respects a good character. She was very quiet and subdued, and said that she infinitely preferred the solitude of the penitentiary to the company with which she must have associated had she been confined in a common gaol. She did not appear at all anxious for the expiration of her term. Her cell was very neat, and ornamented with her own hands in a variety of ways. I observed that she had a lock of hair on her forehead which, from the care taken of it, appeared to be a favourite, and, as I left the cell, I said—"You appear to have taken great pains with that lock of hair, considering that you have no one to look at you?"—"Yes, sir," replied she; "and if you think that vanity will desert a woman, even in the solitude of a penitentiary, you are mistaken."

When I visited this girl a second time, her term was nearly expired; she told me that she had not the least wish to leave her cell, and that, if they confined her for two years more, she was content to stay. "I am quite peaceful and happy here," she said, and I believe she really spoke the truth.

No. 10—a free mulatto girl, about eighteen years of age, one of the most forbidding of her race, and with a physiognomy perfectly brutal; but she evidently had no mean opinion of her own charms: her woolly hair was twisted into at least fifty short plaits, and she grinned from ear to ear as she advanced to meet me. "Pray, may I inquire what you are imprisoned for?" said I.—"Why, sir," replied she, smirking, smiling, and coquetting, as she tossed her head right and left,—"If you please, sir, I was put in here for poisoning a *whole family*." She really appeared to think that she had done a very praiseworthy act. I inquired of her if she was aware of the heinousness of her offence. "Yes, she knew it was wrong, but if her mistress beat her again as she had done, she thought she would do it again. She had been in prison three years, and had four more to remain." I asked her if the fear of punishment—if another incarceration for seven years would not prevent her from committing such a crime a second time. "She didn't know; she didn't like being shut up—found it very tedious, but still she thought—was not quite sure—but she thought that, if ill-treated, she should certainly do it again."

I paid a second visit to this amiable young lady, and asked her what her opinion was then.—"Why, she had been thinking, but had not exactly made up her mind—but she still thought—indeed, she was convinced—that she *should do it again*."

I entered many other cells, and had conversations with the prisoners but I did not elicit from them any thing worth narrating. There is, however, a great deal to be gained from the conversation which I have recorded. It must be remembered, that observations made by one prisoner, which struck me as important, if not made by others, were put as questions by me; and I found that the opinions of the most intelligent, although differently expressed, led to the same result—that the present system of the Philadelphia penitentiary was the best that had been invented. As the schoolmaster said, if it did no good, it could do no harm. There is one decided advantage in this system, which is, that they all learn a trade, if they had not one before; and, when they leave the prison, have the means of obtaining an honest livelihood, if they wish so to do themselves, *and are permitted so to do by others*. Here is the stumbling-block which neutralises almost all the good effects which might be produced by the penitentiary system. The severity and harshness of the world; the unchristianlike feeling pervading society, which denies to the penitent what individually they will have to plead for themselves at the great tribunal, and which will not permit that punishment, awarded and suffered, can expiate the crime; on this point, there is no hope of a better feeling being engendered. Mankind have been, and will be, the same; and it is only to be hoped that we may receive more mercy in the next world than we are inclined to extend toward our fellow-creatures in this.

As I have before observed, I care little for the observations or assertions of directors or of officers entrusted with the charge of the penitentiaries and houses of correction; they are unintentionally biased, and things that appear to them to be mere trifles are very often extreme hardships to the prisoners. It is not only what the body suffers, but what the mind suffers, which must be considered; and it is from the want of this consideration that arise most of the defects in those establishments, not only in America, but everywhere else.

During my residence in the United States, a little work made its appearance, which I immediately procured; it was the production of an American, a scholar, once in the best society, but who, by intemperance, had forfeited his claim to it. He wrote the very best satirical poem I ever read by an American, full of force, and remarkable for energetic versification; but intemperance, the prevalent vice of America, had induced him to beggary and wretchedness, he was (by his own request I understand) shut up in the house of correction at South Boston, that he might, if possible, be reclaimed from intemperance; and, on his leaving it, he published a small work, called "The Rat-Trap, or Cogitations of a Convict in the House of Correction." This work bears the mark of a reflective, although buoyant mind; and as he speaks in the highest terms of Mr Robbins, the master, and bestows praise generally when deserved, his remarks, although occasionally jocose, are well worthy of attention and I shall, therefore, introduce a few of them to the reader.

His introduction commences thus:—

"I take it for granted that one of every two individuals in this *most moral community in the world* has been, will be, or deserves or fears to be, in the house of correction. Give every man his deserts, and who shall escape whipping? This book must, therefore, be interesting, and will have a good circulation—not, perhaps, in this state alone. The state spends its money for the above institution, and, therefore, has a right to know what it is; a knowledge which can never be obtained from the reports of the authorities, the cursory observations of visitors, or the statements of ignorant and exasperated convicts.

"'What thief e'er felt the halter draw, With good opinion of the law.'

"It has been my aim to furnish such knowledge, and it cannot be denied that I have had the best opportunities to obtain it."

To show the prevalence of intemperance in this country among the better classes, read the following:—

"On entering the wool-shop, a man nodded to me, whom I immediately recognised as a lawyer of no mean talent, who had, at no very distant period, been an ornament of society, and a man well esteemed for many excellent qualities, all of which are now forgotten, while his only fault, intemperance, remains engraven on steel. This was not his first term, or his second, or his third. At this time of writing he is discharged, a sober man, anxious for employment, which he cannot get. His having been in the house of correction shuts every door against him, and he must have more than ordinary firmness if he does not relapse again. From my inmost soul I pity him. Another aged man I recognised as a doctor of medicine: his grey hairs would have been venerable in any other place."

The labour in this house of correction which he describes is chiefly confined to wool-picking, stone-cutting, and blacksmiths' work. The fare he states to be plentiful, but not of the very best quality. Speaking of ill-treatment, he says:—

"The convicts all have the privilege of complaint against officers; but while I was there no one used it but myself. I believe they dared not. The officer would probably deny or gloss over the cause of complaint, and his word would be believed rather than that of the convict; and his power of retaliation is so tremendous, that few would care to brave it. The chance is ten to one that a complaint to the directors would be falsified and proved fruitless; and the visit of the governor, council, and magistrates, for the purpose of inquiry, is mere matter of form. When they asked me if I had reason to complain of my treatment, I answered in the negative, because I really had none; but had they asked me if there was any defect in the institution, I would have pointed out a good many."

The monotony of their existence is well described:—

"Few incidents chequered the monotony of our existence. 'Who has got a piece of steel in his eye?'—'Who has gone to the hospital?'—'How many came to-day in the carry-all?' were almost the only questions we could ask. A man falling from the new prison, and breaking his bones in a fashion not to be approved, was a conversational godsend. One day the retiring tide left a small box on the sands at the bottom of the house of correction wharf, which was picked up by a convict, and found to contain the bequest of some woman who had 'loved not wisely, but too well,' namely, a pair of new-born infants. In my mind, their fate was happy. If they never knew woman's tenderness, neither did they ever know woman's falsehood. There is less pleasure than pain in this bad world, and the earlier we take leave of it the better."

He complains of due regard not being paid to the cleanliness of the prisoners:—

"A great defect in the police of the house was the want of baths. We were shaved, or rather scraped, but once a week. Washing one's face and hands in ice-cold water of a winter morning, is little better than no ablution at all. The harbour water is interdicted, lest the convicts should swim away, and in the stone-shop there are no conveniences for bathing whatever: they would cost something! In the wool-shop, forty men have one tubful of warm water once a-week. When I say that shirts are worn a week in summer, and (as well as drawers) two or three weeks in winter, it will at once be conceded that some farther provision for personal cleanliness is imperatively demanded. I hope neither this nor any other remark I may think fit to make will be taken as emanating from a fault-finding spirit, since, while I pronounce upon the disease, I suggest the remedy."

Speaking of his companions, he says:—

"I had expected to find myself linked with a band of most outrageous ruffians, but such did not prove to be the case. Few of them were decidedly of a vicious temperament. The great fault with them seemed to be a want of moral knowledge and principle. Were I to commit a theft I should think myself unworthy to live an instant; but some of them spoke of the felonies for which they were adjudged to suffer with as much *nonchalance* as if they were the every-day business of life, without scruple and without shame. Few of them denied the justice of their sentences; and if they expressed any regret, it was not that they had sinned, but that they had been detected. The duration of the sentence, the time or money lost, the physical suffering, was what filled their estimate of their condition. Many had groans and oaths for a lost dinner, a night in the cells, or a tough piece of work, but none had a tear for the branding infamy of their conviction. Yet some, even of the most hardened, faltered, and spoke with quivering lip and glistening eye, when they thought of their parents, wives, and children. The flinty Horeb of their souls sometimes yielded gushing streams to the force of that appeal. But there were very few who felt any shame on their own account. Their apathy on the point of honour was amazing. A young man, not twenty-five years old, in particular, made his felonies his glory, and boasted that he had been a tenant of half the prisons in the United States. He was sentenced to four years' imprisonment for stealing a great number of pieces of broadcloth, which he unblushingly told me he had lodged in the hands of a receiver of stolen goods, and expected to receive the value at the expiration of his sentence. He relied on the proverbial 'honour among thieves.' That fellow ought to be kept in safe custody the remainder of his natural life."

Certainly those remarks do not argue much for the reformation of the culprit.

By his account, a parsimony in every point appears to be the great desideratum aimed at. Speaking of the chaplain to the institution, he says:—

"Small blame to him; I honour and respect the man, though I laugh at the preacher. And I say, that seven hundred and thirty sermons *per annum*, for three hundred dollars and a weekly dinner, are quite pork enough for a shilling. No man goeth a warfare on his own charges, and the labourer is worthy of his hire. I do not see how he can justify such wear and tear of his pulmonary leather, for so small a sum, to his conscience. What is a sixpenny razor or a nine-shilling sermon? Neither can be expected to cut—not but his sermons would be very good for the use of glorified saints—but, alas! there are none such in the House of Correction. What is the inspiration of a penny-a-liner? I will suppose that one of the hearers is a sailor, who would relish and appreciate a sausage or a lobscouse. Mr — sets *blanc mange* before him.— Messrs of the city government give your chaplain two thousand dollars a-year, so that he may reside in the house of correction, without leaving his family to starvation; let him visit each individual, learn his circumstances and character, and sympathise with him in all his sorrows, and, my word for it, Mr — will have the love and confidence of all. He will be an instrument of great good by his counsel and exhortations. But as for his public preaching, this truly good, pious, and learned man might as well sing psalms to a mad horse. Fishes will not throng to St. Anthony, or swine listen to the exorcism of an apostle, in these godless days. If you think he will be overpaid for his services, you may braze the duty of a schoolmaster, who is very much needed, to that of a ghostly adviser.

"Mr — never fails to pray strenuously that the master and officers may be supported and sustained, which has given rise to the following tin-pot epigram:—

"Support   the   master   and   the   overseers,
O   Lord!   so   runs   our   chaplain's   weekly   ditty;
Unreasonable   prayers   God   never   hears,
He knows that they're supported by the city."

He complains bitterly of the convicts not being permitted the use of any books but the Bible and temperance Almanac. It is rather strange, but he says that he supposes that a full half of the inmates of the house of correction can neither *read* nor *write*.

"Is it pleasant to look back on follies, vices, crimes; presently on blasted hopes, iron bars, and unrequited labour; and forward upon misery, starvation, and a world's scorn? In some degree the malice of this regulation, which ought only to be inscribed on the statute-book of hell, is impotent. The small glimpse of earth, sea, and sky a convict can command, a spider crawling upon the wall, the very corners of his cell, will serve, by a strong effort, for occupation for his thoughts. Read the following tea-pot-graven monologue, written by some mentally-suffering convict, and reflect upon it:—

"Stone walls and iron bars my frame confine,
But the full liberty of thought is mine,
Sad privilege! the mental glance to cast
O'er crimes, o'er follies, and misconduct past.
Oh wretched tenant of a guarded cell,
Thy very freedom makes thy mind a hell.
Come, blessed death; thy grinded dart to me,
Shall the bless'd signal of deliverance be;
With thy worst agonies were cheaply bought,
A last release, a final rest from thought."

"If the pains of a prison be not enough for you, I will teach you a lesson in the art of torture which I learned from our chaplain, or one of his substitutes. —'Make your cells round and smooth; let there be no prominent point for the eye to rest upon, so that it must necessarily turn inward, and I will warrant that you will soon have the pleasure of seeing your victim frantic.' Look well to the temperance trash you physic us with, and you will find, in the Almanac for 1837, a serious attempt to make Napoleon Bonaparte out a drunkard, and to prove that a rum-bottle lost him the battle of Waterloo. The author must himself have been drunk when he wrote it. Are you not ashamed to set such pitiful cant, I will not say such wilful falsehood and slander, before any rational creature? Did you not know that an overcharged gun would knock the musketeer over by its recoil? I do not tell you to give the convicts all and any books they may desire; but pray what harm would an arithmetic do, unless it taught them to refute the statistics of your lying almanac, which gravely advises farmers to feed their hogs with apples, to prevent folks from getting drunk on cider? Why not tell them to feed their cattle with barley and wheat for the same reason? What mind was ever corrupted by Murray's Grammar, or Washington Irving's Columbus? When was ever falsehood the successful pioneer of truth!"

His remarks upon visitors being permitted to see the convicts are good.

"Among the annoyances, which others as well as myself felt most galling, was the frequent intrusion of visitors, who had no object but the gratification of a morbid curiosity. Know all persons, that the most debased convict has human feelings, and does not like to be seen in a parti-coloured jacket. If you want to see any convict for any good reason, ask the master to let you meet him in his office; and even there, you may rely upon it, your visit will be painful enough; to be stared at by the ignorant and the mean with feelings of pity, as if one were some monster of Ind, was intolerable. I hope a certain connexion of mine, who came to see me unasked and unwelcome, and brought a stranger with him to witness my disgrace, may never feel the pain he inflicted on me. To a kind-hearted 'Mac,' who came in a proper and delicate way to comfort when I thought all the world had forsaken me, I tender my most grateful thanks. His kindness shall be remembered by me while memory holds her seat. Let the throng of uninvited fools who swarmed about us, accept the following sally of the house of correction muse, from the pen, or rather the fork, of a fellow convict. It may operate to edification.

"To   Our   Visitors.

"By gazing at us, sirs, pray what do you mean?
Are we the first rascals that ever were seen?
Look into your mirrors—perhaps you may find
All villains are not in South Boston confined.

"I'm not a wild beast, to be seen for a penny;
But a man, as well made and as proper as any;
And what we most differ in is, well I wot,
That I have my merits, and you have them not.

"I own I'm a drunkard, but much I incline
To think that your elbow crooks as often as mine;
Ay, breathe in my face, sir, as much as you will—
One blast of your breath is as good as a gill.

"How kind was our country to find us a home
Where duns cannot plague us, or enemies come!
And you from the cup of her kindness may drain
A *drop* so sufficing, you'll not drink again.

"And now that by staring with mouth and eyes open,
We have bruised the reeds that already were broken;
Go home and, by dint of strict mental inspection,
Let each make his own house a house of correction.

"This *morceau* was signed 'Indignans.'"

The following muster-roll of crime, as he terms it, which he obtained from the master of the prison, is curious, as it exemplifies the excess of intemperance in the United States—bearing in mind that this is the *moral* state of Massachusetts.

"The whole number of males committed to the house of correction from the time it was opened—July 1st, 1833, to September 1st, 1837,—was 1477. Of this number there were common drunkards 783, or more than one-half.

"The whole amount of females committed to this institution from the time it was opened to Sept 1837, was 869. Of this number there were common drunkards 430, very nearly one-half.

"And of the whole number committed there were—"

Natives of Massachusetts	720	England	104

New Hampshire	175	Scotland	38
Maine	130	Ireland	839
Vermont	17	Provinces	69
Rhode Island	35	France	10
Connecticut	28	Spain	2
New York	50	Germany	2
New Jersey	3	Holland	2
Pennsylvania	28	Poland	2
Delaware	6	Denmark	2
Maryland	10	Prussia	1
Virginia	20	Sweden	8

North Carolina	10	West Indies	12
South Carolina	1	Cape de Verde	1
Georgia	5	Island of Malta	1
District of Columbia	3	At Sea	7
		Foreigners	1100
United States	1241	Unknown	5
÷Moral÷ States	1905		
Other States	236	Total	2346

He sums up as follows:—

"I have nearly finished, but I should not do justice to my subject did I omit to advert to the beggarly catch-penny system on which the whole concern is conducted. The convicts raise pork and vegetables in plenty, but they must not eat thereof; these things must be sent to market to balance the debit side of the prison ledger. The prisoners must catch cold and suffer in the hospital, and the wool and stone shops, because it would cost something to erect comfortable buildings. They must not learn to read and write, lest a cent's worth of their precious time should be lost to the city. They may die and go to hell, and be damned, for a resident physician and chaplain are expensive articles. They may be dirty; baths would cost money, and so would books. I believe the very Bibles and almanacks are the donation of the Bible and Temperance societies. Every thing is managed with an eye to money-making—the comfort or reformation, or salvation, of the prisoners are minor considerations. Whose fault is this?

"The fault, most frugal public, is your own. You like justice, but you do not like to pay for it. You like to see a clean, orderly, well conducted prison, and, as far as your parsimony will permit, such is the house of correction. With all its faults, it is still a valuable institution. It holds all, it harms few, and reforms some. It looks well, for the most has been made of matters. If you would have it perfect you must untie your purse-strings, and you will lose nothing by it in the end."

Volume Three—Chapter Four.

Remarks—Army.

Isolated as the officers are from the world, (for these forts are far removed from towns or cities,) they contrived to form a society within themselves, having most of them recourse to matrimony, which always gives a man something to do, and acts as a fillip upon his faculties, which might stagnate from such quiet monotony. The society, therefore, at these outposts is small, but very pleasant. All the officers being now educated at West Point, they are mostly very intelligent and well informed, and soldiers' wives are always agreeable women all over the world. The barracks turned out also a very fair show of children upon the green sward. The accommodations are, generally speaking, very good, and when supplies can be received, the living is equally so; when they cannot, it can't be helped, and there is so much money saved. A suttler's store is attached to each outpost, and the prices of the articles are regulated by a committee of officers, and a tax is also levied upon the suttler in proportion to the number of men in the garrison, the proceeds of which are appropriated to the education of the children of the soldiers and the provision of a library and news-room. If the government were to permit officers to remain at any one station for a certain period, much more would be done; but the government is continually shifting them from post to post, and no one will take the trouble to sow when he has no chance of reaping the harvest. Indeed, many of the officers complained that they hardly had time to furnish their apartments in one fort when they were ordered off to another—not only a great inconvenience to them, but a great expense also.

The American army is not a favourite service, and this is not to be wondered at. It is ill-treated in every way; the people have a great dislike to them, which is natural enough in a Democracy; but what is worse, to curry favour with the people, the government very often do not support the officers in the execution of their duty. Their furloughs are very limited, and they have their choice of the outposts, where they live out of the world, or the Florida war, when they go out of it. But the greatest injustice is, that they have no half-pay: if not wishing to be employed they must resign their commissions and live as they can. In this point there is a great partiality shown to the navy, who have such excellent half-pay, although to prevent remarks at such glaring injustice to the other service, another term is given to the naval half-pay, and the naval officers are supposed to be always on service.

The officers of the army are paid a certain sum, and allowed a certain number of rations per month; for instance, a major-general has two hundred dollars per month, and fifteen rations: According to the estimated value of the rations, as given to me by one of the officers, the annual pay of the different grades will be, in our money, nearly as follows:—

Army.

Army	pounds	Navy	pounds
Major-General	850		
Brigadier-General	570	Same rank	960
Colonel	340	Do.	830
Lieutenant-Colonel	280		
Major	225	Do.	525
Captain	200	Do.	380

First Lieutenant	150		
Second Lieutenant	140		
Cadet	90	Do.	156

The cavalry officers have a slight increase of pay.

The privates of the American regular army are not the most creditable soldiers in the world; they are chiefly composed of Irish emigrants, Germans, and deserters from the English regiments in Canada. Americans are very rare; only those who can find nothing else to do, and have to choose between enlistment and starvation, will enter into the American army. They do not, however, enlist for longer than three years. There is not much discipline, and occasionally a great deal of insolence, as might be expected from such a collection. Corporal punishment has been abolished in the American army except for desertion; and if ever there was a proof of the necessity of punishment to enforce discipline, it is the many substitutes in lieu of it, to which the officers are compelled to resort—all of them more severe than flogging. The most common is that of loading a man with thirty-six pounds of shot in his knapsack, and making him walk three hours out of four, day and night without intermission, with this weight on his shoulders, for six days and six nights; that is, he is compelled to walk three hours with the weight, and then is suffered to sit down *one*. Towards the close this punishment becomes very severe; the feet of the men are so sore and swelled, that they cannot move for some days afterwards. I inquired what would be the consequence if a man were to throw down his knapsack and refuse to walk. The commanding-officer of one of the forts replied, that he would be hung up by the thumbs till he fainted—a variety of piquetting. Surely these punishments savour quite as much of severity, and are quite as degrading as flogging.

The pay of an American private is good—fourteen dollars a month, out of which his rations and regimentals take eight dollars, leaving him six dollars a month for pleasure. Deserters are punished by being made to drag a heavy ball and chain after them, which is never removed day or night. If discharged, they are flogged, their heads shaved, and they are drummed out at the point of the bayonet.

From the conversations I have had with many deserters from our army, who were residing in the United States or were in the American service, I am convinced that it would be a very well-judged measure to offer a free pardon to all those who would return to Canada and re-enter the English service. I think that a good effective regiment would soon be collected, and one that you might trust on the frontiers without any fear of their deserting again; and it would have another good effect, that is, that their statements would prevent the desertion of others.

America, and its supposed freedom, is, to the British soldiers, an Utopia in every sense of the word. They revel in the idea; they seek it and it is not to be found. The greatest desertion from the English regiments is among the musicians composing the bands. There are so many theatres in America, and so few musicians, except coloured people, that instrumental performers of all kinds are in great demand. People are sent over to Canada, and the other British provinces to persuade these poor fellows to desert, promising them very large salaries, and pointing out to them the difference between being a gentleman in America and a slave in the English service. The temptation is too strong; they desert; and when they strive, they soon learn the value of the promises made to them, and find how cruelly they have been deceived.

The Florida war has been a source of dreadful vexation and expense to the United States, having already cost them between 20,000,000 and 30,000,000 of dollars, without any apparent prospect of its coming to a satisfactory conclusion. The American government has also very much injured its character, by the treachery and disregard of honour shown by it to the Indians, who have been, most of them, captured under a flag of truce. I have heard so much indignation expressed by the Americans themselves at this conduct that I shall not comment farther upon it. It is the Federal government, and not the officers employed, who must bear the *onus*. But this war has been mortifying, and even dangerous to the Americans in another point. It has now lasted three years and more. General after general has been superseded, because they have not been able to bring it to a conclusion; and the Indians have proved, to themselves and to the Americans, that they can defy them when they once get them among the swamps and morasses. There has not been one hundred Indians killed, although many of them have been treacherously kidnapped, by a violation of honour; and it is supposed that the United States have already lost one thousand men, if not more, in this protracted conflict.

The aggregate force under General Jessup, in Florida, in November, 1837, was stated to be as follows:—

Regulars	4,637
Volunteers	4,078
Se	10

a m e n	0
I n d ia n s	1 7 8
	8, 8 9 3

It is supposed that the number of Indians remaining in Florida do not amount, men, women, and children, to more than 1,500 and General Jessup has declared to the government that the war is *impracticable*.

Militia.—The return of the militia of the United States, for the year 1837, is as follows:—

The number of *Militia* in the several states and territories, according to the statement of George Bomford, Colonel of Ordnance, dated 20th November, 1837.

States and Territories	Date of Return	Number of Militia
Maine	1836	42,468

New Hampshire	1836	27,473
Massachusetts	1836	44,911
Louisiana	1830	14,808
Mississippi	1830	13,724
Tennessee	1830	60,982
Vermont	1824	25,581
Rhode Island	1832	1,377
Connecticut	1836	23,826
New York	1836	184,728
New Jersey	1829	39,171
Pennsylvania	1834	202,281
Delaware	1827	9,229
Maryland	1836	46,854
Virginia	1836	101,838

North Carolina	1835	64,415
South Carolina	1833	51,112
Georgia	1834	48,461
Alabama	1829	14,892
Kentucky	1836	71,483
Ohio	1836	146,428
Indiana	1833	53,913
Illinois	1831	27,386
Missouri	1835	6,170
Arkansas	1825	2,028
Michigan	1831	5,478
Florida Territory	1831	827
Wisconsin Territory	—	—

District of Columbia	1832	1,249
		1,333,091

This is an enormous force, but at the commencement of a war not a very effective one. In fact, there is no country in the world so defenceless as the United States, but, once roused up, no country more formidable if any (attempt) is made to invade its territories. At the outbreak of a war, the states have almost everything to provide; and although the Americans are well adapted as materials for soldiers, still they have to be levied and disciplined. At the commencement of hostilities, it is not improbable that a well-organised force of 30,000 men might walk through the whole of the Union, from Maine to Georgia; but it is almost certain that not one man would ever get back again, as by that time the people would have been roused and excited, armed and sufficiently disciplined; and their numbers, independent of their bravery, would overwhelm three or four times the number I have mentioned.

Another point must not pass unnoticed, which is, that in America, the major part of which is still an uncleared country, the system of warfare naturally partakes much of the Indian practices of surprise and ambuscade; and the invaders will always have to labour under the great disadvantage of the Americans having that perfect knowledge of the country which the former have not.

Most of the defeats of the British troops have been occasioned by this advantage on the part of the Americans, added to the impracticability of the country rendering the superior discipline of the British of no avail. Indeed the great advantages of knowing the country were proved by the American attempts to invade Canada during the last war, and which ended in the capitulation of General Hull. In an uncleared country, even where large forces meet, each man, to a certain degree, acts independently, taking his position, perhaps, behind a tree (treeing it, as they term it in America), or any other defence which may offer. Now, it is evident that, skilled as all the Americans are in fire-arms, and generally using rifles, a disciplined English soldier, with his clumsy musket, fights at a disadvantage; and, therefore, with due submission to his Grace, the Duke of Wellington was very wrong when he stated, the other day in the House of Lords, that the militia of Canada should be disbanded, and their place supplied by regular troops from England. The militia of Upper Canada are quite as good men as the Americans, and can meet them after their own fashion. A certain proportion of regulars are advantageous, as they are more steady, and in case of a check can be more depended upon; but it is not once in five times that they will, either in America or Canada, be able to bring their concentrated discipline into play. But if the Americans have not the discipline of our troops, their courage is undoubted, and even upon a clear plain the palm of victory will always be severely disputed. A Vermonter, surprised for a moment at finding himself in a charge of bayonets, with the English troops, eyed his opponents, and said, "Well I calculate my piece of iron is as good as *yourn*, anyhow," and then rushed to the attack. People who "calculate" in that way are not to be trifled with, as the annals of history fully demonstrate.

A war between America and England is always to be deprecated. Notwithstanding that the countries are severed, still the Americans are our descendants; they speak the same language, and (although they do not readily admit it) still look up to us as their mother country. It is true that this feeling is fast wearing away, but still it is not yet effaced. It is true also that, in their ambition and their covetousness, they would destroy the mutual advantages derived by both countries from our commercial relations, that they might, by manufacturing as well as producing, secure the whole profits to themselves. But they are wrong; for great as America is becoming, the time is not yet arrived when she can compete with English capital, or work for herself without it. But there is another reason why a war between the two countries is so much to be deprecated, which is, that is must ever be a cruel and an irritating war. To attack the Americans by invasion will always be hazardous, and must ultimately prove disastrous. In what manner, then, is England to avenge any aggression that may be committed by the Americans? All she can do is to ravage, burn, and destroy; to carry the horrors of war along their whole extended line of coast, distressing the non-combatants, and wreaking vengeance upon the defenceless.

Dreadful to contemplate as this is, and, even more dreadful the system of stimulating the Indian tribes to join us, adding scalping, and the murdering of women and children, to other horrors, still it is the only method to which England could resort, and, indeed, a method to which she would be warranted to resort, in her own behoof. Moreover, in case of a future war, England must not allow it to be of such short duration as was the last; the Americans must be made to feel it, by its being protracted until their commerce is totally annihilated, and their expenses are increased in proportion with the decrease of their means.

Let it not be supposed that England would harass the coasts of America, or raise the Indian tribes against her, from any feeling of malevolence, or any pleasure in the sufferings which must ensue. It would be from the knowledge of the fact that money is the sinews of war; and consequently that, by obliging the Americans to call out so large a force as she must do to defend her coast and to repel the Indians, she would be put to such an enormous expense, as would be severely felt throughout the Union, and soon incline all parties to a cessation of hostilities. It is to touch their pockets that this plan must and *will* be resorted to; and a war carried on upon that plan alone, would prove a salutary lesson to a young and too ambitious a people. Let the Americans recollect the madness of joy with which the hats and caps were thrown up in the air at New York, when, even after so short a war with England, they heard that the treaty of peace had been concluded; and that too at a time when England was so occupied in a contest, it may be said, with the whole world, that she could hardly divert a portion of her strength to act against America: then let them reflect how sanguinary, how injurious, a protracted war with England would be, when she could direct her whole force against them. It is, however, useless to ask a people to reflect who are governed and ruled by the portion who will *not* reflect. The forbearance must be on our part; and, for the sake of humanity, it is to be hoped that we shall be magnanimous enough to forbear, for so long as may be consistent with the maintenance of our national honour.

Volume Three—Chapter Five.

Remarks—American Marine.

It may be inferred that I naturally directed my attention to everything connected with the American marine, and circumstances eventually induced me to search much more minutely into particulars than at first I had intended to do.

The present force of the American navy is rated as follows:—

Ships of the Line

of	1
1	
2	
0	
g	

uns	
80 guns	7
74 guns	3
Total	11

Frigates, 1st Class.

Of 54 guns	1
44 g	14

u n s	
T o t a l	15

Frigates, 2nd Class

O f 3 0 g u n s	2

Sloops

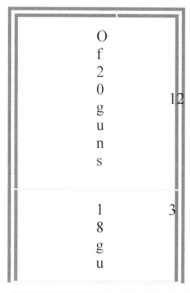

O f 2 0 g u n s	12
1 8 g u	3

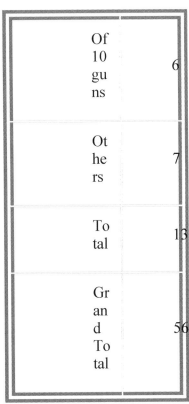

n s	
T o t a l	15

Schooners

Of 10 gu ns	6
Ot he rs	7
To tal	13
Gr an d To tal	56

Navy List.

Vessels of War of the United States Navy, September 1837.

Ships of the Line

Name	Rate	Where built	When	Where employed

Franklin	74	Philadelphia	1815	In ordinary at New York
Washington	74	Portsmouth, NH.	1816	Do. do.
Columbus	74	Washington	1819	At Boston (repaired)
Ohio	80	New York	1820	Do. do.
North Carolina	80	Philadelphia	1820	In commission (Pacific)
Delaware	80	Gosport	1820	At Norfolk (repaired)
Alabama	80			On stocks at Portsmouth, NH.
Vermont	80			Do. at Boston
Virginia	80			Do. do.

New York	80			On stocks, at Norfolk
Penn sylva nia	120	Phila delph ia	1837	At Philadelphia

Frigates, 1st Class

Name	Rate	Where built	When	Where employed
Inde pend ence	54	Bo sto n	1814	On the coast of Brazil
Unit ed State s	44	Ph ila de lp hi a	1797	In commission (Mediterranean)
Cons tituti on	44	Bo sto n	1787	Do. do.
Guer riere	44	Ph ila de lp hi	1814	In ordinary at Norfolk

		a		
Java	44	Baltimore	1814	Receiving ship, do.
Potomac	44	Washington	1821	In ordinary at do.
Brandy Wine	44	Washington	1825	Do. do.
Hudson	44	Purchased	1826	Receiving vessel at New York
Columbia	44	Washington	1836	In ordinary at Norfolk

Santee	44		On stocks, at Portsmouth, NH.
Cumberland	44		Do. at Boston
Sabine	44		Do. at New York
Savannah	44		Do. do.
Raritan	44		Do. at Philadelphia
St. Lawrence	44		Do. at Norfolk

Frigates, 2nd Class

Name	Rate	Where built	When	Where employed
Constellation	36	Baltimore	1797	In commission (West Indies)
Macedo	36	Norfolk	1836	Ready for sea at Norfolk

nian		(rebuilt)		

Sloops of War

Name	Rate	Where built	When	Where employed
John Adams	20	Norfolk (rebuilt)	1820	Ready for sea at New York
Cyane	20	Boston (rebuilding)		
Boston	20	Boston	1825	At sea
Lexington	20	New York	1825	At sea
Vincen	20	New York	1826	In ordinary at Norfolk

ne s				
W ar re n	20	Boston	1826	Do. do.
N at ch es	20	Norfolk	1827	In commission (West Indies)
Fa lm ou th	20	Boston	1827	At sea
Fa irf iel d	20	New York	1828	On the coast of Brazil
V an da lia	20	Philade lphia	1828	In commission (West Indies)
St . L ou is	20	Washin gton	1828	Do. do.
C	20	Portsm	1828	In commission

on co rd		outh		(West Indies)
Er ie	18	New York (rebuilt)	1820	At Boston
O nt ari o	18	Baltim ore	1813	At sea
Pe ac oc k	18	New York	1813	In ordinary at Norfolk

Schooners

Dolph in	10	Ph ila de lp hi a	1821	On the Coast of Brazil
Gram pus	10	W as hi ng to n	1821	In commission (West Indies)

Shark	10	Washington	1821	In the Mediterranean
Enterprise	10	New York	1831	In commission (East Indies)
Boxer	10	Boston	1731	In the Pacific
Porpoise	10	Boston	1836	Atlantic coast
Experiment	4	Washington	1831	Employed near New York
Fox (hulk)	3	Purchased	1823	At Baltimore (condemned)
Sea		Pu	1823	Receiving vessel at

Gull (galliot)		rc ha se d	Philadelphia

Exploring Vessels

Relief		Philadelphia	1836	
Barque Pioneer		Boston	1836	New York (nearly ready for sea)
Barque Consort		Boston	1836	
Schooner Active		Purchased	1837	

The ratings of these vessels will, however, very much mislead people as to the real strength of the armament. The 74's and 80's are in weight of broadside equal to most three-decked ships; the first-class frigates are double-banked of the scantling, and carrying the complement of men of our 74's. The sloops are equally powerful in proportion to their ratings, most of them carrying long guns. Although flush vessels, they are little inferior to a 36-gun frigate in scantling, and are much too powerful far any that we have in our service, under the same denomination of rating. All the line-of-battle ships are named after the several states, the frigates after the principal rivers, and the sloops of war after the towns, or *cities*, and the names are decided by lot.

It is impossible not to be struck with the beautiful architecture in most of these vessels. The Pennsylvania, rated 120 guns, on four decks, carrying 140, is not by any means so perfect as some of the line-of-battle ships.

Note. The following are the dimensions given me of the ship of the line Pennsylvania:—

	feet	inches
In extreme length over all	237	
Between the perpendiculars on the lower gun-deck	220	
Length of keel for tonnage	190	
Moulded breadth of beam	56	9
do. do. from tonnage	57	6
Extreme breadth of beam outside the wales	59	

Depth of lower hold	23
Extreme depth amidships	51

Burthen 3366 tons, and has ports for 140 guns, all long thirty-two pounders, throwing 2240 pounds of ball at each broadside, or 4480 pounds from the whole.

The Ohio is, as far as I am a judge, the perfection of a ship of the line. But in every class you cannot but admire the superiority of the models and workmanship. The dock-yards in America are small, and not equal at present to what may eventually be required, but they have land to add to them if necessary. There certainly is no necessity for such establishments or such store-houses as we have, as their timber and hemp are at hand when required; but they ate very deficient both in dry and wet docks. Properly speaking, they have no great naval depot. This arises from the jealous feeling existing between the several states. A bill brought into Congress to expend so many thousand dollars upon the dock-yard at Boston, in Massachusetts, would be immediately opposed by the state of New York, and an amendment proposed to transfer the works intended to their dock-yard at Brooklyn. The other states which possess dock-yards would also assert their right, and thus they will all fight for their respective establishments until the bill is lost, and the bone of contention falls to the ground.

Her mainmast from the step to the truck	278
Main yard	110
Main-topsail yard	82
Main-top-gallant yard	52

	feet	inches
Main-royal yard	36	
Size of lower shrouds	0	11
Do. of mainstay	0	19
Do. of sheet-cable	0	25

The sheet-anchor, made at Washington, weighs 11,660 pounds

Main-topsail contains 1,531 yards.

The number of yards of canvass for one suit of sails is 18,341, and for bags, hammocks, boat-sails, awnings, etcetera, 14,624; total 32,965 yards.

The Americans considered that in the Pennsylvania they possessed the largest vessel in the world, but this is a great mistake; one of the Sultan's three-deckers is larger. Below are the dimensions of the Queen, lately launched at Portsmouth

	feet	inches
Length on the gun-deck	204	0
Do. of keel for tonnage	166	5.25

Breadth extreme	60	0
Do. for tonnage	59	2
Depth in hold	23	8
Burden in tons (No. 3,099)		
Extreme length aloft	247	6
Extreme height forward	56	4
Do. midships	50	8
Do. abaft	62	6
Launching draught of water, forward	14	1
Do. abaft	19	0
Height from deck to deck, gun-deck	7	3
Do. middle-deck	7	0
Do. main-deck	7	0

Note. There are seven navy yards belonging to, and occupied for the use of the United States, viz.—The navy yard at Portsmouth, NH, is situated on an island, contains fifty-eight acres, cost 5,500 dollars.

The navy yard at Charlestown, near Boston, is situated on the north side of Charles river, contains thirty-four acres, and cost 32,214 dollars.

The navy yard at New York is situated on Long Island, opposite New York, contains forty acres, and cost 40,000 dollars.

The navy yard at Philadelphia is situated on the Delaware river, in the district of Southwark, contains eleven acres to low water mark, and cost 27,000 dollars.

It is remarkable that along the whole of the eastern coast of America, from Halifax in Nova Scotia down to Pensacola in the Gulf of Mexico, there is not one good open harbour. The majority of the American harbours are barred at the entrance, so as to preclude a fleet running out and in to manoeuvre at pleasure; indeed, if the tide does not serve, there are few of them in which a line-of-battle ship, hard pressed, could take refuge. A good spacious harbour, easy of access, like that of Halifax in Nova Scotia, is one of the few advantages, perhaps the only natural advantage, wanting in the United States.

The American navy list is as follows:—

Captains or Commodores	50	Passed Midshipmen	181
Masters Commandant	50	Midshipmen	227
Lieutenants	279	Sailing-Masters	27
Surgeons	50	Sail-makers	25
Passed Assistant Surgeons	24	Boatswains	22
Assistant	33	Gunners	27

Surgeons			
Pursers	45	Carpenters	26
Chaplains	9		

The pay of these officers is on the following scale. It must be observed, that they do not use the term "half pay;" but when unemployed the officers are either attached to the various dockyards or on leave. I have reduced the sums paid into English money, that they may be better understood by the reader:

Senior captain, on service	960
On leave i.e. half-pay	730
Captains, squadron service	830
Navy Yard and other duty, half pay	730
Off duty, ditto	525
Commanders on service	525
Navy-yard and other duty, half pay	440
On leave, ditto	380
Lieutenants commanding	380
Navy-yard and other duty, half pay	315

Waiting orders, ditto	250
Surgeons, according to their length of servitude, from	210
To	500
And half pay in proportion	
Assistant Surgeons, from	200
To	250
Chaplains; sea service	250
On leave, half pay	170
Passed midshipmen, duty	156
Waiting orders, half pay	125
Midshipmen; sea service	33
Navy-yard and other duty, half pay!	72
Leave, ditto!	63
Sailing-masters; ships of the line	228

Other duty, half pay	200
Leave, ditto	156
Boatswains, carpenters, sailmakers, and gunners	
Ships of the line	156
Frigate	125
Other duty, half pay	105
On leave, ditto	75

The navy yard at Washington, in the district of Columbia, is situated on the eastern branch of the Potomac, contains thirty-seven acres, and cost 4,000 dollars. In this yard are made all the anchors, cables, blocks, and almost all things requisite for the use of the navy of the United States.

The navy-yard at Portsmouth, near Norfolk in Virginia, is situated on the south branch of Elizabeth river contains sixteen acres, and cost 13,000 dollars.

There is also a navy-yard at Pensacola in Florida, which is merely used for repairing ships on the West India station.

It will be perceived by the above list how very much better all classes in the American service are paid in comparison with those in our service. But let it not be supposed that this liberality is a matter of choice on the part of the American government; on the contrary, it is one of necessity. There never was, nor never will be, anything like liberality under a democratic form of government. The navy is a favourite service, it is true, but the officers of the American navy have not one cent more than they are entitled to, or than they absolutely require. In a country like America, where any one may by industry, in a few years, become an independent, if not a wealthy man, it would be impossible for the government to procure officers if they were not tolerably paid; no parents would permit their children to enter the service unless they were enabled by their allowances to keep up a respectable appearance; and in America everything, to the annuitant or person not making money, but living upon his income, is much dearer than with us. The government, therefore, are obliged to pay them, or young men would not embark in the profession; for it is not in America as it is with us, where every department is filled up, and no room is left for those who would crowd in; so that in the eagerness to obtain respectable employment, emolument becomes a secondary consideration. It may, however, be worth while to put in juxtaposition the half-pay paid to officers of corresponding ranks in the two navies of England and America:

Officers	America	England
Half-pay post-captains, senior, on leave		
corresponding to commodore or rear-admiral in England	730	456
Post captains off duty—that is duty on shore	730	

On leave	525	191
commanders off sea duty	440	
In yards and on leave	380	155
Lieutenants, shore duty	315	
Waiting orders or on leave	250	90
Passed midshipmen, full pay	156	25
Half-pay	125	0
Midshipmen, full pay	83	25
Half-pay	63	0

My object in making the comparison between the two services is not to gratify an invidious feeling. More expensive as living in America certainly is, still the disproportion is such as must create surprise; and if it requires such a sum for an American officer to support himself in a creditable and gentlemanlike manner, what can be expected from the English officer with his miserable pittance, which is totally inadequate to his rank and station! Notwithstanding which, our officers do keep up their appearance as gentlemen, and those who have no half pay are obliged to support themselves. And I point this out, that when Mr Hume and other gentlemen clamour against the expense of our naval force, they may not be ignorant of one fact, which is, that not only on half-pay, but when on active service, a moiety at least of the expenses necessarily incurred by our officers to support themselves according to their rank, to entertain, and to keep their ships in proper order, is, three times out of four, paid out of their own pockets, or those of their relatives; and that is always done without complaint, as long as they are not checked in their legitimate claims to promotion.

In the course of this employment in the Mediterranean, one of our captains was at Palermo. The American commodore was there at the time, and the latter gave most sumptuous balls and entertainments. Being very intimate with each other, our English captain said to him one day, "I cannot imagine how you can afford to give such parties; I only know that I cannot; my year's pay would be all exhausted in a fortnight." "My dear fellow," replied the American commodore, "do you suppose, that I am so foolish as to go to such an expense, or to spend my pay in this manner; I have nothing to do with them except to give them. My purser provides everything, and keeps a regular account, which I sign as correct, and send home to government, which defrays the whole expenses, under the head of *conciliation* money." I do not mean to say that this is requisite in our service: but still it is not fair to refuse to provide us with paint and other articles, such as leather, etcetera, necessary to fit out our ships; thus, either compelling us to pay for them out of our own pockets, or allowing the vessels under our command to look like anything but men-of-war, and to be styled, very truly, a disgrace to the service. Yet such is the well-known fact. And I am informed that the reason why our admiralty will not permit these necessary stores to be supplied is that, as one of the lords of the admiralty was known to say, "if we *do not*provide them, the captains *most assuredly will*, therefore let us save the government the expense."

During my sojourn in the United States I became acquainted with a large portion of the senior officers of the American navy, and I found them gifted, gentleman-like, and liberal. With them I could converse freely upon all points relative to the last war, and always found them ready to admit all that could be expected. The American naval officers certainly form a strong contrast to the majority of their countrymen, and prove, by their enlightened and liberal ideas, how much the Americans, in general, would be improved if they enjoyed the same means of comparison with other countries which the naval officers, by their profession, have obtained. Their partial successes during the late war were often the theme of discourse, which was conducted with candour and frankness on both sides. No unpleasant feeling was ever excited by any argument with them on the subject, whilst the question, raised amongst their "free and enlightened" brother citizens, who knew nothing of the matter, was certain to bring down upon me such a torrent of bombast, falsehood, and ignorance, as required all my philosophy to submit to with apparent indifference. But I must now take my leave of the American navy, and notice their merchant marine.

Before I went to the United States I was aware that a large proportion of our seamen were in their employ. I knew that the whole line of packets, which is very extensive, was manned by British seamen; but it was not until I arrived in the states that I discovered the real state of the case.

During my occasional residence at New York, I was surprised to find myself so constantly called upon by English seamen, who had served under me in the different ships I had commanded since the peace. Every day seven or eight would come, touch their hats, and remind me in what ships, and in what capacity, they had done their duty. I had frequent conversations with them, and soon discovered that their own expression, "We are all here, sir," was strictly true. To the why and the wherefore, the answer was invariably the same. "Eighteen dollars a-month, sir." Some of them, I recollect, told me that they were going down to New Orleans, because the sickly season was coming on; and that during the time the yellow fever raged they always had a great advance of wages, receiving sometimes as much as thirty dollars per month. I did not attempt to dissuade them from their purpose; they were just as right to risk their lives from contagion at thirty dollars a-month, as to stand and be fired at a shilling a day. The circumstance of so many of my own men being in American ships, and their assertion that there were no other sailors than English at New York, induced me to enter very minutely into my investigation, of which the following are the results:—

The United States, correctly speaking, have no common seamen, or seamen bred up as apprentices before the mast. Indeed a little reflection will show how unlikely it is that they ever should have; for who would submit to such a dog's life (as at the best it is), or what parent would consent that his children should wear out an existence of hardship and dependence at sea, when he could so easily render them independent on shore? The same period of time requisite for a man to learn his duty ay an able seaman, and be qualified for the pittance of eighteen dollars per month, would be sufficient to establish a young man as an independent, or even wealthy, land-owner, factor, or merchant. That there are classes in America who do go to sea is certain, and who and what these are I shall hereafter point out; but it may be positively asserted that, unless by escaping from their parents at an early age, and before their education is complete, they become, as it were, lost, there is in the United States of America hardly an instance of a white boy being sent to sea, to be brought up as a foremast man.

It may be here observed that there is a wide difference in the appearance of an English seaman and a portion of those styling themselves American seamen, who are to be seen at Liverpool and other seaports; tall, weedy, narrow-shouldered, slovenly, yet still athletic men, with their knives worn in a sheath outside of their clothes, and not with a lanyard round them, as is the usual custom of English seamen. There is, I grant, a great difference in their appearance, and it arises from the circumstance of those men having been continually in the trade to New Orleans and the South, where they have picked up the buccaneer airs and customs which are still in existence there; but the fact is, that, though altered also by climate, the majority of them were Englishmen born, who served their first apprenticeship in the coasting trade, but left it at an early age for America. They may be considered as a portion of the emigrants to America, having become in feeling, as well as in other respects, *bona fide* Americans.

The whole amount of tonnage of the American mercantile manner may be taken, in round numbers, at 2,000,000 tons, which may be subdivided as follows:

	Reg ister ed
	Ton

	s
Foreign trade	700,000
Whale fishery	130,000
Enrolled	
Coasting trade	920,000
Steam	150,000
Coast Fisheries	100,000
Total	2,000,000

The American merchant vessels are generally sailed with fewer men than the British calculate five men to one hundred tons, which I believe to be about the just proportion. Mr Carey, in his work, estimates the proportion of seamen in American vessels to be 44 to every one hundred tons, and I shall assume his calculation as correct. The number of men employed in the American mercantile navy will be as follows:—

	Men
Foreign trade	30,333
Whale fishery	5,000
Coasting trade	39,000
Steam	6,500
Coast fisheries	4,333

Total	85,790

And now I will submit, from the examinations I have made, the proportions of American and British seamen which are contained in this aggregate of 85,799 men.

In the foreign trade we have to deduct the masters of the ships, the mates, and the boys who are apprenticed to learn their duty, and rise to mates and masters (not to serve before the mast). These I estimate at:—

Masters	1,500
Mates	3,000
Apprentices	1,500
Ditto, co'ld men, as cooks, stewards, etcetera	2,000
Total	8,

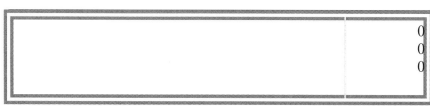

which, deducted from 30,333, will leave 22,333 seamen in the foreign trade; who, with a slight intermixture of Swedes, Danes, and, more rarely, Americans, may be asserted to be all British seamen.

The next item is that of the men employed in the whale fishery; and, as near as I can ascertain the fact, the proportions are two-thirds Americans to one-third British. The total is 5,633; out of which 3,756 art Americans, and 1,877 British seamen.

The coasting trade employs 39,000 men; but only a small proportion of them can be considered as seamen, as *it* embraces all the internal river navigation.

The steam navigation employs 6,500 men, of whom of course not one in ten is a seaman.

The fisheries for cod and herring employ about 4,333 men; they are a mixture of Americans, Nova Scotians, and British, but the proportions cannot be ascertained; it is supposed that about one-half are British subjects, i.e. 2,166.

When, therefore, I estimate that the Americans employ at least *thirty thousand of our seamen* in their service, I do not think, as my subsequent remarks will prove, that I am at all overrating the case.

The questions which are now to be considered are, the nature of the various branches in which the seamen employed in the American marine are engaged, and how far they will be available to America in case of a war.

The coasting trade is chiefly composed of sloops, manned by two or three men and boys. The captain is invariably part, if not whole, owner of the vessel, and those employed are generally his sons, who work for their father, or some emigrant Irishmen, who, after a few months practice, are fully equal to this sort of fresh-water sailing. From the coasting trade, therefore, America would gain no assistance. Indeed, the majority of the coasting trade is so confined to the interior, that it would not receive much check from a war with a foreign country.

The coast fisheries might afford a few seamen, but very few; certainly not the number of men required to man her ships of war. As in the coasting trade, they are mostly owners or partners. In the whale fishery much the same system prevails; it is a common speculation; and the men embarking stipulate for such a proportion of the fish caught as their share of the profits. They are generally well to do, are connected together, and are the least likely of all men to volunteer on board of the American navy. They would speculate in privateers, if they did anything.

From steam navigation, of course, no seamen could be obtained.

Now, as all service is voluntary, it is evident that the only chance America has of manning her navy is from the thirty thousand British seamen in her employ, the other branches of navigation either not producing seamen, or those employed in them being too independent in situation to serve as foremast men. When I was at the different seaports, I made repeated inquiries as to the fact, if ever a lad was sent to sea as foremast-man, and I never could ascertain that it ever was the case. Those who are sent as apprentices, are learning their duty to receive the rating of mates, and ultimately fulfil the office of captains; and it may here be remarked, that many Americans, after serving as captains for a few years, return on shore and become opulent merchants; the knowledge which they have gained during their maritime career proving of the greatest advantage to them. There are a number of free black and coloured lads who are sent to sea, and who, eventually, serve as stewards and cooks; but it must be observed, that the masters and mates are not people who will enter before the mast and submit to the rigorous discipline of a government vessel, and the cooks and stewards are not seamen; so that the whale dependence of the American navy, in case of war, is upon the British seamen who are in her foreign trade and whale fisheries, and in her men-of-war in commission during the peace.

If America brings up none of her people to a seafaring life before the mast, now that her population is upwards of 13,000,000, still less likely was she to have done it when her population was less, and the openings to wealth by other channels were greater: from whence it may be fairly inferred, that, during our continued struggle with France, when America had the carrying trade in her hands, her vessels were chiefly manned by british seamen; and that when the war broke out between the two countries, the same British seamen who were in her employ manned her ships of war and privateers. It may be surmised that British seamen would refuse to be employed against their country. Some might; but there is no character so devoid of principle as the British sailor and soldier. In Dibdin's songs, we certainly have another version, "True to his country and king," etcetera, but I am afraid they do not deserve it: soldiers and sailors are mercenaries; they risk their lives for money; if is their trade to do so; and if they can get higher wages they never consider the justice of the cause, or whom they fight for. Now, America is a country peculiarly favourable for those who have little conscience or reflection; the same language is spoken there; the wages are much higher, spirits are much cheaper, and the fear of dejection or punishment is trifling: nay, there is none; for in five minutes a British seaman may be made a *bona fide* American citizen, and of course an American seaman. It is not surprising, therefore, that after sailing for years out of the American ports, in American vessels, the men, in case of war, should take the oath and serve. It is necessary for any one wanting to become an American citizen, that he should give notice of his intention; this notice gives him, as soon as he has signed his declaration, all the rights of an American citizen, excepting that of voting at elections, which requires a longer time, as specified in each state. The declaration is as follows:
—

"That it is his *bona fide* intention to become a citizen of the United States, and to renounce forever all allegiance and fidelity to any foreign power, potentate, state, or sovereignty whatever, and particularly to Victoria, the Queen of the United Kingdom of Great Britain and Ireland, to whom he is now a subject." Having signed this document, and it being publicly registered, he becomes a citizen, and may be sworn to as such by any captain of merchant vessel or man-of-war, if it be required that he should do so.

During the last war with America, the Americans hit upon a very good plan as regarded the English seamen whom they had captured in our vessels. In the daytime the prison doors were shot and the prisoners were harshly treated; but at night, the doors were left open: the consequence was, that the prisoners whom they had taken added to their strength, for the men walked out, and entered on board their men-of-war and privateers.

This fact alone proves that I have not been too severe in my remarks upon the character of the English seamen; and since our seamen prove to be such "Dugald Dalgettys," it is to be hoped that, should we be so unfortunate as again to come in collision with America, the same plan may be adopted in this country.

Now, from the above remarks, three points are clearly deducible:—

1. That America always has obtained, and for a long period to come will obtain, her seamen altogether from Great Britain.

2. That those seamen can be naturalised immediately, and become American seamen by law.

3. That, under present circumstances, England is under the necessity of raising seamen, not only for her own navy, but also for the Americans; and that, in proportion as the commerce and shipping of America shall increase, so will the demand upon us become more onerous; and that should we fail in producing the number of seamen necessary for both services, the Americans will always be full manned, whilst any defalcation must fall upon ourselves.

And it may be added that, in all cases, the Americans have the choice and refusal of our men; and, therefore, they have invariably all the prime and best seamen which we have raised.

The cause of this is as simple as it is notorious; it is the difference between the wages paid in the navies and merchant vessels of the two nations:

	pounds shils pounds shils
American ships per month	3 10
British ships ditto	2 2 to 2 10
American men-of-war ditto	2 0

British men-of-war	
ditto	1 14

It will be observed, that in the American men-of-war the able-seaman's pay is only 2 pounds; the consequence is that they remain for months in port without being able to obtain men.

But we must now pass by this cause, and look to the origin of it; or, in other words, how is it that the Americans are able to give such high wages to our seamen as to secure the choice of any number of our best men for their service; and how is it that they can compete with, and even under-bid, our merchant vessels in freight, at the same time that they sail at a greater expense?

This has arisen partly from circumstances, partly from a series of mismanagement on our part, and partly from the fear of impressment. But it is principally to be ascribed to the former peculiarly unscientific mode of calculating the tonnage of our vessels; the error of which system induced the merchants to build their ships so as to evade the heavy channel and river duties; disregarding all the first principles of naval architecture, and considering the sailing properties of vessels as of no consequence.

The fact is, that we over-taxed our shipping.

In order to carry as much freight as possible, and, at the same time, to pay as few of the onerous duties, our mercantile shipping generally assumed more the form of floating bores of merchandise than sailing vessels; and by the false method of measuring the tonnage, they were enabled to carry 600 tons, when, by measurement, they were only taxed as being of the burden of 400 tons: but every increase of tonnage thus surreptitiously obtained, was accompanied with a decrease in the sailing properties of the vessels. Circumstances, however, rendered this of less importance during the war, as few vessels ran without the protection of a convoy; and it must be also observed, that vessels being employed in one trade only, such as the West India, Canada, Mediterranean, etcetera, their voyages during the year were limited, and they were for a certain portion of the year unemployed.

During the war the fear of impressment was certainly a strong inducement to our seamen to enter into the American vessels, and naturalise themselves as American subjects; but they were also stimulated even at that period, by the higher wages, as they still are now that the dread of impressment no longer operates upon them.

It appears, then, that from various causes, our merchant vessels have lost their sailing properties, whilst the Americans are the fastest sailers in the world; and it is for that reason, and no other, that, although sailing at a much greater expense, the Americans can afford to outbid us, and take all our best seamen.

An American vessel is in no particular trade, but ready and willing to take freight anywhere when offered. She sails so fast that she can make three voyages whilst one of our vessels can make but two: consequently she has the preference, as being the better manned, and giving the quickest return to the merchant; and as she receives three freights whilst the English vessel receives only two, it is clear that the extra freight wilt more than compensate for the extra expense the vessel sails at in consequence of paying extra wages to the seamen. Add to this, that the captains, generally speaking, being better paid, are better informed, and more active men; that, from having all the picked seamen, they get through their work with fewer hands; that the activity on board is followed up and supported by an equal activity on the part of the agents and factors on shore—and you have the true cause why America can afford to pay and secure for herself all our best seamen.

One thing is evident, that it is a mere question of pounds, shillings, and pence, between us and America, and that the same men who are now in the American service would, if our wages were higher than those offered by America, immediately return to us and leave her destitute.

That it would be worth the while of this country, in case of a war with the United States, to offer 4 pounds a-head to able seamen, is most certain. It would swell the naval estimates, but it would shorten the duration of the war, and in the end would probably be the saving of many millions. But the question is, cannot and ought not something to be done, now in time of peace, to relieve our mercantile shipping interest, and hold out a bounty for a return to those true principles of naval architecture, the deviation from which has proved to be attended with such serious consequences.

Fast-sailing vessels will always be able to pay higher wages than others, as what they lose in increase of daily expense, they will gain by the short time in which the voyage is accomplished; but it is by encouragement alone that we can expect that the change will take place. Surely some of the onerous duties imposed by the Trinity House might be removed, not from the present class of vessels, but from those built hereafter with first-rate sailing properties. These, however, are points which call for a much fuller investigation than I can here afford them; but they are of vital importance to our maritime superiority, and as such should be immediately considered by the government of Great Britain.

Volume Three—Chapter Six.

Remarks—Slavery.

It had always appeared to me as singular that the Americans, at the time of their Declaration of Independence, took no measures for the gradual, if not immediate, extinction of slavery; that at the very time they were offering up thanks for having successfully struggled for their own emancipation from what they considered foreign bondage, their gratitude for their liberation did not induce them to break the chains of those whom they themselves held in captivity. It is useless for them to exclaim, as they now do, that it was England who left them slavery as a curse and reproach us as having originally introduced the system among them. Admitting, as is the fact, that slavery did commence when the colonies were subject to the mother country admitting that the petitions for its discontinuance were disregarded, still there was nothing to prevent immediate manumission at the time of the acknowledgement of their independence by Great Britain. They had then everything to recommence they had to select a new form of government, and to decide upon new laws; they pronounced, in their declaration, that "all men were equal;" and yet, in the face of this declaration, and their solemn invocation to the Deity, the negroes, in *their* fetters, pleaded to them in vain.

I had always thought that this sad omission, which has left such an anomaly in the Declaration of Independence as to have made it the taunt and reproach of the Americans by the whole civilised world, did really arise from forgetfulness; that, as is but too often the case, when we are ourselves made happy, the Americans in their joy at their own deliverance from the foreign yoke, and the repossessing themselves of their own rights, had been too much engrossed to occupy themselves with the undeniable claims of others. But I was mistaken; such was not the case, as I shall presently show.

In the course of one of my sojourns in Philadelphia, Mr Vaughan, of the Athenium of that city, stated to me that he had found the *original draft* of the Declaration of Independence, in the hand-writing of Mr Jefferson, and that it was curious to remark the alterations which had been made previous to the adoption of the manifesto which was afterwards promulgated. It was to Jefferson, Adams, and Franklin, that was entrusted the primary drawing up of this important document, which was then submitted to others, and ultimately to the Convention, for approval and it appears that the question of slavery had *not*been overlooked when the document was first framed, as the following clause, inserted in the original draft by Mr Jefferson, (but *expunged* when it was laid before the Convention,) will sufficiently prove. After enumerating the grounds upon which they threw off their allegiance to the king of England, the Declaration continued in Jefferson's nervous style:

"He (the king) has waged cruel war against human nature itself, violating its most sacred rights of *life and liberty*, in the person of a distant people who never offended him; captivating and carrying them into slavery, in another hemisphere, or to incur miserable death in their transportation thither. This piratical warfare, the opprobrium of infidel powers, is the warfare of the Christian king of Great Britain, determined to keep open a market where men should be bought and sold; he has prostituted his negative for suppressing every legislative attempt to prohibit or restrain this execrable commerce; and that this assemblage of horrors might want no fact of distinguished dye, he is now exciting these very people to rise in arms among us, and to purchase that liberty of which he has deprived them, by murdering the people upon whom he also obtruded them; thus paying off former crimes committed against the liberties of one people, with crimes which he urges them to commit against the lives of another."

Such was the paragraph which had been inserted by Jefferson, in the virulence of his democracy, and his desire to hold up to detestation the king of Great Britain. Such was at that time, unfortunately, the truth; and had the paragraph remained, and at the same time emancipation been given to the slaves, it would have been a lasting stigma upon George the Third. But the paragraph was expunged; and why I because they could not hold up to public indignation the sovereign whom they had abjured, without reminding the world that slavery still existed in a community which had declared that "all men were equal;" and that if, in a monarch, they had stigmatised it as "violating the most sacred rights of life and liberty," and "waging cruel war against human nature," they could not have afterward been so barefaced and unblushing as to continue a system which was at variance with every principle which they professed.

Note. Miss Martineau, in her admiration of democracy, says, that, in the formation of the government, "The rule by which they worked was no less than the golden one, which seems to have been, by some unlucky chance, omitted in the Bibles of other statesmen, '*Do unto others as ye would that they should do unto you*'" I am afraid the American Bible, by some unlucky chance, has also omitted that precept.

It does, however, satisfactorily prove, that the question of slavery was not *overlooked*; on the contrary, their determination to take advantage of the system was deliberate, and, there can be no doubt, well considered—the very omission of the paragraph proves it. I mention these facts to show that the Americans have no right to revile us on being the cause of slavery in America. They had the means, and were bound, as honourable men, to act up to their declaration but they entered into the question, they decided otherwise, and decided that they would retain their ill-acquired property at the expense of their principles.

The degrees of slavery in America are as various in their intensity as are the communities composing the Union. They may, however, be divided with great propriety under two general heads—eastern and western slavery. By eastern slavery, I refer to that in the slave states bordering on the Atlantic, and those slave states on the other side of the Alleghany mountains, which may be more directly considered as their colonies, viz, in the first instance, Maryland, Delaware, Virginia, North and South Carolina; and, secondly, Kentucky and Tennessee. We have been accustomed lately to class the slaves as non-predial and predial,—that is, those who are domestic, and those who work on the plantations. This classification is not correct, if it is intended to distinguish between those who are well, and those who are badly treated. The true line to be drawn is between those who work separately, and those who are worked in a gang and superintended by an overseer. This is fully exemplified in the United States, where it will be found that in all states where they are worked in gangs the slaves are harshly treated, while in the others their labour is light.

Now, with the exception of the rice grounds in South Carolina, the eastern states are growers of corn, hemp, and tobacco; but their chief staple is the breeding of horses, mules, horned cattle, and other stock: the largest portion of these states remain in wild luxuriant pasture, more especially in Virginia, Kentucky, and Tennessee, either of which states is larger than the other four mentioned.

The proportion of slaves required for the cultivation of the purely agricultural and chiefly grazing farms or plantations in these states is small, fifteen or twenty being sufficient for a farm of two hundred or three hundred acres; and their labour, which is mostly confined to tending stock, is not only very light, but of the quality most agreeable to the negro. Half the day you will see him on horseback with his legs idly swinging—as he goes along, or seated on a shaft-horse driving his wagons. He is quite in his glory; nothing delights a negro so much as riding or driving, particularly when he has a whole team under his control. He takes his wagon for a load of corn to feed the hogs, sits on the edge of the shaft as he tosses the cobs to the grunting multitude, whom he addresses in the most intimate terms; in short, everything is done leisurely, after his own fashion.

In these grazing states, as they may very properly be called, the negroes are well fed; they refuse beef and mutton, and will have nothing but pork; and are, without exception, the fattest and most saucy fellows I ever met with in a state of bondage; and such may be said generally to be the case with all the negroes in the eastern states which I have mentioned. The rice grounds in South Carolina are unhealthy, but the slaves are very kindly treated. But the facts speak for themselves. When the negro works in a gang with the whip over him, he may be overworked and ill-treated; but when he is not regularly watched, he will take very good care that the work he performs shall not injure his constitution.

It has been asserted, and generally credited, that in the eastern states negroes are regularly bred up like the cattle for the western market. That the Virginians, and the inhabitants of the other eastern slave states, do sell negroes which are taken to the west, there is no doubt; but that the negroes are bred expressly for that purpose, is, as regards the majority of the proprietors, far from the fact: it is the effect of circumstances, over which they have had no control. Virginia, when first settled, was one of the richest states, but, by continually cropping the land without manuring it, and that for nearly two hundred years, the major portion of many valuable estates has become barren, and the land is no longer under cultivation; in consequence of this, the negroes, (increasing so rapidly as they do in that country.) so far from being profitable, have become a serious task upon their masters, who have to rear and maintain, without having any employment to give them. The small portion of the estates under cultivation will subsist only a certain portion of the negroes; the remainder must, therefore, be disposed of, or they would eat their master out of his home. That the slaves are not willingly disposed of by many of the proprietors I am certain, particularly when it is known, that they are purchased for the west. I know of many instances of this, and wins informed of others; and by wills, especially, slaves have been directed to be sold for *two-thirds* of the price which they would fetch for the western market, on condition that they were not to leave the state. These facts establish two points, viz, that the slaves in the eastern states is well treated, and that in the western states slavery still exists with all its horrors. The common threat to, and ultimate punishment of, a refractory and disobedient slave in the east, is to sell, him for the western market. Many slave proprietors, whose estates have been worn out in the east, have preferred migrating to the west with their slaves rather than sell them, and thus is the severity of the western treatment occasionally and partially mitigated.

But doing justice, as I always will, to those who have been unjustly calumniated, at the same time I must admit that there is a point connected with slavery in America which renders it more odious than in other countries; I refer to the system of amalgamation, which has, from promiscuous intercourse, been carried on to such an extent, that you very often meet with slaves whose skins are whiter than their master's.

At Louisville, Kentucky, I saw a girl, about twelve years old, carrying a child; and, aware that in a slave state the circumstance of white people hiring themselves out to service is almost unknown, I inquired of her if she were a slave. To my astonishment, she replied in the affirmative. She was as fair as snow, and it was impossible to detect any admixture of blood from her appearance, which was that of a pretty English cottager's child.

I afterward spoke to the master, who stated when he had purchased her, and the sum which he had paid.

I took down the following advertisement for a runaway slave, which was posted up in every tavern I stopped at in Virginia on my way to the springs. The expression of, *"in a manner white"* would imply that there was some shame felt it holding a white man in bondage:—

"Fifty Dollars Reward.

"Ran away from the subscriber, on Saturday, the 21st instant, a slave named George, between twenty and twenty-four years of age, five feet five or six inches high, slender made, stoops when standing, a little bow legged; generally wears right and left boots and shoes; had on him when he left a fur cap, a checked stock, and linen roundabout; had with him other clothing, a jean coat with black horn buttons, a pair of jean pantaloons, both coat and pantaloons of handsome grey mixed; no doubt other clothing not recollected. He had with him a common silver watch; he wears his pantaloons generally very tight in the legs. *Said boy* is in a manner *white*, would be passed by *and taken for a white man.* His *hair* is *long and straight*, like that of a *white* person; looks very steady when spoken to, speaks slowly, and would not be likely to look a person full in the face when speaking to him. It is believed he is making his way to Canada by way of Ohio. I will give twenty dollars for the apprehension of said slave if taken in the county, or fifty dollars if taken out of the county, and secured so that I recover him again.

"Andrew Beirne, junior,

"Union Monroe City,

"July 31st, 1838. Virginia."

The above is a curious document, independently of its proving the manner in which man preys upon his fellow-man in this land of liberty and equality. It is a well-known fact, that a considerable portion of Mr Jefferson's slaves were his own children. If any of them absconded, he would smile, thereby implying that he should not be very particular in looking after them; and yet this man, this great and *good* man, as Miss Martineau calls him, this man who penned the paragraph I have quoted, as having been erased from the Declaration of Independence, who asserted that the slavery of the negro was a violation of the most sacred rights of life and liberty, permitted these his slaves and his children, the issue of his own loins, to be sold at auction after his demise, not even emancipating them, as he might have done, before his death. And, but lately, a member of congress for Georgia, whose name I shall not mention, brought up a fine family of children, his own issue by a female slave; for many years acknowledged them us his own children; permitted them to call him by the endearing title of *papa*, and eventually the whole of them were sold by public auction, and that, too, during his own lifetime!

But there is, I am sorry to say, a more horrible instance on record and one well authenticated. A planter of good family (I shall not mention his name or the state in which it occurred, as he was not so much to blame as were the laws), connected himself with one of his own female slaves, who was nearly white; the fruits of this connexion were two daughters, very beautiful girls, who were sent to England to be educated.

They were both grown up when their father died. At his death his affairs were found in a state of great disorder; in fact, there was not sufficient left to pay his creditors. Having brought up and educated these two girls and introduced them as his daughters, it quite slipped his memory that, having been born of a slave, and not manumitted, they were in reality slaves themselves. This fact was established after his decease; they were torn away from the affluence and refinement to which they had been accustomed, sold and purchased as slaves, and with the avowed intention of the purchaser to reap his profits from their prostitution it must not, however, be supposed that the planters of Virginia and the other Eastern states, encourage this intercourse; on the contrary, the young men who visit at the plantations cannot affront them more than to take notice of their slaves, particularly the lighter coloured, who are retained in the house and attend upon their wives and daughters. Independently of the moral feeling which really guides them (as they naturally do not wish that the attendants of their daughters should be degraded) it is against their interest in case they should wish to sell; as a mulatto or light male will not fetch so high a price as a full-blooded negro; the cross between the European and negro; especially the first cross, i.e. the mulatto, is of a sickly constitution, and quite unable to bear up against the fatigue of field labour in the West. As the race becomes whiter, the stamina is said to improve.

Examining into the question of emancipation in America, the first inquiry will be, how far this consummation is likely to be effected by means of the abolitionists. Miss Martineau, in her book, says, "The good work has begun, and will proceed." She is so far right; it has begun, and has been progressing very fast, as may be proved by the single fact of the abolitionists having decided the election in the state of Ohio in October last. But let not Miss Martineau exult; for the stronger the abolition party may become, the more danger is there to be apprehended of a disastrous conflict between the states.

The fact is that, by the constitution of the United States, the federal government have not only no power to *interfere* or to *abolish* slavery, but they are bound to *maintain* it; the abolition of slavery is expressly *withheld*. The citizens of any state may abolish slavery in their own state but the federal government cannot do so without an express violation of the federal compact. Should all the states in the Union abolish slavery, with the exception of one, and that one be Maryland, (the smallest of the whole of the states,) neither the federal government, or the other states could interfere with her. The federal compact binds the general government, "first, not to *meddle* with the slavery of the states where it exists, and next, to *protect* it in the case of runaway slaves, and to *defend* it in case of *invasion* or *domestic violence* on account of it."

It appears, therefore, that slavery can only be abolished by the slave state itself in which it exists; and it is not very probable that any class of people will voluntarily make themselves beggars by surrendering up their whole property to satisfy the clamour of a party. That this party is strong, and is daily becoming stronger, is very true: the stronger it becomes the worse will be the prospects of the United States. In England the case was very different; the government had a right to make the sacrifice to public opinion by indemnification to the slave-holders; but in America the government have not that power; and the efforts of the abolitionists will only have the effects of plunging the country into difficulties and disunion. As an American author truly observes, "The American abolitionists must trample on the constitution, and wade through the carnage of a civil war, before they can triumph—"

Already the abolition party have done much mischief. The same author observes, "The South has been compelled, in self-defence, to rivet the chains of slavery afresh, and to hold on to their political rights with a stronger hand. The conduct of the abolitionists has arrested the improvements which were in progress in the slave states for the amelioration of the condition of the slave; it has broken up the system of intellectual and moral culture that was extensively in operation for the slave's benefit, lest the increase of his knowledge should lend him a dangerous power, in connection with these crusading efforts; it has rivetted the chains of slavery with a greatly increased power, and enforced a more rigorous discipline; it has excluded for the time being the happy moral influence which was previously operating on the South from the North, and from the rest of the world, by the lights of comparison, by the interchange of a friendly intercourse, and by a friendly discussion of the great subject, all tending to the bettering of the slave's condition, and, as was supposed, to his ultimate emancipation. Before this agitation commenced, this subject, in all its aspects and bearings, might be discussed as freely at the South as anywhere; but now, not a word can be said. It has kindled a sleepless jealousy in the South toward the North, and made the slave-holders feel as if all the rest of the world were their enemies, and that they must depend upon themselves for the maintenance of their political rights. We say rights, because they regard them as such; and so long as they do so, it is all the same in their feelings, whether the rest of the world acknowledge them or not. And they are, in fact, *political* rights, guaranteed to them by the constitution of the United States."

It is not, however, impossible that the abolition party in the Eastern and Northern states may be gradually checked by the citizens of those very states. Their zeal may be as warm as ever; but public opinion will compel them, at the risk of their lives, to hold their tongues. This possibility can, however, only arise from the Northern and Eastern states becoming manufacturing states, as they are most anxious to be. Should this happen, the raw cotton grown by slave labour will employ the looms of Massachusetts; and then, as the Quarterly Review very correctly observes, "by a cycle of commercial benefits, the Northern and Eastern states will feel that there is some material compensation for the moral turpitude of the system of slavery."

The slave proprietors in these states are as well aware as any political economist can be, that slavery is a loss instead of a gain, and that no state can arrive at that degree of prosperity under a state of slavery which it would under free labour. The case is simple. In free labour, where there is competition, you exact the greatest possible returns for the least possible expenditure; a man is worked as a machine; he is paid for what he produces, and nothing more. By slave labour, you receive the least possible return for the greatest possible expense, for the slave is better fed and clothed than the freeman, and does as little work as he can. The slave-holders in the eastern states are well aware of this, and are as anxious to be rid of slavery as are the abolitionists; but the time is not yet come, nor will it come until the country shall have so filled up as to render white labour attainable. Such, indeed, are not the expectations expressed in the language of the representatives of their states when in congress; but, it must be remembered, that this is a question which has convulsed the Union, and that, not only from a feeling of pride, added to indignation at the interference, but from if feeling of the necessity of not yielding up one tittle upon this question, the language of determined resistance is in congress invariably resorted to. But these gentlemen have one opinion for congress, and another for their private table; in the first, they stand up unflinchingly for their slave rights; in the other, they reason calmly, and admit what they could not admit in public. There is no labour in the eastern states, excepting that of the rice plantations in South Carolina, which cannot be performed by white men; indeed, a large proportion of the cotton in the Carolinas is now raised by a *free white* population. In the grazing portion of these states, white labour would be substituted advantageously, could white labour be procured at any reasonable price.

The time will come, and I do not think it very distant, say perhaps twenty or thirty years, when, provided America receives no check, and these states are not injudiciously interfered with, that Virginia, Kentucky, Delaware, Maryland, North Carolina, (and, eventually, but probably somewhat later, Tennessee and South Carolina) will, of their own accord, enrol themselves among the free states. As a proof that in the eastern slave states the negro is not held in such contempt, or justice toward him so much disregarded, I extract the following from an American work:—

"An instance of the force of law in the southern states for the protection of the slave has just occurred, in the failure of a petition to his excellency, PM Butler, governor of South Carolina, for the pardon of Nazareth Allen, a white person, convicted of the murder of a slave, and sentenced to be hung. The following is part of the answer of the governor to the petitioners:—

"'The laws of South Carolina make no distinction in cases of deliberate murder, whether committed on a black man or a white man; neither can I. I am not a law-maker, but the executive officer of the laws already made; and I must not act on a distinction which the legislature might have made, but has not thought fit to make.'

"That the crime of which the prisoner stands convicted was committed against one of an inferior grade in society, is a reason for being especially cautious in intercepting the just severity of the law. This class of our population are subjected to us as well for their protection as our advantage. Our rights, in regard to them, are not more imperative than their duties; and the institutions, which for wise and necessary ends have rendered them peculiarly dependent, at least pledge the law to be to them peculiarly a friend and a protector.

"The prayer of the petition is not granted.

"Pierce M Butler."

In the western states, comprehending Missouri, Louisiana, Arkansas, Mississippi, Georgia, and Alabama, the negroes are, with the exception perhaps of the two latter States, in a worse condition than they ever were in the West India islands. This may be easily imagined, when the character of the white people who inhabit the larger portion of these states is considered a class of people, the majority of whom are without feelings of honour, reckless in their habits, intemperate, unprincipled, and lawless, many of them having fled from the eastern states, as fraudulent bankrupts, swindlers, or committers of other crimes, which have subjected them to the penitentiaries—miscreants defying the climate, so that they can defy the laws. Still this representation of the character of the people inhabiting these states must, from the chaotic state of society in America, be received with many exceptions. In the city of New Orleans, for instance, and in Natchez and its vicinity, and also among the planters, there are many most honourable exceptions. I have said the majority: for we must look to the *mass*—the exceptions do but prove the rule. It is evident that slaves, under such masters, can have but little chance of good treatment, and stories are told of them at which humanity shudders.

It appears, then, that the slaves, with the rest of the population of America, are *working their way west*, and the question may now be asked:—Allowing that slavery will be soon abolished in the eastern states, what prospect is there of its ultimate abolition and total extinction in America?

I can see no prospect of exchanging slave labour for free in the western states, as, with the exception of Missouri, I do not think it possible that white labour could be substituted, the extreme heat and unhealthiness of the climate being a bar to any such attempt. The cultivation of the land must be carried on by a negro population, if it is to be carried on at all. The question, therefore, to be considered is, whether these states are to be inhabited and cultivated by a free or a slave negro population. It must be remembered, that not one-twentieth part of the land in the southern states is under cultivation; every year, as the slates are brought in from the east, the number of acres taken into cultivation increases. Not double or triple the number of the slaves at present in America would be sufficient for the cultivation of the whole of these vast territories. Every year the cotton crops increase, and at the same time the price of cotton has not materially lowered; as an everywhere increasing population takes off the whole supply, this will probably continue to be the case for many years, since it must be remembered, that, independently of the increasing population increasing the demand, cotton, from its comparative cheapness, continually usurps the place of some other raw material; this, of course, adds to the consumption. In various manufactures, cotton has already taken the place of linen and fur; but there must eventually be a limit to consumption: and this is certain, that as soon as the supply is so great as to exceed the demand, the price will be lowered by the competition; and, as soon as the price is by competition so lowered as to render the cost and keeping of the slave greater than the income returned by his labour, then, and not till then, is there any chance of slavery being abolished in the western states of America. See Note 4.

The probability of this consummation being brought about sooner is in the expectation that the Brazils, Mexico, and particularly the independent State of Texas, will in a few years produce a crop of cotton which may considerably lower its price. At present, the United States grow nearly, if not more, than half of the cotton produced in the whole world, as the return down to 1831 will substantiate.

Cotton grown all over the world in the years 1821 and 1831; showing the increase in each country in ten years.

	1821	1831 lbs.

	bs.	
United States	180,000,000,000	385,000,000
Brazil	32,000,000,000	38,000,000
West Indies	10,000,000,000	9,000,000

Egypt	6,000,000,000	18,000,000
Rest of Africa	40,000,000,000	36,000,000
India	176,000,000.000	180,000,000
Rest of Asia	185,0	115,000,000

	00,000	
Mexico and South America,	44,000,000	35,000,000
except Brazil		
Elsewhere	8,000,000	4,000,000
In the World	630,000,000	820,000,000

	,
	0
	0
	0

The increase of cotton grown all over the world in ten years is therefore 190,000,000 lbs. Brazil has only increased 6,000,000; Egypt has increased 12,000,000; India, 5,000,000. Africa, West indies, South America, Asia, have all fallen off; but the defalcation has been made good by the United States, which have increased their growth by 205,000,000 of lbs.

In the Southern portion of America there are millions of acres on which cotton can be successfully cultivated, particularly Texas, the soil of which is so congenial that they can produce 1,000 lb. to the 400 lb. raised by the Americans; and the quality of the Texian cotton is said to be equal to the finest sea island produce. It is to Texas particularly that we must look for this produce, as it can there be raised by white labour; (see Note) and being so produced, will, as soon as its population in creases to a certain extent, be able to under sell that which is grown in America by the labour of the slave.

Increase of cotton grown in the United States, from the year 1802 to 1831.

Years	lbs.	Years.	lbs.
1802	55,000,000	1817	130.000,000

180 3	60,001,000	181 8	125,000,000
180 4	65,000,000	181 9	167,000,000
180 5	70,000,000	182 0	160,000,000
180 6	80,000	182 1	180,000,000

	0,000		
1807	80,000,000,000	1822	210,000,000
1808	75,000,000,003	1823	185,000,000
1809	82,000,000,000	1824	215,000,000

181 0	86,000,000,000	182 5	256,000,000
181 1	80,000,000,000	182 6	300,000,000
181 2	75,000,000,006	182 7	270,000,000
181 3	75,000	182 8	325,000,000

	0,000		
1814	70,000,000	1829	365,000,000
1815	100,000,000	1830	360,000,000
1816	124,000,0	1831	385,000,000

It may be asked: how is it, as Texas is so far south, that a white population can labour there? It is because Texas is a prairie country, and situated at the bottom of the Gulf of Mexico. A sea-breeze always blows across the whole of the country, rendering it cool, and refreshing it notwithstanding the power of the sun's rays. This breeze is apparently a continuation of the trade-winds following the course of the sun.

From circumstances, therefore, Texas, which but a few years since was hardly known as a country, becomes a state of the greatest importance to the civilised and moral world.

I am not in this chapter about to raise the question how Texas has been ravished from Mexico. Miss Martineau, with all her admiration of democracy, admits it to have been "the most *high-handed* theft of modern times;" and the letter of the celebrated Dr Charming to Mr Clay has laid bare to the world the whole nefarious transaction. In this letter Dr Charming points out the cause of the seizure of Texas, and the wish to enrol it among the federal states.

"Mexico, at the moment of throwing off the Spanish yoke, gave a noble testimony of her loyalty to free principles, by decreeing 'That no person thereafter should be born a slave, or introduced as such into the Mexican states; that all slaves then held should receive stipulated wages, and be subject to no punishment but on trial and judgment by the magistrate.' The subsequent acts of the government fully carried out these constitutional provisions. It is matter of deep grief and humiliation, that the emigrants from this country, while boasting of superior civilisation, refused to second this honourable policy, intended to set limits to one of the greatest of social evils. Slaves come into Texas with their masters from the neighbouring states of this country. One mode of evading the laws was, to introduce slaves under formal indentures for long periods, in some cases, it is said, for ninety-nine years; but by a decree of the state legislature of Coahuila and Texas, all indentures for a longer period than ten years were annulled, and provision was made for the freedom of children during this apprenticeship. This settled, invincible purpose of Mexico to exclude slavery from her limits, created as strong a purpose to annihilate her authority in Texas. By this prohibition, Texas was virtually shut against emigration from the southern and western portions of this country; and it is well known that the eyes of the south and west had for some time been turned to this province as a new market for slaves, as a new field for slave labour, and as a vast accession of political power to the slave-holding states. That such views were prevalent we know; for, nefarious as they are, they found their way into the public prints. The project of dismembering a neighbouring republic, that slaveholders and slaves might overspread a region which had been consecrated to a free population, was discussed in newspapers as coolly as if it were a matter of obvious right and unquestionable humanity. A powerful interest was thus created for severing from Mexico her distant province."

The fact is this:— America, (for the government looked on and offered no interruption,) has seized upon Texas, with a view of extending the curse of slavery, and of finding a mart for the excess of her negro population: if Texas is admitted into the Union, all chance of the abolition of slavery must be thrown forward to such an indefinite period, as to be lost in the mist of futurity; if, on the contrary, Texas remains an independent province, or is restored to its legitimate owners, and in either case slavery is abolished, she then becomes, from the very circumstance of her fertility and aptitude for white labour, not only the great *check to slavery*, but eventually the means of its *abolition*. Never, therefore, was there a portion of the globe upon which the moral world must look with such interest.

England may, if she acts promptly and wisely, make such terms with this young state as to raise it up as a barrier against the profligate ambition of America. Texas was a portion of Mexico, and Mexico abolished slavery; the Texians are bound (if they are *Texians* and not Americans) to adhere to what might be considered a treaty with the whole Christian world; if not, they can make no demand upon its sympathy or protection, and it should be a *sine qua non* with England and all other European powers previous to acknowledging or entering into commercial relations with Texas, that she should adhere to the law which was passed at the time that she was an integral portion of Mexico, and declare herself to be a Free State—if she does not, unless the chains are broken by the negro himself, the cause and hopes of *emancipation* are lost.

There certainly is one outlet for the slaves, which as they are removed thither and farther to the west will eventually be offered:— that of escaping to the Indian tribes which are spread over the western frontier, and amalgamating with them; such indeed, I think, will some future day be the result, whether they gain their liberty by desertion, insurrection, or manumission.

Of insurrection there is at present but little fear. In the eastern slave states, the negroes do not think of it, and if they did, the difficulty of combination and of procuring arms is so great, that it would be attended with very partial success. The intervention of a foreign power might indeed bring it to pass, but it is to be hoped that England, at all events, will never be the party to foment a servile war. Let us not forget that for more than two centuries we have been *particeps criminis*, and should have been in as great a difficulty as the Americans now are, had we had the negro population on our own soil, and not on distant islands which could be legislated for without affecting the condition of the mother country. Nay, at this very moment, by taking nearly the whole of the American cotton off their hands in exchange for our manufactures, we are ourselves virtually encouraging slavery by affording the Americans such a profitable mart for their slave labour.

There is one point to which I have not yet adverted, which is, Whether the question of emancipation is likely to produce a separation between the Northern and Southern states? The only reply that can be given is, that it entirely depends upon whether the abolition party can be held in check by the federal government. That the federal government will do its utmost there can be no doubt, but the federal government is not so powerful as many of the societies formed in America, and especially the Abolition Society, which every day adds to its members. The interests of the North are certainly at variance with the measures of the society, yet still it gains strength. The last proceedings in congress show that the federal government is aware of its rapid extension, and are determined to do all in its power to suppress it. The following are a portion of the resolutions which were passed last year by an overwhelming majority.

The first resolution was; "That the government is of limited powers, and that by the constitution of the United States, congress has no jurisdiction whatever over the institution of slavery in the several states of the confederacy;" the last was as follows: "Resolved, therefore, that all attempts on the part of congress to *abolish slavery* in the district of Columbia, or the territories, or to prohibit the removal of the slaves from state to state; or to discriminate between the constitution of one portions of the confederacy and another, with the views aforesaid, are in *violation* of the constitutional principles on which the *union* of these States rests, and beyond the jurisdiction of congress; and that every petition, memorial, resolution, proposition, or paper touching or relating in any way or to any extent whatever to slavery as aforesaid, or the abolition thereof, shall without any farther action thereon, be laid on the table, without *printing, reading, debate, or reference*." Question put, "Shall the resolutions pass?" Yeas, 198; Noes, 6—*Examiner*.

These resolutions are very firm and decided, but in England people have no idea of the fanaticism displayed and excitement created in these societies, which are a peculiar feature in the states, and arising from the nature of their institutions. Their strength and perseverance are such that they bear down all before them, and, regardless of all consequences, they may eventually control the government.

As to the question which portion of the States will be the losers by a separation, I myself think that it will be the northern slates which will suffer. But as I always refer to American authority when I can, I had better give the reader a portion of a letter written by one of the southern gentlemen on this subject. In a letter to the editor of the *National Gazette*, Mr Cooper, after referring to a point at issue with the abolitionists, not necessary to introduce here, says—"I shall therefore briefly touch upon the subject once more; and if farther provocation is given, I may possibly enter into more details hereafter; for the present I desire to hint at some items of calculation of the value of the Union *to the North*.

"1. Mr Rhett, in his bold and honest address, has stated that the expenditures of the government for twenty years, ending 1836, have been four hundred and twenty millions of dollars; of which one hundred and thirty were dedicated to the payment of the national debt. Of the remainder, two hundred and ten millions were expended in the northern, and eighty millions in the southern states. Suppose this Union to be severed, I rather guess the government expenditure of what is now about fifteen millions a-year to the North, would be an item reluctantly spared. No people know better what to do with the 'cheese-parings and the candle-ends' than our good friends to the North.

"2. I beg permission to address New York especially. In the year 1836 our exports were one hundred and sixteen millions of dollars, and our imports one hundred and forty millions. It is not too much to assign seventy-five millions of these imports to the state of New York. The South furnishes on an average two-thirds of the whole value of the *exports*. It is fair, therefore, to say, that two-thirds of the *imports* are consumed in the South, that is, fifty millions. The mercantile profit on fifty millions of merchandise, added to the agency and factorage of the Southern products transmitted to pay for them, will be at least twenty per cent. That is, New York is gainer by the South, of at least ten millions of dollars annually; for the traffic is not likely to decrease after the present year. No wonder 'her merchants are like princes!' Sever the Union, and what becomes of them!

"3. The army, the navy, the departments of government, are supported by a revenue obtained from the indirect taxation of custom-house entries, the most fraudulent and extravagant mode of taxation known. Of this the South pays two-thirds. What will become of the system if the South be driven away!

"4. The banking system of the Northern states is founded mainly on the traffic and custom of the South. Withdraw that for one twelve-month, and the whole banking system of the North"

| — | tumbles | all | precipitate |
| Down dash'd. | | | |

"Suppose even one state withdrawn from the Union, would not the pecuniary intercourse with Europe be paralysed at once?

"5. The South even now are the great consumers of New England manufactures. We take her cotton, her woollen goods, her boots and shoes. These last form an item of upwards of fourteen millions annually, manufactured at the North. Much also of her iron ware comes to the South; many other 'notions' are sent among us, greatly to the advantage of that wise people, who know better the value of small gains and small savings than we do.

"6. What supports the shipping of the North but her commerce; and of her commerce two-thirds is Southern commerce. Nor is her *commerce* in any manner or degree *necessary* to the South; *Europe* manufactures what the *South wants*, and the *South* raises what Europe *wants*. Between Europe and the South there is not and cannot be any competition, for there is no commercial or manufacturing, of territorial interference to excite jealousies between them. We want not the North. *We can do without the North*, if we separate to-morrow. We can find carriers and purchasers of *all we have to sell*, and of *all we wish to buy*, without casting one glance to the North.

"7. The North seems to have a strange inclination to quarrel with England. The late war of 1812 to 1814 was a war for Northern claims and Northern interests, now we are in jeopardy from the unjust interference in favour of the patriots of Canada; and a dispute is threatened on account of the north-eastern boundary. The manufacturing and commercial interferences of the north with Europe will always remain a possible, if not a probable, source of disputes. The *North* raises what *Europe* raises; commercially they need not each other —they are two of a trade, they raise not what each other wants—they are *rivals* and *competitors* when they go to war. Does not the South, who is not interested in it, pay most part of the expense, and is not the war expenditure applied to the benefit of the North? Sever, if you please, the Union, and the North will have to pay the whole expense of her own quarrels.

"8. Our system of domestic servitude is a great eye-sore to the fanatics of the North. But there are very many wise and honest men in the North; ay, even in Massachusetts. I ask of these gentlemen, does not at least one-third of the labour produce of every Southern slave ultimately lodge in the purse of the North! If the South works for itself it works also for the Northern merchant, and views his prosperity without grudging.

"9. Nor is it a trifling article of gain that arises from the expenditure of southern visitors and southern travellers, who spend their summers and their money in the north. The quarrelsome rudeness of northern society is fast diminishing this source of expenditure among us. Sever the Union, and we relinquish it altogether. We can go to London, Paris, or Rome, as cheaply and as pleasantly as to Saratoga or Niagara.

"Such are some of the advantages which the north derives from a continuance of that union which her fanatic population is so desirous to sever. A population with whom peace, humanity, mercy, oaths, contracts, and compacts, pass for nothing—whose promises and engagements are as chaff before the wind—to whom bloodshed, robbery, assassination, and murder, are objects of placid contemplation—whose narrow creed of bigotry supersedes all the obligations, of morality, and all the commands of positive law. With such men what valid compact can be made? The appeal must be to those who think that a deliberate compact is mutually binding on parties of any and every religious creed. To such men I appeal, and ask, ought you not resolutely to restore peace, and give the south confidence and repose?

"I have now lived twenty years in South Carolina, and have had much intercourse with her prominent and leading men; not a man among them is ignorant how decidedly in most respects, the south would gain by a severance from the north, and how much more advantageous is this union to the north than to the south. But I am deeply, firmly persuaded that there is not one man in South Carolina that would move one step toward a separation, on account of the superior advantages the north derives from the union. No southern is actuated by these pecuniary feelings; no southern begrudges the north her prosperity. Enjoy your advantages, gentlemen of the north, and much good may they do ye, as they have hitherto. But if these unconstitutional abolition attacks upon us, in utter defiance of the national compact, are to be continued, God forbid this union should last another year.

"I am, sir, your obedient servant,

"Thomas Cooper."

"Many fine looking districts were pointed out to me in Virginia, formerly rich in tobacco and Indian corn, which had been completely exhausted by the production of crops for the maintenance of the slaves. In thickly peopled countries, where the great towns are at hand, the fertility of such soils may be recovered and even improved by manuring, but over the tracts of country I now speak of, no such advantages are within the farmer's reach."—*Captain Hall*.

"Many, very many, with whom I met, would willingly have released their slaves, but the law requires that in such cases they should leave the state; and this would mostly be not to improve their condition, but to banish them from their home, and to make them miserable outcasts. What they cannot at present remove, they are anxious to mitigate, and I have never seen kinder attention paid to any domestics than by such persons to their slaves. In defiance of the infamous laws, making it criminal for the slave to be taught to read, and difficult to assemble for an act of worship, they are instructed, and they are assisted to worship God."—*Rev. Mr Reid.*

"The law declares the children of slaves are to follow the fortunes of the mother. Hence the practice of planters selling and bequeathing their own children."—*Miss Martineau.*

The return at present is very great in these western states; the labour of a slave, after all his expenses are paid, producing on an average 300 dollars (65 pounds) per annum to his master.

Volume Three—Chapter Seven.

Remarks—Religion in America.

In theory nothing appears more rational than that every one should worship the Deity according to his own ideas—form his own opinion as to his attributes, and draw his own conclusions as to hereafter. An established Church *appears* to be a species of coercion, not that you are obliged to believe in, or follow that form of worship, but that, if you do not, you lose your portion of certain advantages attending that form of religion, which has been accepted by the majority and adopted by the government. In religion, to think for yourself wears the semblance of a luxury, and like other luxuries, it is proportionably taxed.

And yet it would appear as if it never were intended that the mass should think for themselves, as everything goes on so quietly when other people think for them, and everything goes so wrong when they do think for themselves: in the first instance where a portion of the people think for the mass, all are of one opinion; whereas in the second, they divide and split into many molecules, that they resemble the globules of water when expanded by heat, and like them are in a state of restlessness and excitement.

That the partiality shown to an established church creates some bitterness of feeling is most true, but being established by law, is it not the partiality shown for the legitimate over the illegitimate? All who choose may enter into its portals, and if the people will remain out of doors of their own accord, ought they to complain that they have no house over their heads? They certainly have a right to remain out of doors if they please, but whether they are justified in complaining afterward is another question. Perhaps the unreasonableness of the demands of the dissenters in our own country will be better brought home to them by my pointing out the effects of the voluntary system in the United States.

In America every one worships the Deity after his own fashion; not only the mode of worship, but even the Deity itself, varies. Some worship God, some Mammon; some admit, some deny, Christ; some deny both God and Christ; some are saved by living prophets only; some go to heaven by water, while some dance their way upwards. Numerous as are the sects, still are the sects much subdivided. Unitarians are not in unity as to the portion of divinity they shall admit to our Saviour; flap-fists, as to the precise quantity of water necessary to salvation; even the Quakers have split into controversy, and the men of peace are at open war in Philadelphia, the city of brotherly love.

The following is the table of the religious denominations of the United States, from the American Almanac of 1838:

Table of the Religious Denominations of the United States

	Congregation	Ministers	Communican	Population

	ns		ts	
Baptists	6,319	4,239	452,000}	
Freewillers	753	612	38,876}	4,300,000
Seventh Day	42	46	4,503}	
Six Principle	16	16	2,117}	
Roman Catholics	43	38		800,

	3	9		00 0
Christians	1 , 0 0 0	8 0 0	1 5 0 , 0 0 0	30 0, 00 0
Congregati onalists	1 , 3 0 0	1 , 1 5 0	1 6 0 , 0 0 0	1, 40 0, 00 0
Dutch Reformed	1 9 7	1 9 2	2 2 , 2 1 5	45 0, 00 0
Episcopalia ns	8 5 0	8 9 9		60 0, 00 0
Friends	5 0 0			10 0, 00 0

German Reformed	600	180	30,000	
Jews				15,000
Lutherans	750	257	62,226	540,000
Mennonites	200		30,000	
Wesleyans		2,764	650,103}	
Protestants		40	50	2,00

		0	,000}	0,000
Moravians	24	33	5,7455	12,000
Mormonites			12,000	12,000
N Jerusalem Church	27	33		5,000
Presbyterians	2,807	2,225	274,084}	
Cumberland	500	450	50,000	

			0}	
Associate	183	87	16,000}	2,175,000
Reformed	40	20	3,000}	
Associate Reformed	214	116	12,000}	
Shakers	15	45	6,000	
Tunkers	40	40	3,000	30,000

			0	
Unitarians	200	174		180,000
Universalists	653	317		600,000

In this list many varieties of sects are blended into one. For instance, the Baptists, who are divided; also the Friends, who have been separated into Orthodox and Hicksite, the Camelites, etcetera, etcetera. But it is not worth while to enter into a detail of the numerous minor sects, or we might add Deists, Atheists, etcetera.—for even *no* religion is a species of *creed*. It must be observed, that, according to this table, out of the whole population of the United States, there are only 1,983,905, (with the exception of the Catholics, who are Communicants,) that is, who have openly professed any creed; the numbers put down as the population of the different creeds are wholly suppositions. How can it be otherwise, when people have not professed? It is computed, that in the census of 1840 the population of the States will have increased to 18,000,000, so that it may be said that only one ninth portion have professed and openly avowed themselves Christians.

Religion may, as to its consequences, be considered under two heads: as it affects the future welfare of the individual when he is summoned to the presence of the Deity, and as it affects society in general, by acting upon the moral character of the community. Now, admitting the right of every individual to decide whether he will follow the usual beaten track, or select for himself a by-path for his journey upward, it must be acknowledged that the results of this free-will are, in a moral point of view, as far as society is concerned, any thing but satisfactory.

It would appear as if the majority were much too frail and weak to go alone upon their heavenly journey; as if they required the support, the assistance, the encouragement, the leaning upon others who are journeying with them, to enable them successfully to gain the goal. The effects of an established church are to cement the mass, cement society and communities, and increase the force of those natural ties by which families and relations are bound together. There is an attraction of cohesion in an uniform religious worship, acting favourably upon the morals of the mass, and binding still more closely those already united. Now, the voluntary system in America has produced the very opposite effects; it has broken one of the strongest links between man and man, for each goeth his own way: as a nation, there is no national feeling to be acted upon; in society, there is something wanting, and you ask yourself what is it? and in families it often creates disunion: I know one among many others, who, instead of going together to the same house of prayer, disperse as soon as they are out of the door: one daughter to an Unitarian chapel, another to a Baptist, the parents to the Episcopal, the sons, any where, or no where. But worse effects are produced than even these: where any one is allowed to have his own peculiar way of thinking, his own peculiar creed, there neither is a watch, nor a right to watch over each other; there is no mutual communication, no encouragement, no parental control; and the consequence is, that by the majority, especially the young, religion becomes wholly and utterly disregarded.

Another great evil, arising from the peculiarity of the voluntary system is, that in any of the principal sects the power has been wrested from the clergy and assumed by the laity, who exercise an inquisition most injurious to the cause of religion: and to such an excess of tyranny is this power exercised, that it depends upon the *laity*, and not upon the *clergy*, whether any individual shall or shall not be admitted as a *communicant* at the table of our Lord.

Miss Martineau may well inquire, "How does the existing state of religion accord with the promise of its birth? In a country which professes to every man the pursuit of happiness in his own way, what is the state of his liberty in the most private and individual of all concerns?"

Referring to religious instruction, Mr Carey in his work attempts to prove the great superiority of religious instruction and church accommodation in America, as compared with those matters in this country. He draws his conclusions from the number of churches built and provided for the population in each. Like most others of his conclusions, they are drawn from false premises: he might just as well argue upon the number of horses in each country, from the number of horse-ponds he might happen to count in each. In the first place, the size of the churches must be considered, and their ability to accommodate the population; and on this point, the question is greatly in favour of England; for, with the exception of the cities and large towns, the churches scattered about the hamlets and large towns are small even to ridicule, built of clap-boards, and so light that, if on wheels, two pair of English post-horses would trot them away, to meet the minister.

Mr Carey also finds fault with the sites of our churches as being unfortunate in consequence of the change of population. There is some truth in this remark: but our churches being built of brick and stone cannot be so easily removed; and it happens that the sites of the majority of the American churches are equally unfortunate, not as in our case, from the population having *left* them, but from the population not having *come* to them. You may pass in one day a dozen towns having not above twenty or thirty private houses, although you will invariably find in each an hotel, a bank, and churches of two or three denominations, built as a speculation, either by those who hold the ground lots or by those who have settled there, and as an inducement to others to come and settle. The churches, as Mr Carey states, exist, but the congregations have not arrived; while you may, at other times, pass over many miles without finding a place of worship for the spare population. I have no hesitation in asserting, not only that our 12,000 churches and cathedrals will hold a larger number of people than the 20,000 stated by Mr Carey to be erected in America, but that as many people, (taking into consideration the difference of the population,) go to our 12,000, as to the 20,000 in the United States.

Neither is Mr Carey correct when he would insinuate that the attention given by the people in America to religious accommodation is greater than with us. It is true, that more churches, such as they are, are built in America; but paying an average of 12,000 pounds for a church built of brick or stone in England, is a very different thing from paying 12,000 dollars for a clap-board and shingle affair in America, and which, compared with those of brick and mortar, are there in the proportion of ten to one. And further, the comparative value of church building in America is very much lowered by the circumstance that they are compelled to multiply them, to provide for the immense variety of creeds which exist under the *voluntary* system. When people in a community are all of one creed, one church is sufficient; but if they are of different persuasions, they must, as they do in America, divide the one large church into four little ones. It is not fair, therefore, for Mr Carey to count *churches*.

(Note. "We know also that large sums are expended annually for the building of churches or places of worship, which in cities cost from 10,000 to 100,000 dollars each; and in the country from 500 to 5,000 dollars."—*Voice from America, by an American Gentleman*. (What must be the size of a church which costs 500 dollars?))

But, although I will not admit the conclusions drawn from Mr Carey's premises, nor that, as he would attempt to prove, the Americans are a more religious people than the English, I am not only ready, but anxious to do justice to the really religious portion of its inhabitants. I believe that in no other country is there more zeal shown by its various ministers, zeal even to the sacrifice of life; that no country sends out more zealous missionaries; that no country has more societies for the diffusion of the gospel and that in no other country in the world are larger sums subscribed for the furtherance of those praise-worthy objects as in the Eastern States of America. I admit all this, and admit it with pleasure; for I know it to be a fact: I only regret to add that in no other country are such strenuous exertions so incessantly required to stem the torrent of atheism and infidelity, which so universally exists in this. Indeed this very zeal, so ardent on the part of the ministers, and so aided by the well-disposed of the laity, proves that what I have just now asserted is, unfortunately, but too true.

It is not my intention to comment upon the numerous sects, and the varieties of worship practised in the United States. The Episcopal church is small in proportion to the others, and as far as I can ascertain, although it may increase its members with the increase of population, it is not likely to make any vigorous or successful stand against the other sects. The two churches most congenial to the American feelings and institutions are the Presbyterian and Congregationalist.

"The Congregationalists answer to the Independents of England and are sympathetically, and to a great extent, lineally descendants of the Puritans."—*Voice from America*, p. 62.

They may, indeed, in opposition to the hierarchy of the Episcopal, be considered as Republican churches; and admitting that many errors have crept into the established church from its too intimate union with the State, I think it will be proved that, in rejecting its errors and the domination of the mitre, the seceders have fallen into still greater evils; and have, for the latter, substituted a despotism to which every thing, even religion itself, must in America succumb.

In a republic, or democracy, the people will rule in every thing: in the Congregational church they rule as deacons; in the Presbyterian as elders. Affairs are litigated and decided in committees and councils, and thus is the pastoral office deprived of its primitive and legitimate influence, and the ministers are tyrannised over by the laity, in the most absurd and most unjustifiable manner. If the minister does not submit to their decisions, if he asserts his right as a minister to preach the word according to his reading of it, he is arraigned and dismissed. In short, although sent for to instruct the people, he must consent to be instructed by them, or surrender up his trust. Thus do the ministers lose all their dignity and become the slaves of the congregation, who give them their choice, either to read the Scriptures according to *their* reading, or to go and starve. I was once canvassing this question with an American, who pronounced that the laity were quite right, and that it was the duty of the minister to preach as his congregation wished. His argument was this:—"If I send to Manchester for any article to be manufactured, I expect it to be made exactly after the pattern given; if not, I will not take it: so it is with the minister: he must find goods exactly suited to his customers, or expect them to be left on his hands!"

And it really would appear as if such were the general opinion in the United States. Mr Colton, an American minister, who turned from the Presbyterian to the Episcopal church, in his "Reasons for Episcopacy," makes the following remarks:—

(I must request the reader's forbearance at the extreme length of the quotations, but I cannot well avoid making them. Whatever weight my opinion, as the opinion of an observant traveller may have, it must naturally be much increased if supported, as it always is when opportunity offers, by *American* authority.)

Speaking of the deacons and elders of their churches, he says—"They may be honest and good men, and very pious: but in most churches they are men of little intellectual culture; and the less they have, the more confident and unbending are they in their opinions. If a minister travels an inch beyond the circle of their vision in theology, or startles them with a new idea in his interpretation of Scripture, it is not unlikely that their suspicions of his orthodoxy will be awakened. If he does any thing out of the common course, he is an innovator. If, from the multiplicity of his cares and engagements, he is now and then obliged to preach an old sermon, or does not visit so much as might be expected, he is lazy. For these and for other delinquencies, as adjudged by these associates, it becomes their conscientious duty to admonish him. He who is appointed to supervise the flock, is himself supervised. 'I have a charge to give you,' said a deacon to me once, the first time and the moment I was introduced to him, after I had preached one or two Sabbaths in the place, and, as it happened, it was the first word he said after we shook hands, adding, 'I often give charges to ministers.' I knew him to be an important man, and the first in the church; but as I had nothing at stake there that depended on his favour, I could not resist the temptation of replying to him in view of his consequential airs, 'You may use your discretion, sir, in this particular instance; but I can tell you that ministers are sometimes overcharged.' However, I did not escape.

"The American clergy are the most backward and timid class in the society in which they live; self-exiled from the great moral question of the time; the least informed with true knowledge—the least efficient in virtuous action—the least conscious of that Christian and republican freedom which, as the native atmosphere of piety and holiness, it is their prime duty to cherish and diffuse,"—*Miss Martineau.* I quote this paragraph to *contradict it.* The American clergy are, in the mass, equal, if not superior, to any in the world: they have to struggle with difficulties almost insurmountable, (as I shall substantiate) and worthily do they perform their tasks.

"It seems to be a principle in Presbyterian and Congregational churches, that the minister must be overlooked by the elders and deacons; and if he does not quietly submit to their rule, his condition will be uncomfortable. He may also expect visitations from *women* to instruct him in his duty; at least, they will contrive to convey to him their opinions. It is said of Dr Bellamy, of Bethlehem, Connecticut, who was eminently a peace-maker, and was always sent for by all the churches in the country around, or a great distance, to settle their difficulties, that having just returned from one of these errands, and put up his horse, another message of the same kind came from another quarter —'And what is the matter?' said the Doctor to the messenger. 'Why,' said he, 'Deacon has—' 'Has—that's enough—There never is a difficulty in a church, but some old deacon is at the bottom of it.'

"Unquestionably, it is proper, wise, and prudent, for every minister to watch and consult the popular opinion around him, in relation to himself, his preaching, and his conduct. But, if a minister is worthy to be the pastor of a people, he is also worthy of some confidence, and ought to receive deference. In his own proper work he may be helped, he may be sustained, but he cannot be instructed by his people; he cannot in general be instructed by the wisest of them. Respectful and kind hints from competent persons he may receive, and should court—he may profit by them. But, if he is a man fit for his place, he should retain that honour that will leave him scope, and inspire him with courage to act a manly part. A Christian pastor can never fulfil his office, and attain its highest ends, without being free to act among his people according to the light of his conscience and his best discretion. To have elders and deacons to rule over him, is to be a slave—is not to be a man. The responsibilities, cares, burdens, and labours of the pastoral office are enough, without being impeded and oppressed by such anxieties as these. In the early history of New England, a non-conformist minister, from the old country, is represented to have said, after a little experience on this side of the water, 'I left England to get rid of my lords the bishops; but here I find in their place my lords, the brethren and sisters; save me from the latter, and let me have the former.'

"It has actually happened—within a few years—in New England, and I believe in other parts of the country, that there has been a system of lay visitation of the clergy for the purpose of counselling, admonishing, and urging them up to their duty; and that these self-commissioned apostles, two and two, have gone from town to town, and from district to district of the country, making inquisition at the mouth of common rumour, and by such methods as might be convenient, into the conduct and fidelity of clergymen whom they never saw; and, having exhausted their means of information, have made their way into the closets of their adopted protégés; to advise, admonish, pray with, and for them; according as they might need. Having fulfilled their office, they have renewed their march, 'staff and script,' in a straightforward way, to the next parish, in the assigned round of their visitations, to enact the same scene, and so on till their work was done.

"Of course, they were variously received; though, for the most part, I believe they have been treated civilly, and their title to this enterprise not openly disputed. There has been an unaccountable submission to things of this kind, proving indeed that the ministers thus visited were not quite manly enough; or that a public opinion, authorising these transactions, had obtained too extensive a sway in their own connexion, and among their people, to be resisted. By many, doubtless, it was regarded as one of the hopeful symptoms of this age of religious experiment.

"I have heard of one reception of these lay apostles, which may not be unworthy of record. One pair of them—for they went forth 'two and two,' and thus far were conformed to scripture—both of them mechanics, and one a shoemaker, having abandoned their calling to engage in this enterprise, came upon a subject who was not well disposed to recognise their commission. They began to talk with him: 'We have come to stir you up.'—'How is the shoe business in your city?' said the clergyman to the shoemaker, who was the speaker: for it was a city from which they came. The shoemaker looked vacant, and stared at the question, as if he thought it not very pertinent to his errand; and, after a little pause, proceeded in the discharge of his office: 'We have come to give your church a shaking.'—'Is the market for shoes good?' said the clergyman. Abashed at this apparent obliquity, the shoemaker paused again; and again went on in like manner. To which the clergyman: 'Your business is at a stand, sir, I presume; I suppose you have nothing to do.' And so the dialogue went on; the shoemaker confining himself to his duty, and the clergyman talking only of shoes: in varied and constantly-shifting colloquy, till the perverse and wicked pertinacity of the latter discouraged the former; and the shoemaker and his brother took up their hats, 'to shake off the dust of their feet,' and turn away to a more hopeful subject. The clergyman bowed them very civilly out of doors, expressing his wish, as they departed, that the shoe business might soon revive. Of course, these lay apostles, in this instance, were horror-struck; and it cannot be supposed they were much inclined to leave their blessing behind them.

"I believe I do not mistake in expressing the conviction that there are hundreds, not to say thousands, of the Presbyterian and Congregational clergy, who will sympathise with me thoroughly in these strictures on the encroachments of the laity upon pastoral prerogative; who groan under it; who feel that it ought to be rebuked and corrected, but despair of it; and who know that their usefulness is abridged by it to an account that cannot be estimated."

(The Reverend Mr Reid mentions a very whimsical instance of the interference of the laity in every possible way. He says, that being at church one Sabbath, there was one reverend old man, certainly a leader among them, who literally, as the preacher went on with his sermon, kept up a sort of recitation with him as, for instance, the preacher continuing his sermon—

The duty here inferred is, to deny ourselves—

Elder. And enable us to do it.

Preacher. It supposes that the carnal mind is enmity against God—

Elder. Ah, indeed, Lord, it is.

Preacher. The very reverse of what God would have us to be—

Elder. God Almighty knows it's true.

Preacher. How necessary, then, that God should call upon us to renounce everything—

Elder. God help us!

Preacher. Is it necessary for me to say more?

Elder. No—oh—no!

Preacher. Have I not said enough?

Elder. Oh, yes, quite enough.

Preacher. I rejoice that God calls me to give up every thing—

Elder. Yes, Lord, I would let it all go.

Preacher. You *must* give up all—

Elder. Yes—all.

Preacher. Your pride—

Elder. My pride.

Preacher. Your envy.

Elder. My envy.

Preacher. Your covetousness—

Elder. My covetousness.

Preacher. Your anger.

Elder. Yes—my anger.

Preacher. Sinner, then; how awful is your condition!

Elder. How awful!

Preacher. What reason for all to examine themselves.

Elder. Lord, help us to search our hearts!

Preacher. Could you have more motives? I have done.

Elder. Thank God.—Thank God for his holy word. Amen.)

"It can hardly be denied, I think, that the prevalence of this spirit has greatly increased within a few years, and become a great and alarming evil. This increase is owing, no doubt, to the influence and new practices introduced into the religious world by a certain class of ministers, who have lately risen and taken upon themselves to rebuke, and set down as unfaithful, all other ministers who do not conform to their new ways, or sustain them in their extravagant career."

The interference, I may say the tyranny, of the laity over the ministers of these democratic churches is, however, of still more serious consequences to those who accept such arduous and repulsive duty. It is a well-known fact, that there is a species of *bronchitis*, or affection of the lungs, peculiar to the ministers in the United States, arising from their excessive labours in their vocation. I have already observed, that the zeal of the minister is even unto death: the observations of Mr Colton fully bear me out in my assertion:—

"There is another serious evil in the Presbyterian and Congregational denominations, which has attained to the consequence of an active and highly influential element in these communities. I refer to the excessive amount of labour that is demanded of the clergy, which is undermining their health, and sending scores to their graves every year, long before they ought to go there. It is a new state of things, it must be acknowledged, and might seem hopeful of good, that great labours and high devotion to the duties of the Christian ministry in our country will not only be tolerated, but are actually demanded and imperatively exacted. At first glance, it is a most grateful feature. But, when the particulars come to be inquired into, it will be found that the mind and health-destroying exactions now so extensively made on the energies of the American clergy, particularly on these two classes I am now considering, are attributable, almost entirely, to an appetite for certain novelties, which have been introduced within a few years, adding greatly to the amount of ministerial labour, without augmenting its efficiency, but rather detracting from it. Sermons and meetings without end, and in almost endless variety, are expected and demanded; and a proportionate demand is made on the intellect, resources, and physical energies of the preacher. He must be as much more interesting in his exercises, and exhibitions as the increased multiplicity of public religious occasions tend to pall on the appetite of hearers. Protracted meetings from day to day, and often from week to week, are making demands upon ministers, which no human power can sustain and, where these are dispensed with, it is often necessary to introduce something tantamount, in other forms, to satisfy the suggestions and wishes of persons so influential as to render it imprudent not to attempt to gratify them. In the soberest congregations, throughout nearly all parts of the land, these importunate, and, without unkindness, I am disposed to add, morbid minds are to be found, often in considerable numbers. Almost everywhere, in order to maintain their ground and satisfy the taste of the times, labours are demanded of ministers in these two denominations enough to kill any man in a short period. It is as if Satan had come into the world in the form of an angel of light, seeming to be urging on a good work, but pushing it so hard as to destroy the labourers by over exaction.

"The wasting energies—the enfeebled, ruined health—the frequent premature deaths—the failing of ministers in the Presbyterian and Congregational connexions from these causes all over the country, almost as soon as they have begun to work—all which is too manifest not to be seen, which everybody feels that takes any interest in this subject, are principally, and with few exceptions, owing to the unnecessary exorbitant demands on their intellectual powers, their moral and physical energies. And the worst of it is, we not only have no indemnification for this amazing, immense sacrifice, by a real improvement of the state of religion, but the public mind is vitiated: an unnatural appetite for spurious excitements, all tending to fanaticism, and not a little of it the essence of fanaticism, is created and nourished. The interests of religion in the land are actually thrown backward. It is a fever, a disease which nothing but time, pains, and a change of system can cure. A great body of the most talented, best educated, most zealous, most pious, and purest Christian ministers in the country—not to disparage any others—a body which in all respects will bear an advantageous comparison with any of their class in the world, is threatened to be enervated, to become sickly, to have their minds wasted, and their lives sacrificed out of season, and with real loss to the public, by the very means which prostrates them, even though we should leave out of the reckoning the premature end to which they are brought. This spectacle, at this moment before the eyes of the wide community, is enough to fill the mind of an enlightened Christian with dismay. I have myself been thrown ten years out of the stated use of the ministry by this very course, and may, therefore, be entitled to feel and to speak on the subject. And when I see my brethren fallen and falling around me, like the slain in battle, the plains of our land literally covered with these unfortunate victims, I am constrained to express a most earnest desire, that some adequate remedy may be applied."

It is no matter of surprise, then, that I heard the ministers at the camp meeting complain of the excess of their labours, and the difficulty of obtaining young men to enter the church; (The Rev. Mr Reid observes, speaking of the Congregationalists, "When I rose to support his resolution, as requested, all were generously attentive. At the close I alluded emphatically to one fact in the report, which was, That out of 4,500 churches there were 2,000 not only void of educated pastors, but void of pastors, and I insisted that, literally, they ought not to sleep on such a state of things."—*Reid and Matheson's Tour*) who, indeed, unless actuated by a holy zeal, would submit to such a life of degradation? what man of intellect and education could submit to be schooled by shoemakers and mechanics, to live poor, and at the mercy of tyrants, and drop down dead like the jaded and over laden beast from excess of fatigue and exertion? Let me again quote the same author:

"It is these excessive, multitudinous, and often long *protracted* religious occasions, together with the spirit that is in them, which have been for some years breaking up and breaking down the clergy of this land? It has been breaking them *up*. It is commonly observed, that a new era has lately come over the Christian congregations of our country in regard to the permanence of the pastoral relation. Times was, in the memory of those now living, when the settlement of a minister was considered of course a settlement for life. But now, as every body knows, this state of things is entirely broken up; and it is, perhaps, true that, on an average, the clergy of this country do not remain more than five years in the same place." ("I was sorry to find that, in this part of the State, the ministers are so frequently changing the scene of their pastoral labours. The fault may sometimes be in themselves: but from conversations I have heard on the subject, I am inclined to believe that the *people* are fond of a change."—*Rev. Mr Reid*) And it is impossible they should, in the present state of things. They could not stand it. So numerous are their engagements; so full of anxiety is their condition in a fevered state of the public mind acting upon them from all directions; so consuming are their labours in the study and in public, pressed and urged upon them by the demands of the time; and, withal, so fickle has the popular mind become under a system that is forever demanding some new and still more exciting measure—some new society— some new monthly or weekly meeting, which perhaps soon grows into a religious holiday—some special effort running through many days, sometimes lasting for weeks, calling for public labours of ministers, of the most exciting kind throughout each day, from the earliest hour of the morning to a late hour of night; for reasons and facts of this kind, so abundant, and now so obvious to the public, that they need only to be referred to, to be seen and appreciated, it is impossible that ministers should remain long in the same place. Their mental and physical energies become exhausted, and they are compelled to change; first, because it is not in the power of man to satisfy the appetite for novelties which is continually and from all quarters making its insatiate demands upon them; and next; that, if possible, they may purchase a breathing time and a transient relief from the overwhelming pressure of their cares and labours.

"But, alas! there is no relief: they are not only broken up, but they find themselves fast breaking down. Wherever they go, there is the same demand for the same scene to be acted over. There is—there can be—no stability in the pastoral relation, in such a state of the public mind: and, what is still more melancholy and affecting, the pastors themselves cannot endure it—they cannot live. They are not only constantly fluctuating—literally afloat on the wide surface of the community—but their health is undermined—their spirits are sinking—and they are fast treading upon each others' heels to the grave, their only land of rest.

"Never since the days of the apostles, was a country blessed with so enlightened, pious, orthodox, faithful, willing clergy, as the United States of America at this moment; and never did a ministry, so worthy of trust, have so little independence to act according to their conscience and best discretion. They are literally the victims of a spiritual tyranny that has started up and burst upon the world in a new form—at least, with an extent of sway that has never been known. It is an influence which comes up from the lowest conditions of life, which is vested in the most ignorant minds, and, therefore, the more unbending and uncontrollable. It is an influence which has been fostered and blown into a wide-spread flame by a class of itinerating ministers, who have suddenly started up and overrun the land, decrying and denouncing all that have not yielded at once to their sway; by direct and open efforts shaking and destroying public confidence in the settled and more permanent ministry, leaving old paths and striking out new ones, demolishing old systems and substituting others, and disturbing and deranging the whole order of society as it had existed before. And it is to this new state of things, so harassing, so destructive to health and life, that the regular ministry of this country (the best qualified, most pious, most faithful, and in all respects the most worthy Christian ministry that the church has ever enjoyed in any age) are made the victims. They cannot resist it, they are overwhelmed by it."

The fact is, that there is little or no healthy religion in their most numerous and influential churches; it is all excitement. Twenty or thirty years back, the Methodists were considered as extravagantly frantic, but the Congregationalists and Presbyterians in the United States have gone far ahead of them; and the Methodist church in America has become to a degree Episcopal, and softened down into, perhaps, the most pure, most mild, and most simple of all the creeds professed.

I have said that in these two churches the religious feeling was that of excitement: I believe it to be more or less the case in *all* religion in America; for the Americans are a people who are prone to excitement, not only from their climate, but constitutionally, and it is the *caviare* of their existence. If it were not so, why is it necessary that revivals should be so continually called forth—a species of stimulus, common, I believe, to almost every sect and creed, promoted and practised in all their colleges, and considered as most important and salutary in their results. Let it not be supposed that I am deprecating that which is to be understood by a revival, in the true sense of the word; not those revivals which were formerly held the benefit of all, and for the salvation of many: I am raising my voice against the modern system, which has been so universally substituted for the reality; such as has been so fully exposed by Bishop Hopkins, of Vermont, and, by Mr Colton, who says—

"Religious excitements, called revivals of religion, have been a prominent feature in the history of this country from its earliest periods, more particularly within a hundred years and the agency of man has always had more or less to do in their management, or in their origination, or in both. Formerly, in theory, (for man is naturally a philosopher, and will always have his theory for every event, and every fact,) they were regarded as Pentecostal seasons—as showers from heaven; with which this world below had nothing to do but to receive, and be refreshed by them as they came. A whole community, or the great majority of them, absorbed in serious thoughts about eternal things, inquiring the way to heaven, and seeming intent on the attainment of that high and glorious condition, presents a spectacle as solemn as it is interesting to contemplate. Such, doubtless, has been the condition of many communities in the early and later history of American revivals; and it is no less true that the fruits have been the turning of many to God and his ways.

"The revivals of the present day are of a very different nature." (The American clergymen are supported in their opinion on the present revivals and their consequences by Doctors Reid and Matheson, who, otherwise favourable to them, observe, "These revival preachers have denounced pastors with whom they could not compare, as dumb dogs, hypocrites, and formalists, leading their people to hell. The consequences have been most disastrous. Churches have become the sport of derision, distraction, and disorder. Pastors have been made unhappy in their dearest connexions. So extensive has been this evil, that, in one presbytery of nineteen churches, there were only three who had settled pastors; and in one synod, in 1832, of a hundred and three churches, only fifty-two had pastors.") "There are but two ways by which the mind of man can be brought to a proper sense of religion—one is by love, and the other by fear; and it is by the latter only that modern revivals become at all effective. Bishop Hopkins says, very truly—'Have we any example in the preaching of Christ and his apostles, of the use of strong individual denunciation? Is there one sentence in the word of inspiration to justify the attempt to excite the feelings of a public assembly, until every restraint of order is forgotten, and confusion becomes identified with the word of God." ("The Primitive Church Compared," etcetera, by the Bishop of Vermont.) Yet such are the revivals of the present day, as practised in America. Mr Colton calls them—"Those startling and astounding shocks which are constantly invented, artfully and habitually applied, under all the power of sympathy, and of a studied and enthusiastic elocution, by a large class of preachers among us. To startle and to shock is their great secret—their power."

The same author then proceeds:

"Religion is a dread and awful theme in itself. That is, as all must concede, there are revealed truths belonging to the category. To invest these truths with terrors that do not belong to them, by bringing them out in distorted shapes and unnatural forms; to surprise a tender and unfortified mind by one of awful import, without exhibiting the corresponding relief which Christianity has provided; to frighten, shock, and paralyse the mind with alternations and scenes of horror, carefully concealing the ground of encouragement and hope, till reason is shaken and hurled from its throne, for the sake of gaining a convert, and in making a convert to make a maniac (as doubtless sometimes occurs under this mode of preaching, for we have the proof of it,) involves a fearful responsibility. I have just heard of an interesting girl thus driven to distraction, in the city of New York, at the tender age of fourteen, by being approached by the preacher after a sermon of this kind, with a secretary by his side with a book and pen in his hand, to take down the names and answers of those who, by invitation, remained to be conversed with. Having taken her name, the preacher asked, 'Are you for God or the devil?' Being overcome, her head depressed, and in tears, she made no reply. 'Put her down, then, in the devil's book,' said the preacher to his secretary. From that time the poor girl became insane; and, in her simplicity and innocence, has been accustomed to tell the story of her misfortunes."

And yet these revivals are looked up to and supported as the strong arm of religion. It is not only the ignorant or the foolish, but the enlightened and the educated also, who support and encourage them, either from a consideration of their utility, or from that fear, so universal in the United States, of expressing an opinion contrary to the majority. How otherwise could they be introduced once or twice a year into all the colleges, the professors of which are surely most of them men of education and strong mind? Yet such is the fact. It is announced that some minister, peculiarly gifted to work in revivals, is to come on a certain day. Books are thrown on one side, study is abandoned, and ten days perhaps are spent in religious exercises of the most violent and exciting character. It is a scene of strange confusion, some praying, some pretending to pray, some scoffing. Day after day it is carried on, until the excitement is at its height, as the exhortations and the denunciations of the preacher are poured into their ears. A young American who was at one of the colleges, and gave me a full detail of what had occurred, told me that on one occasion a poor lad, frightened out of his senses, and anxious to pray, as the vengeance and wrath of the Almighty was poured out by the minister, sunk down upon his knees and commenced his prayer with "Almighty and *diabolical* God!" No misnomer, if what the preacher had thundered out was the *truth*.

As an example of the interference of the laity, and of the description of people who may be so authorised, the same gentleman told me that at one revival a deacon said to him previous to the meeting, "Now, Mr —, if you don't take advantage of this here revival and lay up a little salvation for your soul, all I can say is, that you ought to have your (something) confoundedly well kicked."

What I have already said on this subject will, I think, establish two points, first, that the voluntary system does not work well for society; and secondly, that the ministers of the churches are treated with such tyranny and contumely, as to warrant the assertion, that in a country, like the United States, where a man may, in any other profession, become independent in a few years, the number of those who enter into the ministry must decrease at the very time that the population and demand for them will increase.

We have now another question to be examined, and a very important one, which is:— Are those who worship under the voluntary system supplied at a cheaper rate than those of the established churches in this kingdom?

I say this is an important question, as there is no doubt that one of the principal causes of dissenting has been the taxes upon religion in this country, and the wish, if it were attainable, of worshipping at free cost. In entering into this question, there is no occasion to refer to any particular sect, as the system is much the same with them all, and is nearly as follows:

Some pious and well disposed people of a certain persuasion, we will say, imagine that another church might, if it were built, be well filled with those of their own sect: and that, if it is not built, the consequences will be that many of their own persuasion will, from the habit of attending other churches, depart from those tenets which they are anxious should not only be retained by those who have embraced them, but as much as possible promulgated, so as to gather strength and make converts—for it should be borne in mind that the sectarian spirit is one great cause of the rapid church-building in America. (Churches are also built upon speculation, as they sometimes are in England.) One is of Paul, another of Apollos. They meet, and become the future deacons and elders, in all probability, to whom the minister has to bow; they agree to build a church at their own risque: they are not speculators, but religious people, who have not the least wish to make money, but who are prepared, if necessary, to lose it.

Say then that a handsome church (I am referring to the cities) of brick or stone, is raised in a certain quarter of the city, and that it costs 75,000 dollars. When the interior is complete, and the pews are all built, they divide the whole cost of the church upon the pews, more or less value being put upon them according to their situations. Allowing that there are two hundred pews, the one hundred most eligible being valued at five hundred dollars each; and the other one hundred inferior at two hundred and fifty dollars; these prices would pay the 75,000 dollars, the whole expense of the church building.

The pews are then put up to auction; some of the most eligible will fetch higher prices than the valuation, while some are sold below the valuation. If all are not sold, the residue remains upon the hands of the parties who built the church, and who may for a time be out of pocket. They have, however, to aid them, the extra price paid for the best pews, and the sale of the vaults for burial in the church-yard. Most of the pews being sold, the church is partly paid for. The next point is to select a minister, and, after due trial, one is chosen. If he be a man of eloquence and talent, and his doctrines acceptable to the many, the church fills, the remainder of the pews are sold, and so far the expenses of building the church are defrayed; but they have still to pay the salary of the minister, the heating and lighting of the church, the organist, and the vocalists: this is done by an assessment upon the pews, each pew being assessed according to the sum which it fetched when sold by auction.

I will now give the exact expenses of an American gentleman in Boston, who has his pew in one of the largest churches.

He purchased his pew at auction for seven hundred and fifty dollars, it being one of the best in the church. The salaries of the most popular ministers vary from fifteen hundred to three or four thousand dollars. The organist receives about five hundred; the vocalists from two to three hundred dollars each. To meet his share of these and the other expenses, the assessment of this gentleman is sixty-three dollars per annum. Now, the interest of seven hundred and fifty dollars in America is forty-five dollars, and the assessment being sixty-three—one hundred and eight dollars per annum, or twenty-two pounds ten shillings sterling for his yearly expenses under the voluntary system. This, of course, does not include the offerings of the plate, charity sermons, etcetera, all of which are to be added, and which will swell the sum, according to my friend's statement, to about thirty pounds per annum. ("A great evil of our American churches is, their great respectability or exclusiveness. Here, being of a large size and paid by Government, the church is open to all the citizens, with an equal right and equal chance of accommodation. In ours, the dearness of pew-rent, especially in Episcopal and Presbyterian, turns poverty out of doors. Poor people have a sense of shame, and I know many a one, who, because he cannot go to Heaven decently, will not go at all."—*Sketches of Paris by an American Gentleman*.)

It does not appear by the above calculations that the voluntary system has cheapness to recommend it, when people worship in a respectable manner, as you might hire a house and farm of fifty acres in that State for the same rent which this gentleman pays for going to church; but it must also be recollected that it is quite optional and that those who do not go to church need not pay at all.

It was not, however, until late years that such was the case. In Massachusetts, and in most of the Eastern States, the system was not voluntary, and it is to this cause that may be ascribed the superior morality and reverence for religion still existing, although decaying, in these States. By former enactments in Massachusetts, landowners in the country were compelled to contribute to the support of the church.

Pews in cities or towns are mentioned in all deeds and wills as *personal* property; but in the country, before the late Act, they were considered as *real* estate.

A pew was allotted each farm, and whether the proprietor occupied it or not, he was obliged to pay for it; but by an Act of the Massachusetts State legislature, passed within these few years, it was decided that no man should be compelled to pay for religion. The consequence has been, that the farmers now refuse to pay for their pews, the churches are empty, and a portion of the clergy have been reduced to the greatest distress. An itinerant ranter, who will preach in the open air, and send his hat round for cents, suits the farmers much better as it is much cheaper. Certainly this does not argue much for the progressive advancement of religion, even in the moral State of Massachusetts.

In other points the cause of morality has, till lately, been upheld in these Eastern States. It was but the other day that a man was discharged from prison, who had been confined for disseminating atheistical doctrines. It was, however, said at the time, that that was the last attempt that would ever be made by the authorities to imprison a man for liberty of conscience; and I believe that such will be the case.

The *Boston Advocate* says—"Abner Kneeland came out of prison yesterday, where he has been for sixty days, under the barbarous and bigoted law of Massachusetts, which imprisons men for freedom of opinions. As was to have been expected, Kneeland's liberation was made a sort of triumph. About three hundred persons assembled, and were addressed by him at the jail, and he was conveyed home in a barouche. During his persecution in prison, liberal sums of money have been sent to him. How much has Christianity gained by this foul blot on the escutcheon of Massachusetts?"

It is however worthy of remark, that those States that have *enforced* religion and morality, and have punished infidelity, (Miss Martineau complains of this as contrary to the unalienable rights of man:—"Instead of this we find laws framed against speculative atheists; opprobrium directed against such as embrace natural religion otherwise than through Christianity, and a yet more bitter oppression exercised by those who view Christianity in one way over those who regard it in another.") are now the most virtuous, the most refined, and the most intellectual, and are quoted as such by American authors, like Mr Carey, who by the help of Massachusetts alone can bring out his statistics to anything near the mark requisite to support his theories.

It is my opinion that the voluntary system will never work well under any form of government, and still less so under a democracy.

Those who live under a democracy have but one pursuit, but one object to gain, which is wealth. No one can serve God and Mammon. To suppose that a man who has been in such ardent pursuit of wealth, as is the American for six days in the week, can recall his attention and thoughts to serious points on the seventh, is absurd; you might as well expect him to forget his tobacco on Sunday.

Under a democracy, therefore, you must look for religion among the women, not among the men, and such is found to be the case in the United States. As Sam Slick very truly says, "It's only women who attend meeting: the men folks have their politics and trade to talk over and havn't *time*." Even an established church would not make people as religious under a democratic form of government as it would under any other. (Mrs Trollope observes, "A stranger taking up his residence in any city in America, must think the natives the most religious people upon earth." This is very true; the *outward* observances are very strict; why so will be better comprehended when the reader has finished my remarks upon the country. The author of Mammon very truly observes, that the only vice which we can practise without being arraigned for it in this world, and at the same time go through the *forms* of religion, is *covetousness*.)

I have yet to point out how slander and defamation flourish under a democracy. Now, this voluntary system, from the interference of the laity, who judge not only the minister, but the congregation, gives what appears to be a legitimate sanction to this tyrannical surveillance over the conduct and behaviour of others. I really believe that the majority of men who go to church in America do so, not from zeal towards God, but from fear of their neighbours; and this very tyranny in the more established persuasions, is the cause of thousands turning away to other sects which are not subjected to scrutiny. The Unitarian is in this point the most convenient, and is therefore fast gaining ground. Mr Colton observes, "Nothing can be more clear, than that scripture authority against meddling, tattling, slander, scandal, or in any way interfering with the private concerns, conduct, and character of our neighbours, except as civil or ecclesiastical authority has clothed us with legitimate powers, is specific, abundant, decided, emphatic. It is founded in human nature; it is essential to the peace of society a departure from it would be ruinous to social comfort. If therefore it is proper to introduce any rule on this point into a mutual church covenant, it seems to me that the converse of that which is usually found in that place ought to be substituted. Even the apostles, as we have seen, found it necessary to rebuke the disposition prevalent in their time to meddle with the affairs, and to make inquisition into the conduct of others. But it should be recollected, that the condition of Christians and the state of society then were widely different from the same things with us. Christianity was a new religion, and its disciples were generally obnoxious. They were compelled by their circumstances to associate most intimately; they were bound together by those sympathies and ties, which a persecuted and suffering class always feel, independent of Christian affection. Hence in part we account for the holy and exemplary candour (?an dour) of their attachments to their religion and to each other. But even in these circumstances, and under these especial intimacies, or rather, perhaps, on account of them, the apostles found it necessary to admonish them against the abuse of that confidence so generally felt and reciprocated by those who confessed Christ in those unhappy times; an abuse so naturally developed in the form of meddling and private inquisition."

I quote the above passage, as, in the United States, the variety of sects, the continual splitting and breaking up of those sects, and their occasional violent altercations, have all proved most injurious to society, and to the cause of religion itself. Indeed religion in the States may be said to have been a source of continual discord and the unhinging of society, instead of that peace and good-will inculcated by our divine Legislator. It is the division of the Protestant church which has occasioned its weakness in this country, and will probably eventually occasion, if not its total subversion, at all events its subversion in the western hemisphere of America.

The subjugation of the ministry to the tyranny of their congregations is another most serious evil; for either they must surrender up their consciences or their bread. In too many instances it is the same here in religion as in politics: before the people will permit any one to serve them in any office, he must first prove his unfitness, by submitting to what no man of honesty or conscientious rectitude would subscribe to. This must of course, in both cases, be taken with exceptions, but it is but too often the fact. And hence has arisen another evil, which is, that there are hundreds of self-constituted ministers, who wander over the western country, using the word of God as a cloak, working upon the feelings of the women to obtain money, and rendering religion a by-word among the men, who will, in all probability, some day rise up and lynch some dozen of them, as a hint for the rest to *clear out*.

It would appear as if Locofoco-ism and infidelity had formed an union, and were fighting under the same banner. They have recently celebrated the birth-day of Tom Paine, in Cincinnati, New York, and Boston. In Cincinnati, Frances Wright Darusmont, better known as Fanny Wright, was present, and made a violent politico-atheistical speech on the occasion, in which she denounced banking, and almost every other established institution of the country. The nature of the celebration in Boston will be understood from the following toast, given on the occasion:

By George Chapman:—"*Christianity* and the *banks*, tottering on their last legs: May their *downfall* be speedy," etcetera, etcetera.

Miss Martineau informs us that "The churches of Boston, and even the other public buildings, being guarded by the dragon of bigotry, so that even Faith, Hope, and Charity, are turned back from the doors, a large building is about to be erected for the use of all, Deists not excepted, who may desire to meet for free discussion." She adds, *This at least is in advance!*" And in a few pages further:—"The eagerness in pursuit of speculative truth is shown by the *rapid sale of every heretical work*. The clergy complain of the enormous spread of bold books, from the infidel tract to the latest handling of the miracle question, as sorrowfully as the most liberal members of society lament the unlimited circulation of the false morals issued by certain Religious Tract Societies. Both testify to the interest taken by the public in religion. The love of truth is also shown by the outbreak of heresy in all directions!"

Having stated the most obvious objections to the voluntary system, I shall now proceed to show how far my opinions are corroborated by American authorities. The author of "A Voice from America," observes very truly, that the voluntary system of supporting religion in America is inadequate to the purpose, and he closes his argument with the following observation:—

"How far that part of the system of supporting religion in America, which appeals to the pride and public spirit of the citizens, in erecting and maintaining religious institutions on a respectable footing, in towns, cities, and villages, and among rival sects—and in this manner operating as a species of constraint—is worthy to be called voluntary, we pretend not to say. But this comprehends by far the greatest sum that is raised and appropriated to these objects. All the rest is a mere fraction in comparison. And yet it is allowed, and made a topic of grievous lamentation, that the religious wants of the country are most inadequately supplied; and such, indeed, we believe to be the fact."

The next point referred to by this author is, "that the American system of supporting religion has brought about great instability in the religious world, and induced a ruinous habit of change."

This arises from the caprice of the congregation, for Americans are naturally capricious and fond of change: whether it be concerning a singer, or an actor, or a clergyman, it is the same thing. This American author observes, "There are few clergymen that can support their early popularity for a considerable time; and as soon as it declines, they must begin to think of providing elsewhere for themselves. They go—migrate—and for the same reason, in an equal term of time, they are liable to be forced to migrate again. And thus there is no stability, but everlasting change, in the condition of the American clergy. *They* change, the *people* change—all is a round of change—because all depends on the voluntary principle. The clerical profession in America is, indeed, like that of a soldier; always under arms, frequently fighting, and always ready for a new campaign—a truly militant state. A *Clergyman's Guide* would be of little use, so far as the object might be to direct where to find him: he is not this year where he was last." And, as must be the consequence, he justly observes, "Such a system makes the clergy servile, and the people tyrannical." "When the enmity of a single individual is sufficient to destroy a resident pastor's peace, and to break him up, how can he be otherwise than servile, if he has a family about him, to whom perpetual change is inconvenient and disastrous? There is not a man in his flock, however mean and unworthy of influence, whom he does not fear; and if he happens to displease a man of importance, or a busy woman, there is an end to his peace; and he may begin to pack up. This perpetual bondage breaks down his mind, subdues his courage, and makes a timid nervous woman of one who is entitled, and who ought to be, a man. He drags out a miserable existence, and dies a miserable slave. There are exceptions to this rule, it is true; because there are clergymen with talent enough to rise above these disadvantages, enforce respect, and maintain their standing, in spite of enemies."

But there is another very strong objection, and most important one, to the voluntary system, which I have delayed to bring forward: which is, that there is *no provision for the poor* in the American voluntary church system. Thus only those who are rich and able to afford religion can obtain it. At present, it is true that the majority of the people in America have means sufficient to pay for seats in churches, if they choose to expend the money; but as America increases her population, so will she increase the number of her poor; and what will be the consequence hereafter, if this evil is to continue? The author I am now quoting from observes, "At best the *poor are unprovided for*, and the talents of the clergy are always in the market to the highest bidder." (This is true. When I was in the States one of the most popular preachers quitted his church at Boston to go to New York, where he was offered an increase of salary; telling his parishioners "that he found *he would be more useful elsewhere*"—the very language used by the Laity to the clergyman when *they* dismiss *him*.) There have been many attempts to remedy this evil, in the dense population of cities, by setting up a still more voluntary system, called 'free churches,' in which the pews are not rented, but free to all. But they are uniformly *failures*.

Two other remarks made by this author are equally correct; first, that the voluntary system tends to the multiplication of sects without end; and next, that the voluntary system is a mendicant system, and involves one of the worst features of the church of Rome, which is, that it tends to the production of pious frauds. But I have already, in support of my arguments, quoted so much from this book that I must refer the reader to the work itself.

At present, Massachusetts, and the smaller Eastern States, are the strong-hold of religion and morality; as you proceed from them farther south or west, so does the influence of the clergy decrease, until it is totally lost in the wild States of Missouri and Arkansas. With the exception of certain cases to be found in Western Virginia, Kentucky, and Ohio, the whole of the States to the westward of the Alleghany Mountains, comprising more than two-thirds of America, may be said to be either in a state of neglect and darkness, or professing the Catholic religion.

Although Virginia is a slave state, I think there is more religion there than in some of the more northern free states; but it must be recollected that Virginia has been long settled, and the non-*predial* state of the slaves is not attended with demoralising effects; and I may here observe that the *black* population of American is decidedly the most religious, and sets an example to the white, particularly in the free states.

(Mr Reid, in his Tour, describes a visit which he paid to a black church in Kentucky:—

"By the laws of the state, no coloured persons are permitted to assemble for worship, unless a white person be present and preside.

"One of the black preachers, addressing me as their 'strange master,' begged that I would take charge of the service. I declined doing so. He gave out Dr Watts' beautiful psalm, 'Shew pity, Lord, oh! Lord forgive.' They all rose immediately. They had no books, for they could not read; but it was printed on their memory, and they sung it off with freedom and feeling.

"The senior black, who was a preacher among them, then offered prayer and preached; his prayer was humble and devotional. In one portion, he made an affecting allusion to their wrongs. 'Thou knowest,' said the good man, with a broken voice, 'our state—that it is the meanest—that we are as mean and low as man can be. But we have sinned—we have forfeited all our rights to **Thee**, and we would submit before *Thee*, to these marks of thy displeasure.'"

Mr Reid subsequently asserts, that the sermon delivered by the black was an "earnest and efficient appeal;" and, afterward, hearing a sermon on the same day from a white preacher, he observes that it was a "*very sorry affair*," in contrast with what he had before witnessed.)

It may be fairly inquired, can this be true? Not fifty years back, at the time of the Declaration of Independence, was not the American community one of the most virtuous in existence? Such was indeed the case, as it is now equally certain that they are one of the most demoralised. The question is, then, what can have created such a change in the short period of fifty years?

The only reply that can be given, is, that as the Americans, in their eagerness to possess new lands, pushed away into the West, so did they leave civilisation behind, and return to ignorance and barbarism; they scattered their population, and the word of God was not to be heard in the wilderness.

That as she increased her slave states, so did she give employment, land, and power to those who were indifferent to all law, human or divine. And as, since the formation of the Union, the people have yearly gained advantages over the *government* until they now control it, so have they controlled and fettered*religion* until it produces no good fruits.

Add to this the demoralising effects of a democracy which turns the thoughts of all to Mammon, and it will be acknowledged that this rapid fall is not so very surprising.

But, if the Protestant cause is growing weaker every day from disunions and indifference, there is one creed which is as rapidly gaining strength; I refer to the Catholic church, which is silently, but surely advancing. (Although it is not forty years since the first Roman Catholic see was created, there is now in the United States a Catholic population of 800,000 souls under the government of the Pope, or Archbishop, 12 Bishops, and 433 priests. The number of churches is 401; mass houses, about 300; colleges, 10; seminaries for young men, 9; theological seminaries, 5; noviciates for Jesuits, monasteries, and converts, with academies attached, 31; seminaries for young ladies, 30; schools of the Sisters of Charity, 29; an academy for coloured girls at Baltimore; a female infant school, and 7 Catholic newspapers.) Its great field is in the West, where, in some states, almost all are Catholics, or from neglect and ignorance altogether indifferent as to religion. The Catholic priests are diligent, and make a large number of converts every year, and the Catholic population is added to by the number of Irish and German emigrants to the West, who are almost all of them of the Catholic persuasion.

Mr Tocqueville says—

"I think that the Catholic religion has erroneously been looked upon as the natural enemy of democracy. Among the various sects of Christians, Catholicism seems to me, on the contrary to be one of those which are most favourable to equality of conditions. In the Catholic church, the religious community is composed of only two elements—the priest and the people. The priest alone rises above the rank of his flock, and all below him are equal. On doctrinal points, the Catholic faith places all human capacities upon the same level. It subjects the wise and the ignorant, the man of genius and the vulgar crowd, to the details of the same creed: it imposes the same observances upon the rich and the needy; it inflicts the same austerities upon the strong and the weak; it listens to no compromise with mortal man; but, reducing all the human race to the same standard, it confounds all the distinctions of society at the foot of the same altar, even as they are confounded in the sight of God. If Catholicism predisposes the faithful to obedience, it certainly does not prepare them for inequality; but the contrary may be said of Protestantism, which generally tends to make men independent, more than to render them equal."

And the author of a Voice from America observes—

"The Roman Catholic church bids fair to rise to importance in America. Thoroughly democratic as her members are, being composed for the most part, of the lowest orders of European population, transplanted to the United States with a fixed and implacable aversion to everything bearing the name and in the shape of monarchy, the priesthood are accustomed *studiously to adapt themselves to this state of feeling*, being content with that authority that is awarded to their office by their own communicants and members."

(The Rev. Dr Reid observes:—

"I found the people at this time under some uneasiness in relation to the spread of Romanism. The partisans of that system are greatly assisted from Europe by supplies of money and teachers. The teachers have usually more acquired competency than the native instructors; and this is a temptation to parents who are seeking accomplishments for their children, and who have a high idea of European refinements. It appeared, that out of four schools, provided for the wants of the town (Lexington, Kentucky) three were in the hands of Catholics."

To which we may add Miss Martineau's observations:—

"The Catholics of the country, thinking themselves now sufficiently numerous to be an American Catholic church, a great stimulus has been given to proselytism. This has awakened fear and persecution; which last has again been favourable to the increase of the sect. While the Presbyterians preach a harsh, ascetic, persecuting religion, the Catholics dispense a mild and indulgent one; and the prodigious increase of their numbers is a necessary consequence. It has been so impossible to supply the demand for priests, that the term of education has been shortened by two years.")

Now, I venture to disagree with both these gentlemen: It is true, as Mr Tocqueville observes, that the Catholic church reduces all the human race to the same standard, and confounds all distinctions—not, however, upon the principle of equality or democracy, but because it will ever equally exert its power over the high and the low, assuming its right to compel princes and kings to obedience, and their dominions to its subjection. The equality professed by the Catholic church, is like the equality of death, all must fall before its power; whether it be to excommunicate an individual or an empire is to it indifferent; it assumes the power of the Godhead, giving and taking sway, and its members stand trembling before it, as they shall hereafter do in the presence of the Deity.

The remark of the author of the *Voice from America*, "that aware of the implacable aversion of the people to monarchy, the priesthood are accustomed *studiously to adapt themselves to this state of feeling*," proves rather to me the universal subtlety shown by the Catholic clergy, which, added to their zeal and perseverance, so increases the power of the church. At present Catholicism is, comparatively speaking, weak in America, and the objects of that church is, to become strong; they do not, therefore, frighten or alarm their converts by any present show of the invariable results; but are content to bide their time, until they shall find themselves strong enough to exert their power with triumphant success. The Protestant cause in America is weak, from the evil effects of the voluntary system, particularly from its division into so many sects. A house divided against itself cannot long stand; and every year it will be found that the Catholic church will increase its power: and it is a question whether a hierarchy may not eventually be raised, which, so far from *advocating the principles of equality*, may serve as a *check* to the spirit of democracy becoming more powerful than the government, curbing public opinion, and reducing to better order the present chaotic state of society.

Judge Haliburten asserts, that all America will be a Catholic country. That all America west of the Alleghanies will eventually be a Catholic country, I have no doubt, as the Catholics are already in the majority, and there is nothing, as Mr Cooper observes, to prevent any state from establishing that, or any other religion, as the *Religion of the State*; ("There is nothing in the constitution of the United States to prevent all the states, or any particular state, from possessing an established religion."—*Cooper's Democrat*) and this is one of the dark clouds which hang over the destiny of the western hemisphere.

The reverend Mr Reed says:—"It should really seem that the Pope, in the fear of expulsion from Europe, is anxious to find a reversion in this new world. The crowned heads of the continent, having the same enmity to free political institutions which his holiness has to free religious institutions, willingly unite in the attempt to enthral this people. They have heard of the necessities of the West; they have the foresight to see that the West will become the heart of the country, and ultimately determine the character of the whole; and they have resolved to establish themselves there. Large, yea *princely, grants* have been made from the Leopold society, and other sources, chiefly, though by no means exclusively, in favour of this portion of the empire that is to be. These sums are expended in erecting showy churches and colleges, and in sustaining priests and emissaries. Everything is done to captivate, and to liberalise in appearance, a system essentially despotic. The sagacity of the effort is discovered, in avoiding to attack and shock the prejudices of the adult, that they may direct the education of the young. They look to the future; and they really have great advantages in doing so. They send out teachers excellently qualified; superior, certainly, to the run of native teachers. (The Catholic priests who instruct are, to my knowledge, the best educated men in the states. It was a pleasure to be in their company.) Some value the European modes of education as the more excellent, others value them as the mark of fashion; the demand for instruction, too, is always beyond the supply, so that they find little difficulty in obtaining the charge of protestant children. This, in my judgment, is the point of policy which should be especially regarded with jealousy; but the actual alarm has arisen from the disclosure of a correspondence which avows designs on the West, beyond what I have here set down. It is a curious affair, and is one other evidence, if evidence were needed, that popery and jesuitism are one."

I think that the author of Sam Slick may not be wrong in his assertion, that *all* America will be a Catholic country. I myself never prophesy; but, I cannot help remarking, that even in the most anti-Catholic persuasions in America there is a strong Papistical *feeling*; that is, there is a vying with each other, not only to obtain the best preachers, but to have the best organs and the best singers. It is the system of excitement which, without their being aware of it, they carry into their devotion. It proves that, to them there is a weariness in the church service, a tedium in prayer, which requires to be relieved by the stimulus of good music and sweet voices. Indeed, what with their *anxious seats*, their *revivals*, their *music* and their *singing*, every class and sect in the states have even now so far fallen into Catholicism, that religion has become more of an appeal to the *senses* than to the calm and *sober judgment*.

Volume Three—Chapter Eight.

Remarks—Societies and Associations.

Although in a democracy the highest stations and preferments are open to all, more directly than they may be under any other form of government, still these prizes are but few and insufficient, compared with the number of total blanks which must be drawn by the ambitious multitude. It is, indeed, a stimulus to ambition (and a matter of justice, when all men are pronounced equal), that they all should have an equal chance of raising themselves by their talents and perseverance; but, when so many competitors are permitted to enter the field, few can arrive at the goal, and the mass are doomed to disappointment. However fair, therefore, it may be to admit all to the competition, certain it is that the competition cannot add to the happiness of a people, when we consider the feelings of bitterness and ill-will naturally engendered among the disappointed multitude.

In monarchical and aristocratical institutions, the middling and lower classes, whose chances of advancement are so small that they seldom lift their eyes or thoughts above their own sphere, are therefore much happier, and it may be added, much more virtuous than those who struggle continually for preferment in the tumultuous sea of democracy. Wealth can give some importance, but wealth in a democracy gives an importance which is so common to many that it loses much of its value; and when it has been acquired, it is not sufficient for the restless ambition of the American temperament, which will always spurn wealth for power. The effects, therefore, of a democracy are, first to raise an inordinate ambition among the people, and then to cramp the very ambition which it has raised; and, as I may comment upon hereafter, it appears as if this ambition of the people, *individually* checked by the nature of their institutions, becomes, as it were, concentrated and collected into a focus in upholding and contemplating the success and increase of power in the federal government. Thus has been produced a species of demoralising reaction; the disappointed *units* to a certain degree satisfying themselves with any advance in the power and importance of the whole Union, wholly regardless of the means by which such increase may have been obtained.

But this unsatisfied ambition has found another vent in the formation of many powerful religious and other associations. In a country where there will ever be an attempt of the people to tyrannise over everybody and everything, power they will have; and if they cannot obtain it in the various departments of the States Governments, they will have it in opposition to the Government; for all these societies and associations connect themselves directly with politics. (See Note 1.) It is of little consequence by what description of tie "these sticks in the fable" are bound up together; once bound together, they are, not to be broken. In America religion severs the community, but these societies are the bonds which to a certain degree reunite it.

To enumerate the whole of these societies actually existing, or which have been in existence, would be difficult. The following are the most prominent:—

List of Benevolent Societies, with their Receipts in the Year 1834.

	Dolls Cts.
American Board of Commissioners for Foreign Missions	155,0 02 24
American Baptist Board of Foreign Missions	63,00 0 00
Western Foreign Mission Society	
at Pittsburgh, Pennsylvania	16,29 6 46
Methodist Episcopal Missionary Society	35,70 0 15
Protestant Episcopal Foreign	
and Domestic Missionary Society	26,00

	7 97
American Home Missionary Society	78,91 1 24
Baptist Home Missionary Society	11,44 8 28
Board of Missions of the	
Reformed Dutch Church (Domestic)	5,572 97
Board of Missions of the General Assembly of the	
Presbyterian Church (Domestic) estimated	40,00 0 00
American Education Society	57,12 2 20
Board of Education of the General Assembly of the	
Presbyterian churches	38,00 0 00
Northern Baptist Education Society	4,681 11
Board of Education of the Reformed Dutch Church	1,270 20

American Bible Society	88,600 82
American Sunday School Union	136,855 58
General Protestant Episcopal Sunday School Union	6,641 00
Baptist General Tract Society	6,126 97
American Tract Society	66,485 83
American Colonisation Society	48,939 17
Prison Discipline Society	2,364 00
American Seamen's Friend Society	16,064 00
American Temperance Society	5,871 12
	8,910,961 31

Many of these societies had not been established more than ten years at the date given; they must have increased very much since that period. Of course many of them are very useful, and very well conducted. There are many others: New England Non-resistance Society, Sabbath Observance Society, etcetera; in fact, the Americans are society mad. I do not intend to speak with the least disrespect of the societies, but the zeal or fanaticism, if I may use the term, with which many, if not all, of them are carried on, is too remarkable a feature in the American character to be passed over without comment. Many of these societies have done much good, particularly the religious societies; but many others, from being pushed too far, have done great mischief, and have very much assisted to demoralise the community. I remember once hearing a story of an ostler who confessed to a Catholic priest; he enumerated a long catalogue of enormities peculiar to his profession, and when he had finished, the priest inquired of him "whether he had ever greased horses' teeth to prevent their eating their corn?" this peculiar offence not having been mentioned in his confession. The ostler declared that he never had, absolution was given, and he departed. About six months afterwards, the ostler went again to unload his conscience; the former crimes and peccadilloes were enumerated, but added to them were several acknowledgments of having at various times "*greased horses' teeth*" to prevent their eating their corn. "Ho-ho!" cried the priest, "why, if I recollect aright, according to your former confession you had never been guilty of this practice. How comes it that you have added this crime to your many others?" "May it please you, Father," replied the ostler, "I had *never heard of it*, until you told me."

Now this story is very *apropos* to the conduct pursued by many of these societies in America: they must display to the public their statistics of immorality and vice; they must prove their usefulness by informing those who were quite ignorant, and therefore innocent, that there are crimes of which they had no idea; and thus, in their fanatic wish to improve, they demoralise. Such have been the consequences among this excitable yet well-meaning people. The author of "A voice from America" observes:—

It has been thought suitable to call the attention of mothers and daughters over the wide country to the condition and evils of brothels and of common prostitution, in towns and cities; to send out agents—young men—to preach on the subject; and to organise subsidiary societies after the fashion of all reforms. The annual report of "The New York Female Moral Reform Society" for 1838, (a very decent name certainly for the object), announces 361 auxiliaries and 20,000 members, with 16,500 subscribers (all females!) to the "*Advocate of Moral Reform*," a semi-monthly paper, published by the parent society, devoted to the text of the seventh commandment, and to the facts and results growing out of its violation. "This same class of reformers have heretofore been accustomed to strike off prints of the most unmentionable scenes of these houses of pollution in their naked forms, and in the very acts of crime, for public display, that the public might know what they are: in other words, as may be imagined, to make sport for the initiated, to tempt the appetites and passions of the young, who otherwise would have known little or nothing about it, into the same vortex of ruin, and to cause the decent and virtuous to turn away with emotions of ineffable regret."

I cannot help inquiring, how is it, if the Americans are, as they assert, both orally and in their printed public documents, a *very moral nation*, that they find it necessary to resort to all these societies for the improvement of their brother citizens; and how is it that their reports are full of such unexampled atrocities, as are printed and circulated in evidence of the necessity of their stemming the current of vice! The Americans were constantly twitting me about the occasional cases of adultery and divorce which appear in our newspapers, assuring me at the same time, that there was hardly ever such a thing heard of in their own moral community. Now, it appears that this subject has not only been taken up by the clergy, (for Dr Dwight, late president of Yale College, preached a sermon on the seventh commandment, which an American author asserts "was heard with pain and confusion of face, and which never can be read in a promiscuous circle without exciting the same feelings;") but by one of their societies also; and, although they have not assumed the name of the *Patent Anti-Adultery Society*, they are positively doing the work of such a one, and the details are entered into in promiscuous assemblies without the least reservation.

The author before mentioned says:

"The common feeling on the subject has been declared false delicacy; and, in order to break ground against its sway, females have been forced into the van of this enterprise; and persuaded to act as agents, not only among their own sex, but in circumstances where they must necessarily agitate the subject with men,—not wives with husbands, which would be bad enough, but *young and single women* with *young and single men*! And we have been credibly informed, that attempts have been made to form associations among *wives* to regulate the privileges, and so attain the end of temperance, in the *conjugal relation*. The next step, of course, will be teetotalism in this particular; and, as a consequence, the extinction of the human race, unless peradventure the failure of the main enterprise of the *Moral Reform Society* should keep it up by a progeny not to be honoured." ("A Voice from America.")

Let it be remembered that this is not a statement of my own, but it is an *American* who makes the assertion, which I could prove to be true, might I publish what I must not.

From the infirmity of our natures, and our proneness to evil, there is nothing so corrupting as the statistics of vice. Can young females remain pure in their ideas, who read with indifference details of the grossest nature? Can the youth of a nation remain uncontaminated, who are continually poring over pages describing sensuality; and will they not, in their desire of "something new," as the Prophet says, run into the very vices of the existence of which they were before unconscious! It is this dangerous running into extremes which has occasioned so many of these societies to have been productive of much evil. A Boston editor remarks: "The tendency of the leaders of the moral and benevolent reforms of the day to run into fanaticism, threatens to destroy the really beneficial effects of all associations for these objects. The spirit of propagandism, when it becomes over zealous, is next of kin to the spirit of persecution. The benevolent associations of the day are on the brink of a danger that will be fatal to their farther usefulness if not checked."

Of the Abolition Society and its tendency, I have already spoken in the chapter on slavery. I must not, however, pass over another which at present is rapidly extending its sway over the whole Union, and it is difficult to say whether it does most harm or most good—I refer to the Temperance Society.

The Rev. Mr Reid says:

"In the short space of its existence, upwards of seven thousand Temperance Societies have been formed, embracing more than one million two hundred and fifty thousand members. More than three thousand distilleries have been stopped, and more than seven thousand persons who dealt in spirits have declined the trade. Upwards of one thousand vessels have abandoned their use. And, most marvellous of all! it is said that above ten thousand drunkards have been reclaimed from intoxication." And he adds—"I really know of no one circumstance in the history of this people, or of any people, so exhilarating as this. It discovers that power of self-government, which is the leading element of all national greatness, in an unexampled degree. Now here is a remarkable instance of a traveller taking for granted that what is reported to him is the truth." The worthy clergyman, himself, evidently without guile, fully believed a statement which was absurd, from the simple fact, that only one side of the balance sheet had been presented.

That 7,000 Temperance Societies have been formed is true. That 3,000 distilleries have stopped from principle may also be true; but the Temperance Society reports take no notice of the many which have been *set up in their stead* by those who felt no compunction at selling spirits. Equally true it may be that 7,030 dealers in spirits have ceased to sell them; but if they have declined the trade, *others have taken it up*. That the crews of many vessels have abandoned the use of spirituous liquors is also the fact, and that is the greatest benefit which has resulted from the efforts of the Temperance Society; but I believe the number to be greatly magnified. That 10,000 drunkards have been reclaimed—that is, that they have signed papers and taken the oath—may be true; but how many have fallen away from their good resolutions, and become more intemperate than before, is not recorded; nor how many who, previously careless of liquor, have, out of pure opposition, and in defiance of the Society, actually become drunkards, is also unknown. In this Society, as in the Abolition Society, they have canvassed for legislative enactments, and have succeeded in obtaining them. The legislature of Massachusetts, which state is the stronghold of the society, passed an act last year by which it prohibited the selling of spirits in a smaller quantity than fifteen gallons, intending thereby to do away with the means of dram-drinking, at the groceries, as they are termed; a clause, however, permitted apothecaries to retail smaller quantities, and the consequence was that all the grog-shops commenced taking out apothecaries' licences. That being stopped, the *striped pig* was resorted to: that is to say, a man charged people the value of a glass of liquor to see a *striped pig*, which peculiarity was exhibited as a sight, and, when in the house, the visitors were offered a glass of spirits for nothing. But this act of the legislature has given great offence, and the state of Massachusetts is now divided into two very strange political parties, to wit, the *topers* and the *teetotalers*. It is asserted that, in the political contest which is to take place, the topers will be victorious; and if so, it will be satisfactorily proved that, in the very enlightened and moral state of Massachusetts the pattern of the Union, there are more intemperate than sober men.

In this dispute between sobriety and inebriety the clergy have not been idle: some denouncing alcohol from the pulpit; some, on the other hand denouncing the Temperance Societies as not being Christians. Among the latter the Bishop of Vermont has led the van. In one of his works, "The Primitive Church," he asserts that:—

"The Temperance Society is not based upon religious, but worldly principles.

"That it opposes vice and attempts to establish virtue in a manner which is not in accordance with the word of God," etcetera, etcetera.

His argument is briefly this:— The Scriptures forbid drunkenness. If the people will not do right in obedience to the word of God, but only from the fear of public opinion, they show more respect to man than God.

The counter argument is:— The Bible prohibits many other crimes, such as murder, theft, etcetera; but if there were not punishments for these offences agreed upon by society, the fear of God would not prevent these crimes from being committed.

That in the United States public opinion has more influence than religion I believe to be the case; and that in all countries present punishment is more to be considered than future is, I fear, equally true. But I do not pretend to decide the question, which has occasioned great animosities, and on some occasions, I am informed, the dismissal of clergymen from their churches.

The teetotalers have carried their tenets to a length which threatens to invade the rites of the church, for a portion of them, calling themselves the Total Abstinence Society, will not use any wine which has alcohol in it, in taking the sacrament, and as there is no wine without a portion of alcohol; they have invented a harmless mixture which they call wine. Unfortunately, many of these Temperance Societies in their zeal, will admit of no medium party—you must either abstain altogether, or be put down as a toper.

It is astonishing how obstinate some people are, and how great is the diversity of opinion. I have heard many anecdotes relative to this question. A man who indulged freely was recommended to join the society. "Now," said the minister, "you must allow that there is nothing so good, so valuable to man as water. What is the first thing you call for in sickness but water? What else can cool your parched tongue like water? What did the rich man ask for when in fiery torments? What does the wretch ask for when on the rack? You cannot always drink spirits, but water you can. Water costs nothing; and you save your money. Water never intoxicates, or prevents you from going to your work. There is nothing like water. Come now, Peter, let me hear your opinion."

"Well, then, sir, I think water is very good, very excellent indeed—for navigation."

An old Dutchman, who kept an inn at Hoboken, had long resisted the attacks of the Temperance Societies, until one night he happened to get so very drunk, that he actually signed the paper and took the oath. The next morning he was made acquainted with what he had unconsciously done, and, much to the surprise of his friends, he replied, "Well, if I have signed and have sworn, as you tell me I have, I must keep to my word;" and from that hour the old fellow abstained altogether from his favourite schnapps. But the leaving off a habit which had become necessary had the usual result. The old man took to his bed, and at last became seriously ill. A medical man was called in, and when he was informed of what had occurred, perceived the necessity of some stimulus, and ordered that his patient should take one ounce of French brandy every day.

"An ounce of French brandy," said the old Dutchman, looking at the prescription. "Well, dat is goot; but how much is an ounce?" Nobody who was present could inform him. "I know what a quart, a pint, or a gill of brandy is," said the Dutchman, "but I never yet have had a customer call for an ounce. Well, my son, go to the schoolmaster; he is a learned man, and tell him I wish to know how much is one ounce."

The message was carried. The schoolmaster, occupied with his pupils, and not liking the interruption, hastily, and without further inquiries of the messenger, turned over his Bonnycastle, and arriving at the table of avoirdupois weight, replied, "Tell your father that *sixteen drams* make an *ounce*."

The boy took back the message correctly, and when the old Dutchman heard it, his countenance brightened up. "A goot physician, a clever man—I only have drank twelve drams a-day, and he tells me to take sixteen. I have taken one oath when I was drunk, and I keep it; now dat I am sober I take anoder, which is, I will be very sick for de remainder of my days, and never throw my physic out of window."

There was a *cold water* celebration at Boston, on which occasion the hilarity of the evening was increased by the singing of the following ode. Nobody will venture to assert that there is any *spirit* in the composition, and, judging from what I have seen of American manners and customs, I am afraid that the sentiments of the last four lines will not be responded to throughout the Union.

Ode.

In   Eden's   green   retreats
 A   water-brook   that   played
Between   soft,   and   mossy   seats
 Beneath   a   plane-tree's   shade,
  Whose   rustling   leaves
Danced   o'er   its   brink,
Was   Adam's   drink,
 And   also   Eve's.

Beside   the   parent   spring
 Of   that   young   brook,   the   pair
Their   morning   chaunt   would   sing;
 And   Eve,   to   dress   her   hair,
  Kneel   on   the   grass
That   fringed   its   side,
 And   made   its   tide
  Her   looking-glass.

And   when   the   man   of   God
From   Egypt   led   his   flock,
They   thirsted,   and   his   rod
 Smote   the   Arabian   rock,
 And   forth   a   rill
Of   water   gushed,
And   on   they   rushed,
 And   drank   their   fill.

Would   Eden   thus   have   smil'd
 Had *wine* to   Eden   come?
Would   Horeb's   parching   wild
Have   been   refreshed   with *rum*
 And   had   Eve's   hair
Been   dressed   in *gin*
Would   she   have   been
 Reflected   fair?

Had   Moses   built   a   still
 And   dealt   out   to   that   host,
To   every   man   his   gill,
 And   pledged   him   in   a   toast,

How large a band
Of Israel's sons
Had laid their bones
In Canaan's land?

Sweet fields, beyond Death's flood,
Stand dressed in living green,
For, from the throne of God,
To freshen all the scene,
A river rolls,
Where all who will
May come and fill
Their crystal bowls.

If Eden's strength and bloom
Cold water thus hath given—
If e'en beyond the tomb,
It is the drink of heaven—
Are not *good wells,*
And *crystal springs,*
The very *things*
For our hotels?

As I shall return to the subject of intemperance in my examination of society, I shall conclude this chapter with an extract from Miss Martineau, whose work is a strange compound of the false and the true:—"My own convictions are, that associations, excellent as they are for mechanical objects, are not fit instruments for the achievement of moral aims; that there has been no proof that the principle of self-restraint has been exalted and strengthened in the United States by the Temperance movement while the already too great regard to *opinion*, and subservience to spiritual encroachment, have been much increased; and, therefore, great as may be the visible benefits of the institution, it may at length appear that they have been dearly purchased."

Note 1. Not long afterwards a prominent Presbyterian clergyman of Philadelphia thought fit to preach and publish a sermon, wherein it was set forth and conclusively proved, that on such and such contingencies of united religious effort of the religious public, the majority of the American people could be made*religious*; consequently they might carry their *religious influence* to the *polls*; consequently the religious would be able to turn all the profane *out of office*; and consequently, the American people would become a *Christian nation!—Voice from America by an American Gentleman.*

Volume Three—Chapter Nine.

Remarks—Law.

The lawyers are the real aristocracy of America; they comprehend nearly the whole of the gentility, talent, and liberal information of the Union. Any one who has had the pleasure of being at one of their meetings, such as the Rent Club at New York, would be satisfied that there is no want of gentlemen with enlightened, liberal ideas in the United States; but it is to the law, the navy, and the army, that you must chiefly look for this class of people. Such must ever be the case in a democracy, where the mass are to be led; the knowledge of the laws of the country, and the habit of public speaking being essential to those who would reside at the helm or assist in the evolutions: the consequence has been, that in every era of the Union, the lawyers have always been the most prominent actors; and it may be added that they ever will play the most distinguished parts. Clay and Webster of the present day are, and all the leading men of the former generation were, lawyers. Their presidents have almost all been lawyers, and any deviation from this custom has been attended with evil results; witness the elevation of General Jackson to the presidency, and the heavy price which the Americans have paid for their phantom glory. The names of Judge Marshall and of Chancellor Kent are well known in this country, and most deservedly so: indeed, I am informed it has latterly been the custom in our own law courts, to cite as cases the decisions of many of the superior American judges—a just tribute to their discrimination and their worth.

The general arrangement of that part of the American constitution relating to the judicature is extremely good, perhaps the best of all their legislative arrangements, yet it contains some great errors; one of which is, that of district and inferior judges being *elected*, as it leaves the judge at the mercy of an excitable and overbearing people, who will attempt to dictate to him as they do to their spiritual teacher. Occasionally he must choose whether he will decide as they wish, or lose his situation on the ensuing election. Justice as well as religion will be interfered with by the despotism of the democracy.

The Americans are fond of law in one respect, that is, they are fond of going to law. It is excitement to them, and not so expensive as in this country. It is a pleasure which they can afford, and for which they cheerfully pay.

But, on the other hand, the very first object of the Americans, after a law has been passed, is to find out how they can evade it; this exercises their ingenuity, and it is very amusing to observe how cleverly they sometimes manage it. Every state enactment to uphold the morals, or for the better regulation of society, is immediately opposed by the sovereign people.

An act was passed to prohibit the playing of *nine pins*, (a very foolish act, as the Americans have so few amusements): as soon as the law was put in force, it was notified every where, "*Ten* pins played here," and they have been played every where, ever since.

Another act was passed to put down billiard tables, and in this instance every precaution was taken by an accurate description of the billiard table, that the law might be enforced. Whereupon an extra *pocket* was added to the billiard table, and thus the law was evaded.

When I was at Louisville, a bill which had been brought in by congress, to prevent the numerous accidents which occurred in steam navigation, came into force. Inspectors were appointed to see that the steam-boats complied with the regulations; and those boats which were not provided according to law, did not receive the certificate from the inspectors, and were liable to a fine of five hundred dollars if they navigated without it. A steam-boat was ready to start; the passengers clubbed together and subscribed half the sum, (two hundred and fifty dollars), and, as the informer was to have half the penalty, the captain of the boat went and informed against himself and received the other half; and thus was the fine paid.

At Baltimore, in consequence of the prevalence of hydrophobia, the civic authorities passed a law, that all dogs should be muzzled, or, rather, the terms were, "that all dogs should wear a muzzle," or the owner of a dog not wearing a muzzle, should be brought up and fined; and the regulation farther stated that anybody convicted of having, "removed the muzzle from off a dog should also be severely fined." A man, therefore, tied a muzzle to his dog's tail (the act not stating where the muzzle was to be placed). One of the city officers, perceiving this dog with his muzzle at the wrong end, took possession of the dog and brought it to the town-hall; its master being well known, was summoned, and appeared. He proved that he had complied with the act, in having fixed a muzzle on the dog; and, farther, the city officer having taken the *muzzle off* the dog's tail, he insisted that he should be fined five dollars for so doing.

The *striped* pig, I have already mentioned; but were I to relate all I have been told upon this head, it would occupy too much of the reader's time and patience.

The mass of the citizens of the United States have certainly a very great dislike to all law except their own, i.e., the decision of the majority; and it must be acknowledged that it is not only the principle of equality, but the parties who are elected as district judges, that, by their own conduct, contribute much to that want of respect with which they are treated in their courts. When a judge on his bench sits half-asleep, with his hat on, and his coat and shoes off; his heels kicking upon the railing or table which is as high or higher than his head; his toes peeping through a pair of old worsted stockings, and with a huge quid of tobacco in his cheek, you cannot expect that much respect will be paid to him. Yet such is even now the practice in the interior of the western states. I was much amused at reading an English critique upon a work by Judge Hall (a district judge), in which the writer says, "We can imagine his honour in all the solemnity of his flowing wig," etcetera, etcetera. The last time I saw his *honour* he was cashier to a bank at Cincinnati, thumbing American bank-notes—dirtier work than is ever practised in the lowest grade of the law, as any one would say if he had ever had any American bank-notes in his possession.

As may be supposed, in a new country like America, many odd scenes take place. In the towns in the interior, a lawyer's office is generally a small wooden house, of one room, twelve feet square, built of clapboards, and with the door wide open; and the little domicile with its tenant used to remind me of a spider in its web waiting for flies.

Not forty years back, on the other side of the Alleghany mountains, deer skins at forty cents per pound, and the furs of other animals at a settled price, were *legal* tender, and received both by judges and lawyers as fees. The lawyers in the towns on the banks of the Susquehannah, where it appears the people, (notwithstanding Campbell's beautiful description,) were extremely litigious, used to receive all their fees in kind, such as skins, corn, whiskey, etcetera, etcetera, and, as soon as they had sufficient to load a raft, were to be seen gliding down the river to dispose of their cargo at the first favourable mart for produce. Had they worn the wigs and gown of our own legal profession, the effect would have been more picturesque.

There is a record of a very curious trial which occurred in the state of New York. A man had lent a large iron, kettle, or boiler, to another, and it being returned *cracked*, an action was brought against the borrower for the value of the kettle. After the plaintiff's case had been heard, the counsel for the defendant rose and said:—"Mister Judge, we defend this action upon three counts, all of which we shall most satisfactorily prove to you.

"In the first place, we will prove, by undoubted evidence, that the kettle was cracked when we borrowed it.

"In the second, that the kettle, when we returned it was whole and sound.

"And in the third, we will prove that we never borrowed the kettle at all."

There is such a thing as proving too much, but one thing is pretty fairly proved in this case, which is, that the defendant's counsel must have originally descended from the Milesian stock.

I have heard many amusing stories of the peculiar eloquence of the lawyers in the newly settled western states, where metaphor is so abundant. One lawyer was so extremely metaphorical upon an occasion, when the stealing of a pig was the case in point, that at last he got to "coruscating rays." The judge (who appeared equally metaphorical—himself) thought proper to pull him up by saying:—"Mr —, I wish you would take the feathers from the wings of your imagination, and put them into the tail of your judgment."

Extract from an American paper:—

"Scene.—A Court-house not fifty miles from the city of Louisville. Judge presiding with great dignity. A noise is heard before the door. He looks up, fired with indignation.—'Mr Sheriff, sir, bring them men in here; this in the temple of liberty—this in the sanctuary of justice, and it shall not be profaned by the cracking of nuts and the eating of gingerbread.'"—*Marblehead Register*.

I have already observed that there is a great error in the office of the inferior and district judges being elective, but there are others equally serious. In the first place the judges are not sufficiently paid. Captain Hamilton remarks:—

"The low salaries of the judges constitute matter of general complaint among the members of the bar, both at Philadelphia and New York. These are so inadequate, when compared with the income of a well-employed barrister, that the state is deprived of the advantage of having the highest legal talent on the bench. Men from the lower walks of the profession, therefore, are generally promoted to the office; and for the sake of a wretched saving of a few thousand dollars, the public are content to submit their lives and properties to the decision of men of inferior intelligence and learning.

"In one respect, I am told, the very excess of democracy defeats itself. In some states the judges are so inordinately underpaid, that no lawyer who does not possess a considerable private fortune can afford to accept the office. From this circumstance, something of aristocratic distinction has become connected with it, and a seat on the bench is now more greedily coveted than it would be were the salary more commensurate with the duties of the situation."

The next error is, that political questions are permitted to interfere with the ends of justice. It is a well-known fact that, not long ago, an Irishman, who had murdered his wife, was brought to trial upon the eve of an election; and, although his guilt was undoubted, he was acquitted, because the Irish party, which were so influential as to be able to turn the election, had declared that, if their countryman was convicted, they would vote on the other side.

But worst of all is the difficulty of finding an *honest* jury—a fact generally acknowledged. Politics, private animosities, bribery, all have their influence to defeat the ends of justice, and it argues strongly against the moral standard of a nation that such should be the case; but that it is so is undoubted. (See Note 1.) The truth is that the juries, have no respect for the judges, however respectable they may be, and as many of them really are. The feeling "I'm as good as he" operates everywhere. There is no shutting up a jury and starving them out as with us; no citizen, "free and enlightened, aged twenty-one, white," would submit to such an invasion of his rights. Captain Hamilton observes:—

"It was not without astonishment, I confess, that I remarked that three-fourths of the jury-men were engaged in eating bread and cheese, and that the foreman actually announced the verdict with his mouth full, ejecting the disjointed syllables during the intervals of mastication! In truth, an American seems to look on a judge exactly as he does on a carpenter or coppersmith; and it never occurs to him, that an administrator of justice is entitled to greater respect than a constructor of brass knockers, or the sheather of a ship's bottom. The judge and the brazier are paid equally for their work; and Jonathan firmly believes that, while he has money in his pocket, there is no risk of suffering from the want either of law or warming pans."

One most notorious case of bribery, I can vouch for, as I am acquainted with the two parties, one of whom purchased the snuff-box in which the other enclosed the notes and presented to the jurymen. A gentleman at New York of the name of Stoughton, had a quarrel with another of the name of Goodwin: the latter followed the former down the street, and murdered him in open day by passing a small sword through his body. The case was as clear as a case could be, but there is a great dislike to capital punishment in America, and particularly was there in this instance, as the criminal was of good family and extensive connections. It was ascertained that all the jury except two intended to acquit the prisoner upon some pretended want of evidence, but that these two had determined that the law should take its course, and were quite inexorable. Before the jury retired to consult upon the verdict, it was determined by the friends of the prisoner that an attempt should be made by bribery to soften down the resolution of these two men. As they were retiring, a snuff-box was put into the hands of one of them by a gentleman, with the observation that he and his friend would probably find a pinch of snuff agreeable after so long a trial. The snuff-box contained bank notes to the amount of 2,500 dollars (500 pounds sterling). The snuff-box and its contents were not returned, and the prisoner was acquitted.

The unwillingness to take away life is a very remarkable feature in America, and were it not carried to such an extreme length, would be a very commendable one. An instance of this occurred just before my arrival at New York. A young man by the name of Robinson, who was a clerk in an importing house, had formed a connection with a young woman on the town, of the name of Ellen Jewitt. Not having the means to meet her demands upon his purse, he had for many months embezzled from the store goods to a very large amount, which she had sold to supply her wants or wishes. At last, Robinson, probably no longer caring for the girl, and aware that he was in her power, determined upon murdering her. Such accumulated crime can hardly be conceived! He went to sleep with her, made her drunk with champagne before they retired to bed, and then as she lay in bed murdered her with an axe, which he had brought with him from his master's store. The house of ill-fame in which he visited her was at that time full of other people of both sexes, who had retired to rest—it is said nearly one hundred were there on that night, thoughtless of the danger to which they were exposed, fearful that the murder of the young woman would be discovered and brought home to him, the miscreant resolved to set fire to the house, and by thus sending unprepared into the next world so many of his fellow creatures, escape the punishment which he deserved. He set fire to the bed upon which his unfortunate victim laid, and having satisfied himself that his work was securely done, locked the door of the room, and quitted the premises. A merciful Providence, however, directed otherwise; the fire was discovered, and the flames extinguished, and his crime made manifest. The evidence in an English court would have been more than sufficient to convict him; but in America, such is the feeling against taking life that, strange to say, Robinson was acquitted, and permitted to leave for Texas, where it is said, he still lives under a false name. I have heard this subject canvassed over and over again in New York; and, although some, with a view of extenuating to a foreigner such a disgraceful disregard to security of life, have endeavoured to show that the evidence was not quite satisfactory, there really was not a shadow of doubt in the whole case. See Note 2.

But leniency towards crime is the grand characteristic of American legislation. Whether it proceeds, (as I much suspect it does,) from the national vanity being unwilling to admit that such things can take place among "a very moral people," or from a more praiseworthy feeling, I am not justified in asserting: the reader must form his own opinion, when he has read all I have to say upon other points connected with the subject.

I have been very much amused with the reports of the sentences given by my excellent friend the recorder of New York. He is said to be one of the soundest lawyers in the Union, and a very worthy man; but I trust say, that as recorder, he does not add to the dignity of the bench by his facetious remarks, and the peculiar lenity he occasionally shows to the culprits. See Note 3.

I will give an extract from the newspapers of some of the proceedings an his court, as they will, I am convinced, be as amusing to the reader as they have been to me.

The Recorder then called out—"Mr Crier, make the usual proclamation;" "Mr Clerk, call out the prisoners, and let us proceed to sentencing them!"

Clerk. Put Stephen Schofield to the bar.

It was done.

Clerk. Prisoner, you may remember you have heretofore been indicted for a certain crime by you committed; upon your indictment you were arraigned; upon your arraignment you pleaded guilty, and threw yourself upon the mercy of the court. What have you now to say, why judgment should not be passed upon you according to law.

The prisoner, who was a bad-looking mulatto, was silent.

Recorder. Schofield, you have been convicted of a very bad crime; you attempted to take liberties with a young white girl—a most serious offence. This is getting to be a very bad crime, and practised, I am sorry to say, to a great extent in this community: it must be put a stop to. Had you been convicted of the whole crime, we should have sent you to the state-prison for life. As it is, we sentence you to hard labour in the state-prison at Sing Sing for five years; and that's the judgment of the court; and when you come out, take no more liberties with white girls.

Prisoner. Thank your honour it ain't no worse.

Clerk. Bring out Mary Burns.

It was done.

Clerk. Prisoner, you may remember, etcetera, etcetera, upon your arraignment you pleaded not guilty, and put yourself on your country for trial; which country hath found you guilty. What have you now to say why judgment should not be pronounced upon you according to law?

(Silent).

Recorder. Mary Burns, Mrs Forgay gave you her chemise to wash.

Prisoner. No, she didn't give it to me.

Recorder. But you got it somehow, and you stole the money. Now, you see, our respectable fellow-citizens, the ladies, must have their chemises washed, and, to do so, they must put confidence in their servants; and they have a right to sew their money up in their chemise if they think proper, and servants must not steal it from them. As you're a young woman, and not married, it would not be right to deprive you of the opportunity to get a husband for five years; so we shall only send you to Sing Sing for two years and six months; the keeper will work you in whatever way he may think proper.—Go to the next.

Charles Liston was brought out and arraigned, *pro formâ*. He was a dark negro.

Clerk. Liston, what have you to say why judgment, etcetera?

Prisoner. All I got to say to his honour de honourable court is, dat I see de error of my ways, and I hope dey may soon see de error of deirs. I broke de law of my free country, and I must lose my liberty, and go to Sing Sing. But I trow myself on de mercy of de Recorder; and all I got to say to his honour, de honourable Richard Riker, is, dat I hope he'll live to be de next mayor of New York till I come out of Sing Sing.

Recorder (laughing). A very good speech! But, Liston, whether I'm mayor or not, you must suffer some. This stealing from entries is a most pernicious crime, and one against which our respectable fellow-citizens can scarcely guard. Two-thirds of our citizens hang their hats and coats in entries, and we must protect their hats and coats. We, therefore, sentence you to Sing Sing for five years,—Go to the next.

John Mcdonald and Godfrey Crawluck were put to the bar.

Recorder. Mcdonald and Crawluck, you stole two beeves. Now, however much I like beef, I'd he very hungry before I'd steal any beef. You are on the high road to ruin. You went up the road to Harlem, and down the road to Yorkville, and you'll soon go to destruction. We shall send you to Sing Sing for two years each; and when you come out, take your mother's maiden name, and lead a good life, and don't eat any more beef—I mean, don't steal any more beeves—Go to the next.

Luke Staken was arraigned.

Recorder.—Staken, you slept in a room with Lahay, and stole all his gold (1000 dollars). This sleeping in rooms with other people, and stealing their things, is a serious offence, and practised to a great extent in this city; and what makes the matter worse, you stole one thousand dollars in specie, when specie is so scarce. We send you to Sing Sing for five years.

Jacob Williams was arraigned. He looked as if he had not many days to live, though a young man.

Recorder. Williams, you stole a lot of kerseymere from a store, and ran off with it—a most pernicious crime! But, as your health is not good, we shall only send you to Sing Sing for three years and six months.

John H Murray was arraigned.

Recorder. Murray, you're a deep fellow. You got a Green Mountain boy into an alley, and played at "shuffle and burn," and you burned him out of a hundred dollars. You must go to Sing Sing for five years; and we hope the reputable reporters attending for the respectable public press will warn our respectable country friends, when they come into New York, not to go into Orange street, and play at "shuffle and burn" among bad girls and bad men, or they'll very likely get burnt, like this Green Mountain boy.—Go to the next.

William Shay, charged with shying glasses at the head of a tavern-keeper. Guilty.

Recorder. This rioting is a very bad crime, Shay, and deserves heavy punishment; but as we understand you have a wife and sundry little Shays, we'll let you off, provided you give your solemn promise never to do so any more.

Shay. I gives it—wery solemnly.

Recorder. Then we discharge you.

Shay. Thank your honour—your honour's a capital judge.

John Bowen, charged with stealing a basket. Guilty.

Recorder. Now, John, we've convicted you; and you'll have to get out stone for three months on Blackwell's Island—that's the judgment of the court.

Buckley and Charles Rogers, charged with loafing, sleeping in the park, and leaving the gate open, were discharged, with a caution to take care how they interfered with corporation rights in future, or they would get their corporation into trouble.

Ann Boyle, charged with being too *lively* in the street. Let off on condition of being quiet for the time to come.

Thomas Dixon, charged with petty larceny. Guilty.

Dixon. I wish to have judgment suspended.

Recorder. It's a bad time to talk about suspension; why do you request this?

Dixon. I've an uncle I want to see, and other relations.

Recorder. In that case we'll send you to Black well's island for six months, you'll be sure to find them all there. Sentence accordingly.

Charles Enroff, charged with petty larceny—coming Paddy over an Irish shoemaker, and thereby cheating him out of a pair of shoes.—Guilty.

Sentenced to the penitentiary, Blackwell's island, for six months, to get out stone.

Charles Thorn, charged with assaulting Miss Rachael Prigmore.

Recorder. Miss Prigmore, how came this man to strike you?

Rachael. Because I wouldn't have him. (A laugh.) He was always a teasing me, and spouting poetry about roses and thorns; so when I told him to be off he struck me.

Prisoner (theatrically). Me strike you! Oh, Rachael—

"Perhaps   it   was   right   to   dissemble   your   love,
But why did you kick me down stairs?"

Prisoner's Counsel. That's it, your honour. Why did she kick him down stairs?

This the fair Rachael indignantly denied, and the prisoner was found guilty.

Recorder. This striking of women is a very bad crime, you must get out stone for two months.

Prisoner. She'll repent, your honour. She loves me—I know she does.

"On   the   cold   flinty   rock,   when   I'm   busy   at   work,
Oh, Rachael, I'll think of thee."

Thomas Ward, charged with petty larceny. Guilty. Ward had nothing to offer to *ward* off his sentence, therefore he was sent to the island for six months.

Maria Brandon, charged with petty larceny. Guilty. Sentenced to pick oakum for six months.

Maria. Well, I've friends, that's comfort, they'll sing—

"Oh, come to this bower, my own stricken deer."

Recorder. You're right, Maria, it's an *oakum* bower you're going to.

The court then adjourned. See Note 4.

But all these are nothing compared with the following, which at first I did not credit. I made the strictest inquiry, and was informed by a legal gentleman present that it was correct. I give the extract as it stood in the newspapers.

Influence of a Pretty Girl.—"Catherine Manly," said the Recorder yesterday, in the sessions, "you have been convicted of a very bad crime. This stealing is a very serious offence; but, *as you are a pretty girl*! we'll suspend judgment, in hopes you will do better for the future." We have often heard that justice was blind. What a fib to say so!

Mr Carey, in his publication on Wealth, asserts, that security of property and or person are greater in the United States than in England. How far he is correct I shall now proceed to examine. Mr Carey says, in his observations on security of person:—"Comparing Massachusetts with England and Wales, we find in the former 1 in 86,871 sentenced to one year's imprisonment or more; whereas, in the latter 1 in 70,000 is sentenced to more than one year. The number sentenced to one year or more in England is greater than in Pennsylvania. It is obvious, therefore, that security is much greater in Massachusetts than in England, and consequently greater than in any other part of the world."

Relative to crimes against security of property, he asserts:—

Of crimes against property, involving punishments of one year's imprisonment, or more, we find:—

In Pennsyl vania	1 in 4, 40 0

In New York	1 in 5,900
In Massachusetts	1 in 5,932

While in England, in the year 1834, their convictions for offences against property, involving punishments exceeding one year's imprisonment, was 1 in 3,120.

Now, that these numbers are fairly given, as far as they go, I have no doubt; but the comparison is not just, because, first, in America crime is not so easily detected; and, secondly, when detected, conviction does not always follow.

Mr Carey must be well aware that, in the American newspapers, you *continually* meet with a paragraph like this:—"A body of a white man, or of a negro, was found floating near such and such a wharf, on Saturday last, with evident marks of violence upon it, etcetera. etcetera, and the coroner's inquest is returned either found drowned, or violence by person or persons unknown." Now, let Mr Carey take a list from the coroner's books of the number of bodies found in this manner at New York, and the number of instances in which the perpetrators have been discovered; let him compare this list with a similar one made for England and Wales, and he will then ascertain the difference between the *crimes committed* in proportion to the *convictions* which take place through the activity of the police in our country, and, it may be said, the total want of police in the United States.

As to the second point, namely, that when crimes are detected, conviction does not follow, (see Note 5) I have only to refer back to the cases of Robinson and Goodwin, two instances out of the many in which criminals in the United States are allowed to escape, who, if they had committed the same offence in England, would most certainly have been hanged. But there is another point which renders Mr Carey's statement unfair, which is, that he has no right to select one, two, or even three states out of twenty-six, and compare them all with England and Wales.

The question is, the comparative security of person and property in Great Britain and the United States. I acknowledge that, if Ireland were taken into the account, it would very much reduce our proportional numbers; but, then, there crime is *fomented* by traitors and demagogues—a circumstance which must not be overlooked.

Still, the whole of Ireland would offer nothing equal in atrocity to what I can prove relative to one small town in America: that of Augusta, in Georgia, containing only a population of 3,000, in which, in one year, there were *fifty-nine assassinations* committed in open day, without any notice being taken of them by the authorities.

This, alone, will exceed all Ireland, and I therefore do not hesitate to assert, that if every crime committed in the United States were followed up by conviction, as it would be in Great Britain, the result would fully substantiate the fact, that, in security of person and property, the advantage is considerably in favour of my own country.

Note 1. Miss Martineau, speaking of the jealousy between the Americans and the French creoles, says—"No American expects to get a verdict, on *any evidence*, from a jury of French creoles."

Note 2. America though little more than sixty years old as a nation, has already published an United States Criminal Calendar (Boston, 1835.) I have this book in my possession, and, although in number of criminals it is not quite equal to our Newgate Calendar, it far exceeds it in atrocity of crime.

Note 3. Some allowance must be made for the license of the reporters, but in the main it is a very fair specimen of the recorder's style and language.

Note 4. There is, as will appear by the quotations, as much fun in the police reports in New York as in the best of ours: the *style* of the Recorder is admirably taken off.

Note 5. Miss Martineau, speaking of a trial for murder in the United States, says, "I observed that no one seemed to have a doubt of his guilt." She replied, that there never was a clearer case: but that he would be acquitted; the examination and trial were a mere form, of which everyone knew the conclusion beforehand. The people did not choose to see any more hanging, and till the law was so altered as to allow an alternative of punishment, no conviction for a capital offence would be obtainable. I asked on what pretence the young man would be got off, if the evidence against him was as clear as it was represented. She said some one would be found to swear an *alibi*.

"A tradesman swore an *alibi*; the young man was acquitted, and the next morning he was on his way to the West."

Volume Three—Chapter Ten.

Remarks—Lynch Law.

Englishmen express their surprise that in a moral community such a monstrosity as Lynch law should exist; but although the present system, which has been derived from the original Lynch law, cannot be too severely condemned, it must, in justice to the Americans, be considered that the original custom of Lynch law was forced upon them by circumstances. Why the term of Lynch law has been made use of, I do not know; but in its origin the practice was no more blameable than were the laws established by the Pilgrim fathers on their first landing at Plymouth, or any law enacted amongst a community left to themselves, their own resources, and their own guidance and government. Lynch law, as at first constituted, was nothing more than punishment awarded to offenders by a community who bed been injured, and who had no law to refer to, and could have no redress if they did not take the law into their own hands; the *present*system of Lynch law is, on the contrary, an illegal exercise of the power of the majority in opposition to and defiance of the laws of the country, and the measure of justice administered and awarded by those laws.

It must be remembered that fifty years ago, there were but a few white men to the westward of the Alleghany Mountains; that the states of Kentucky and Tennessee were at that time as scanty in population, as even now are the districts of Ioway and Columbia; that by the institutions of the Union a district required a certain number of inhabitants before it could be acknowledged as even a district; and that previous to such acknowledgment, the people who had*squatted* on the land had no claim to protection or law. It must also be borne in mind, that these distant territories offered an asylum to many who fled from the vengeance of the laws, men without principle, thieves, rogues, and vagabonds, who escaping there, would often interfere with the happiness and peace of some small yet well-conducted community, which had migrated and settled on these fertile regions. These communities had no appeal against personal violence, no protection from rapacity and injustice. They were not yet within the pale of the Union; indeed there are many even now in this precise situation (that of the Mississippi for instance,) who have been necessitated to make laws of government for themselves, and who acting upon their own responsibilities, do very often condemn to death, and execute. (Note 1.) It was, therefore, to remedy the defect of their being no established law, that Lynch law, as it is termed, was applied to; without it, all security, all social happiness would have been in a state of abeyance. By degrees, all disturbers of the public peace, all offenders against justice met with their deserts; and as it is a query, whether on its first institution, any law from the bench was more honestly and impartially administered than this very Lynch law, which has now had its name prostituted by the most barbarous excesses and contemptuous violation of all law whatever. The examples I am able to bring forward of Lynch law, in its primitive state, will be found to have been based upon necessity, and a due regard to morals and to justice. For instance, the harmony of a well-conducted community would be interfered with by some worthless scoundrel, who would entice the young men to gaming, or the young women to deviate from virtue. He becomes a nuisance to the community, and in consequence the heads or elders would meet and vote his expulsion. Their method was very simple and straight-forward; he was informed that his absence would be agreeable, and that if he did not "clear out" before a certain day, he would receive forty lashes with a cow-hide. If the party thought proper to defy this notice, as soon as the day arrived he received the punishment, with a due notification that, if found there again after a certain time, the dose would be repeated. By these means they rid the community of a bad subject, and the morals of the junior branches were not contaminated. Such was in its origin the practice of Lynch law.

A circumstance occurred within these few years in which Lynch law was duly administered. At Dubuque, in the Ioway district, a murder was committed. The people of Dubuque first applied to the authorities of the state of Michigan, but they discovered that the district of Ioway was not within the jurisdiction of that State; and, in fact, although on the opposite side of the river there was law and justice, they had neither to appeal to. They would not allow the murderer to escape; they consequently met, selected among themselves a judge and a jury, tried the man, and, upon their own responsibility, hanged him.

There was another instance which occurred a short time since at Snakes' Hollow, on the western side of the Mississippi, not far from the town of Dubuque. A band of miscreants, with a view of obtaining possession of some valuable diggings (lead mines,) which were in the possession of a grocer who lived in that place, murdered him in the open day. The parties were well known, but they held together and would none of them give evidence. As there were no hopes of their conviction, the people of Snakes' Hollow armed themselves, seized the parties engaged in the transaction, and ordered them to quit the territory on pain of having a rifle-bullet through their heads immediately. The scoundrels crossed the river in a canoe, and were never after heard of.

I have collected these facts to show that Lynch law has been forced upon the American settlers in the western states by *circumstances*; that it has been acted upon in support of morality and virtue, and that its awards have been regulated by strict justice. But I must now notice this practice with a view to show how dangerous it is that any law should be meted out by the majority, and that what was commenced from a sense of justice and necessity, has now changed into a defiance of law, where law and justice can be readily obtained. The Lynch law of the present day, as practised in the states of the west and south, may be divided into two different heads: the first is, the administration of it in cases in which the laws of the states are considered by the majority as not having awarded a punishment adequate, in their opinion, to the offence committed; and the other, when from excitement the majority will not wait for the law to act, but inflict the punishment with their own hands.

The following are instances under the first head.

Every crime increases in magnitude in proportion as it affects the welfare and interest of the community. Forgery and bigamy are certainly crimes, but they are not such heavy crimes as many others to which the same penalty is decreed in this country. But in a commercial nation forgery, from its effects, becomes most injurious, as it destroys confidence and security of property, affecting the whole mass of society. A man may have his pocket *picked* of 1000 pounds or more, but this is not a capital offence, as it is only the individual who suffers; but if a man *forges* a bill for 5 pounds he is (or rather, was) sentenced by our laws to be hanged. Bigamy may be adduced as another instance: the heinousness of the offence is not in having more than one wife, but in the prospect of the children of the first marriage being left to be supported by the community. Formerly, that was also pronounced a capital offence. Of punishments, it will be observed that society has awarded the most severe for crimes committed against itself, rather than against those which most offend God. Upon this principle, in the southern and western states, you may murder *ten* white men and no one will arraign you or trouble himself about the matter; but *steal one nigger*, and the whole community are in arms, and express the most virtuous indignation against the sin of theft, although that of murder will be disregarded.

One or two instances in which Lynch law was called in to *assist* justice on the bench, came to my knowledge. A Yankee had stolen a slave, but as the indictment was not properly worded, he knew that he would be acquitted, and he boasted so, previous to the trial coming on. He was correct in his supposition; the flaw in the indictment was fatal, and he was acquitted. "I told you so," said he, triumphantly smiling as he left the court, to the people who had been the issue of the trial.

"Yes," replied they, "it is true that you have been acquitted by Judge Smith, but you have not yet been tried by *Judge* Lynch." The latter judge was very summary. The Yankee was tied up, and cow-hided till he was nearly dead; they then put him into a *dug-out* and sent him floating down the river. Another instance occurred which is rather amusing, and, at the same time, throws some light upon the peculiar state of society in the west.

There was a bar-keeper at some tavern in the state of Louisiana (if I recollect right) who was a great favourite; whether from his judicious mixture of the proportions of mint juleps and gin cocktails, or from other causes, I do not know; but what may appear strange to the English, he was elected to an office in the law courts of the state, similar to our *Attorney-General*, and I believe was very successful, for an American can turn his hand or his head to almost anything. It so happened that a young man who was in prison for stealing a negro, applied to this attorney-general to defend him in the court. This he did so successfully that the man was acquitted; but Judge Lynch was as usual waiting outside, and when the attorney came out with his client, the latter was demanded to be given up. This the attorney refused, saying that the man was under his protection. A tumult ensued, but the attorney was firm; he drew his Bowie-knife, and addressing the crowd, said, "My men, you all know me: no one takes this man, unless he passes over my body." The populace were still dissatisfied, and the attorney not wishing to lose his popularity, and at the same time wanting to defend a man who had paid him well, requested the people to be quiet a moment until he could arrange the affair. He took his client aside, and said to him, "These men will have you, and will Lynch you, in spite of all my efforts, only one chance remains for you, and you must accept it: you know that it is but a mile to the confines of the next state, which if you gain you will be secure. You have been in prison for two months, you have lived on bread and water, and you must be in good wind, moreover, you are young and active. These men who wish to get hold of you are half drunk, and they never can run as you can. Now, I'll propose that you have one hundred and fifty yards law, and then if you exert yourself, you can easily escape." The man consented, as he could not help himself: the populace also consented, as the attorney pointed out to them that any other arrangement would be injurious to his honour. The man, however, did not succeed; he was so frightened that he could not run, and in a short time he was taken, and had the usual allowance of cow-hide awarded by Judge Lynch. Fortunately he regained his prison before he was quite exhausted, and was sent away during the night in a steamer.

At Natchez, a young man married a young lady of fortune, and, in his passion, actually flogged her to death. He was tried, but as there were no witnesses but negroes, and their evidence was not admissible against a white man, he was acquitted: but he did not escape; he was seized, tarred and feathered, *scalped*, and turned adrift in a canoe without paddles.

Such are the instances of Lynch law being superadded, when it has been considered by the majority that the law has not been sufficiently severe. The other variety of Lynch law is, when they will not wait for law, but, in a state of excitement, proceed to summary punishment.

The case more than once referred to by Miss Martineau, of the burning alive of a coloured man at St. Louis, is one of the gravest under this head. I do not wish to defend it in any way, but I do, for the honour of humanity, wish to offer all that can be said in extenuation of this atrocity: and I think Miss Martineau, when she held up to public indignation the monstrous punishment, was bound to acquaint the public with the cause of an excitable people being led into such an error. This unfortunate victim of popular fury was a free coloured man, of a very quarrelsome and malignant disposition; he had already been engaged in a variety of disputes, and was a nuisance in the city. For an attempt to murder another coloured man, he was seized, and was being conducted to prison in the custody of Mr Hammond, the Sheriff, and another white person who assisted him in the execution of his duty. As he arrived at the door of the prison, he watched his opportunity, stabbed the person who was assisting the Sheriff, and, then passing his knife across the throat of Mr Hammond, the carotid artery was divided, and the latter fell dead upon the spot. Now, here was a wretch who, in one day, had three times attempted murder, and had been successful in the instance of Mr Hammond, the sheriff, a person universally esteemed. Moreover, when it is considered that the culprit was of a race who are looked upon as inferior; that this successful attempt on the part of a black man was considered most dangerous as a precedent to the negro population; that, owing to the unwillingness to take away life in America, he might probably have escaped justice; and that this occurred just at the moment when the abolitionists were creating such mischief and irritation: — although it must be lamented that they should have so disgraced themselves, the summary and cruel punishment which was awarded by an incensed populace is not very surprising. Miss Martineau has, however, thought proper to pass over the peculiar atrocity of the individual who was thus sacrificed: to read her account of the transaction, it would appear as if he were an unoffending party, sacrificed on account of his *colour* alone.

Another remarkable instance was the execution of five gamblers at the town of Vicksburgh, on the Mississippi. It may appear strange that people should be lynched for the mere vice of gambling: but this will be better understood when, in my second portion of this work, I enter into a general view of society in the United States. At present it will be sufficient to say, that as towns rise in the South and West, they gradually become peopled with a better class; and that, as soon as this better class is sufficiently strong to accomplish their ends, a purification takes place much to the advantage of society. I hardly need observe; that these better classes come from the Eastward. New Orleans, Natchez, and Vicksburgh are evidences of the truth of observations I have made. In the present instance, it was resolved by the people of Vicksburgh that they would no longer permit their city to be the resort of a set of unprincipled characters, and that all gamblers by profession should be compelled to quit it. But, as I have the American account of what occurred, I think it will be better to give it in detail, the rather as I was informed by a gentleman residing there that it is perfectly correct:—

Our city has for some days past been the theatre of the most novel and startling scenes that we have ever witnessed. While we regret that the necessary for such scenes should have existed, we are proud of the public spirit and indignation against offenders displayed by the citizens, and congratulate them on having at length banished a class of individuals, whose shameless vices and daring outrages have long poisoned the springs of morality, and interrupted the relations of society. For years past, professional gamblers, destitute of all sense of moral obligation—unconnected with society by any of its ordinary ties, and intent only on the gratification of their avarice —have made Vicksburgh their place of rendezvous—and, in the very bosom of our society, boldly plotted their vile and lawless machinations. Here, as everywhere else, the laws of the country were found wholly ineffectual for the punishment of these individuals; and, emboldened by impunity, their numbers and their crimes have daily continued to multiply. Every species of transgression followed in their train. They supported a large number of tippling-houses, to which they would decoy the youthful and unsuspecting, and, after stripping them of their possessions, send them forth into the world the ready and desperate instrument of vice. Our streets were ever resounding with the echoes of their drunken and obscene mirth, and no citizen was secure from their villainy. Frequently, in armed bodies, they have disturbed the good order of public assemblages, insulted our citizens, and defied our civil authorities. Thus had they continued to grow bolder in their wickedness, and more formidable in their numbers, until Saturday, the 4th of July (inst), when our citizens had assembled together, with the corps of Vicksburg volunteers, at a barbecue, to celebrate the day by the usual festivities. After dinner, and during the delivery of the toasts, one of the officers attempted to enforce order and silence at the table, when one of these gamblers, whose name is Cabler, who had impudently thrust himself into the company, insulted the officer, and struck one of the citizens. Indignation immediately rose high, and it was only by the interference of the commandant that he was saved from instant punishment. He was, however, permitted to retire, and the company dispersed. The military corps proceeded to the public square of the city, and were there engaged in their exercises, when information was received that Cabler was coming up, armed, and resolved to kill one of the volunteers, who had been most active in expelling him from the table. Knowing his desperate character, two of the corps instantly stepped forward and arrested him. A loaded pistol and a large knife and dagger were found upon his person, all of which he had procured since he separated from the company. To liberate him would have been to devote several of the most respectable members of the company to his vengeance, and to proceed against him at law, would have been mere mockery, inasmuch as, not having had the opportunity of consummating his design, no adequate punishment could be inflicted on him. Consequently, it was determined to take him into the woods and *Lynch* him, which is a mode of punishment provided for such as become obnoxious in a manner which the law cannot reach. He was immediately carried out under a guard, attended by a crowd of respectable citizens, tied to a tree, punished with stripes, tarred and feathered, and ordered to leave the city in forty-eight hours. In the meantime, one of his comrades, the Lucifer of his gang, had been endeavouring to rally and arm his confederates for the purpose of rescuing him—which, however, he failed to accomplish.

"Having thus aggravated the whole band of these desperadoes, and feeling no security against their vengeance, the citizens met at night in the Court-house, in a large number, and there passed the following resolutions:—

"*Resolved*, That a notice be given to all professional gamblers, that the citizens of Vicksburg are *resolved* to exclude them from this place and its vicinity; and that twenty-four hours' notice be given them to leave the place.

"*Resolved*, That all persons permitting faro-dealing in their houses, he also notified that they will be prosecuted therefore.

"*Resolved*, That one hundred copies of the foregoing resolutions be printed and stuck up at the corners of the streets—and that this publication be deemed a notice.

"On Sunday morning, one of these notices was posted at the corners of each square of the city. During that day (the 5th) a majority of the gang, terrified by the threats of the citizens, dispersed in different directions, without making any opposition. It was sincerely hoped that the remainder would follow their example and thus prevent a bloody termination of the strife which had commenced. On the morning of the 6th, the military corps, followed by a file of several hundred citizens, marched to each suspected house, and sending in an examining committee, dragged out every faro-table and other gambling apparatus that could be found. At length they approached a house which occupied by one of the most profligate of the gang, whose name was North, and in which it was understood that a garrison of armed men had been stationed. All hoped that these wretches would be intimidated by the superior numbers of their assailants, and surrender themselves at discretion rather than attempt a desperate defence. The house being surrounded, the back door was burst open, when four or five shots were fired from the interior, one of which instantly killed Dr Hugh S Bodley, a citizen universally beloved and respected. The interior was so dark that the villains could not be seen; but several of the citizens, guided by the flash of their guns, returned their fire. A yell from one of the party announced that one of the shots had been effectual, and by this time a crowd of citizens, their indignation overcoming all other feelings, burst open every door of the building, and dragged into the light those who had not been wounded.

"North the ringleader, who had contrived this desperate plot, could not be found in the building, but was apprehended by a citizen, while attempting, in company with another, to make his escape at a place not fir distant. Himself, with the rest of the prisoners, was then conducted *in silence* to the scaffold. One of them, not having been in the building before it was attacked, nor appearing to be concerned with the rest, except that he was the brother of one of them, was liberated. The remaining number of five, among whom was the individual who had been shut, but who still lived, were *immediately executed* in presence of the assembled multitude. All sympathy for the wretches was completely merged in detestation and horror of their crime. The whole procession then returned to the city, collected all the faro-tables into a pile, and burnt them. This being done, a troop of horsemen set out for a neighbouring house; the residence of J Hord the individual who had attempted to organise a force on the first day of the disturbance for the rescue of Cabler, who had since been threatening to fire the city. He had, however, made his escape on that day, and the next morning crossed the Big Black at Baldwin's Ferry, in a state of indescribable consternation. We lament his escape, as his whole course of life for the last three years has exhibited the most shameless profligacy, and been a series of continual transgressions against the laws of God and man.

"The names of the individuals who perished were as follow:— North, Hullams, Dutch Bill, Smith, and Mccall.

"Their bodies were cut down on the morning after the execution, and buried in a ditch.

"It is not expected that this act will pass without censure from those who had not an opportunity of knowing and feeling the dire necessity out of which it originated. The laws, however severe in their provision, have never been sufficient to correct a vice which must be established by positive proof, and cannot, like others, be shown from circumstantial testimony. It is practised, too, by individuals whose whole study is to violate the law in such a manner as to evade its punishment, and who never are in want of secret confederates to swear them out of their difficulties, whose oaths cannot be impeached for any specific cause. We had borne with their enormities until to suffer them any longer would not only have proved us to be destitute of every manly sentiment, but would also have implicated us in the guilt of necessaries to their crimes. Society may be compared to the elements, which, although 'order is their first law,' can sometimes be purified only by a storm. Whatever, therefore, sickly sensibility or mawkish philanthropy may say against the course pursued by us, we hope that our citizens will not relax the code of punishment which they have enacted against this infamous and baleful class of society; and we invite Natchez, Jackson, Columbus, Warrenton, and all our sister towns throughout the State, in the name of our insulted laws, of offended virtue, and of slaughtered innocence, to aid us in exterminating this deep-rooted vice from our land. The revolution has been conducted here by the most respectable citizens, heads of families, members of all classes, professions, and pursuits. None have been heard to utter a syllable of censure against either the act or the manner in which it was performed.

"An Anti-Gambling Society has been formed, the members of which have pledged their lives, fortunes, and sacred honours for the suppression of gambling, and the punishment and expulsion of gamblers.

"Startling as the above may seem to foreigners, it will ever reflect honour on the insulted citizens of Vicksburg, among those who best know how to appreciate the motives by which they were actuated. Their city now stands redeemed and ventilated from all the vices and influence of gambling and assignation houses; two of the greatest curses that ever corrupted the morals of any community."

That the society in the towns on the banks of the Mississippi can only, like the atmosphere, "be purified by storm," is, I am afraid, but too true.

I have now entered fully, and I trust impartially, into the rise and progress of Lynch Law, and I must leave my readers to form their own conclusions. That it has occasionally been beneficial, in the peculiar state of the communities in which it has been practised, must be admitted; but it is equally certain that it is in itself indefensible, and that but too often, not only the punishment is much too severe for the offence, but what is still more to be deprecated, the innocent do occasionally suffer with the guilty.

"A similar case is to be found at the present day, west of the Mississippi. Upon lands belonging to the United States, not yet surveyed or offered for sale, are numerous bodies of people who have occupied them, with the intention of purchasing them when they shall be brought into the market. These persons are mailed *squatters*, and it is not to be supposed that they consist of the *élite* of the emigrants to the West; yet we are informed that they have organised a government for themselves, and regularly elect magistrates to attend to the execution of the laws. They appears in this respect, to be worthy descendants of the pilgrims."—*Carey on Wealth*.

Volume Three—Chapter Eleven.

Remarks—Climate.

I wish the remarks in this chapter to receive peculiar attention, as in commenting upon the character of the Americans, it is but justice to them to point out that many of what may be considered their errors, arise from *circumstances* over which they have no control; and one which has no small weight in this scale is the peculiar climate of the country; for various as is the climate, in such an extensive region, certain it is, that in one point, that of *excitement*, it has, in every portion of it, a very pernicious effect.

When I first arrived at New York, the effect of the climate upon me was immediate. On the 5th of May, the heat and closeness were oppressive. There was a sultriness in the air, even at that early period of the year, which to me seemed equal to that of Madras. Almost every day there were, instead of our mild refreshing showers, sharp storms of thunder and lightning; but the air did not appear to me to be cooled by them. And yet, strange to say, there were no incipient signs of vegetation: the trees waved their bare arms, and while I was throwing off every garment which I well could, the females were walking up and down Broadway wrapped up in warm shawls. It appeared as if it required twice the heat we have in our own country, either to create a free circulation in the blood of the people, or to stimulate nature to rouse after the torpor of a protracted and severe winter. In a week from the period I have mentioned, the trees were in full foliage, the *belles* of Broadway walking about in summer dresses and thin satin shoes; the men calling for ice, and rejoicing in the beauty of the weather, the heat of which to me was most oppressive. In one respect there appears to be very little difference throughout all the States of the Union; which is, in the extreme heat of the summer months, and the rapid changes of temperature which take place in the twenty-four hours. When I was on Lake Superior the thermometer stood between 90 degrees and 100 degrees during the day, and at night was nearly down to the freezing point. When at St. Peter's, which is nearly as far north, and farther west, the thermometer stood generally at 100 degrees to 106 degrees during the day, and I found it to be the case in all the northern States when the winter is most severe, as well as in the more southern. When on the Mississippi and Ohio rivers, where the heat was most insufferable during the day, our navigation was almost every night suspended by the thick dank fogs, which covered not only the waters but the inland country, and which must be anything but healthy. In fact, in every portion of the States which I visited, and in those portions also which I did not visit, the extreme heat and rapid changes in the weather were (according to the information received front other persons) the same.

But I must proceed to particulars. I consider the climate on the sea coasts of the eastern States, from Maine to Baltimore, as the most unhealthy of all parts of America; as, added to the sudden changes, they have cold and damp easterly winds, which occasion a great deal of consumption. The inhabitants, more especially the women, shew this in their appearance, and it is by the inhabitants that the climate must be tested. The women are very delicate, and very pretty; but they remind you of roses which have budded fairly, but which a check in the season has not permitted to blow. Up to sixteen or seventeen, they promise perfection; at that age their advance appears to be checked. Mr Sanderson, in a very clever and amusing work, which I recommend to every one, called "Sketches of Paris," says: "Our climate is noted for three eminent qualities—extreme heat and cold, and extreme suddenness of change. If a lady has bad teeth, or a bad complexion, she lays them conveniently to the climate; if her beauty, like a tender flower, fades before noon, it is the climate; if she has a bad temper, or a snub nose; still it is the climate. But our climate is active and intellectual, especially in winter, and in all seasons more pure and transparent than the inking skies of Europe. It sustains the infancy of beauty— why not its maturity? It spares the bud—why not the opened blossom, or the ripened fruit? Our negroes are perfect in their teeth—why not the whites? The chief preservation of beauty in any country is health, and there is no place in which this great interest is so little attended to as in America. To be sensible of this, you must visit Europe—you must see the deep bosomed maids of England upon the Place Vendome and the Rue Castiglione."

I have quoted this passage, because I think Mr Sanderson is not just in these slurs upon his fair countrywomen. I acknowledge that a bad temper does not directly proceed from climate, although sickness and suffering, occasioned by climate, may directly produce it. As for the snub nose, I agree with him, that climate has not so much to do with that. Mr Sanderson is right in saying, that the chief preservative of beauty is health; but may I ask him, upon what does health depend but upon *exercise*? and if so, how many days are there in the American summer in which the heat will admit of exercise, or in the American winter in which it is possible for women to *walk* out? for carriage driving is not exercise, and if it were, from the changes in the weather in America, it will always be dangerous. The fact is, that the climate will not admit of the exercise necessary for health, unless by running great risks, and very often contracting cold and chills, which end in consumption and death. To accuse his countrywomen of natural indolence, is unfair; it is an indolence forced upon them. As for the complexions of the females, I consider they are much injured by the universal use of close stoves, so necessary in the extremity of the winters. Mr S's implication, that because negroes have perfect teeth, therefore so should the whites, is another error. The negroes were born for, and in, a torrid clime, and there is some difference between their strong ivory masticators and the transparent pearly teeth which so rapidly decay in the eastern states, from no other cause than the variability of the climate. Besides, do the teeth of the women in the western states decay so fast? Take a healthy situation, with an intermediate climate, such as Cincinnati, and you will there find not only good teeth, but as deep-bosomed maids as you will in England; so you will in Virginia, Kentucky, Missouri, and Wisconsin, which, with a portion of Ohio, are the most healthy states in the Union. There is another proof, and a positive one, that the women are affected by the *climate* and not through any fault of their own, which is, that if you transplant a delicate American girl to England, she will in a year or two become so robust and healthy as not to be recognised upon her return home; showing that the even temperature of our damp climate is from the capability of constant exercise, more conducive to health, than the sunny, yet variable atmosphere of America.

The Americans are fond of their climate, and consider it, as they do every thing in America, as the very best in the world. They are, as I have said before, most happy in their delusions. But if the climate be not a healthy one, it is certainly a beautiful climate to the eye; the sky is so clear, the air so dry, the tints of the foliage so inexpressibly beautiful in the autumn and early winter months: and at night, the stars are so brilliant, hundreds being visible with the naked eye which are not to be seen by us, that I am not surprised at the Americans praising the *beauty* of their climate. The sun is terrific in his heat, it is true, but still one cannot help feeling the want of it, when in England, he will disdain to shine for weeks. Since my return to this country, the English reader can hardly form an idea of how much I have longed for the sun. After having sojourned for nearly two years in America, the sight of it has to me almost amounted to a necessity, and I am not therefore at all astonished at an American finding fault with the climate of England; nevertheless, our climate, although unprepossessing to the eye, and depressive to the animal spirits, is much more healthy than the exciting and changeable atmosphere, although beautiful in appearance, which they breathe in the United States.

One of the first points to which I directed my attention on my arrival in America, was to the diseases most prevalent. In the eastern States, as may be supposed, they have a great deal of consumption; in the western, the complaint is hardly known: but the general nature of the American diseases are *neuralgic*, or those which affect the nerves, and which are common to almost all the Union. Ophthalmia, particularly the disease of the ophthalmic nerve, is very common in the eastern States. The medical men told me that there were annually more diseases of the eye in New York city alone, than perhaps all over Europe. How far this may be correct I cannot say; but this I can assert, that I never had any complaint in my eyes until I arrived in America, and during a stay of eighteen months, I was three times very severely afflicted. The oculist who attended me asserted that he had *seven hundred* patients.

The *tic douloureux* is another common complaint throughout America,—indeed so common is it, that I should say that one out of ten suffers from it, more or less; the majority, however, are women.

I saw more cases of *delirium tremens* in America, than I ever *heard* of before. In fact, the climate is one of *extreme excitement*. I had not been a week in the country before I discovered how impossible it was for a foreigner to drink as much wine or spirits as he could in England, and I believe that thousands of emigrants have been carried off by making no alteration in their habits upon their arrival. See Note 1.

The winters in Wisconsin, Ioway, Missouri, and Upper Canada, are dry and healthy, enabling the inhabitants to take any quantity of exercise, and I found that the people looked forward to their winters with pleasure, longing for the heat of the summer to abate.

Michigan, Indiana, Illinois, and a portion of Ohio, are very unhealthy in the autumns from the want of drainage; the bilious congestive fever, ague, and dysentery, carrying off large numbers, Virginia, Kentucky, North Carolina, and the eastern portions of Tennessee, are comparatively healthy. South Carolina, and all the other southern States, are, as it is well known, visited by the yellow fever, and the people migrate every fall to the northward, not only to avoid the contagion, but to renovate their general health, which suffers from the continual demand upon their energies, the western and southern country being even more exciting than the east. There is a fiery disposition in the Southerners which is very remarkable; they are much more easily excited than even the Spaniard or Italian, and their feelings are more violent and unrestrainable, as I shall hereafter show. That this is the effect of climate I shall now attempt to prove by one or two circumstances, out of the many which fell under my observation. It is impossible to imagine a greater difference in character than exists between the hot-blooded Southerner, and the cold calculating Yankee of the eastern States. I have already said that there is a continual stream of emigration from the eastern States to the southward and westward the farmers of the eastern States leaving their comparatively barren lands to settle down upon the more grateful soils of the interior. Now, it is a singular, yet a well known fact, that in a very few years the character of the Eastern farmer is completely changed. He arrives there a hard-working, careful, and sober man; for the first two or three years his ground is well tilled, and his crops are abundant; but by degrees he becomes a different character: he neglects his farm, so that from rich soil he obtains no better crops than he formerly did upon his poor land in Massachusetts; he becomes indolent, reckless, and often intemperate. Before he has settled five years in the Western country, the climate has changed him into a Western man, with all the peculiar virtues and vices of the country.

A Boston friend of mine told me that he was once on board of a steamboat on the Mississippi, and found that an old schoolfellow was first mate of the vessel. They ran upon a snag, and were obliged to lay the vessel on shore until they could put the cargo on board of another steamboat, and repair the damage. The passengers, as usual on such occasions, instead of grumbling at what could not be helped, as people do in England, made themselves merry; and because they could not proceed on their voyage they very wisely resolved to drink champagne. They did so: a further supply being required, this first mate was sent down into the hold to procure it. My Boston friend happened to be at the hatchway when he went down with a flaring candle in his hand, and he observed the mate creep over several small barrels until he found the champagne cases, and ordered them up.

"What is in those barrels?" inquired he of the mate when he came up again.

"Oh, *gunpowder*!" replied the mate.

"Good Heavens!" exclaimed the Bostonian, "is it possible that you could be so careless? why I should have thought better of you; you used to be a prudent man."

"Yes, and so I was, until I came into this part of the country," replied the mate, "but somehow or another, I don't care for things now, which, when I was in my own State, would have frightened me out of my wits." Here was a good proof of the Southern recklessness having been imbibed by a cautious Yankee.

I have adduced the above instances, because I consider that the excitement so general throughout the Union, and forming so remarkable a feature in the American character, is occasioned much more by climate than by any other cause: that the peculiarity of their institutions affords constant aliment for this excitement to feed upon is true, and it is therefore seldom allowed to repose. I think, moreover, that their climate is the occasion of two bad habits to which the Americans are prone, namely, the use of tobacco and of spirituous liquors. An Englishman could not drink as the Americans do; it would destroy him here in a very short time, by the irritation it would produce upon his nerves. But the effect of tobacco is narcotic and anti-nervous; it allays that irritation, and enables the American to indulge in stimulating habits without their being attended with such immediate ill consequences.

To the rapid changes of the climate, and to the extreme heat, must be also to a great degree ascribed the excessive use of spirituous liquors; the system being depressed by the sudden changes demanding stimulus to equalise the pulse. The extraordinary heat during the summer is also another cause of it. The Rev. Mr Reid says, in his Tour through the States, "the disposition to drink now became intense; we had only to consider how we might safely gratify it; the thermometer rose to low, and the heat and perspiration were intolerable." Now, if a Christian divine acknowledged this feeling, it is not to be supposed but that others must be equally affected. To drink pure water during this extreme heat is very dangerous: it must be qualified with some wine or spirit; and thus is an American led into a habit of drinking, from which it is not very easy, indeed hardly possible, for him to abstain, except during the winter, and the winters in America are too cold for a man to leave off *any* of his *habits*. Let it not be supposed that I wish to excuse intemperance: far from it; but I wish to be just in my remarks upon the Americans, and show, that if they are intemperate (which they certainly are), there is more excuse for them than there is for other nations, from their temptation arising out of circumstances.

There is but one other point to be considered in examining into the climate of America. It will be admitted that the American stock is the very best in the world, being originally English, with a favourable admixture of German, Irish, French, and other northern countries. It moreover has the great advantage of a continual importation of the same varieties of stock to cross and improve the breed. The question then is, have the American race improved or degenerated since the first settlement? If they have degenerated, the climate cannot be healthy.

I was very particular in examining into this point, and I have no hesitation in saying, that the American people are not equal in strength or in form to the English. I may displease the Americans by this assertion, and they may bring forward their backwoodsmen and their Kentuckians, who live at the spurs of the Alleghany Mountains, as evidence to the contrary; but although they are powerful and tall men they are not well made, nor so well made as the Virginians, who are the finest race in the Union. There is one peculiar defect in the American figure common to both sexes, which is, *narrowness of the shoulders*, and it is a very great defect; there seems to be a check to the expansion of the chest in their climate, the physiological causes of which I leave to others. On the whole, they certainly are a taller race than the natives of Europe, but not with proportionate muscular strength. Their climate, therefore, I unhesitatingly pronounce to be bad, being injurious to them in the two important points, of healthy vigour in the body, and healthy action of the mind; enervating the one, and tending to demoralise the other.

Note 1. Vermont, New Hampshire, the interior portion of the State of New York, and all the portions of the other States which abut on the great lakes, are healthy, owing to the dryness of the atmosphere being softened down by the proximity of such large bodies of water.

Volume Three—Chapter Twelve.

Remarks—Education.

Mr Carey, in his statistical work, falls into the great error of most American writers—that of lauding his own country and countrymen, and inducing them to believe that they are superior to all nations under heaven. This is very injudicious, and highly injurious to the national character: it upholds that self-conceit to which the Americans are already so prone, and checks that improvement so necessary to place them on a level with the English nation. The Americans have gained more by their faults having been pointed out by travellers than they will choose to allow; and, from his moral courage in fearlessly pointing out the truth, the best friend to America, among their own countrymen, has been Dr Charming. I certainly was under the impression, previous to my visit to the United States, that education was much more universal there than in England; but every step I took, and every mile I travelled, lowered my estimate on that point. To substantiate my opinion by statistical tables would be difficult; as, after much diligent search, I find that I can only obtain a correct return of a portion of our own establishments; but, even were I able to obtain a general return, it would not avail me much, as Mr Carey has no general return to oppose to it. He gives us, as useful, Massachusetts and one or two other States, but no more; and, as I have before observed, Massachusetts is not America. His remarks and quotations from English authors are not fair; they are loose and partial observations, made by those who have a case to substantiate. Not that I blame Mr Carey for making use of those authorities, such as they are; but I wish to show that they have misled him.

I must first observe that Mr Carey's estimate of education in England is much lower than it ought to be; and I may afterwards prove that his estimate of education in the United States is equally erroneous on the other side.

To estimate the amount of education in England by the number of *national schools* must ever be wrong. In America, by so doing, a fair approximation may be arrived at, as the education of all classes is chiefly confined to them; but in England the case is different; not only the rich and those in the middling classes of life, but a large proportion of the poor, sending their children to private schools. Could I have obtained a return of the private seminaries in the United Kingdom, it would have astonished Mr Carey. The small parish of Kensington and its vicinity has only two national schools, but it contains 292 (I believe this estimate is below the mark) private establishments for education; and I might produce fifty others, in which the proportion would be almost as remarkable. I have said that a large portion of the poorer classes in England send their children to private teachers. This arises from a feeling of pride; they prefer paying for the tuition of their children rather than having their children educated by the *parish*, as they term the national schools. The consequence is, that in every town, or village, or hamlet, you will find that there are "dame schools," as they are termed, at which about one half of the children are educated.

The subject of national education has not been warmly taken up in England until within these last twenty-five years, and has made great progress during that period. The Church of England Society for National Education was established in 1813. Two years after its formation there were only 230 schools, containing 40,484 children. By the Twenty-seventh Report of this Society, ending the year 1838, these schools had increased to 17,341, and the number of scholars to 1,003,087. But this, it must be recollected, is but a small proportion of the public education in England; the Dissenters having been equally diligent, and their schools being quite as numerous in proportion to their numbers. We have, moreover, the workhouse schools, and the dame schools before mentioned, for the poorer classes; and for the rich and middling classes, establishments for private tuition, which, could the returns of them and of the scholars be made, would, I am convinced, amount to more than five times the number of the national and public establishments. But as Mr Carey does not bring forward his statistical proof; and I cannot produce mine, all that I can do is to venture my opinion from what I learnt and saw during my sojourn in the United States, or have obtained from American and other authorities.

The State of Massachusetts is a *school*; it may be said that all there are educated, Mr Reid states in his work:—

"It was lately ascertained by returns from 131 towns in Massachusetts, that the number of scholars was 12,393; that the number of persons in the towns between the ages of fourteen and twenty-one who are unable to write was fifty-eight; and in one town there were only three persons who could not read or write, and those three were dumb."

I readily assent to this, and I consider Connecticut equal to Massachusetts; but as you leave these two states, you find that education gradually diminishes. (See Note 1.) New York is the next in rank, and thus the scale descends until you arrive at absolute ignorance.

I will now give what I consider as a fair and impartial tabular analysis of the degrees of education in the different states in the Union. It may be cavilled at, but it will nevertheless be a fair approximation. It must be remembered that it is not intended to imply that there are not a certain portion of well-educated people in those states put down in class 4, as ignorant states, but they are included in the Northern states, where they principally receive their education.

Degrees of Education in the different States in the Union.

1st Class.	Population.
Massachusetts	700,000
Connecticut	298,000
	998,000
2nd Class.	
New York	2,400,00

	0
Maine	555,000
New Hampshire	300,000
Vermont	330,000
Rhode Island	110,000
New Jersey	360,000
Ohio	1,300,000
	5,355,000
3rd Class	
Virginia	1,360,000

North Carolina	800,000
South Carolina	650,000
Pennsylvania (note)	1,600,000
Maryland	500,000
Delaware	80,000
Columbia (district)	50,000
Kentucky	800,000
	5,840,000
4th Class	
Tennessee	900,000
Georgia	620,

	000
Indians	650,000
Illinois	320,000
Alabama	600,000
Louisiana	350,000
Missouri	350,000
Mississippi	150,000
Michigan	120,000
Arkansas	70,000
Wisconsin	20,000
Florida (territory)	50,000

	5,000,000

If I am correct, it appears then that we have:—

Highly educated	998,000
Equal with Scotland	5,355,000
Not equal with England	5,840,000
Uneducated	6,000,000

This census is an estimate of 1836, sufficiently near for the purpose. It is supposed that the population of the united States has since increased about two millions, and of that increase the great majority is in the Western states, where the people are wholly uneducated. Taking, therefore, the first three classes, in which there is education in various degrees, we find that they amount to 12,193,000; against which we may fairly put the 5,000,000 uneducated, adding to it, the 2,000,000 increased population, and 3,000,000 of slaves.

I believe the above to be a fair estimate, although nothing positive can be collected from it. In making a comparison of the degree of education in the United States and in England, one point should not be overlooked. In England, children may be sent to school, but they are taken away as soon as they are useful, and have little time to follow up their education afterwards. Worked like machines, every hour is devoted to labour, and a large portion forget, from disuse, what they have learnt when young. In America, they have the advantage not only of being educated, but of having plenty of time, if they choose, to profit by their education in after life. The mass in America ought, therefore, to be better educated than the mass in England, where *circumstances* are against it. I must now examine the nature of education given in the United States.

It is admitted as an axiom in the United States, that the only chance they have of upholding their present institutions is by the education of the mass; that is to say, a people who would govern themselves must be enlightened. Convinced of this necessity, every pains has been taken by the Federal and State governments to provide the necessary means of *education* (See Note 4.) This is granted; but we now have to inquire into the nature of the education, and the advantages derived from such education as is received in the United States.

In the first place, what is education? Is teaching a boy to read and write education? If so, a large proportion of the American community may be said to be educated; but, if you supply a man with a chest of tools, does he therefore become a carpenter! You certainly give him the means of working at the trade, but instead of learning it, he may only cut his fingers. Reading and writing without the farther assistance necessary to guide people aright, is nothing more than a chest of tools.

Then, what is education? I consider that education commences before a child can walk: the first principle of education, the most important, and without which all subsequent are but as leather and prunella, is the lesson of *obedience* —of submitting to parental control—"*Honour thy father and thy mother*!"

Now, any one who has been in the United States must have perceived that there is little or no parental control. This has been remarked by most of the writers who have visited the country; indeed to an Englishman it is a most remarkable feature. How is it possible for a child to be brought up in the way that it should go, when he is not obedient to the will of his parents? I have often fallen into a melancholy sort of musing after witnessing such remarkable specimens of uncontrolled will in children; and as the father and mother both smiled at it, I have thought that they little knew what sorrow and vexation were probably in store for them, in consequence of their own injudicious treatment of their offspring. Imagine a child of three years old in England behaving thus:—

"Johnny, my dear, come here," says his mamma.

"I won't," cries Johnny.

"You must, my love, you are all wet, and you'll catch cold."

"I won't," replies Johnny.

"Come, my sweet, and I've something for you."

"I won't."

"Oh! Mr —, do, pray make Johnny come in."

"Come in, Johnny," says the father.

"I won't."

"I tell you, come in directly, sir—do you hear?"

"I won't," replies the urchin taking to his heels.

"A sturdy republican, sir," says his father to me, smiling at the boy's resolute disobedience.

Be it recollected that I give this as one instance of a thousand which I witnessed during my sojourn in the country.

It may be inquired, how is it that such is the case at present, when the obedience to parents was so rigorously inculcated by the puritan fathers, that by the blue laws, the punishment of disobedience was *death*? Captain Hall ascribes it to the democracy, and the rights of equality therein acknowledged; but I think, allowing the spirit of their institutions to have some effect in producing this evil, that the principal cause of it is the total neglect of the children by the father, and his absence in his professional pursuits, and the natural weakness of most mothers, when their children are left altogether to their care and guidance.

Mr Sanderson, in his Sketches of Paris, observes:— "The motherly virtues of our women, so eulogised by foreigners, is not entitled to unqualified praise. There is no country in which maternal care is so assiduous; but also there is none in which examples of injudicious tenderness are so frequent." This I believe to be true; not that the American women are really more injudicious than those of England, but because they are not supported as they should be by the authority of the father, of whom the child should always entertain a certain portion of fear mixed with affection, to counterbalance the indulgence accorded by natural yearnings of a mother's heart.

The self-will arising from this fundamental error manifests itself throughout the whole career of the American's existence, and, consequently, it is a self-willed nation *par excellence*.

At the age of six or seven you will hear both boys and girls contradicting their fathers and mothers, and advancing their own opinions with a firmness which is very striking.

At fourteen or fifteen the boys will seldom remain longer at school. At college, it is the same thing; (note 6) and they learn precisely what they please, and no more. Corporal punishment is not permitted; indeed, if we are to judge from an extract I took from an American paper, the case is reversed.

The following "Rules" are posted up in New Jersey school-house:—

"No kissing girls in school-time; no *licking* the *master* during holy days."

At fifteen or sixteen, if not at college, the boy assumes the man; he enters into business, as a clerk to some merchant, or in some store. His father's home is abandoned, except when it may suit his convenience, his salary being sufficient for most of his wants. He frequents the bar, calls for gin cocktails, chews tobacco, and talks politics. His theoretical education, whether he has profited much by it or not, is now superseded by a more practical one, in which he obtains a most rapid proficiency. I have no hesitation in asserting that there is more practical knowledge among the Americans than among any other people under the sun. (note 7).

It is singular that in America, everything, whether it be of good of evil, appears to assist the country in *going a-head*. This very want of parental control, however it may affect the morals of the community, is certainly advantageous to America, as far as her rapid advancement is concerned. Boys are working like men for years before they would be in England; time is money, and they assist to bring in the harvest.

But does this independence on the part of the youth of America end here? On the contrary, what at first was *independence*, assumes next the form of*opposition*, and eventually that of *control*.

The young men before they are qualified by age to claim their rights as citizens, have their societies, their book-clubs, their political meetings, their resolutions, all of which are promulgated in the newspapers; and very often the young men's societies are called upon by the newspapers to come forward with their opinions. Here is *opposition*. Mr Cooper says, on page 152 of his "Democrat":—

"The defects in American deportment are, notwithstanding, numerous and palpable. Among the first may be ranked, *insubordination in children*, and a great want of respect for age. The former vice may be ascribed to the business habits of the country, which leave so little time for parental instruction, and, perhaps, in some degree to the acts of political agents, who, with their own advantages in view, among the other expedients of their cunning, have resorted to the artifice of separating children from their natural advisers by calling meetings of the young to decide on the fortunes and policy of the country."

But what is more remarkable, is the fact that society has been usurped by the young people, and the married and old people have been, to a certain degree, excluded from it. A young lady will give a ball, and ask none but young men and young women of her acquaintance; not a *chaperon* is permitted to enter, and her father and mother are requested to stay upstairs, that they may not interfere with the amusement. This is constantly the case in Philadelphia and Baltimore, and I have heard bitter complaints made by the married people concerning it. Here is *control*. Mr Sanderson, in his "Sketches of Paris," observes:—

"They who give a tone to society should have maturity of mind; they should have refinement of taste, which is a quality of age. As long as *college beaux and boarding-school misses* take the lead, it must be an insipid society, in whatever community it may exist. Is it not villainous in your Quakerships of Philadelphia, to lay us, before we have lived half our time out, upon the shelf! Some of the native tribes, more merciful, eat the old folks out of the way."

However, retribution follows: in their turn they marry, and are ejected; they have children, and are disobeyed. The pangs which they have occasioned to their own parents are now suffered by them in return, through the conduct of their own children; and thus it goes on, and will go on, until the system is changed.

All this is undeniable; and thus it appears that the youth of America, being under no control, acquire just as much as they please, and no more, of what may be termed theoretical knowledge. Thus is the first great error in American education, for how many boys are there who will learn without coercion, in proportion to the number who will not? Certainly not one in ten, and, therefore it may be assumed that not one in ten is properly instructed. (See note 6.)

Now, that the education of the youth of America is much injured by the want of control on the part of the parents, is easily established by the fact that in those states where the parental control is the greatest, as in Massachusetts, the education is proportionably superior. But this great error is followed by consequences even more lamentable: it is the first dissolving power of the kindred attraction, so manifest throughout all American society. Beyond the period of infancy there is no endearment between the parents and children; none of that sweet spirit of affection between brother and sisters; none of those links which unite one family; of that mutual confidence; that rejoicing in each other's success; that refuge, when they are depressed or afflicted, in the bosoms of those who love us—the sweetest portion of human existence, which supports us wider, and encourages us firmly to brave, the ills of life—nothing of this exists. In short, there is hardly such a thing in America as "Home, sweet home." That there are exceptions to this, I grant but I speak of the great majority of cases, and the results upon the character of the nation. Mr Cooper, speaking of the weakness of the family tie in America, says—

"Let the reason be what it will, the effect is to cut us off from a large portion of the happiness that is dependent on the affections."

The next error of American education is, that in their anxiety to instil into the minds of youth a proper and ardent love of their own institutions, feelings and sentiments are fostered which ought to be most carefully checked. It matters little whether these feelings (in themselves vices) are directed against the institutions of other countries; the vice once engendered remains, and *hatred* once implanted in the breast of youth, will not be confined in its action. Neither will national conceit remain only *national* conceit, or *vanity* be confined to admiration of a form of government; in the present mode of educating the youth of America, all sight is lost of humility, good-will, and the other Christian virtues, which are necessary to constitute a good man, whether he be an American, or of any other country.

Let us examine the manner in which a child is taught. Democracy, equality, the vastness of his own country, the glorious independence, the superiority, of the Americans in all conflicts by sea or land, are impressed upon his mind before he can well read. All their elementary books contain garbled and false accounts of naval and land engagements, in which every credit is given to the Americans, and equal vituperation and disgrace thrown upon their opponents. Monarchy is derided, the equal rights of man declared—all is invective, uncharitableness, and falsehood.

That I may not in this be supposed to have asserted too much, I will quote a reading-lesson from a child's book, which I purchased in America as a curiosity, and is now in my possession. It is called the "Primary Reader for Young Children," and contains many stories besides this, relative to the history of the country.

"Lesson" 62.

"Story about the 4th of July".

6. "I must tell you what the people of New York did. In a certain spot in that city there stood a large statue, or representation of King George III. It was made of lead. In one hand he held a sceptre, or kind of sword, and on his head he wore a crown."

7. "When the news of the Declaration of Independence reached the city, a great multitude were seen running to the statue."

8. "The cry was heard, 'Down with it—down with it!' and soon a rope was placed about its neck, and the leaden King George came tumbling down."

9. "This might fairly be interpreted as a striking prediction of the downfall of the monarchical form of government in these United States."

10. "If we look into history, we shall frequently find great events proceeding from as trifling causes as the fall of the *leaden* statue, which not unaptly represents the character of a despotic prince."

11. "I shall only add, that when the statue was fairly down, it was cut to pieces, and converted into musket-balls to kill the soldiers whom his majesty had sent over to fight the Americans."

This is quite sufficient for a specimen. I have no doubt that it will be argued by the Americans—"We are justified in bringing up our youth to *love* our institutions." I admit it; but you bring them up to *hate* other people, before they have sufficient intellect to understand the merits of the case.

The author of "*A Voice from America*," observes:—

"Such, to a great extent is the unavoidable effect of that political education which is *indispensable* to all classes of a self-governed people. They must be trained to it from their cradle; it must go into all schools; it must thoroughly leaven the national literature, it must be 'line upon line, and precept upon precept,' here a little and there a little; it must be sung, discoursed, and thought upon everywhere and by every body."

And so it is; and as if this scholastic drilling were not sufficient, every year brings round the 4th of July, on which is read in every portion of the states the act of independence, in itself sufficiently vituperative, but invariably followed-up by one speech (if not more) from some great personage of the village, hamlet, town, or city, as it may be, in which the more violent he is against monarchy and the English, and the more he flatters his own countrymen, the more is his speech applauded.

Every year is this drilled into the ears of the American boy, until he leaves school, when he takes a political part himself, connecting himself with young men's society, where he spouts about tyrants, crowned heads, shades of his forefathers, blood flowing like water, independence, and glory.

The Rev. Mr Reid very truly observes, of the reading of the Declaration of Independence:— "There is one thing, however, that may justly claim the calm consideration of a great and generous people. Now that half a century has passed away, is it necessary to the pleasures of this day to revive feelings in the children which, if they were found in the parent, were to be excused only by the extremities to which they were pressed? Is it generous, now that they have achieved the victory, not to forgive the adversary? Is it manly, now that they have nothing to fear from Britain, to indulge in expressions of hate amid vindictiveness, which are the proper language of fear? Would there be less patriotism, because there was more charity? America should feel that her destinies are high and peculiar. She should scorn the patriotism which cherishes the love of one's own country, by the hatred of all others."

I think, after what I have brought forward, the reader will agree with me, that the education of the youth in the United States is immoral, and the evidence that it is so, is in the demoralisation which has taken place in the United States since the era of the Declaration of Independence, and which fact is freely admitted by so many American writers:—

"Aetas parentum pejor avis tulit
Nos nequieres, mox daturos
    Progeniem vitiosiorem."
        Horace, book iii, *ode* 6.

I shall by and by shew some of the effects produced by this injudicious system of education; of which, if it is necessary to uphold their democratical institutions, I can only say, with Dr Franklin, that the Americans "pay much too dear for their *whistle*."

It is, however, a fact, that education (such as I have shown it to be) is in the United States more equally diffused. They have very few citizens of the States (except a portion of those in the West) who may be considered as "hewers of wood and drawers of water," those duties being performed by the emigrant Irish and German, and the slave population. The education of the higher classes is not by any means equal to that of the old countries or Europe. You meet very rarely with a good classical scholar, or a very highly educated man, although some there certainly are, especially in the legal profession. The Americans have not the leisure for such attainments: hereafter they may have; but at present they do right to look principally to Europe for literature, as they can obtain it thence cheaper and better. In every liberal profession you will find that the ordeal necessary to be gone through is not such as it is with us; if it were, the difficulty of retaining the young men at college would be much increased. To show that such is the case, I will now just give the difference of the acquirements demanded in the new and old country to qualify a young man as an MD.

English Physician	American Physician
1. A regular classical education at college	1. Not required
2. Apprenticeship of not less than five years	2. One year's apprenticeship
3. Preliminary examination in the classics, etcetera	3. Not required
4. Sixteen months' attendance at lectures in 2.5 years	4. Eight months in two years
5. Twelve months' hospital practice	5. Not required
6. Lectures on botany, natural philosophy, etcetera	6. Not required

If the men in America enter so early into life that they have not time to obtain the acquirements supposed to be requisite with us, it is much the same thing with the females of the upper classes, who, from the precocious ripening by the climate and consequent early marriages, may be said to throw down their dolls that they may nurse their children.

The Americans are very justly proud of their women, and appear tacitly to acknowledge the want of theoretical education in their own sex, by the care and attention which they pay to the instruction of the other. Their exertions are, however, to a certain degree, checked by the circumstance, that there is not sufficient time allowed previous to the marriage of the females to give that solidity to their knowledge which would ensure its permanency. They attempt too much for so short a space of time. Two or three years are usually the period during which the young women remain at the establishments, or colleges I may call them (for in reality they are female colleges.) In the prospectus of the Albany Female Academy, I find that the classes run through the following branches:— French, book-keeping, ancient history, ecclesiastical history, history of literature, composition, political economy, American constitution, law, natural theology, mental philosophy, geometry, trigonometry, algebra, natural philosophy, astronomy, chemistry, botany, mineralogy, geology, natural history, and technology, besides drawing, penmanship, etcetera, etcetera.

It is almost impossible for the mind to retain, for any length of time, such a variety of knowledge, forced into it before a female has arrived to the age of sixteen or seventeen, at which age, the study of these sciences, as is the case in England, should *commence* not *finish*. I have already mentioned that the examinations which I attended were highly creditable both to preceptors and pupils; but the duties of an American woman as I shall hereafter explain, soon find her other occupation, and the *ologies* are lost in the realities of life. Diplomas are given at most of these establishments, on the young ladies completing their course of studies. Indeed, it appears to be almost necessary that a young lady should produce this diploma as a certificate of being qualified to bring up young republicans. I observed to an American gentlemen how youthful his wife appeared to be—"Yes," replied he, "I married her a month after she had *graduated*." The following are the terms of a diploma, which was given to a young lady at Cincinnati, and which she permitted me to copy:—

"In testimony of the zeal and industry with which Miss M— T— has prosecuted the prescribed course of studies in the Cincinnati Female Institution, and the honourable proficiency which she has attained in penmanship, arithmetic, English grammar, rhetoric, belles-lettres, composition, ancient and modern geography, ancient and modern history, chemistry, natural philosophy, astronomy, etcetera. etcetera. etcetera, of which she has given proofs by examination.

"And also as a mark of her amiable deportment, intellectual acquirements, and our affectionate regard, we have granted her this letter—the *highest honour* **bestowed** in this institution."

(Seal.) "Given under our hands at Cincinnati, this 19th day of July, Anno Domini 1837."

The ambition of the Americans to be a-head of other nations in every thing, produces, however, injurious effects, so far as the education of the women is concerned. The Americans will not "*leave well alone*," they must "gild refined gold," rather than not consider themselves in advance of other countries, particularly of England. They *alter* our language, and think that they have *improved* upon it; as in the same way they would raise the standard of morals higher than with us, and consequently fall much below us, appearances supplying the place of the reality. In these endeavours they sink into a sickly sentimentality, and, as I have observed before, attempts at refinement in language, really excite improper ideas. As a proof of the ridiculous excess to which this is occasionally carried, I shall insert an address which I observed in print; had such a document appeared in the English newspapers, it would have been considered as a hoax.

"Mrs Mandelle's Address:—

"To the young ladies of the Lancaster Female Academy, at an examination on the 3rd March, 1838.

"Affectionate Pupils:— With many of you this is our final meeting in the relative position of teacher and pupil, and we must part perhaps to meet no more. That this reflection *filtrates from my mind to my heart* with saddening influence, I need scarce assure you. But *Hope*, in a voice sweet as 'the wild strains of the Eolian harp,' whispers in dulcet accents, '*we may again meet.*' In youth the impressions of sorrow are fleeting and evanescent as '*the vapery sail*,' that momentarily o'ershadows the *luciferous orb of even*, vanishes and leaves her disc untarnished in its lustre: so may it be with you—may the gloom of this moment, like the elemental prototype, be but the precursor of reappearing radiance undimmed by the transitory shadow.

"Happy and bright indeed has been this small portion of your time occupied, not only in the interesting pursuit of science, but in a reciprocation of attentions and sympathies, endeared by that holiest *ligament* of earthly sensibilities, *religion*, which so oft has united us in soul and sentiment, as the aspirations of our hearts simultaneously ascended to the mercy-seat of the great Jehovah! The remembrance of emotions like these are ineffaceable by care or sorrow, and only blotted out by the immutable hand of death. These *halcyon hours of budding existence* are to memory as the *oasis* of the desert, where we may recline beneath the soothing *influence* of their umbrage, and quaff in *the goblet of retrospection* the lucid draught that refreshes for the moment, and is again forgotten. Permit me to solicit, that the immaculate principles of *virtue*, I have so often and so carefully inculcated, may not be forgotten, but perseveringly cherished and practised. May the divine dictates of reason *murmur in harmonious cadence*, bewitching as the fabled melody of the musical bells on the trees of the Mahomedan Paradise. She dwells not alone beneath the glittering star, nor is always encircled by the diamond cestus and the jewel'd tiara! indeed not! and the brilliancy *emulged* from the spangling gems, but make more hideous the dark, black spot enshrined in the effulgence. The traces of her peaceful footsteps are found alike in the dilapidated hovel of the beggared peasant, and the velveted saloon of the coroneted noble; who may then apportion her a home or assign her a clime? In making my acknowledgments for the attentive interest with which you received my instructions; and the respectful regard you manifested in appreciating my advice, it is not as a compliment to your vanity, but a debt due to your politeness and good sense. Long, my beloved pupils, may my precepts and admonitions live in your hearts; and hasten you, in the language of Addison, to commit yourself to the care of Omnipotence, and when the morning calls again to toil, cast all your cares upon him the author of your being, who has conducted you through one stage of existence, and who will always be present to guide and attend your progress through eternity."

An advertisement of Mr Bonfil's Collegiate Institute for Young Ladies, after enumerating the various branches of literature to be taught, winds up with the following paragraph:—

"And finally, it will be constantly inculcated, that their education will be completed when they have the power to extend unaided, a spirit of investigation, searching and appreciating truth, *without passing the bounds assigned to the human understanding.*"

I have now completed this volume, and although I omitted the major portion of my Diary, that I might not trespass too long upon the reader my task is still far from its termination. The most important parts of it—an examination into the American society and their government, and the conclusions to be drawn from the observations already made upon several subjects; in short, the working out of the problem, as it were, is still to be executed. I have not written one line of this work without deliberation and examination. What I have already done has cost me much labour—what I have to do will cost me more. I must, therefore, claim for myself the indulgence of the public, and request that, in justice to the Americans, they will not decide until they have perused the second portion, with which I shall, as speedily as I can, wind up my observations upon the United States and their Institutions.

Note 1. A church-yard with its mementos of mortality is sometimes a fair criterion by which to judge of the degree of the education of those who live near it. In one of the church-yards in Vermont, there is a tomb stone with an inscription which commences as follows: "Paws, *reader*, Paws."

Note 2. New York is superior to the other states in this list; but Ohio is not quite equal. I can draw the line no closer.

Note 3. Notwithstanding that Philadelphia is the capital, the state of Pennsylvania is a great *dunce*.

Note 4. Miss Martineau says: "Though, as a whole, the nation is probably better informed than any other entire nation, it cannot be denied, that their knowledge is far inferior to what their safety and their virtue require."

Note 5. The master of a school could not manage the gab, they being exceedingly contumacious. Beat them, he dared not; so he hit upon an expedient. He made a very strong decoction of wormwood, and for a slight offence, poured one spoonful down their throats: for a more serious one, he made them take two.

Note 6. Mrs Trollope says: "At sixteen, often much earlier, education ends and money making begins; the idea that more learning is necessary than can be acquired by that time, is generally ridiculed as absolute monkish bigotry to which, if the seniors willed a more prolonged discipline, the juniors would refuse submission. When the money getting begins, leisure ceases, and all the lore which can be acquired afterwards is picked up from novels, magazines, and newspapers."

Captain Hall also remarks upon this point:— "I speak now from the authority of the Americans themselves. There is the greatest possible difficulty in fixing young men long enough at college. Innumerable devices have been tried with considerable ingenuity to remedy this evil, and the best possible intentions by the professors and other public-spirited persons who are sincerely grieved to see so many incompetent, half-qualified men in almost every corner of the country."

Captain Hamilton very truly observes:— "Though I have unquestionably met in New York with many most intelligent and accomplished gentlemen, still I think the fact cannot be denied,—that the average of acquirement resulting from education is a good deal lower in this country than in the better circles in England. In all the knowledge which must be taught, and which requires laborious study for its attainment, I should say the Americans are considerably inferior to my countrymen. In that knowledge, on the other hand, which the individual acquires for himself by actual observation, which bears an immediate marketable value and is directly available in the ordinary avocations of life, I do not imagine that the Americans are excelled by any people in the world."

The End.

Made in the USA
Middletown, DE
06 January 2024